Chartered Banker

STUDY TEXT

Risk Management in Banking

In this 2014/15 edition

- A **user-friendly format** for easy navigation
- **Updated** on recent developments
- A **chapter review** at the end of each chapter
- A full **index**

Chartered Banker
Leading financial professionalism

Published October 2014

ISBN 978 1 4727 0497 9

British Library Cataloguing-in-Publication Data
A catalogue record for this book
is available from the British Library

Published by

BPP Learning Media Ltd
BPP House, Aldine Place
London W12 8AA

www.bpp.com/learningmedia

Printed in the United Kingdom by Ricoh

Unit 2
Wells Place
Merstham
RH1 3LG

Your learning materials, published by BPP Learning Media Ltd, are printed on paper obtained from traceable sustainable sources.

The contents of this book are intended as a guide and not professional advice. Although every effort has been made to ensure that the contents of this book are correct at the time of going to press, BPP Learning Media makes no warranty that the information in this book is accurate or complete and accept no liability for any loss or damage suffered by any person acting or refraining from acting as a result of the material in this book.

A note about copyright

Dear Customer

What does the little © mean and why does it matter?

Your market-leading BPP books, course materials and e-learning materials do not write and update themselves. People write them: on their own behalf or as employees of an organisation that invests in this activity. Copyright law protects their livelihoods. It does so by creating rights over the use of the content.

Breach of copyright is a form of theft – as well being a criminal offence in some jurisdictions, it is potentially a serious beach of professional ethics.

With current technology, things might seem a bit hazy but, basically, without the express permission of BPP Learning Media:

- Photocopying our materials is a breach of copyright.
- Scanning, ripcasting or conversion of our digital materials into different file formats, uploading them to facebook or emailing them to your friends is a breach of copyright.

You can, of course, sell your books, in the form in which you have bought them – once you have finished with them. (Is this fair to your fellow students? We update for a reason.) But the e-products are sold on a single user license basis: we do not supply 'unlock' codes to people who have bought them secondhand.

And what about outside the UK? BPP Learning Media strives to make our materials available at prices students can afford by local printing arrangements, pricing policies and partnerships which are clearly listed on our website. A tiny minority ignore this and indulge in criminal activity by illegally photocopying our material or supporting organisations that do. If they act illegally and unethically in one area, can you really trust them?

CONTENTS

INTRODUCTION

The aim of this module is to provide an extensive, detailed and critical knowledge and understanding of risk management in the banking industry and develop the practitioner's skills and ability to synthesise complex issues, evaluate information, apply principles and techniques, and make professional judgements and informed decisions in relevant work situations.

Learning outcomes

The main learning outcomes associated with this module should enable you to:

- critically analyse key risk management concepts in banking
- distinguish between different types of risk and how these can be identified, monitored and mitigated
- evaluate the central credit risk function of a bank and its role within the risk management framework
- assess credit risk and apply credit risk practices
- assess and manage operational risks
- critically review the International and UK regulatory risk environment
- examine the impact of the global banking crisis of 2007/08 and subsequent events in banking that have affected the industry.

Assessment structure

Your online extended response examination will be worth 70% of your overall result and your summative assignment will make up the remaining 30%.

Introduction to this Study Text

If you want to gain the attention of a bank or even a single banker these days simply mention one of two subjects close to their heart – costs or risk. In many ways they are intertwined. This book focuses on the second topic.

What is risk?

Risk – the possibility of incurring misfortune or loss. There are many definitions, but the key issues which emerge from using this particular definition are that there is:

Possibility. This is the chance or likelihood of an event happening in the future. The event has not yet happened – it exists as one of a number of possible outcomes that may occur in the future, some quite likely and others not so probable. This is important because it suggests that people can put in place a plan or take an action today that may reduce the chance of the event occurring in the future.

Misfortune or loss. The potential outcome is regarded as negative. It is a potential occurrence that people are trying to avoid. This is also called the downside of risk, some may be extremely serious and others of relatively minor significance.

Phrases such as run the risk and taking a risk are commonplace in our normal conversation. As we all know life is risky! We learn from an early age and throughout our professional lives that mistakes, errors of strategy and downright foolhardy behaviour can lead to calamity. We shall explore some examples of this from the world of banking throughout this book. Risk is all around us in our daily lives and as financial markets struggle to emerge from the economic turmoil of the global financial crisis, which delivered an unprecedented impact upon the global industry in 2008 and beyond, we are all more attuned to the risks businesses face, particularly in the banking and financial sector.

This phenomenon of risk is not new but so much more demonstrably powerful today. As a result, the managers of financial institutions, indeed anyone in a senior position, must contribute to the overall duty of a firm to manage its risks. Executive managers must have a firm grasp of the businesses for which they are responsible. They should set in place an environment and a structure of control processes which looks critically at risk sources and addresses them effectively. This book aims to present a guide to the sources from which risks may emerge and to explore effective strategies to face and overcome business risks.

Risk manifests itself in several differing ways and one of the basic steps for firms to take is to understand the nature of the different types of risks, their sources, the events which can occur and the resultant impacts. The modern banking industry and its variety of products can be broken down into three general sectors of risk – credit risk, market risk and operational risk, each of which are examined in greater detail in this book. However there are also other vitally important areas, such as regulatory risk and liquidity risk, which are also addressed in this book.

Managing risk is therefore an essential skill (and responsibility) of those who run banks and other financial institutions. Those who do manage risk well will benefit from significant rewards and those which do not may well see their businesses fail completely.

Overseeing the whole process are a firm's shareholders and governments and their appointed regulators, all of whom have learned a thing or two about risk in the recent past as they have borne the brunt of the cost of rescuing or bailing out failing firms. Risk management is right at the top of the agenda of the banking industry and regulators across the global financial marketplace.

It is generally accepted that there are three main categories of risk in the financial services industry.

Market risk is manifested by exposure to the uncertain market value of a portfolio. For example, a trader may hold a position or portfolio of securities. They know what their market value is today, but are uncertain as to what their market value will be a week from today. The market may move in price. Therefore the trader faces market risk. Market risk represents the potential risk of loss of earnings or capital arising from a reduction in the value of financial instruments. In simple terms, an investor is exposed to market risk as soon as a financial product is purchased, sold or a market position is taken. This is intrinsic in all markets and across all products.

Credit risk relates to lending to or agreeing to trade with another counterparty. Will the other counterparty pay or deliver the asset they have undertaken to deliver on the due date? Traditionally, the primary risk for financial institutions has been credit risk or the potential for loss that results from lending. Institutions accept credit risk in order to earn revenue. They lend to firms with a higher risk because of the potential for higher returns.

Operational risk addresses almost everything else; a good basic definition, which is widely accepted today is, 'The risk of loss resulting from inadequate or failed internal processes, people and systems or from external events'. This is the concise, formal definition which has been drawn up by the Basel Committee on Banking Supervision.

All of these fundamental types of risks plus others will be explored in this book.

As you will be well aware, the global banking industry has experienced a number of very turbulent years and that situation could prevail for some time yet. Whilst the contents of this book are up to date at the time of writing, you should be aware that some of the examples discussed will change and develop during the lifetime of this book. It is therefore important that you keep yourself fully appraised of these ongoing developments.

chapter 1

RISK MANAGEMENT CONCEPTS

Contents

Learning objectives

On completion of this chapter, you should be able to:

- critically analyse key risk management concepts in banking
- identify the key risk sources in banking and establish the interconnections between global financial markets
- explain how the concept of economic capital relates to the management of risk in banking.

Introduction

In the first chapter of this study text, we will consider some of the basic concepts associated with risk management. The chapter starts by developing the risk – reward continuum, before moving on to consider the various categories of risks that can be faced by banks in the early 21st century, for example, regulatory risk, credit risk, liquidity risk, technology risk. The next section will consider the interconnections between the global financial markets. As you will be aware, economies no longer operate in isolation, but due to advances in technology, events in one part of the world can have an immediate impact on the other side of the globe.

Throughout this course, use is made of statistics, so it is useful at this early stage to explain some key financial and statistical techniques and concepts that will be used later on such as probability and distribution. Having introduced some statistical material, we can now turn our attention to financial and non-financial quantification. Firms can assess risk both on a qualitative and quantitative basis and examples of this will be given in the text. Firms will also use models and the importance of having the correct data in these models is described next, along with a discussion on the drawbacks of using models and scenarios.

Economic capital is examined next – with the differences between economic capital and regulatory capital being explained. This chapter then concludes with a description of the ten major risk areas faced by organisations across a number of different industries.

1 The importance of risk taking

Risk taking is an integral part of business and life, but so few people know how to manage it properly. The word **risk** has a slightly negative connotation to it – it implies danger, tension, and possible loss. However risk also has a positive side, the chance of achieving success or future reward being greater than the initial investment.

So the basic question to contemplate is risk vs. reward. If banks did not take any risks, they would not be able to generate any profit. This is the fundamental conundrum of banking and finance: How much of each are we comfortable in facing or taking? What are the obstacles to achieving reward and what could be the downside of failing to do so? How do we assess and manage the risk and the reward?

We are searching for a positive outcome but we know that a negative hurdle or even disaster may potentially await us.

This concept of the risk-reward continuum manifests itself in the pricing of loans granted by banks.

QUICK QUESTION

How do you think we can see this concept in action when pricing loans?

Write your answer here before reading on.

When the banker feels that there is a higher risk associated with a loan, then the rate of interest charged to the customer should be higher. If you are about to lend a customer £10,000 and they do not offer you any security then the risk of default can be quite high as, should the customer not repay the loan, then the bank is facing a bad debt. On the other hand, if you are going to lend £10,000 to another customer but this customer is offering the bank security (for example, by pledging a life policy with a surrender value of say £17,500) then the risk of loss to the bank will be lower, as in the second instance, should the customer not repay the loan, then the bank is in a position to either surrender or sell the life policy and use this money to repay the loan. In this example, the first loan represents a higher risk to the bank and so the rate of interest charged to the customer will be higher than in the second – lower risk – example. In this case, the potential reward to the bank is the income they will receive from the customer, so in the riskier scenario, the potential reward is higher.

Another example in this area can be seen when the bank credit scores lending applications. The fundamental purpose of credit scoring is to determine the probability of repayment of the proposed loan. You may have come across examples at work where the level of the credit score will determine the rate of interest that the borrowing customer will be charged – the same principle applies with the high risk applications being charged a higher rate of interest.

We therefore need to be able to exploit risk to our advantage. To exploit risk, a firm needs an edge over its competitors who are also exposed to that same risk. A firm's edge can come from five possible sources:

1. Having more timely and reliable information when confronted with a crisis, allowing the firm to map out a superior plan of action in response.
2. The speed of the response to the risk, since not all firms, even when provided with the same information, are equally effective at acting quickly and appropriately.
3. Experience in weathering similar crises in the past. The institutional memories as well as the individual experiences of how the crises unfolded may provide an advantage over competitors who are new to the risk.
4. The resources of the firm, since firms with access to capital markets or large cash balances, superior technology and better trained personnel can survive risks better than their competitors.
5. Firms that have more operating, production or financial flexibility built into their responses, as a result of choices made in earlier periods, will be able to adjust better than their more rigid competitors.

Let us consider a practical, yet hypothetical, example of risk taking. We'll keep it simple.

CASE STUDY

Special Bank

In the early 2000s Special Bank a long-established institution with a history of solid performance (and a slightly old-fashioned brand image) had a moderate trading book of strongly rated assets and a banking book of medium-sized loans to highly-rated customers. This was supported by a sizeable set of loyal depositor customers on the other side of its balance sheet. To many observers this seemed to be a satisfactory position. However, a new chief executive was appointed to drive the bank onwards in the 21st century with added vigour and to build Special Bank into a major global player within a few short years. He therefore needed to make greater returns on the banking book and by moving into new products demonstrating greater leverage to make the trading book generate significantly higher rewards. Therefore, with his board and senior executive team, he set in train an expansion policy and advanced mortgages and loans (in greater size and number) to new customers on easier terms for which the bank had to borrow to acquire the necessary funds. He also set up an investment banking arm to enter the world of corporate finance plus a proprietary dealing operation which geared up the bank's trading positions in the global marketplace. One can see at a glance that the appetite for taking risk had been transformed. The question was whether the new policy could deliver greater rewards. So the essence of the issue is whether Special Bank is able to manage the risks that it is taking on.

There is nothing inherently wrong in taking a risk as long as it can be and is managed satisfactorily. All banks are in the business of taking risk. No one bank controls the market; no one bank can have all the customers as markets offer choice in a fully competitive arena. Markets must be competitive. There are many moving parts therefore and the successful navigation of the labyrinthine sets of challenges and risks is the big challenge.

2 Key sources of risk in banking

All major banks will have their own way of describing the risks that they believe that they are facing. This section will define the principal risks faced by most major banks and it will be noted that these range across a very wide spectrum of concerns.

At the heart of this analysis, much will depend upon the business mix of the bank. For the purposes of this analysis we shall assume that the bank is a major bank, commonly known as a universal bank with activities ranging from current accounts of personal customers to international corporate, government and institutional clients. Similarly a large universal bank will have different geographical pressures which will clearly not be the case for a localised bank operating in one particular country or region.

The first issue therefore will be the general economic conditions and performance of the general economy in which the bank wholly or partly operates. This will create pressures on the activities of the bank and will manifest itself in operational risk issues and the credit quality of the operating corporate portfolios. In 2014, the major global economies are experiencing a recovery after the recession caused by the financial crisis of 2008 and its aftermath. However, the economic environment for banks has become tougher due to increased regulation and greater scrutiny on their activities due to a number of high profile scandals (these will be covered throughout the text).

Against this backdrop therefore, there were a number of principal risk factors which major banks needed to consider and have in place effective procedures to identify, assess, manage and report risks that may have affected their business and be impacted by general operating conditions in the marketplace.

QUICK QUESTION

Reflect upon the organisation that you work in and list as many sources of risk that you think the business faces.

Write your answer here before reading on.

Risk type	Definition	Characteristics
Credit Risk	Credit risk is the risk of the bank suffering financial loss if any of its customers, clients or market counterparties fails to repay their debt obligations.	Credit Risk and Wholesale Credit Risk results from concentrations of exposure to poorly performing debtors. This risk can also arise when an entity's credit rating is downgraded, leading to a fall in the value of the bank's investment in its issued financial instruments.
Market Risk	Market risk is the risk that the bank's earnings or capital, or its ability to meet business objectives, will be adversely affected by changes in the level or volatility of market rates and prices.	These include interest rates, credit spreads, commodity prices, equity prices and foreign exchange rates. The bank is exposed to market risk through traded market risk, non-traded interest rate risk and its pension fund.
Capital Risk	Capital risk is the risk that the bank has insufficient capital resources to ensure the bank is well capitalised relative to the minimum regulatory capital requirements set out by the bank's regulator(s).	Also known as Prudential Risk. Capital Risk must be addressed in each of the bank's prime locations of business. It must ensure that locally regulated subsidiaries can meet their minimum regulatory requirements also.
Liquidity Risk	Liquidity risk is the risk that the bank is unable to meet its financial obligations as they fall due.	Failure may result in an inability to: support normal business activity; failing to meet liquidity regulatory requirements; or rating agency concerns.

Risk type	Definition	Characteristics
Operational Risk	The classic Basel Committee definition is 'The risk of loss resulting from inadequate or failed internal processes, people and systems or from external events'. Banks may interpret this literally or add their own specific slant to their definition.	This will cover a wide range of activities – transactions, new products, premises and security, external suppliers it and systems, outsourcing, legal, payments processing plus information and data management.
Financial Crime Risk	Financial crime risk is the risk that the bank suffers losses as a result of internal and external fraud or intentional damage, loss or harm to people, premises or moveable assets.	Fraud may be perpetrated by third parties or internally.
Technology Risk	Technology risk includes the non-availability of IT systems, inadequate design and testing of new and changed IT solutions and inadequate IT system security.	System capacity and scalability. Lack of a strategic IT policy. Software change control. Lack of support. Dependence on third party suppliers.
People Risk	People risk arises from failures of a bank to manage its key risks as an employer. This could result from poor training, recruitment or motivation of staff.	This will include lack of appropriate people resources, failure to manage performance and reward, unauthorised or inappropriate employee activity and failure to comply with employment related requirements.
Regulatory Risk	Regulatory risk arises from a failure or inability to comply fully with the laws, regulations or codes applicable specifically to the financial services industry.	This will exist across all locations in which the bank operates. Banks may well report to large numbers of regulatory bodies internationally if they operate in more than one country.
Financial Reporting Risk	Financial reporting risk arises from a failure or inability to comply fully with the laws, regulations or codes that cover the bank's operations and reporting requirements.	The risk of sanction by a regulator should any form of reporting not be fulfilled or acceptable to the regulator.
Legal Risk	The risk of losses or misfortune occurring as a result of failure to comply with the laws governing the bank's operations.	This will include business conduct standards, enforceability of contracts, intellectual property rights and liabilities to third parties.

Risk type	Definition	Characteristics
Strategic Risk	Banks devote substantial management and planning resources to the development of strategic plans for organic growth and identification of possible acquisitions. This will be supported by substantial expenditure to generate growth in customer business. Strategic risk is the risk of losses or misfortunes occurring as a result of these strategic plans.	If strategic plans are not delivered as anticipated, the bank's earnings could grow more slowly or decline. In addition, the bank's strategy could be impacted by revenue volatility due to factors such as macroeconomic conditions, inflexible cost structures, uncompetitive products or pricing and structural inefficiencies.
Change Risk	Arises when a bank needs to make extensive changes to its operations. The cost of implementation projects may overrun, or they may fail to achieve their objectives.	Examples of situations in which change risk arises include the integration of acquired businesses, significant business unit restructuring, changes in target operating models, the roll-out of new and potentially disruptive technologies, the introduction of a single currency such as the euro, and Group-wide projects to implement significant new regulation such as Basel III.
Reputational Risk	The risk arising from loss of or impacted reputation. Reputational risk means the risk to earnings and capital from negative public opinion. Negative public opinion can result from the actual or perceived manner in which a bank conducts its business activities.	Negative public opinion may adversely affect a bank's ability to keep and attract customers and, in particular, corporate and retail depositors. Failure to meet expectations of stakeholders.
Model Risk	The risk of losses occurring due using models to make decisions. The model may result in incorrect decisions because of the model inputs used or because the model itself has fundamental flaws. Also, models cannot always correctly predict the future.	Models are used for a variety of different purposes, from credit scoring through to predicting the probabilities of events occurring. Models need to be updated regularly to ensure that they produce relevant information for decision making.
Insurance Risk	The risk of financial loss through fluctuations in the timing, frequency and/or severity of insured events, relative to the expectations at the time of underwriting.	Frequent small losses and infrequent large material losses.

3 The interconnections between global financial markets

Everyone realises that we live in a global financial marketplace; indeed a global village. It is not uncommon for customers to undertake cross border business between different continents through banking institutions in a third continent. Capital can move at a moment's notice from one part of the world to another and this has been achieved by the inter-connections between global financial markets across the countries of the world.

While inter-connections between global financial markets bring many benefits to the global economy, they also result in risks transcending national boundaries. One such example is the Foreign Corrupt Practises Act (FCPA) in the US. FCPA aims to prevent bribery of foreign officials and increase transparency of accounting information. The Act does not just cover US companies, but any company that that is required to file reports under the Securities and Exchange Act 1934. Therefore many foreign companies are subject to the provisions of FCPA, even though their operations in the US may be small. As a result of legislation such as FCPA, banks that trade with clients across the globe must ensure that they adhere to the rules and regulation in both their domestic markets and in all of the different global markets where they operate.

QUESTION TIME 1

Consider all of the risk categories listed in this section and assess how they apply to your organisation.

The following table will help you:

Risk Area	Application to my firm
Credit	
Market	
Capital	
Liquidity	
Operational	
Financial Crime	
Technology	
People	
Regulatory	
Financial reporting	
Legal	
Strategic	
Change	
Reputational	
Insurance	
Information	

Write your answer above then check with the answer at the back of the book.

CASE STUDY

Japanese Tsunami 2011

This was a natural event of cataclysmic significance to those in Japan who were directly impacted by the disaster. Nevertheless the ramifications of the tsunami reverberated throughout the world and affected oil prices, oil consumption and the rebalancing of Japanese demand for such things as oil and energy and impacted other economies throughout the world. One of the first markets to react to events of that kind is of course the foreign exchange market where currencies are traded across the globe. Droughts or floods, hurricanes or tsunamis in one part of the world can impact agricultural commodities and financial markets in places thousands of miles away. The closure of a port or a mine owing to natural events or economic circumstances such as labour strikes can have an impact on other parts of the world. The financial meltdown that began in 2007 and 2008, whilst starting in the United States, had global repercussions.

We are all linked as both consumers and nation states. Sovereign issues with law, rules and regulations in one country will impact others. For example major new financial regulation in the United States will impact what is happening in Brazil, or China, in the European Union and Asia-Pacific. One of the best examples in recent times of interconnectedness has been the impact of the heightening European sovereign debt crisis which has had a major impact upon stock exchanges and bond markets throughout the world. This is because the trading patterns between one part of the globe and another are inextricably linked in the ability to borrow money, create investment and to effect trading agreements. This relationship is referred to as systematic risk. This is risk that affects all market participants and it cannot be diversified away. Therefore, global markets will always be vulnerable to systematic risk.

3.1 The importance of technology

One of the reasons why financial markets and economies are so interconnected today is because of technology. Most market dealing has now migrated to electronic trading using computers. They have the distinct advantage of being able to communicate across vast distances at minimal speed. Algorithmic programmes enable high frequency traders and others to scalp micro dollars in nanoseconds. It is amazing to consider how quickly and to what a huge extent electronic market trading in the United States has resulted in excess of 90% of trading was being done by this medium. As a subset of electronic trading, high frequency traders probably account for about 50% of the trades in the European Union and roughly a third of the trades in the United States' equity markets.

Through this technology and accelerated by high frequency trading, liquidity has grown in markets. Liquidity measures how the ease with which securities can be bought the sold – the higher the liquidity, the easier it is to trade in markets. Much of the new liquidity is intra-day liquidity. It is short-lived and may be fleeting but nevertheless it is still liquidity. This is the essence of flourishing successful markets.

Technology enables connectivity and access. It is not uncommon to find the largest contributing traders for a market in the United States to be found in Europe or for a major customer of a market in South Korea to come from the Middle East. That has all been achieved by computer systems and the communication that connects them. Technology is welcomed by regulators because it provides an electronic audit trail of the data.

However technology has also brought with it other issues that are presenting issues for regulators and practitioners alike. A good example is the flash crash in the United States on May 6th 2010. This was where the Dow Jones Industrial Average fell by over 1,000 points and recovered these losses almost immediately. Imagine that if this event had occurred in the European morning of that same day then the world might have seen a global economic event but because it took place in the mid-afternoon it was primarily limited to American markets due to time differences. Regulators, particularly in the United States have been addressing remedies such as circuit breakers and other methods to eliminate the potential danger of markets becoming out of control.

3.2 The importance of information

Information is a source of competitive advantage in global financial markets. An organisation that can access, store and analyse useful information will have an edge over competitors. For example, a bank that can analyse the borrowing trends and habits of different customers and can use this information to tailor new products and services to suit customer needs. Similarly, banks will use information to make strategic decisions: they may decide to withdraw from a certain market because their research tells them that revenues in that market are likely to contract in the coming years. Because information is such a valuable asset it poses some important security risks, such as information being lost or stolen. These issues will be discussed later on in the course.

Banks share and transmit information with a variety of stakeholders, such as customers and suppliers. This carries the risk that information may be lost, stolen or manipulated in transit, be it an email, telephone conversation or information logged on a website. Whilst a bank can do everything within its powers to ensure that all information is secure, they must also help stakeholders to understand the importance of information security. For example, banks try and educate customers on the importance of confidential information security, such as using secure passwords and not sharing this information with others. This helps to reduce risks for the bank and the stakeholders.

3.3 The global marketplace

As indicated earlier, investors will want to invest their capital where it can be put to good use. Technology allows capital to be invested instantaneously. Therefore institutional money and funds, particularly that of a speculative nature, can create exposures in markets very rapidly. Consider the financial crisis of 2008 where a huge swell of money entered the futures markets. It is understood that roughly US$200 billion in speculative money entered those markets. Crude oil reached US$147 a barrel. Gasoline at the pump exceeded US$4 a gallon. The evidence was that the upsurge in investment money had an effect in driving up prices in those markets and once the institutional money moved on the prices decreased.

A particularly worrying issue in global markets is the impact of fluid capital into commodities markets. Commodities prices, and in particular those of foodstuffs, have seen an upswing in value and volatility. Price growth has occurred in products such as wheat, rice and corn. This has created issues whereby some governments have found it difficult to be able to feed their populations. This powerful example demonstrates the interconnected world we live in.

The case of the collapse of MF Global at the end of October 2011 is another good example of interconnections in modern financial markets. MF Global, a brokerage company with its headquarters in the US, collapsed. The main issue that needed to be dealt with in the marketplace was the ability to pay back to the thousands of traders and trading companies who had their assets tied up in accounts at the collapsed firm. These were customers from all over the world. The criticism of MF Global's London subsidiary resulted from compromised clients. This also resulted in some reputational damage to the United Kingdom with respect to its laws concerning segregation of client assets and the manner in which the British regulator, the FSA (which has since been replaced by the FCA), and its rules did not facilitate a smooth repatriation of client funds where required. A period of some four months had passed with receivers being unable to repatriate any assets satisfactorily.

Thus we live in a world of interconnected markets where customers are doing business around the world and capital is highly transportable and fast-moving. It is against this back-drop that modern financial institutions including most banks are operating and need to make themselves resilient with respect to the management of their business because asset classes and market infrastructures systems upon which everything is based together with the regulatory environment is being modified and changing its shape all the time.

From studying this section, you will appreciate the truly global nature of financial services in the modern world. This presents challenges not only to firms, but also to those who seek to regulate the industry as events in one country can have far reaching effects in others. This phenomenon is compounded by the impact of technology whereby markets may be affected by automatic responses programmed into the systems used by traders and fund managers. For example, it may have been programmed that should the price of a particular security reach a specified price, then instructions to sell any such security in the fund manager's portfolio will be automatically generated. Depending upon the size of the holding, this could have implications for the value of the share index in which this particular security is held.

3.4 Regulatory initiatives

Since the global financial crisis, governments in leading marketplaces have addressed the shortcomings that led, by virtue of market infrastructure and procedure together with the regulatory governance structures, to the systemic risk problems. An example of this in the UK this has been the Independent Commission on Banking chaired by Sir John Vickers, which recommended a split between a banking group's retail business and their investment business. We do not have a world of globally harmonised regulation and there is to some extent a regulatory arbitrage in place across diverse parts of the world which are at different stages of development with respect to their regulatory infrastructure.

A major development that the financial world is now preparing for is the Wall Street Reform and Consumer Protection Act of 2010 in the United States, commonly referred to as the Dodd-Frank Act. This is a sweeping piece of financial market regulatory reform legislation that has been designed to address amongst other things markets such as the OTC markets (this is the name for an over the counter market, whereby financial instruments are traded directly through two parties) that had had no regulatory oversight whatsoever before but wads the market mechanism for trading credit default swaps and collateralised debt obligations. These markets created difficulties and losses in a range of countries that were impacted by the momentous events of 2008. What has been recognised more recently is that regulatory scrutiny together with increased transparency and accountability are necessary in financial markets to provide benefits to consumers and businesses alike. It has also been recognised how systemically important certain parts of the market infrastructure are – and in particular large banks. One of the phenomena that is being discussed is that of Globally Significant International Financial Institutions (GSIFIs), a group which includes many large banks. The acceptance that such institutions are systemically important links back to a phrase made famous during the global financial crisis of some banks being too big to fail. A good example of these in the UK were the Royal Bank of Scotland and Lloyds Banking Group, both of which had to be rescued by taxpayers' funds in order to protect the British economy and the British public from the systemic risk of the financial machinery of the country falling apart.

We will return to this theme of regulation later in the course when we discuss Regulatory Risk.

4 Key financial and statistical techniques

4.1 Financial risk modelling

Financial risk modelling refers to the use of formal econometric techniques to determine the aggregate risk in a financial portfolio. Risk modelling is a subset of the broader discipline of financial modelling.

Many financial firms use risk modelling to help portfolio managers assess the amount of capital reserves to maintain, and to help guide their purchases and sales of various classes of financial assets.

Formal risk modelling is required under Basel II for all the major international banking institutions by the various national depository institution regulators. In the past, risk analysis was done qualitatively but now with the advent of powerful computing software, quantitative risk analysis can be done quickly and effortlessly.

4.2 Distribution analysis

This refers to a statistical means of using historical data to predict future events and relies on an understanding of probability distributions. These are mathematical functions that describe the probability of possible outcomes. They are depicted as graphs with the probability of occurrence on the vertical axis and the possible outcome on the horizontal axis. Many types of distribution are used for analysis but, for the purposes of this course, only an understanding of the most common form is needed, which is called a normal distribution or bell curve.

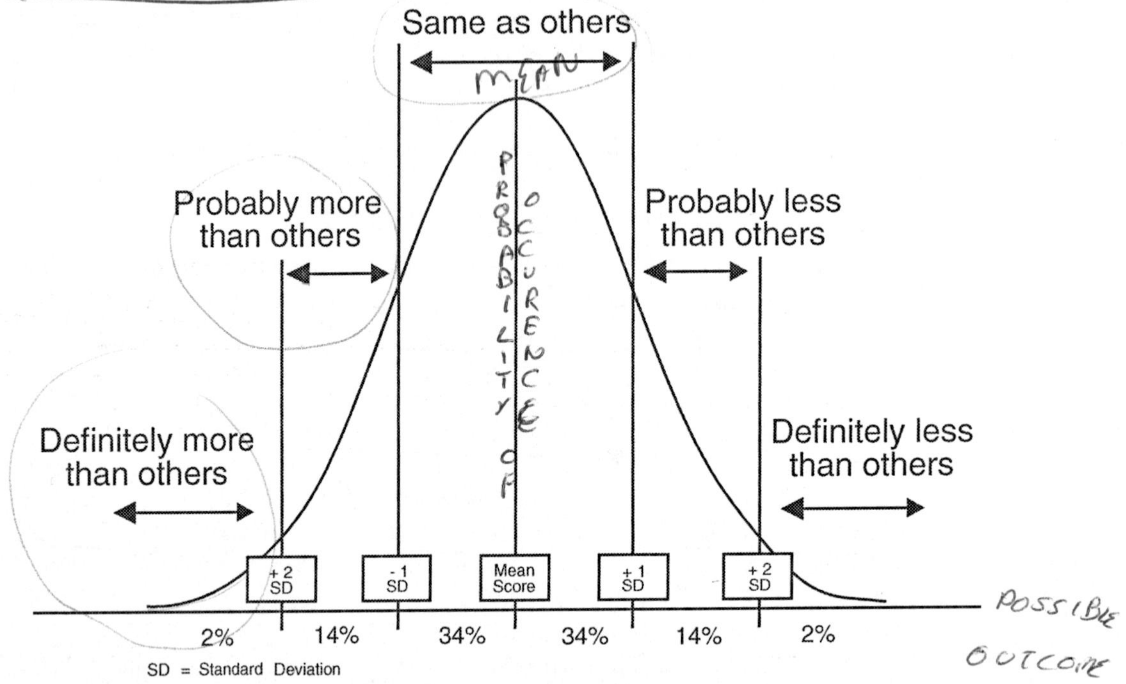

Many social phenomena occur in the population in the distribution called the bell curve. This picture shows the scores of a sample population, for a performance test of some sort, as a symmetrical bell curve, in which the average score (i.e. the mean) would be plotted in the middle of the curve, where the bell shape is the tallest. Most of the people (i.e. 68% of them, or 34% + 34%) have performance within 1 segment (i.e. a standard deviation) of the average score.

For the measures, typical performance is the same as the middle sections on the bell curve, or 68% of the population under review.

As we move farther away from the average performance (towards the ends of the curve – known as the tails), less and less people will have this higher or lower performance. As you can see on the diagram, approximately 16% (i.e. 14% + 2%) of the people will be higher than the average and 16% will be lower than the average.

The measures, **'definitely more than others'** and **'definitely less than others'** represents the 2% sections at the extremes on the bell curve. This is why we can say 'definitely' because not very many people will perform at these levels.

The measures, **'probably more than others'** and **'probably less than others'** represents the 14% sections to the right and left of the bell curve – the outliers.

The same distribution analysis can be undertaken on any set of market data in a similar manner. We could plot, say, the movements up or down of the FTSE 100 share index on a daily basis or the credit spreads between gilts and UK corporate bonds.

QUICK QUESTION

Write down some examples of where you have encountered a normal distribution curve.

Write your answer here before reading on.

Some relevant examples where we can see a normal distribution curve are:

When we look at the finishing times of athletes in a Marathon, you will find that a very small percentage of the overall finishers (the elite runners) will complete the race in under 2 hours 20 minutes. This group may account for around 5% of the total field. The next group will be larger, but still quite small when we compare it to the total amount of participants. These runners (the good club runners) will complete the race between 2 hours 20 minutes and 3 hours 15 minutes and could account for 20% of the field. The next group are the masses – those runners who compete for a favourite charity and complete the course between 3 hours 15 minutes and 4 hours 30 minutes. If you watch a race like the London Marathon on television, you will have seen at this time that a huge number of runners are crossing the finishing line at the same time. We would expect to see 50% of the field completing at this point. After 4 hours 30 minutes, the number of finishers will start to diminish. These runners, who complete the race between 4 hours 30 minutes and 5 hours 30 minutes are perhaps those who didn't train quite hard enough, or perhaps suffered some injury during the race but have still managed to complete the course. Around 20% of the field will fall into this category. Finally we have the stragglers – those who have been slowed down perhaps by the fancy dress costumes that they have worn or perhaps they have chosen to walk the course. This final 5% of the field can take all day to complete.

If we plot these results on a graph, the result will be the same as the normal distribution curve illustrated above.

Another example, perhaps a little closer to home is the desire by organisations to obtain a range of scores in their performance management system. Assume that the firm's system has a range of scores from 1 (poor performance) to 5 (outstanding performance). The firm will argue that if performance is being assessed fairly across the organisation, then all of these scores should be represented, probably along the following lines:

Score	Description	Percentage of staff in this category
1	Poor performance	5%
2	Requires improvement	20%
3	Meets expectations	50%
4	Exceeds expectations	20%
5	Outstanding performance	5%

Again, if plotted on a graph, we should see a normal distribution curve. However, in many firms few managers are comfortable with awarding scores of 1, 2 or 5 and so the curve would become skewed.

4.3 Confidence levels

Before we can start modelling any Variance at Risk (VaR), there are some basic decisions that must be taken so that we can know what the final number is telling us.

The first decision is about what **confidence level** (C/L) we want the model to work to. Commonly used levels are 99%, 97.5% and 95%.

What the figure indicates is that when using for instance a 99% C/L we will produce a VaR figure where in normal trading the loss figure will only be exceeded on one day out a sample of 100. Similarly a 95% C/L can expect a loss figure of greater than the figure predicted to occur on five days out of a sample of 100.

4.4 Holding periods

The second decision is over what period the price changes should be observed. Should it be a daily price change, should it be a weekly price change or should it be an even longer period?

The product or asset type drives how long this period should be. For example a position in government bonds can probably be liquidated in less than a day, so a one-day **holding period** would be appropriate. However if you had a position in corporate bonds in which there was a relatively illiquid market, then a holding period of perhaps 20 days would be appropriate – this would reflect the anticipated time between making an instruction to sell and receiving the cash for the sale of the security. The issue with holding periods is how long would it take you to close out your position in the event of a crisis? This is directly linked to liquidity in the market for the asset concerned.

The decision is thus driven by the type of asset held and subsequently the amount of time to carry out an orderly liquidation of the position. Clearly, when we are talking about an orderly liquidation, the actual size of the position is relevant. If the asset holding is very substantial, more time will be needed to liquidate it without distorting the normal market.

An example of how large positions can distort markets on liquidation was when the hedge fund Long Term Capital Management (LTCM) was closed down. Because they held so many large securities positions, it took more than four months to unwind the asset and derivative positions.

When talking about time horizons for financial assets, we have to recognise that for the vast majority of markets, trading only takes place from Monday to Friday, with breaks for national holidays.

This means that a two-week time horizon would normally be described as a ten-day horizon. Similarly a one-year time horizon is normally allocated between 250-252 days. This reflects 52 weeks X 5 days = 260 less between 8 and 10 days national holidays depending on which country you are monitoring.

4.5 Observation period

This is the period over which data are gathered with a view to finding the pattern from which future market prices are to be predicted. One of the fundamental decisions to be made is how far to go back when looking at the historic pricing history. It is evident how difficult predictions will be when volatility has changed suddenly. It is generally accepted that the most recent price history has greatest relevance to assessing the probability of future price moves.

This being said, there must be a reasonable level of clean historic data to justify the projections.

4.6 Regulatory requirements

Basel recommends that the following parameters are used when banks are calculating capital requirements to cover market risk:

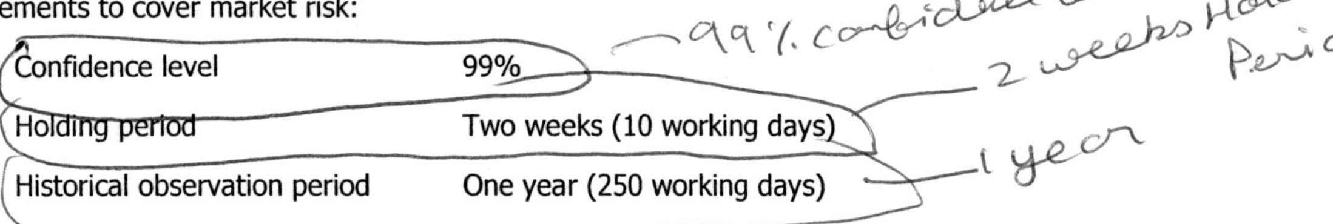

Confidence level	99%
Holding period	Two weeks (10 working days)
Historical observation period	One year (250 working days)

4.7 Normal distribution

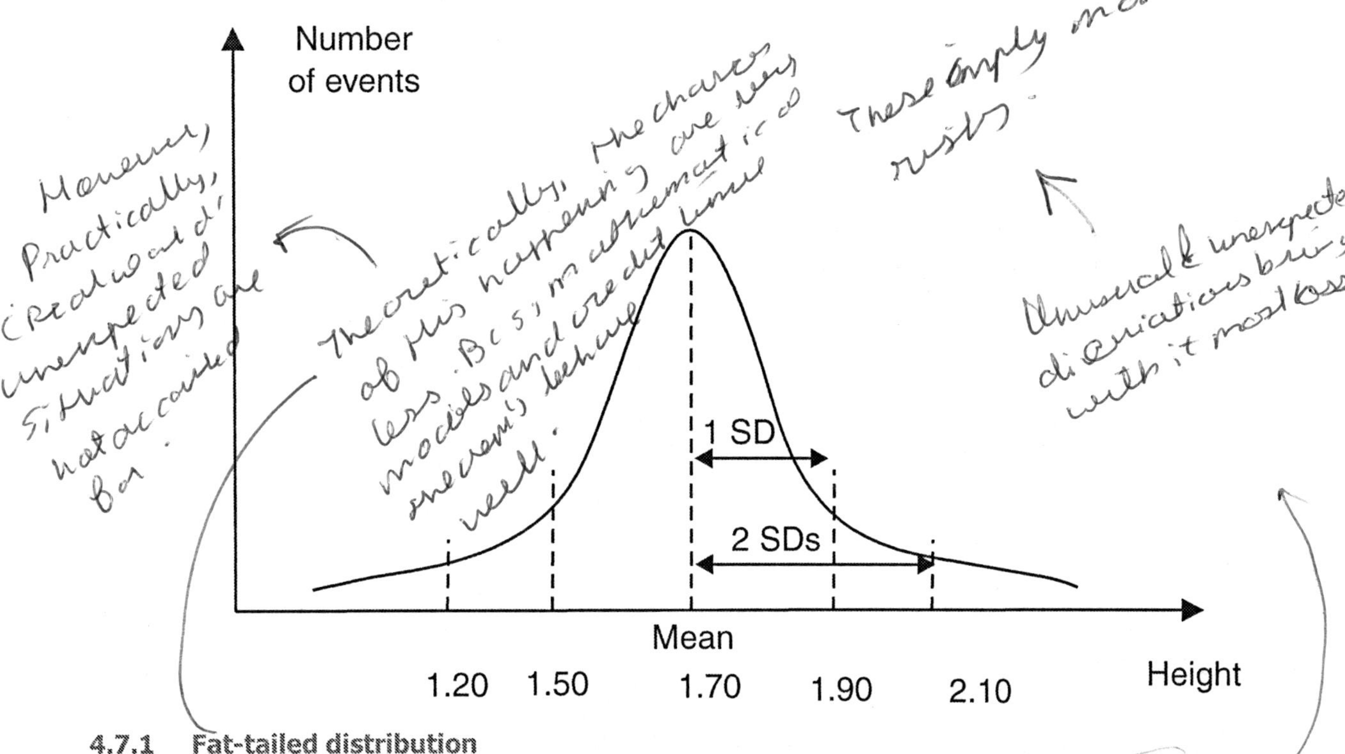

4.7.1 Fat-tailed distribution

The typical bell curve shape as described earlier is well-known. The property known as a fat tail illustrates how models may mislead. The deviations which are unusual and unexpected will be sudden and perhaps unpublicised but they might bring with them the worst losses. Such risks may be unsuitable for normal VaR modelling and may need a different approach.

In finance, fat tails are considered undesirable because of the additional risk they imply. For example, an investment strategy may have an expected return, after one year that is five times its standard deviation. Assuming a normal distribution, the likelihood of its failure (negative return) is less than one in a million; in practice, it may be higher. Normal distributions that emerge in finance generally do so because the factors influencing an asset's value or price are mathematically well-behaved, and the central limit theorem provides for such a distribution. However, traumatic 'real-world' events (such as an oil shock, a large corporate bankruptcy, or an abrupt change in a political situation) are usually not mathematically well-behaved. The bankruptcy of US energy firm Enron is an example of a traumatic fat-tailed event.

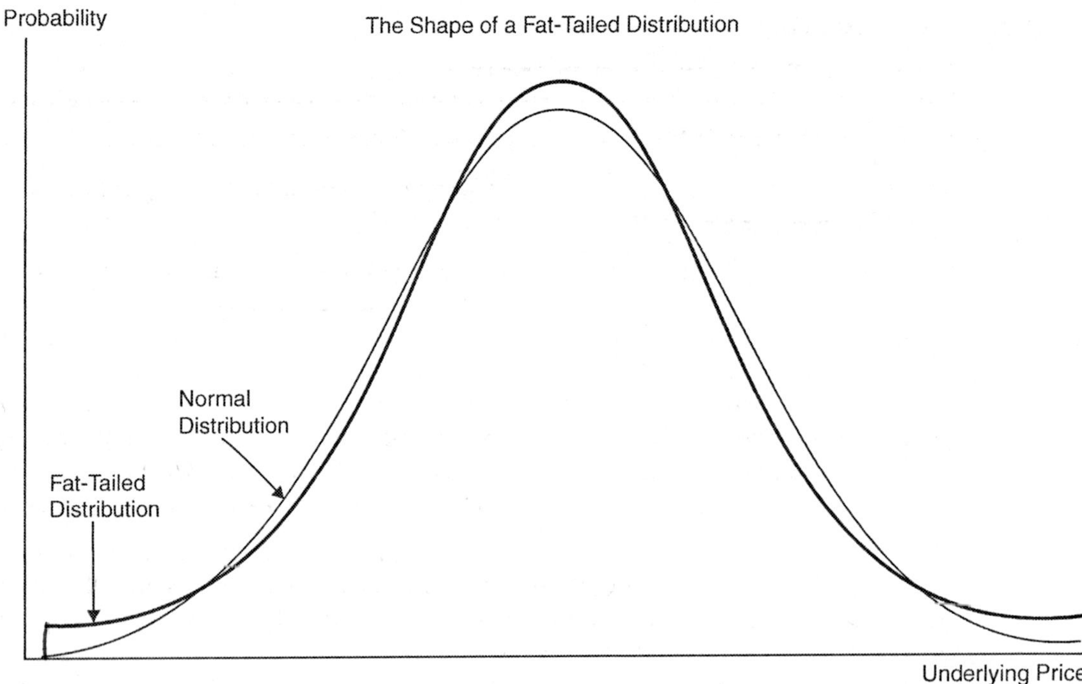

4.8 Probability

Probability is a way of expressing knowledge or belief that an event will occur or has occurred. In mathematics the concept has been given an exact meaning in probability theory, which is used extensively in such areas of study as mathematics, statistics and finance to draw conclusions about the likelihood of potential events.

A probability provides a quantitative description of the likely occurrence of a particular event. Probability is conventionally expressed on a scale from 0 to 1; a rare event has a probability close to 0, a very common event has a probability close to 1.

The probability of an event has been defined as its long-run relative frequency. It has also been thought of as a personal degree of belief that a particular event will occur (subjective probability).

In some experiments, all outcomes are equally likely. For example if you were to choose one winner in a raffle from a hat, all raffle ticket holders are equally likely to win, that is, they have the same probability of their ticket being chosen. This is the equally-likely outcomes model and is defined to be:

$$P(E) = \frac{\text{number of outcomes corresponding to event E}}{\text{total number of outcomes}}$$

EXAMPLE

1. The probability of drawing a spade from a pack of 52 well-shuffled playing cards is 13/52 = 1/4 = 0.25 since:
   - Event E = a spade is drawn
   - The number of outcomes corresponding to E = 13 (spades)
   - The total number of outcomes = 52 (cards)
2. When tossing a coin, we assume that the results 'heads' or 'tails' each have equal probabilities of 0.5.

4.8.1 Sensitivity analysis

Some of the estimates made in risk analysis are imprecise. A sensitivity analysis should be carried out to test the effect of uncertainty in assumptions and data. Sensitivity analysis is also a way of testing the appropriateness and effectiveness of potential controls and risk treatment options.

The process always needs to start by looking at sensitivity analysis and looking to extreme values. This is based on probability and distributions.

Sensitivity analysis is the study of how the variation in the output of a model (numerical or otherwise) can be apportioned, qualitatively or quantitatively, to different sources of variation. Sensitivity analysis looks at a key variable in a business and tries to vary it by a unitary amount. Consider a typical bank and think through the type of things that can vary and would change the risk profile for the organisation. Interest rates and foreign exchange rates should be the first things that we think of. We might consider credit risk issues and think about downgrades or changes in the economy. After that we might suggest things like operations. In these areas issues cover matters such as the volume of transactions undertaken, the number of errors occurring and the number of types of deals being captured.

So the sensitivity analysis is a sensible starting point. It is effectively the variation of a single variable in a complex model, viewing the impact of such a unitary movement. It can be regarded as a way to look at the impact of a changing variable on a total data population. Typically one variable is moved by a standardised amount and its impact measured. For example, the potential effect of a two percent rise in interest rates could be measured. Two or more variables can be varied leading to two and three-dimensional solutions.

Effectively this is the expected movements and their impacts. It enables a firm to understand profitability and costs, the resources that are required in terms of cash and liquidity, software and hardware capacity, people and equipment. If the 1% increases results in losses going up by 5% then this is the type of concern that needs to be identified.

As such, sensitivity analysis is good risk management but requires a firm to have fully modelled and understood risk environment.

4.9 Earnings risk

This originates from the interest rate gap between loans and bonds (assets) and deposits and other funding (liabilities). The difference (known as the spread) in interest rates between a bank's assets and liabilities will impact on its earnings. Off-balance sheet exposures, such as mortgage servicing and transaction processing fees can also be an important source of earnings risk.

Traditionally, commercial banks are asset sensitive; their floating rate loans (assets) have shorter durations or re-price more frequently than their core deposits (liabilities). Earnings models focus on the impact of changes in interest rates on accrual or reported earnings.

One such model is known as **earnings at risk (EAR),** which refers to the impact on net income over the following 12 months of a one-time change in market rates/prices. Earnings risk is more akin to market risk. However, it avoids the arbitrary assumptions of economic valuations. A firm's accounting earnings are a well-defined notion. A problem with looking at earnings risk is that earnings are non-economic. Earnings may be suggestive of economic value, but they can be misleading and are often easy to manipulate. A firm can report high earnings while its long term franchise is eroded away by lack of investment or competing technologies. Financial transactions can boost short-term earnings at the expense of long-term earnings. After all, traditional techniques of Asset and Liability Management (ALM) focus on earnings, and their shortcomings remain today.

Gap models and re-pricing schedules analyse earnings risk in terms of the gap or mismatch between assets and liabilities over duration or maturity buckets. Such models usually make simplifying assumptions about interest rate and cash flow behaviour. For example, they often do not take account of mortgage prepayments or potential disintermediation from rising interest rates. Further, gap models generally assume perfect correlations between products.

ALM managers measure market risk with duration-gap models and/or market value simulation models. Similar to the distinction between earnings gap and simulation models, market value simulation models rely more heavily upon assumptions than do duration-gap models. Different from earnings simulation models, market value simulation cash flows are not static, e.g. cash flows are dynamically simulated over the entire expected lives of the bank's holdings.

Dynamic simulation models, such as earnings at risk warn of potential earnings shortfalls over a range of maturity buckets over longer periods of time and manage option-like returns.

5 Financial and non-financial quantification

5.1 Quantitative risk calculation

Risk can be assessed on a qualitative or a quantitative basis. The former type of assessment will typically present a range of values which do not contain figures. These might be for example high, medium-high, medium, medium-low and low. On the other hand a quantitative assessment will contain only figures. This could be done perhaps in ranges; for example, up to £5 million, £5-10 million, and £10-25 million and additionally by using likelihood figures. The monetary amounts refer to risk impact values and percentage figures would be used to address likelihood, for example 10%, 25%, 30%.

Some managers and their organisations are more comfortable with figures. It is also very common for a risk assessment approach to use a colour coding, for example red, amber, green and generating what is known as RAG statuses with no numeric definitions. At a later date a move to a quantitative basis can be added as the organisation builds its knowledge and confidence and gains better loss data and information about the risks and its experience of losses.

Operational risk generates both quantitative and qualitative data. Therefore a particular challenge for the risk managers involved in operational risk management is the collecting and blending together of both quantitative and qualitative data in the reports that are presented to management.

5.2 Application of modelling approaches

As large operational risk losses continue to occur they always attract a lot of media attention and regulatory interest. This has given rise to the requirement for better ways of achieving the satisfactory quantification of operational risk and this is expounded in initiatives such as Basel III. However a sound operational risk model is definitely going to require more than just a formula because the underlying operational profile of the firm needs to be explored by various means that are available to generate data to feed the model and to interpret its outputs. All components of the model, both its input data and its expert judgement, the design of the calculation itself and the analysis and treatment of results must be surrounded by an appropriate governance framework.

For banks in particular, the stringent capital requirements of both Basel II and III raise the potential benefits of the advanced measurement approach (AMA) for operational risk. For this technique, modelling must be performed and that requires the utilisation of forms of financial quantification. These measurements will be looked at in more detail when we consider Regulatory Risk.

5.3 The importance of data

The first of the components is the data that is available for modelling. This data can be information on loss events directly experienced by the company, known as **internal loss databases**. This can be enhanced by information on loss events experienced by peer companies (these are the **external loss databases**). The information required for integration appropriately into the operational risk model is very extensive and includes amongst other things the definition of a convention regarding dates, a clear description of the loss event itself, the amount of loss involved and the link to controls.

Data may be collected locally say at branch offices or business divisions or from subsidiaries but then should be converted into a central database where quality control checks can be carried out. This information, provided by means of loss data, is not only important for the quantification of operational risk but also delivers the fundamental inputs for qualitative risk management. The definition of investigations and control measures can only be efficiently applied if the quality of loss data information is reliable and detailed particularly for external loss events.

5.4 Scenario modelling

The next stage of modelling involves adding the expert interpretation and judgement which is applied by essentially a non-quantification based upon managers' expertise and experience. This is commonly applied in the form of scenario modelling. It is important that expert judgement be regarded as complementary in addition to the loss database and available industry information. The definition of scenario should cover all potentially high severity risks and result in a longer term interpretation of the model itself. In the tails of the model the worst case scenarios will exist. These should be challenging yet should not be changed frequently. As with all risk management it is essential to carry out reviews of both models and scenarios on a regular basis. For example, there should as a minimum be an annual review based on changing business environments and utilising new information that occurs as time moves on. Perhaps the two most common modelling scenario approaches are known as the loss distribution approach and the scenario approach.

QUICK QUESTION

What do you think could be common problems encountered when using models?

Write your answer here before reading on.

Common issues with modelling:

- Limited internal loss data history
- Limited information on low frequency yet high impact events
- Limited descriptive information about loss events
- Unsystematic data collection
- Loss of information.

With respect to the design of scenarios, these issues commonly occur:

- Non-availability or inconsistency or lacking of an aggregated view
- Outdated information
- Failure to generate sufficiently challenging scenarios.

Various modelling methods exist. Internal measurement models are normally deterministic in nature whereas loss distribution models are typically using Value at Risk type structures. A third technique is known as scorecards which are derived from the concept of the balance scorecard.

5.5 Drawbacks with modelling

A fundamental point that is often experienced is that masses of loss data are necessary in order for the model to have something solid to work on and produce some meaningful results. It may also be that loss data for certain types of risk are sparse because the company has simply no loss data experience. It is essential to apply modelling consistently and therefore it is important to be assured that all losses are collected and correctly recorded. To do this generates an incentive for the organisation and the fundamental question exists as to whether there is a suitable degree of incentive in place.

Sometimes the changing nature of the firm's business will prevent this task from being fulfilled owing to the changes that the business is experiencing. A business that has been very similar for many years will have a greater chance of generating more meaningful data than one that is constantly changing. Most losses that are experienced by companies are those in the high likelihood and low impact area. Another point that can be stated as a disadvantage is that using past loss data history is all very well but it is the future that we are seeking to model and therefore can the past records generate a meaningful picture for what is to come in the future? This is particularly relevant when we consider that we are operating in a fast-changing environment. Similarly every firm is different so therefore when applying external loss data from peers there may be an issue about the relevance to any particular firm.

5.6 The scorecard approach

The scorecard approach presents a more qualitative view which can be challenged and supported by real loss data. It is essential to discuss this with the business managers and for a review to be performed centrally by the risk managers additionally. The technique is relatively fast to put in place - both to set up and review – and can generate some confidence about treating worst case scenarios well in that the scorecard approach is realistic and traps the big risks.

On the other hand the scorecard approach does have some downside. The first of these is that extensive training and competence is essential amongst both the business managers and the risk professionals to make the system work. There just has to be a sufficient degree of understanding as to how to apply the technique. There is also an issue about the quality of business judgement on hand within the firm to apply to the task together with the degree of management commitment to the approach in the first place.

5.7 General issues with models

With all models, data quality is far more important than the mathematics of the model. It is also necessary to recognise the correlations between risks.

There are many practical problems with models. Some of the major ones normally encountered are as follows:

- Gaps in the data
- Scaling issues
- Is the data clean? There will be a requirement for data scrubbing (particularly with external loss data)
- Applying weighting to different risk buckets
- The insurance effect, i.e. has insurance mitigated the total loss for certain losses where insurance was in place and did indeed pay out?
- Modifying fat tails in that models producing distribution analysis will sometimes generate higher figures in the tails of the diagram
- Confidence levels and ratings
- Comparing the actual results of the model – how to ensure that the model is producing sensible and relevant information.

5.8 Application of scenarios

Stress tests and scenarios have been referred to because they help to improve models and historic data. Scenarios must involve the business and they should not just be conducted by the risk managers. They are important because they feed into capital and liquidity planning, particularly under the Basel rules.

Scenarios challenge assumptions and indeed as pointed out elsewhere in this text, have to be challenging. Scenarios also link in with business continuity activities.

5.9 Issues with scenarios

Very often scenarios take too short a view. It must be remembered that, for example, taking a change in interest rates as a scenario could become the status quo for a long time. It is also possible for scenarios to present an outcome that is too modest because the analysis has been limited by the inexperience of those conducting the evaluation. A particular point to stress with scenarios is that they must involve the business and failure to do so will threaten the validity of the outcome. Remember that, with scenarios, time will need to pass in order for the scenarios to fulfil their course and be played out. As a general rule scenarios must work hand in hand and assess historic data carefully. Do not forget to address reputational risk as part of the challenge and above all review scenarios frequently with a view to making consistent improvements in the techniques and skill deployed.

5.10 Using scenarios successfully

This is a short list of the sorts of ideas for applications of scenarios that could be applied:

- The broader environment – extreme events
- Fraud in loans or payments
- Accidents to staff and customers
- Litigation
- Regulatory breaches
- IT failures
- Project failure
- Data theft
- Mis-selling.

The learning outcomes of successful scenario modelling might include:

- Failure to meet objectives
- Funding issues
- Fraud
- Capacity problems
- Ratings and reputational damage
- Impact on the environment
- Competitive threats
- Delivery difficulties
- Loss of customers/business.

6 Economic capital

In financial services firms, economic capital can be thought of as the capital level shareholders would choose in the absence of capital regulation.

More specifically, it is the amount of risk capital, assessed on a realistic basis, which a firm requires to cover the risks that it is running or collecting as a going concern, across market risk, credit risk, and operational risk. Firms and financial services regulators should then aim to hold risk a capital of an amount at least equal to economic capital.

Typically, economic capital is calculated by determining the amount of capital that the firm needs to ensure that its balance sheet stays solvent over a certain time period within a pre-specified probability. Therefore, economic capital is often calculated as value at risk. The balance sheet, in this case, would be prepared showing market value (rather than book value) of assets and liabilities.

Economic capital and regulatory capital are two terms that are frequently used in the analysis of the banks under modern day regulation. Regulatory capital is the minimum amount required, particularly by the Basel Committee, for banks as a result of regulatory requirement. Economic capital is the level of capital that is effectively chosen by the bank shareholders without impact of regulation. The normal meaning of the phrase economic capital is to be able to define the level of capital that is required to cover a bank's potential losses with a certain confidence level. In some ways economic capital can be thought of as the level of capital that banks' shareholders would choose in the absence of external capital regulation.

Regulatory capital on the other hand is a clear concept. It is the minimum capital required by the regulator which may be the capital charge required by the Basel Committee.

Economic capital in the eyes of a bank's shareholders is the amount of capital that is required to operate the bank for the maximisation of the shareholders wealth. For regulatory capital, on the other hand, the primary stakeholders would be the bank's depositors and their objective would be to minimise the possibility of their receiving a loss of their capital by the failure of the bank.

The concept of economic capital differs from regulatory capital in the sense that regulatory capital is the mandatory capital the regulators require to be maintained while economic capital is the best estimate of required capital that financial institutions use internally to manage their own risk and to allocate the cost of maintaining regulatory capital among different units within the organisation.

To compute economic capital therefore, a dynamic model would be used by which the shareholders would choose at the beginning of the financial year the level of capital that they need in order to maximise the value of the bank taking into account the possibility that the bank could be closed if its losses during the financial year might exceed the initial level of capital.

A further concept could identify the amount of actual capital held by a bank, which could be defined as the level of capital chosen by the bank's shareholders taking into account regulatory constraints as well as their views with respect to economic capital.

Using the approaches under Basel II and Basel III will derive a regulatory capital figure for banks.

7 Application of risk in other companies

The management of risk is central to running any business enterprise, regardless of size. Most risks can be considered to be financial.

In 2012 economies and companies were attempting to build a recovery from the global financial crisis. It was not surprising that economic slowdown was regarded as the top risk across the world.

QUICK QUESTION

What do you think are the major risks facing businesses across all sectors?

Write your answer here before reading on.

Top ten risks facing businesses of all types are as follows (source: *Aon 2013 Global Risk Management Survey*):

1. Weak economies
2. Regulatory and legislative changes
3. Increasing competition
4. Damage to reputation
5. Failure to attract top talent
6. Failure to innovate
7. Business interruption
8. Commodity price risk
9. Cashflow and liquidity risk
10. Political risk

These top ten risks show the major risks of a much longer list which could be drawn up covering anything from pension scheme funding through to pandemic risk health crises and mergers and acquisitions and restructuring. A large proportion of risks faced by general business are operational risks; these involve keeping customers happy, managing staff resources, managing technology and the demands of protecting assets including succession planning and physical damage to plants etc. The types of risks involved in banking in addition to operational risk are credit risk and market risk but these, by and large, are of far less significance in other types of business. The essence of banking is investment, making loans and trading and this exposes firms directly to the credit risk of providing loans to other businesses and individuals and also to trading exposures in any markets where trading positions are taken.

Risk should firmly be on the agenda of the Board. Three out of four major companies in 2011 would have stated that the Board or a Board committee has established or partially established policies on risk oversight or management. Risk management therefore, as an element of corporate governance, is being recognised more and more by those that manage firms.

Firms will seek to have a formal risk management department reporting in the main to the chief financial officer or to finance or the treasury department. This is even true of firms where no formal risk management department is in existence.

Covering the top ten risks in turn.

7.1 Weak economies

Organisations are concerned about how economies will rise out of the recession. Fuelling this concern are continued high rates of unemployment and unease over the debt sustainability of many of the largest economies supported by monetary and fiscal policies that cannot be maintained in perpetuity. This is particularly true of the Eurozone, which has suffered greatly.

7.2 Regulatory and legislative changes

Risks related to regulatory and legislative changes involve the inability of an organisation to comply with current, changing or new regulations. Failure in compliance can result in severe consequences, including direct penalties in the short-term and the loss of markets, reputation and customers in the long-term.

Regulatory changes, even small ones, can add huge compliance costs to organisations. This is well known similarly to those involved in the banking industry.

7.3 Increasing competition

A large number of variables can impact the competitive position of an organisation in any industry sector – economic trends, regulatory changes, emergence of new competitors, changes in consumer trends, advances in technology, use of lower cost resources from emerging economies and aggressive strategies by competitors.

It is a rapidly changing marketplace and failure adequately to address all these changes and other market developments can lead to an irreversible loss of market share.

7.4 Damage to reputation

Corporate reputation is one of the most important corporate assets and also one of the most difficult to protect. The economic crisis and various high profile cases involving industrial accidents, product recalls and the like have made organisations realise the urgency of protecting their reputation. Reputations can take years to build but can be destroyed rapidly, even overnight. In the modern world complex global supply chains and an internet-fed 24-hour news cycle fuelled by the demands of social media have posed additional challenges for companies to manage risks related to their reputation and brand.

It is perfectly correct to consider a damaged reputation as a risk in its own right but also it can be a consequence of other risks. Either way, it is clear that all risks may impact or be impacted by damage to reputation.

When thinking about reputational risk, we need look no further than the damage to the reputation of those banks that needed public funds to support then during the banking crisis.

7.5 Failure to attract top talent

This has always been a major risk in the government sector which regularly loses its talented staff to the better paying private sector. Changing business environments similarly strain the processes of recruiting top industry talent and force organisations to develop strategic plans that address shifts in the workforce, talent shortages, economic pressures and organisation.

Securing, retaining and maximising talent requires a thoughtfully designed strategy which includes rigorous and appropriate recruitment, assessment and development of individuals. As the global pool of available candidates becomes increasingly smaller, the ability to attract top talent has significant implications to the financial results of organisations.

Business interruption refers to an anticipated or unanticipated interruption of an organisation's normal operations. Losses can arise from many sources, some man-made and others natural. The factors that contribute to business interruption are often sudden and can change rapidly, making it a challenging risk to understand and manage.

Some of these exposures can be insured against while others can only be mitigated.

As companies expand abroad or acquire components from abroad, the interdependence of global business partners as well as outsourcing and off shoring has increased their international exposures. At the very least they are more volatile and complex. The tsunami in Japan in 2011 provided a clear example of this and reinforced further the importance of having risk mitigation strategies for business interruption exposure. Another example is the BP Gulf of Mexico oil spill in 2012.

7.6 Failure to innovate

Innovation plays a vital role in the development of new business concepts, processes and products. Innovation drives growth and opportunity in new markets and breathes life into a mature industry. Innovation is a pre-requisite for success, even for survival. Companies can rapidly lose market share if they fail to invest in innovation.

More than ever innovation, speed and flexibility are essential to compete successfully in the global economy.

7.7 Business interruption

Any interruption to business can cause havoc and in the worst cases cause business failures. Interruptions range from delays in key suppliers through to natural disasters.

With the heavy reliance on technology infrastructure, businesses are becoming more vulnerable to system failures which have led to business interruptions, damaged reputation and loss of customers. Such issues are often exacerbated by companies that temporarily delay improvements and maintenance on existing systems to manage earnings during difficult times.

An inherent problem with the technology infrastructure of large blanks is their huge size and fragmented nature. RBS for example has grown through mergers and acquisitions and in the UK is made up of The Royal Bank of Scotland, NatWest, Ulster Bank, Drummonds Bank and Coutts. This makes managing and maintaining a multitude of legacy and often non-integrated of banking systems complicated and expensive. Therefore, attempts to upgrade and integrate the banking systems are often untried and high risk.

In June 2012, customers of RBS were unable to use their online bank accounts for over a week, causing widespread disruption for customers – for some Ulster Bank customers, disruption lasted for up to two weeks. Similarly, in January 2014, 3,500 Lloyds, Bank of Scotland and TSB cash machines working. In this instance, the failure was not due to an upgrade and was a random hardware failure. This goes to show how reliant banks are on technology and that technology failure causes widespread disruption for customers.

Hopefully, with the economic recession abating and IT investments on the rise improvements in this area will help to mitigate this risk.

7.8 Commodity price risk

Commodity prices surged towards the end of 2010. As a result the requirement for stability of commodity prices creates an even bigger concern for many organisations, such as airlines, who are exposed to fuel prices.

Principally among these is the price of energy which is influenced globally by potential political conflicts and natural disasters in the regions of major oil producers. It is difficult to think of any corporation that is not affected either directly or indirectly by commodity prices in general and specifically by the price of energy.

Commodity price risk will be one of the highest risks for the natural resources sector (oil, gas and mining) and food processing and distribution industries. It is also a threat to the wider economy because the cost of energy has to be factored in and priced into the eventual prices paid by the end consumer.

7.9 Cash flow and liquidity risks

The prolonged period of low interest rates globally, organisational planning, restructuring and revival of investor confidence have enabled corporations to access relatively cheap short to medium-term funding sources.

Even though the rate of corporate defaults dropped from 2009 organisations still consider this to be a substantial risk in the aftermath of the financial crisis.

Higher concerns exist for companies with revenues under one billion US dollars because smaller companies have fewer assets against which to borrow.

7.10 Political risk

Political risk relates to any complications or implications faced by businesses due to political decisions. A recent example is the tensions between Russia and Ukraine over Russia wishing to take control of the Crimean Peninsula. The tensions caused chaos for any businesses that traded with Russia and Ukraine: The US placed economic sanctions on Russia and jeopardised Russian gas imports to Europe (who rely on Russian gas for half of their gas supply).

Political risk is hard to quantify and it tricky to fully plan for all political risks. For example, imagine if the European Union was disbanded. The widespread global economic impact would be impossible to quantify, but the effects would be far reaching.

7.11 Global organisations' risk management policies

The following extract is from a major international company describing its risk management policy:

'Risk is inherent in our business. The identification and management of risk is central to delivering on the Corporate Objective.

Risk will manifest itself in many forms and has the potential to impact the health and safety, environment, community, reputation, regulatory, operational, market and financial performance of the Group and, thereby, the achievement of the Corporate Objective.

By understanding and managing risk we provide greater certainty and confidence for our shareholders, employees, customers and suppliers, and for the communities in which we operate.

Successful risk management can be a source of competitive advantage.

Risks faced by the Group shall be managed on an enterprise-wide basis. The natural diversification in the Group's portfolio of commodities, geographies, currencies, assets and liabilities is a key element in our risk management approach.

We will use our risk management capabilities to maximise the value from our assets, projects and other business opportunities and to assist us in encouraging enterprise and innovation.

Risk management will be embedded into our critical business activities, functions and processes. Risk understanding and our tolerance for risk will be key considerations in our decision making.

Risk issues will be identified, analysed and ranked in a consistent manner. Common systems and methodologies will be used.

Risk controls will be designed and implemented to reasonably assure the achievement of our Corporate Objective. The effectiveness of these controls will be systematically reviewed and, where necessary, improved.

Risk management performance will be monitored, reviewed and reported. Oversight of the effectiveness of our risk management processes will provide assurance to executive management, the Board and shareholders.

The effective management of risk is vital to the continued growth and success of our Group.'

The company in question is BHP Billiton, the global mining conglomerate. It could so easily have been a bank too, judging by the style and the nature of the remarks it contains.

QUICK QUESTION

Reflect upon the organisation that you work in and list some the risk management policies of the bank you work in, or a large global bank

Write your answer here before reading on.

The purpose of a policy is to communicate an organisation's principles. Therefore risk management policies communicate how an organisation wants to manage risks. A global bank will face a multitude of risks, ranging from technology risk through to reputational risk. To try and jot down every risk facing a bank would be an impossible task, not least because the risks are evolving. In order to have a coherent and understandable set of risk management policies, banks use a defined framework. The types of frameworks that can be used will be explored in detail in later chapters.

The framework will contain the high level risk management policies and break them down into procedures. Procedures define a set of actions required to achieve an end result – the 'how' to complement the policy. For example, a bank may have a risk management principle of not lending to customers with poor credit ratings. The procedure to complement this policy could be to run detailed credit rating and credit history checks and to ensure management sign-off of all new customer loans.

KEY WORDS

Key words in this chapter are given below. There is space to write your own revision notes and to add any other words or phrases that you want to remember.

- Credit risk
- Market risk
- Capital risk
- Liquidity risk
- Operational risk
- Financial crime risk
- Technology risk
- People risk
- Regulatory risk
- Financial reporting risk
- Legal risk
- Strategic risk
- Change risk
- Reputational risk
- Insurance risk
- Systematic risk
- Distribution analysis
- Normal distribution
- Sensitivity analysis
- Earnings risk
- Internal loss database
- External loss database
- Economic capital
- Regulatory capital

REVIEW

Now consider the main points that were introduced in this section. These are listed below. Tick each one as you go through them.

- The business of banking is fundamentally concerned with the balancing of risk versus reward.
- Risks can be categorised under a number of headings – for example, credit risk, liquidity risk, strategic risk, etc.
- The finance industry is a global industry with events in one part of the world having possible ramifications in many other places. Technology has been a key driver in the development of this phenomenon.
- Distribution analysis is a method of using past data to predict the future.
- Probability is a way of expressing the knowledge or belief that an event will or has occurred.
- Sensitivity analysis is used by banks to assess the impact of a change in a variable from a complex model.
- Firms will use both quantitative and qualitative data to assess risk.
- When using models, the data used must have integrity.
- Economic capital is the amount of capital shareholders would want to maintain without regulation – regulatory capital is the minimum amount of capital the bank must maintain as laid down by Basel.
- Risks faced by organisations can be broadly similar across a number of industry sectors.

Top 10 Risks

-> Slowing of Economy
-> Reputational Risk — 3
-> Regulatory Risk
-> Commodity Prices
-> Interruption of Business — 3
-> Liquidity and Cash Flow
-> Political Risk
-> Increased competition — 3
-> Inability to Recruit new talent
-> Inability to innovate -> 1

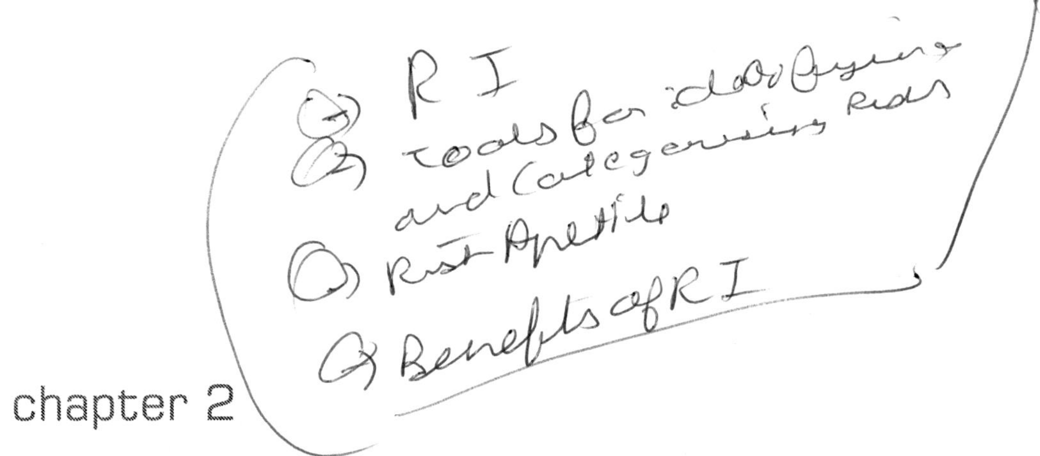

chapter 2

RISK IDENTIFICATION

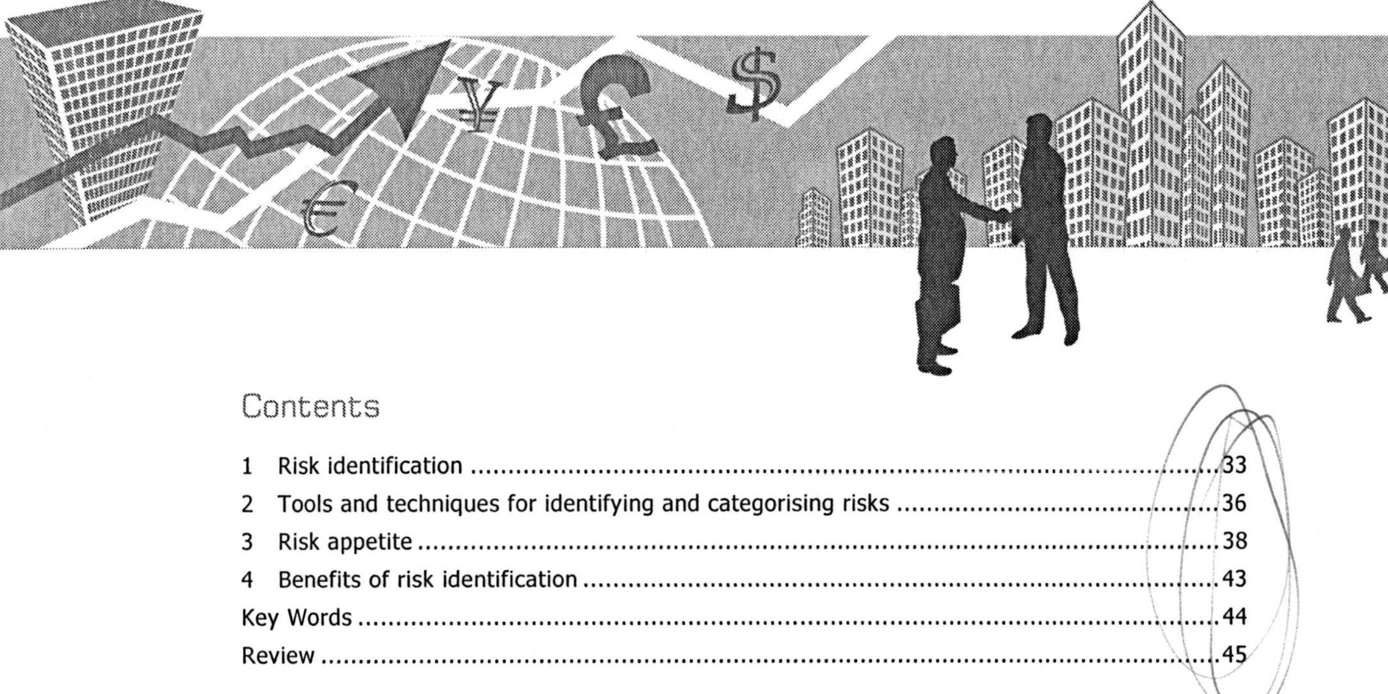

Contents

Learning objectives

On completion of this chapter, you should be able to:

- distinguish between different types of risk and how these can be identified, monitored and mitigated
- examine a range of tools and techniques to identify risk and explain how these can be implemented in the workplace.

Introduction

In the forthcoming chapters we will be exploring the Risk Management Lifecycle which is illustrated and explained below:

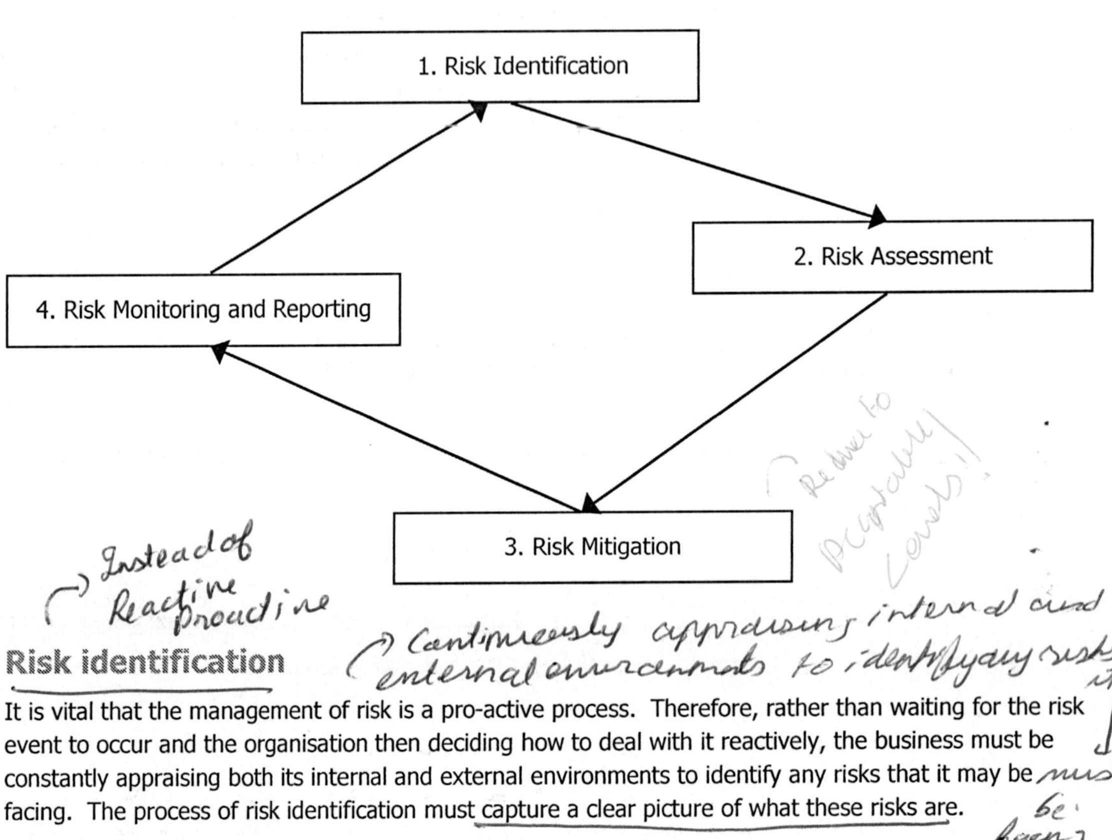

Risk identification

It is vital that the management of risk is a pro-active process. Therefore, rather than waiting for the risk event to occur and the organisation then deciding how to deal with it reactively, the business must be constantly appraising both its internal and external environments to identify any risks that it may be facing. The process of risk identification must capture a clear picture of what these risks are.

Risk assessment

Once the business is clear as to the risks it faces, it then has to decide how likely it is that these risks will occur and if they do occur, what is the likely effect of these risks on the business?

Mitigation

Having assessed the probability and impact of the risk, the organisation can move on to decide how best to mitigate the risks to a level it is comfortable with.

Monitoring and reporting

The management of risk should be an on-going process; therefore risk should be monitored on an on-going basis. This may be in the shape of key risk indicators that tell us if a risk is moving from one of the categories described above to another. The firm must also be clear about what it should be reporting on and to whom.

In the following chapters, we are going to develop on these themes by looking at each section of the Risk Management Lifecycle in turn. To do this, we will start with this chapter on Risk Identification, where we will consider the different ways in which risk can be identified, looking at the techniques that allow us not only to identify risk, but also to think about how these risks can be categorised under common headings. As it is impossible for either organisations or individuals to exist in a risk free environment, the topic of risk appetite will be introduced next. This allows us to consider what risks we are willing to accept in differing sets of circumstances. The chapter will then conclude with a short discussion around the benefits of risk identification – which should be apparent to you by then!

1 Risk identification

Risk identification is at the heart of the development of a risk management project. If you fail to identify a risk you will fail to measure it, mitigate it, monitor and report on it and so on.

It is important to recognise that risk identification will not be just a single exercise that can be completed and then forgotten about; it is clear that operational risks change over time both in their likelihood and in their type. Risk identification will therefore need to be a live and dynamic process that is regularly revisited to ensure that it remains current and applicable to the nature of the business being conducted.

1.1 The regulatory imperative

The Prudential Regulatory Authority (PRA) (the current regulator for the UK financial sector responsible for risk oversight) – states that, '...(a firm) will need to notify the PRA of any operational risk matter that has a significant regulatory impact. ....this requirement includes, but is not limited to, notification of:

1. a significant failure in its systems and controls
2. a significant operational loss
3. its intention to enter into, or significantly change, a material outsourcing arrangement.

A firm may also wish to notify the PRA of:

1. any significant operational exposures that it has identified
2. the invocation of a business continuity plan
3. any other significant change to its organisation, infrastructure or business operating environment.

Therefore operational risk is central to the PRA's regulatory requirements.

The PRA has stated that, 'The operational risk management function is responsible for developing strategies to identify, assess, monitor and control/mitigate operational risk...'.

It also states that, 'In order to understand its operational risk profile, a firm should identify the types of operational risk that it is exposed to as far as reasonably possible. This might include, but is not limited to consideration of:

1. the nature of a firm's customers, products and activities, including sources of business, distribution mechanisms, and the complexity and volumes of transactions.
2. the design, implementation, and operation of the processes and systems used in the end-to-end operating cycle for a firm's products and activities'.

So in terms of the risk identification that needs to be undertaken there are a series of risks to consider. A system could be designed incorrectly. If that is the case the blame may well lie with the design team. The system might have been perfectly designed, but implementation could be poor. You would neither want to blame the design people for this, not the operations people who will then be spending additional time trying to correct a poor system. The blame could sit with the IT professionals, or their equivalent. Finally the system could be well designed and implemented, but the staff just operate it inappropriately. In this case the loss would be for the operations department to consider. Other PRA requirements are:

3. the risk culture and human resource management practices at a firm; and
4. the business operating environment, including political, legal, socio-demographic, technological, and economic factors as well as the competitive environment and market structure.

The regulator has plenty to say about risk management. The PRA goes on to state, 'A firm should recognise that it may face significant operational exposures from a product or activity that may not be material to its business strategy. A firm should consider the appropriate level of detail at which risk identification is to take place, and may wish to manage the operational risks that it faces in risk categories that are appropriate to its organisational and legal structures.'

1.2 Understanding of risk

You cannot manage something that you do not understand. If one cannot define the risk at the outset then the remainder of the risk management cycle is meaningless. The principles start with understanding of risk – risk identification. Only having implemented effective risk identification can a firm move on to consider a risk profile. It is intended that the framework should cover the bank's appetite and tolerance for operational risk, including the extent of, and the manner in which, operational risk is transferred outside the bank – perhaps by the use of a joint-venture initiative with another organisation.

There is a need for an operational risk structure; the structure would be sufficient to set out how risks will be identified, measured, controlled and reported – you will recall that these are the headings from the Risk Management Lifecycle.

QUICK QUESTION

In your organisation with whom does the ultimate responsibility for the implementation of the Risk Management Lifecycle lie?

Write your answer here before reading on.

The responsibility for this framework will always sit with the Board of Directors and they will be answerable for any failure to implement the structure. They will certainly delegate some of the responsibilities under the framework – it is unrealistic for the Board to check every system and process. What they are not able to do is to walk away from their responsibilities in this vital area. Consequently it will be necessary for the Board to document the nature of the delegated actions and responsibilities properly and for this delegation to be included within job descriptions for the individual employees concerned.

The Board also needs to implement some form of monitoring system to ensure that the delegated authorities are operating successfully. This could include input from both internal and external auditors, but must be supplemented by detailed reporting together with clear questioning of assumptions.

Furthermore it would be expected that there would be some form of back testing based upon actual experience – if a significant operational loss occurs, why was this the case? Was it properly considered so that it was within the risk tolerance of the institution as approved by the Board? What does it tell the Board about the risk framework that they are applying and the nature of the delegations they have implemented?

1.3 Developing better standards

By using terms like assessing, tolerance and appetite, the Basel Committee is clearly moving institutions towards some form of modelling and numeric solutions to the problem. Whilst they are not explicit in this, it would be difficult to come up with a non-numeric appetite or tolerance to or for operational risk. Basel is looking for Boards to have clear lines of responsibility, accountability and reporting. In addition, there must be segregated responsibilities and reporting lines between control functions and the revenue generating business lines. This all sounds rather like good corporate governance (which we will cover later) and the type of things that are required to meet the demands of the Hampel and Turnbull committees, which were concerned with the concept of good corporate governance.

When considering how often the framework should be revised, the objective is to ensure that the bank is managing the operational factors arising from external market changes and other environmental factors, as well as those operational risks associated with new products, activities or systems. The review process should also aim to incorporate industry innovations in operational risk management appropriate for the bank's activities, systems and processes.

What they are looking for is for the Board to really take ownership of operational risk, rather than simply pass this on to the Operational Risk function of the bank. As mentioned above, whilst they can delegate the operational aspects of this work to other parts of the firm, responsibility for operational risk lies ultimately with the Board The framework needs to be capable of being sufficiently flexible to meet changing requirements and the differing needs of senior and junior staff – so there is a lot of planning to consider at the outset prior to developing the framework – and part of that is down to what the bank's objectives are for the framework.

Effective risk identification considers both internal factors (such as the complexity of the bank's structure, the nature of its activities, the quality of personnel, organisational changes and employee turnover) and external factors (such as changes in the industry and technological advances) that could adversely affect the achievement of the bank's objectives. There will be many different scenarios to consider and the more remote the likelihood of a particular risk is considered, the harder it may be to imagine or evaluate. However just because something is difficult to imagine or to evaluate, does not mean that the risk goes away. The London riots that occurred in the summer of 2011 were difficult to imagine in advance, but the possibility of such events occurring need to be evaluated and plans considered. It is important to start to evaluate the firm's vulnerability to certain risks. Creating a risk profile where risks are understood, controlled, mitigated or accepted is part of effective and efficient management of the business and its resources.

There are several processes commonly used by banks to help them identify and assess operational risk. Those identified in the Basel Accord are self or risk assessment, risk mapping, risk indicators and measurement.

Basel recognises that banks are quantifying their operational risks and trying to come up with meaningful measures. What is also clear is that there will need to be an involvement of the operational risk team when new business initiatives are being considered/developed to ensure that the impact of any new development on the total operational risk framework is properly considered. However there are other drivers to consider in such a scenario, such as being able to measure the additional operational risk applying to a new product to be introduced will enable appropriate product pricing. There are many examples of transactions or types of activity that have looked profitable in credit risk or market risk terms, only to incur disproportionate levels of operational risk – perhaps settlement problems and penalties or excessive legal work being required.

Involving the operational risk team at an early stage will ensure that matters are properly considered prior to activity being undertaken.

2 Tools and techniques for identifying and categorising risks

When identifying risks, a firm needs to consider not only its own processes and systems, but also its relationships with its clients, the nature of its products and the wider business environment.

Risk identification is the fundamental first step in understanding how operational risk affects the firm, raising awareness of risk issues and assessing the culture of the organisation. It can be a difficult exercise due to the diverse nature of risk causes and the difficulty in distinguishing cause from effect. Risk identification lies at the heart of the development of an operational risk management project. As mentioned before, if we fail to identify a risk, then we will fail to measure it, mitigate it and consider it and so on. As you can appreciate, effective risk identification is the cornerstone of the operational risk activities in any firm. We also need to remember the point made earlier in this chapter – namely that risk identification is not something that should only happen on occasion – risk is a dynamic area and so risk identification needs to be carried out on an on-going basis. Even once a risk has been identified, both the internal and external influences on the organisation can change, and with these changes, the level of risk can also change.

2.1 Why risk identification is important

The purpose of identifying operational risks is to understand, record and categorise a firm's operational risks. By doing this the firm can create a basis for establishing its risk profile (the level and nature of risks that the firm is exposed to) and risk appetite (the level of risk it is willing to accept), an understanding of the types of risk it faces and its level of exposure.

QUICK QUESTION

Why do you think it is of such importance for a firm to invest in the identification of risk?

Write your answer here before reading on.

There is a need to do this in order to:

- provide information to management on which to make decisions and take action to ensure a controlled environment
- establish the chain of events relationship of operational risk and understand where they occur throughout the firm
- provide a basis for risk measurement and assessment which may, for example, be used for capital allocation purposes
- set boundaries to differentiate between operational risk and other risk types (such as market and credit) and assign ownership for their mitigation
- develop a common language for discussing, assessing and managing risk that allows clear and transparent communication and decision-making.

2.2 The self-assessment (self-certification) method

Self-assessment (also known as self-certification) can be regarded as an extension of the risk identification process. Once a list of risks has been compiled, managers make their own assessment of their exposure to each risk on a regular basis.

QUICK QUESTION

What do you think is the major drawback of this self-assessment?

Write your answer here before reading on.

A major benefit of self-assessment is empowering managers to take responsibility of the risks in their area. It will increase awareness of risks and enable managers to highlight areas where they feel they may need support and guidance to mitigate important risks. It also encourages communication between managers and the risk function and gives managers a forum where they can voice their opinions and concerns on the risk matters that affect them.

Assessment as a single method of measurement has limitations because it can be subjective and possibly open to abuse and manipulation. It can also lead to a conflict of interest. A lending manager may deliberately underestimate risks in his business area as they may feel that giving a true assessment of the risks will result in their capacity to issue loans being reduced. This in turn will reduce their ability to generate profits and achieve bonus targets.

Therefore it is often used in conjunction with other techniques and the results are independently validated. A further drawback is that it can also be difficult to apply consistently across the various business units and multiple locations that exist within a large firm as different areas and different people may approach this task in diverse ways. It must also be considered that some members at staff will be more adept to assessing risk than others. Staff may over or under estimate risk assessment because they have insufficient knowledge and experience in this area.

Classifying operational risk using common categories is the first step in developing a common risk language. It also helps to distinguish causes from effects and can be used as a basis for the development of a risk capture, identification and measurement system.

Organisations will put their different emphases on risks and will therefore categorise risks in different ways. It is not important what categories are chosen, provided they are relevant, logical understood and consistent. Therefore it will be important to make the categorisation common across the whole organisation, taking a holistic approach.

Here is an example of risk categories, drawn together under the broad headings of process, people, technology and environment:

Process	People	Technology	Environment
Procedures	Role and responsibilities	Availability	Technology
Capacity	Authority to act	Design	Volumes
Volume sensitivity	Supervision	Security	Integration
Controls	Escalation procedures	System integrity	Pace of change
Documentation	Accountability	System controls	Vendors
Delivery mechanisms	Human error	Testing	Catastrophe
	Integrity/honesty	Denial of service attacks	Fraud
	Customer focus	Identity theft	Competition
	Training	Viruses	Political climate
	Communication		
	Expertise concentration		
	Culture		
	Uncertainty		
	Labour		

There are a variety of methods used for the practical capture and identification of risk. The most widely used are:

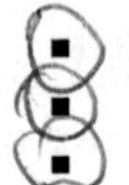

- Self-assessment
- Reviews and audits
- Focus workshops
- Historical loss data
- Management information statistics and key risk indicators (KRIs).

In order to capture the complete risk profile, all of these methods require the involvement and partnership of risk owners and risk experts. Risk owners include senior management, process and product heads and the line staff who deal with the risks on a daily basis. Risk experts can be staff employed in the Operational Risk function of the firm. They can be used either individually or in combination.

3 Risk appetite

3.1 Inherent risk

Inherent risk is risk related to the nature of the activities being undertaken. This may include almost anything you care to think of but let us use as an example a complex project or a complex corporate structure – they both present inherent risk.

Logically following inherent risk is the control environment and the fact that this may not be efficient. This can be referred to as the control strategy. This in turn presents control risk. **Control risk** is the threat that errors or irregularities in the underlying transactions will not be prevented, detected and corrected by the internal control systems (either at the desk or on the spot). This may be caused by relatively inexperienced staff managing and controlling the risk management activity, inadequate staffing (owing to workload or time pressure) or if the control strategy does not take sufficient account of risks or misses a key risk area.

3.2 Residual risk

QUICK QUESTION

How would you describe residual risk?

Write your answer here before reading on.

Residual risk occurs as it is impossible to reduce risks to zero. Without taking some level of risk, there are no opportunities for success and gain in business, politics, government or life itself. No matter how much control you exert, there will always be a finite level of risk that remains – the risk that these controls will fail under extreme circumstances. This is known as **residual risk**. Provided that the residual risk is within the organisation's risk appetite or risk tolerance, residual risk is acceptable risk.

Inherent risk x Control risk = Residual risk

Zero risk in any activity is not achievable; therefore the residual risk (after considering controls) has to be defined by management; who may decide whether or not to reduce residual risk further. The additional benefit of extra controls must be weighed against their cost. Acceptable residual risk must be understood as the end result of the conjunction of a particular control environment and an adequate, cost-effective control structure. The control system put in place reaches its breakeven point at which additional controls are not in the interest of the firm, since they give no positive net benefit.

3.3 Risk appetite

Risk appetite is a term that is frequently used throughout the risk management community. Financial risk areas and some other risks can easily be translated into financial terms; others are much more difficult. Risk appetite, at the organisational level, is the amount of risk exposure, or potential adverse impact from an event, that the organisation is willing to accept/retain. Once the risk appetite threshold has been breached, risk management treatments and business controls are implemented to bring the exposure level back within the accepted range.

To define an organisation's risk appetite and determine the acceptable level of risk, the management should answer the following questions.

- Where do we feel we should allocate our limited time and resources to minimise risk exposures? Why?
- What level of risk exposure requires immediate action? Why?
- What level of risk requires a formal response strategy to mitigate the potentially material impact? Why?
- What events have occurred in the past, and at what level were they managed? Why?

Each question is followed by a 'Why' because the organisation should be able to articulate the quantitative and/or qualitative basis for the appetite, or it will be backward-looking (based only on historical events) or, worse still, even arbitrary.

The process to adopt in order to achieve a meaningful result will involve these steps:

- Deciding upon key metrics relevant to the organisation
- Back test the data over time
- Look for consistency
- Discuss with key officers
- Attempt to reach a consensus
- Communicate the decision.

The total risk appetite for the firm will need to be calculated. It will have to cover all risk types – credit, market and operational risk, together with any other risk types that the firm has identified.

In most firms there is a range of risk appetites amongst the senior individuals. There will be those that are more comfortable taking risks and those that are naturally risk averse. These two groups must work together in order to achieve a sensible result for the organisation overall. Remember what happened to banks such as HBOS during the Credit Crunch when the risk appetites within banking firms were dramatically reduced as a result of falling confidence levels.

The exercise must be to balance the various factors, both positive and negative. Questions to be asked might include:

- Is the risk consistent with the company's policy and basic philosophy?
- What does our history of gains and losses tell us? How does it compare?
- Is our management capable and sufficiently competent to manage the risks?
- Do all stakeholders understand the risks and why the organisation is taking them? Note that this will include external stakeholders, such as customers and regulators.
- How will the risk impact the cash flow and balance sheet of the organisation?
- How will the risk impact our operations?

Distributing Risk Appetite

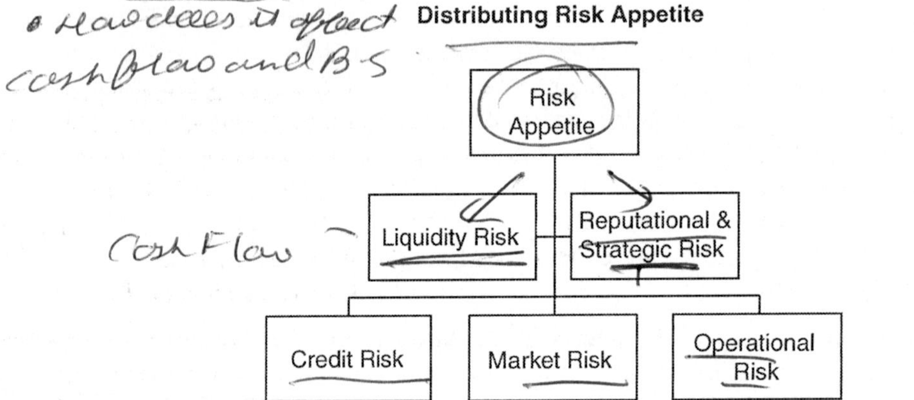

3.4 The firm's risk appetite

Within a bank, the Board is responsible to approve the overall risk appetite for the organisation. Remember that the term risk appetite refers to the level of risk that a firm chooses itself to take in pursuit of its own business objectives. In doing this it needs to recognise a range of possible outcomes as its business plans are implemented. This might be done using a top-down view of the firm's capacity to take risk in parallel with a bottom-up view of the business risk profile associated with each individual business area's medium-term plans.

Risk appetite is very important in that it helps the bank to ascertain and achieve the following:

- Risk(s) to be avoided
- Insurance – to help reduce the potential risk exposure to an acceptable level

- Setting limits and thresholds
- Setting the quality criteria for processing systems
- Dealing with non-goal-correlated events.

A study of impact and likelihood will be required, as is mentioned elsewhere in this text, and the following diagram shows how the risk appetite is likely to shape across a typical outlook. You may have encountered this diagram elsewhere, described as an impact and probability matrix.

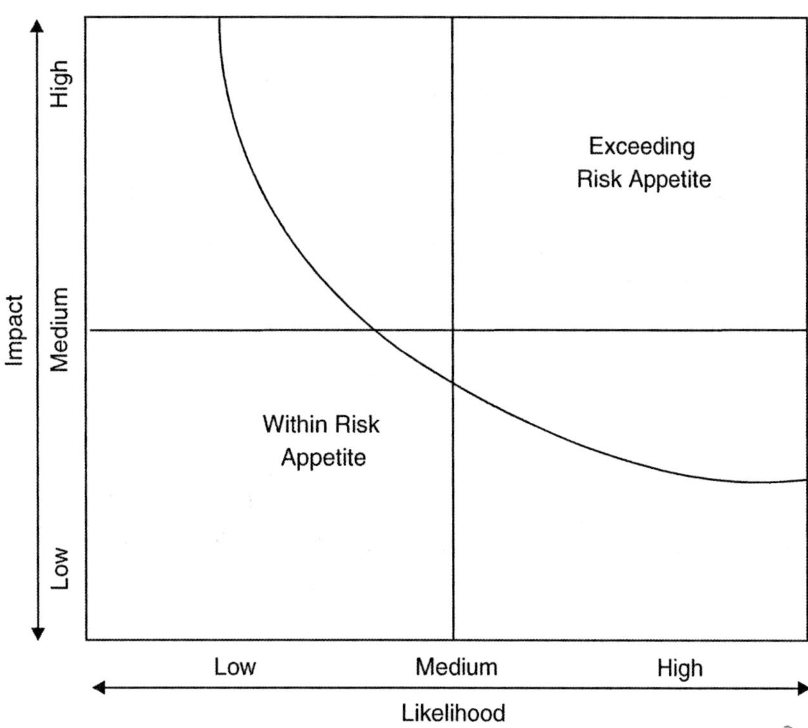

3.5 A realistic risk appetite

It is impossible to reduce risks to zero as without taking some level of risk in banking, as otherwise there are no opportunities for success and gains. For example a bank has to lend money in order to receive interest on its loans and some of the loans will default. No matter how much control the bank exerts, there will always be a finite level of risk that remains. The risk is that a bank's controls will fail under extreme circumstances. This is known as residual risk. Provided that the residual risk is within the organisation's risk appetite, residual risk is an acceptable risk. However, if the bank chose not to lend at all – for fear that some borrowers would not repay – then it would not make profit.

A more formal definition of risk appetite could be that it is the risk of loss that a bank is willing to accept for a given risk-reward ratio (or continuum as described in Chapter 1). It is also important to understand how risk appetite and risk tolerance are slightly different concepts. Clearly a bank might have no appetite for fraud but nevertheless the Board accepts that from time to time some fraud take place and within certain bounds there is a tolerance of a certain degree of fraud risk.

Most likely any particular bank would argue that is has no appetite for financial crime and has no appetite for reputational damage and has minimal appetite with respect to regulatory risks.

The concept of risk appetite can be applied to all types of risks. Largely it is used to address credit risk, market risk, operational risk and any other type of recognised risk.

Comparing banking with other industries such as the oil exploration, mining or construction industries immediately highlights the risk appetite for death or injuries to employees would be a zero tolerance of death or injury of employees whilst working for a firm. However in the financial services industry employees are not exposed to risk of death or serious injury in their normal course of work. In the other industries mentioned however owing to the use of heavy machinery and far more difficult operating environments such risks are far more real.

Remember that risk appetite is not something that only applies to businesses. Every individual has an appetite for risk that varies from person to person as well as varying within the same person as circumstances change. For example, you may have a fear of heights that would make you unwilling to spend an afternoon on a zipwire at Go Ape whereas your colleague may relish such an opportunity. However, your risk appetite may have changed with circumstances. An example would be as a result of witnessing a road accident, you may have decided to change your car to one with higher specifications of safety features.

3.6 The risk appetite framework

Barclays Bank operates a risk appetite framework which consists of two elements – financial volatility and mandate and scale.

Financial volatility is defined as the level of deviation from expected financial performance that Barclays is prepared to sustain at relevant points on the risk profile. However, under mandate and scale Barclays sets an approach that seeks to review formally all its business activities to ensure that they remain within their given mandate and are of an appropriate scale relative to the risk and reward of the underlying activities. This is achieved by using limits and triggers to avoid concentrations which would be out of line with external expectations. The limits are set by an independent risk function formally monitored and reporting to Board level.

3.7 The link with capital

Capital requirements are part of the regulatory framework governing how banks and depository institutions are managed. Capital ratios express a bank's capital as a percentage of its risk-weighted assets. Both Core Tier 1 and Tier 1 capital resources are defined by the UK's regulator – the PRA. Core Tier 1 is broadly tangible shareholders' funds less certain capital deductions from Tier 1.

A bank's capital management activities seek to maximise shareholders' value by prudently optimising the level and mix of its capital resources. The bank's capital management objectives are to maintain sufficient capital resources to: ensure the financial holding company is well capitalised relative to the minimum regulatory capital requirements set by the UK's PRA and other regulators such as the US Federal Reserve (should the bank also operate in the United States); ensure locally regulated subsidiaries can meet their minimum regulatory capital requirements; support the bank's risk appetite and economic capital requirements; and support its credit rating.

3.8 Application to different types of risk

A different approach when establishing risk appetite applies to credit and market risks compared to operational risk.

Whereas taking credit or market risk is likely to be encouraged up to the stated level as established under the risk appetite analysis, operational risk is more likely to be mitigated downwards as long as the cost of mitigation/control does not exceed the expected loss of the particular risk.

By and large, credit or market risk can be capped using systems but operational risk cannot be constrained in a similar way. Having entered a business activity, a bank is committed to managing the associated operational risk unless it withdraws from the marketplace altogether.

3.9 Setting thresholds

A key element in the risk appetite process is to establish agreed thresholds. These provide specific definitions for each expression of appetite of what constitutes an acceptable level of risk. Beyond that a tolerable level or an unacceptable level of risk could similarly declared so whenever a bank establishes any measures with respect to key risk indicators of confidence levels it is also making an expression of its risk appetite for those particular risks.

Setting appropriate thresholds can be done with the assistance of industry and market data that is widely available. For example, industry data with regards to operational losses in banking is compiled on a regular basis. Analysing this data will help management to decide on operational risk thresholds that is both acceptable to the organisation and realistic as compared to competitors.

4 Benefits of risk identification

4.1 Achieving risk identification that works

As you will now be aware, the whole process of risk management starts with the on-going identification of risk. Without this step in the lifecycle being carried out properly and carefully, then the rest of the process is based on flawed information. Whilst it is important to note that the ultimate responsibility for this lies at the top of the organisation, risk identification is something that should be embedded in the culture of the firm – if this is the case, relevant risks will be captured and managed on a pro-active basis.

As with any process, if rigorous planning does not take place at the start, then the system will be fundamentally flawed.

QUESTION TIME 1

Reflect upon the major themes in this chapter and consider a range of ways in which you have recently identified risk and what steps you have then taken to reduce that risk to an acceptable level.

Write your answer here then check with the answer at the back of the book.

KEY WORDS

Key words in this chapter are given below. There is space to write your own revision notes and add any other key words or phrases you want to remember.

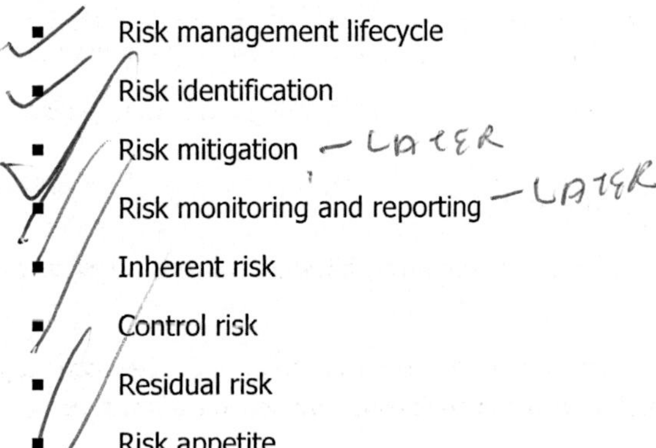

- Risk management lifecycle
- Risk identification
- Risk mitigation
- Risk monitoring and reporting
- Inherent risk
- Control risk
- Residual risk
- Risk appetite

REVIEW

Now consider the main points that were introduced in this section. These are listed below. Tick each one as you go through them.

- The management of risk works around the risk management lifecycle. This starts with the identification or risk, before moving to risk assessment, mitigation and concluding with risk monitoring and reporting.
- Responsibility for the management of risk lies with the Board of Directors, although they may allocate tasks in this regard to staff in the organisation.
- Risk must be identified to allow the firm to make informed risk decisions.
- It is impossible to remove all danger of risk. That level of risk remaining after control measures have been put in place is called residual risk.
- Risk appetite is the level of risk that an organisation or an individual is willing to accept. This can vary from organisation to organisation or person to person. It also varies with changes in circumstances.

chapter 3

RISK ASSESSMENT

Contents

Learning objectives

On completion of this chapter, you should be able to:

- create a plan that details a methodical approach to risk assessment.

Introduction

This chapter will move on to consider the next stage of the risk management lifecycle – risk assessment. In order to do this we will start by considering why we need to carry out this activity and introduce some of the terminology used in risk assessment. We will then move on to discuss what can cause a risk event to occur and what the impact of such an event can be. The next area to think about is how we can record this work, so the Risk Register will be introduced in this chapter. Impact and probability was introduced in the last chapter and we turn our attention to these themes again when we consider what the effect of a risk event could be on the firm. This theme is developed further in the final section of the chapter when a number of tools and techniques that can be used to assess operational risk are explained.

1 The purpose and benefits of risk assessment

Why do we measure risk at all? Two immediate conclusions would be that it gives the organisation the ability to understand the likelihood of risks occurring and to understand the impact that such risks would deliver (both direct and indirect).

QUICK QUESTION

Why is it so important to carefully and accurately assess risks in an organisation?

Write your answer here before reading on.

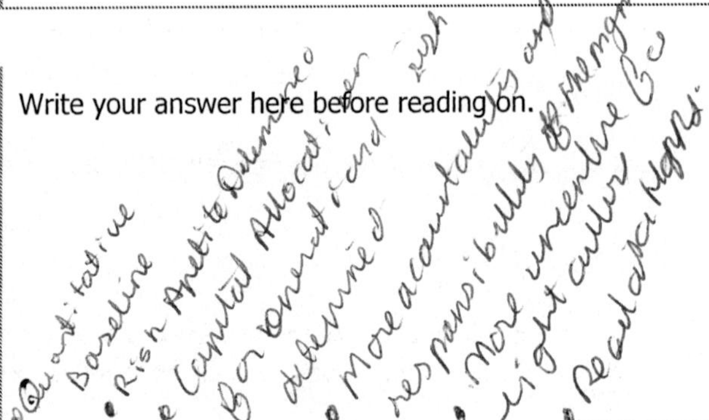

Risk management and the assessment of identified risks allow the following to take place within the firm:

- A quantitative baseline can be established of the potential risks that the business faces.
- Accountability and responsibility for the responsibility for the management of those risks can be assigned to the relevant people within the firm.
- An incentive for the right culture and change within the firm can be established as risk is pushed up the agenda in the business and becomes more visible.
- The risk appetite for the firm can be established and the decision-making process improved.
- The Regulator can be satisfied as this fits in with their overall risk management objectives and requirements.
- A capital allocation figure with respect to operational risk can be established.

Risk assessment and risk measurement are concerned with understanding the likelihood of risks occurring and their impact on the business in terms of direct or indirect loss. Once an understanding of the size of a problem has been gained, appropriate action can be taken to address it.

QUICK QUESTION

Why do you think we need to measure and assess operational risk?

Write your answer here before reading on.

The reasons for measuring and assessing operational risk are to:

- establish a quantitative baseline for operating and improving the control environment
- ensure there is appropriate accountability and responsibility for risk management. By understanding where risk occurs and measuring how big it is, accountability and responsibility can be assigned to the people that are in the best position to manage it
- provide an incentive for risk management and the development of a risk-aware culture within the business. The development of the right environment and culture cannot be overemphasised as a key aspect of managing operational risk. Measuring risk can powerfully demonstrate the impact of operational risk issues and help to gain the commitment that is essential for driving cultural change, emphasising the importance of risk management within the organisation
- improve management decision-making. By knowing the size of risks they face, firms are in a position to decide how much risk they wish to take, as described in the last chapter
- satisfy regulators and stakeholders that the firm is adopting a proactive and transparent approach to risk management
- make an assessment of the financial risk exposure that can be used for capital allocation purposes.

1.1 Risk measurement approaches

With measurement of risk, in principle where any risk is quantifiable the firm should measure the potential loss at three levels – expected loss, statistical loss and stress loss. These levels can be described as follows:

- **Expected loss** is the loss that is expected to arise on average in connection with an activity. It is an inherent cost of such activity and is budgeted and, where permitted, deducted directly from revenues.
- **Statistical loss** (also known as **unexpected loss**) is an estimate of the amount that actual loss can exceed expected loss over a specified time horizon measured to a specific level of confidence (probability).
- **Stress loss** is the loss that could arise from extreme events. Stress situations can arise from many sources and when extreme events do occur, quantitative and qualitative risk assessments alone are not sufficient. In these cases, the essential elements are a tried and tested disaster recovery process and well-prepared business continuity plans. These will be discussed later on in the chapter dedicated to business continuity management.

1.2 Assessment and measurement working together

Risk assessment is closely linked to risk measurement. It delivers an assessment of risk at a point in time with appropriate controls in place. Measurement is associated with the use of quantitative techniques to understand the size of risk such as measuring losses, measuring the frequency and impact of risk events and making statistical predictions. Assessment has more to do with evaluating measurement data and estimating the impact on the business. It is especially useful for considering those risks which cannot be actuarially or statistically measured, given the lack of appropriate data.

For instance, a firm's risk measurement system might record that the front office trading system is 98.5% reliable. Assessment would make the judgement as to whether this is acceptable for normal business performance. Put another way, measurement is objective and assessment is subjective.

These terms are closely linked and are often used interchangeably – both address the question: how big is the problem?

1.3 Don't set up a blame culture

Basel focuses on loss and loss databases, but in terms of building a robust operational risk management structure, it is not only losses that need to be considered. Abnormal profits could be just as symptomatic of a problem with an operational risk control framework as an unexpected loss. Also a near miss, or an unexpected event that has not resulted in a loss, may also yield significant information concerning the adequacy of a control environment and appropriate actions taken. The risk register is an integral tool in a risk management system that helps organisations to categorise and report risks. The risk register is discussed in detail in section 3 of this chapter.

The objective is to see if the operational risk system is working effectively, not to blame people for failures. If a blame culture is introduced the effect will be to reduce the likelihood that staff will report losses in the first place – the tendency will be for the organisation's people to sweep issues under the carpet, rather than face a potential reprimand. If losses are disguised, this will have the effect that the business will be unable to act to prevent recurrence. So the aim is to investigate actual unexpected losses, unexpected profits and near misses to understand what caused the event and to see what this tells us about our control environment – without introducing a blame culture.

Just because an event has occurred will not in itself mean that we will want to change our control environment, rather it will provide additional information that we may wish to consider.

1.4 Terms used in the assessment and measurement of operational risk

QUICK QUESTION

What steps do you think a business could take when assessing risks?

Write your answer here before reading on.

Firms should address these steps when assessing risks:

- Review actual operational losses – or events that could have resulted in significant losses
- Consider the effectiveness of controls
- Undertake an internal assessment of risks inherent in its operations
- Consider other risk indicators
- Consider reported external operational losses and exposures
- Review changes in its operational environment.

2 Cause and effect

A cause is something which creates a risk event. It can be regarded potentially as a trigger for a risk to take place, whilst the effect is the consequence of this event. For example, in June 2012, there were problems with a software upgrade at RBS/NatWest and Ulster Bank – this can be described as a cause.

QUICK QUESTION

What was the effect of this cause?

Write your answer here before reading on.

The effect was the well-publicised delay in payments being processed for customers, resulting, for example, in the customers salary credits being delayed by up to two weeks. The outcome of this was that the Group set aside £125m to make compensation payments to affected customers.

There is always a logical relationship between a cause, an event and its effect (or consequence). These are the three logical stages of a risk incident. Something has caused an event to happen and the event itself has created an impact.

Causes are helpful in identifying risk events and in avoiding confusion between a cause and an event. However, causes are much more useful in assisting the identification of an action plan since if one can prevent a cause that will by definition prevent a similar risk event occurring in the future. Risk events can be triggered by different causes and circumstances change over time so it is necessary to bear that in mind when examining causes. In the example above, action can be taken to remedy a repetition of the cause event happening again, but this will not guarantee that the bank will never again have a delay in making payments to its customers' accounts. Such a delay could be caused either by different causes in the future or changes to the original cause which would make a repetition of these events immune to the control measures put in place in 2012.

A risk effect or consequence is an occurrence which is brought about by a risk event taking place. These can be confused with risk events as they demonstrate the outcome of the risk event itself. They can sometimes be easier to control and manage than the risk event itself.

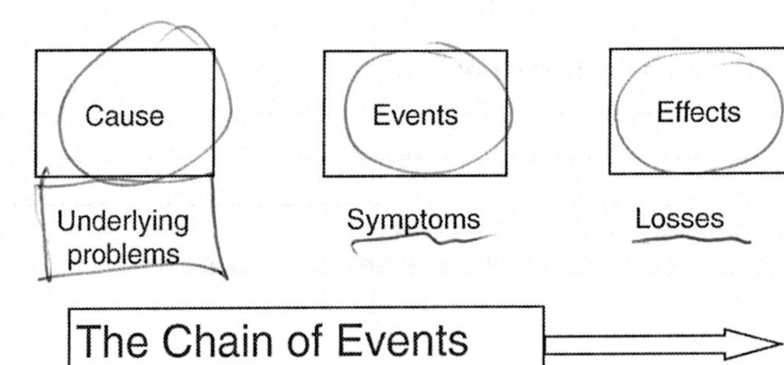

3 The Risk Register

The risk register lies at the centre of the risk management system. Its objective is to summarise risk and the potential for scoring and the approach for managing that risk.

QUICK QUESTION

Use a common sense approach to list what headings should appear in a risk register.

Write your answer here before reading on.

It will typically include the following:

- Description and overview of the risk
- Owner of the risk
- Division/business area exposed to the risk
- Geographical location(s) exposed to the risk
- Legal and regulatory requirements (e.g. Sarbanes Oxley) associated with the risk
- When the risk might occur
- The impact assuming that the risk does occur
- Link to existing procedures and policies relating to the risk
- An assessment of the risk's likelihood or probability of occurrence
- A priority rating or score, obtained from the impact and probability assessment
- The management's strategy as to how the risk will be addressed
- The containment strategy defining what exactly will happen if the risk occurs.

This figure shows a simple example:

Function/Activity:		Compiled by:		Date:	
Date of risk review:		Reviewed by:		Date:	

Reference	The risk	What can happen? (event)	How can it happen?	What can happen? (consequences)	Identify existing controls	Effectiveness and implementation of existing controls	Analysis			Risk priority	Treat risk Y/N	Further action
							Likelihood	Consequences	Level of risk			

NOTE: Indicative example only.

In compiling the risk register the firm must describe the risk in a clear manner so that everyone in the firm who needs to be aware of the risk understands it and not just the person who is most directly involved in its management.

3.1 The importance of the risk register

A risk register lists all the risks identified by a firm according to risk categories. It can be regarded as an inventory and it might be described as a library or list of risks. It acts as a basic component of the risk and control assessment process in order to record identified risks. The existence of a risk register illustrates that risks have been identified that relate to specific activities.

The design and implementation of a risk register in a bank needs to be carefully considered. Rather than having different geographic regions and business areas keeping separate risk registers, an integrated risk register should contain risk information for the entire bank. Therefore the risk register needs to be robust and well managed. Some banks will use a specialist piece of risk register software or may design a bespoke database in-house to meet their exact requirements.

As the risk register is likely to include a large volume of information, it should be capable of providing different levels of visibility. For example while risk managers will be involved in the detail of the risk register, senior managers will concentrate on higher level risks. Similarly, the information in the risk register will need to be reviewed by various departments across the organisation, from risk owners through to the control functions.

3.2 Building the risk register

However in a broader context in the risk and control assessment process it is necessary to consider risks that might occur rather than purely risks that have occurred. Therefore a risk register (or a list of risks) may not reflect the full picture.

A risk register would take an individual event and state what the loss value might be should the risk occur and then will apply an impact assessment to it. Consider for example a case of potential fraud where the risk impact might be assessed at say £5 million with a 15% chance of its occurrence in any one individual year. Multiplying these together £5 million x 15% would give a severity of £0.75million in any one individual year. Of course this would not mean that the company would expect a loss of £5 million or even £0.75 million. The actual cost would be based upon the distribution of losses. So the loss could be at least £0.25 million with a 75% likelihood or up to £2 million with a 25% likelihood. Any assessments are based upon actual knowledge from real loss events that have occurred together with additional assessment made by management and risk specialists regarding the quality of the control environment and control and risk self assessment key performance indicators.

The severity could be calculated by assessors who might be asked to choose from say a number in the range of 1 to 10 for each of the risk issues that they are addressing. These expectation (or likelihood) levels would then be multiplied to come up with a severity. Hence expectation multiplied by impact would deliver the severity figure.

The risk manager or the person administrating the risk register and the assessment would be the person who would then take the different expectations and convert them into something more meaningful in terms of real values rather than levels of severity. An expectation of 6 could equate to say 30% and an impact of 5 could equate to £10 million. This then would give the severity of £3 million i.e. 30% of £10 million. The point of this exercise would be to translate the general severity analysis from the managers who initially assessed the issue into real numbers to apply to the business. At the next level however, one is faced with the change of other events, for example business volumes. Should business volumes go up by 1% would the expectation increase by 1%? Would the impact increase by 1%? It could be that the expectation changes but not the impact or vice versa. It could also be that both of these might occur but that one is more than a 1% increase rather than the other. This is the beginning of the concept of stress testing which even at its most simple level is not straightforward.

4 Probability

4.1 Definition of risk

The concept of risk includes both undesirable consequences and likelihoods, e.g. the amount of money lost, the number of customers lost, the number of people harmed, and the probability of occurrence of this loss or harm. Sometimes, risk is defined as a set of single values, e.g. the expected values of these consequences. This is a summary measure and not a general definition. Producing probability distributions for the consequences affords a much more detailed description of risk.

A very common definition of risk represents it as a set of: scenarios, likelihoods and consequences. Determining risk generally amounts to answering the following questions:

1. What can go wrong?
2. How likely is it?
3. What are the associated consequences?

The answer to the first question is a set of accident or loss scenarios. The second question requires the evaluation of the probabilities of these scenarios, while the third estimates their consequences. Implicit within each question is that there are uncertainties. The uncertainties pertain to whether all the significant accident scenarios have been identified, and whether the probabilities of the scenarios and associated consequence estimates have properly taken into account the sources of variability and the limitations of the available information.

4.2 Probability and uncertainty

In understanding risk management we need to get to grips with some basic definitions or risk, certainty, probability and uncertainty.

Risk refers to any adverse consequence or loss. This is the chance that damage, loss, injury or disaster may occur.

Certainty refers to an absolute fact, which can be depended upon with conviction.

Probability refers to the degree of likelihood, the extent to which an event is likely to occur, measured by the ration of favourable cases to all possible cases.

Uncertainty refers to something that cannot be accurately predicted or known – being uncertain or any restriction on the accuracy of measurement.

So while we know that risks may occur, and indeed will occur, we may be uncertain as to the frequency of the risk occurrence or the severity of the impact of that risk.

QUESTION TIME 1

Think about the activities that you have engaged in today and describe events using the headings below.

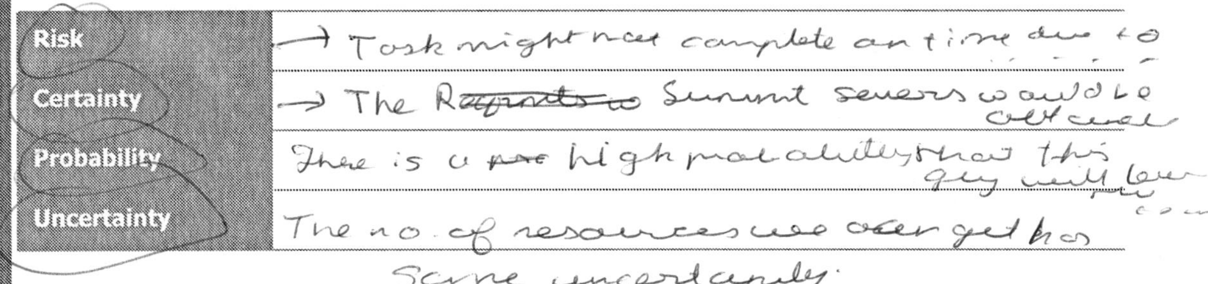

Risk	
Certainty	
Probability	
Uncertainty	

Write your answer here then check with the answer at the back of the book.

4.3 Risk maps

A summary risk profile is a simple mechanism to increase the visibility of risks; it is a graphical representation of information normally found on an existing risk register. In some industry sectors it is referred to as a risk map. The risk manager needs to update the risk register on a regular basis and then regenerate the graph, showing risks in terms of probability and impact with the effects of mitigating action taken into account. The summary risk profile illustrated below shows all key risks as one picture, so that managers can gain an overall impression of the total exposure to risk. It is essential for the graph to reflect current information as documented in the risk register. The profile must be used with extreme care and should not mislead the reader. If an activity has over 200 risks it will be impractical to illustrate all of the risks. It will be more appropriate to illustrate the top 20 risks, for example, making it clear what is and is not illustrated.

A key feature of this picture is the risk tolerance line, indicated here as a bold line. It shows the overall level of risk that the organisation is prepared to tolerate in a given situation. If exposure to risk is above this line, managers can see that they must take prompt action such as upward referral of relevant risks. Setting the risk tolerance line is a task for experienced risk managers; it reflects the organisation's attitudes to risk in general and to a specific set of risks within a particular situation. The parameters of the risk tolerance line should be agreed at the outset of an activity and regularly reviewed to allow for changes in the environment and other circumstances.

4.4 Using risk status codes

The use of RAGB indicators (Red, Amber, Green, Blue) status can be useful for incorporating the status reporting from risk registers into risk profiles, and can provide a quick and effective means of monitoring. Typically RAG statuses (simply red, amber or green) are used by most firms, omitting the additional blue level. The degree of sophistication will be designed to suit the individual firm.

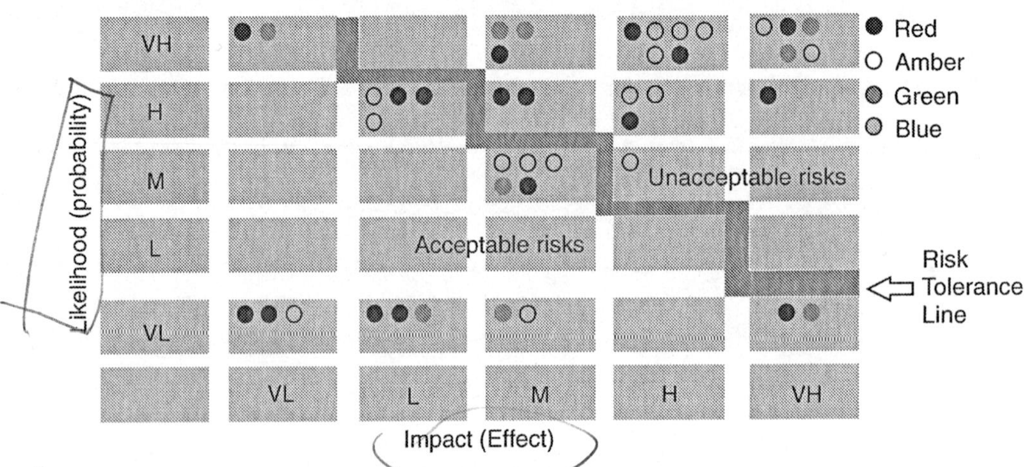

Example – summary risk profile

The end result is a matrix that looks like this. This is helpful for management to assess what is the risk that they should look at first – clearly those that are high are marked accordingly. The severity, which is the product of the probability and the impact, will give a value and there are a series of these for each of the risks. Effectively by totalling up all risks a firm is able to come up with the level of loss that it expects – but this is the unexpected type of losses not the expected type of losses.

Example – Probability/impact matrix

Probability	Impact: Low	Impact: Medium	Impact: High
High	risk 6	risk 9	risk 1 risk 4
Medium	risk 3 risk 7	risk 2 risk 5 risk 11	
Low		risk 8 risk 10	risk 12

4.5 Heat maps

The following diagram shows the probability and severity in a different form – known as a heat map. This shows that the further from the origin, the higher will be the loss resulting from the product of the probability and consequence.

Example – heat map

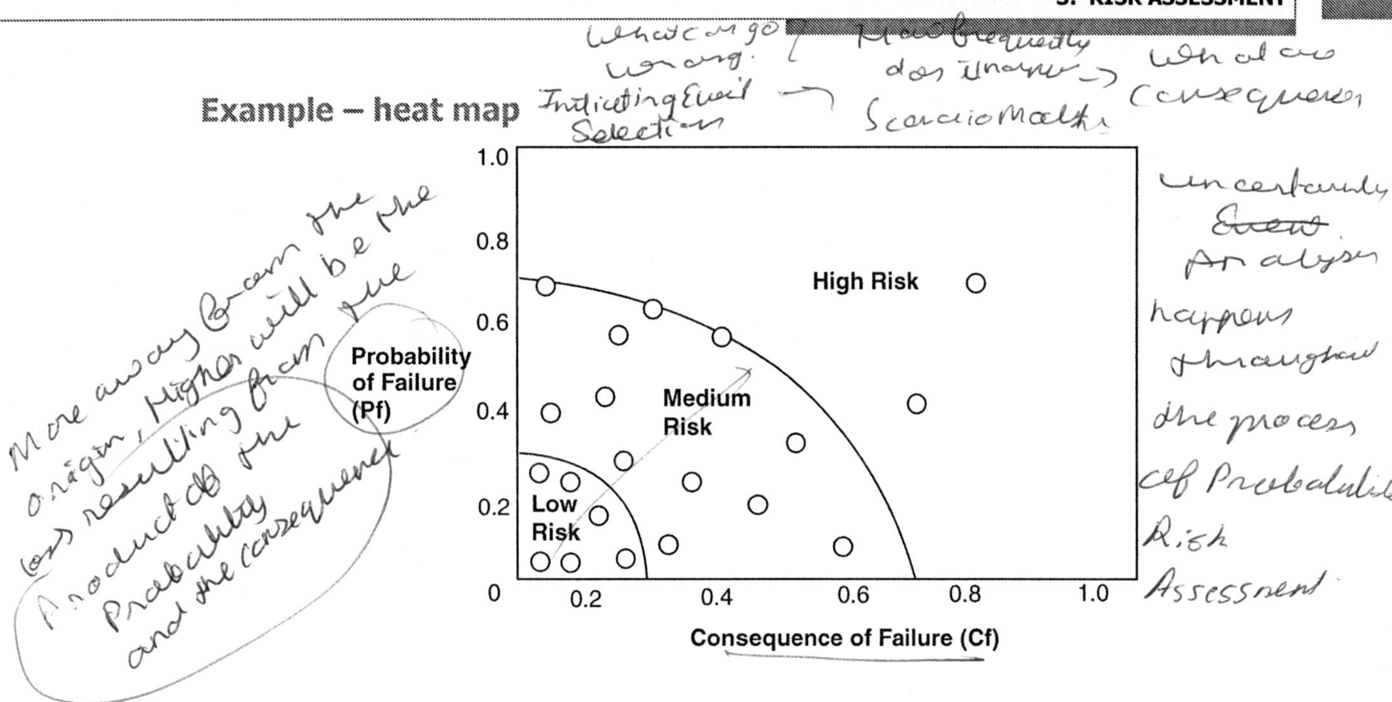

4.6 The triplet definition

Scenarios and uncertainties are among the most important components of a risk assessment. The diagram below shows the implementation of these concepts in Probabilistic Risk Assessment (PRA). In this diagram, uncertainty analysis is shown to be an integral part of each step of the process rather than just a calculation that is performed at the end of the risk quantification.

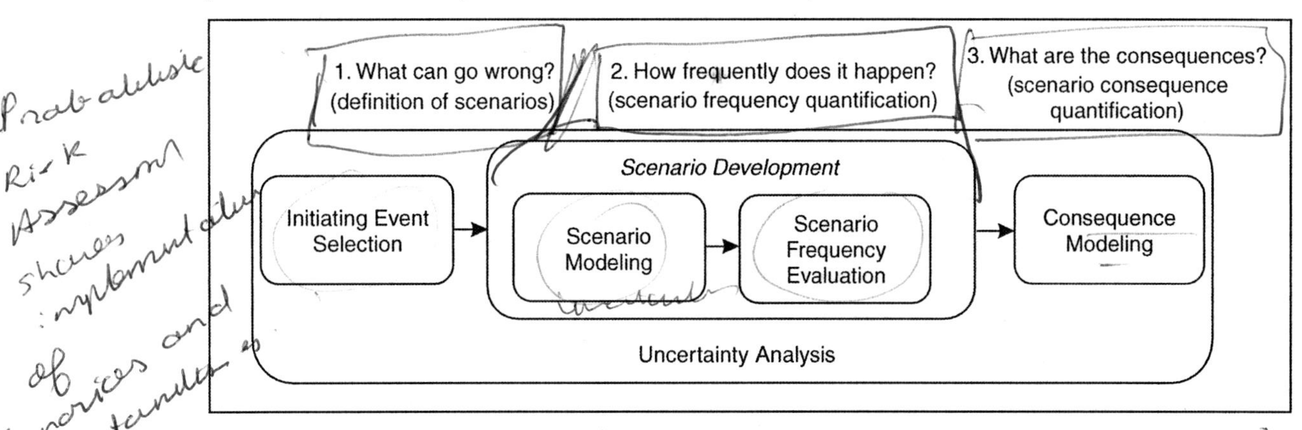

Uncertainty analysis will seek to quantify the uncertainties contained within assessment of risk. Therefore rather than simply stating we cannot be certain what is going to happen in a particular situation, we see to quantify some of these uncertainties – for example by building scenarios of potential situations or events that could occur. Associated with uncertainty analysis is the concept of sensitivity analysis. This is the tool which considers how the output of a particular model can be affected by changes to inputs to that model. For example, we can consider what the effects of different levels of interest rate changes would be on the lending book of a bank. It is sometimes known as what if analysis, as we are considering what would happen to the model if certain events occur.

QUESTION TIME 2

Carry out an uncertainty analysis for your commute to work.

What can go wrong?	How frequently does it happen?	What are the consequence?

Write your answer here then check with the answer at the back of the book.

5 The risk assessment approach

5.1 Methods of assessing operational risk

Quantifying risk in terms of the precise financial impact it has on the business would be the ideal basis for decision-making. However, the problem with using financial measures and models is supporting them with accurate, comprehensive data. The acquisition of this data is the most difficult aspect of measurement due to operational risk's complex nature and the fact that much of the data is difficult to derive automatically from the firm's systems. Objective measurement is difficult because of the same practical problems explained in the previous section on risk identification.

Objectivity is further complicated by the multi-dependencies between functional areas and processing activities. For these reasons it is hard to measure and assess operational risk precisely with confidence, so both qualitative and quantitative methods are commonly used. Some methods are:

- Ranking
- Scenario analysis
- Bottom-up analysis
- Key risk indicators
- Historical loss data.

The rest of this chapter will look at each of these methods in turn.

5.2 Ranking

A firm assesses its operations and activities against a menu of potential operational risk vulnerabilities. This process is internally driven and often incorporates checklists and/or workshops to identify the strengths and weaknesses of the operational risk environment.

The basic idea of control and risk self assessment is to create a structured way to obtain management's opinions regarding operational risk. The idea is to ensure that the necessary decisions are made in a consistent manner to enable judgements to be made. You will remember from earlier the importance of this consistency across the firm. This style of approach recognises that there is a lack of information regarding the true impact and therefore replaces financial assessment with general opinion assessment, albeit that such assessment is likely to be supported by some level of actual data. It is worth obtaining the views of both users and owners of controls on their adequacy. Differences in opinion could tell a lot about the business and the attitudes of different parts of the business. However this process must not be too onerous.

The key business risks facing the firm must be determined. The firm must decide what is necessary to achieve corporate objectives, where the organisation is falling short and where and how performance can be improved. It is helpful to examine existing process controls and determine changes to improve their efficiency and effectiveness. This may involve the investigation of a business process to see where it can be improved. Examining business processes and risks is necessary in order to understand them from multiple perspectives such as employee satisfaction, customer impact, business risk and efficiency of operations points of view in order to obtain a comprehensive overview.

There are two main approaches to control and risk assessment techniques:

- The first takes a series of questionnaires as the basis for establishing that an adequate control environment is in place and then some form of modelling is undertaken to provide a level of support. In some situations the questionnaires are available as standard, whereas in others they need to be produced from the control environment of the firm.
- The other approach is to look at individual key risks in isolation and provide a High, Medium, Low type of assessment of the adequacy of the control environment associated with such a risk.

From the control perspective, one of the simplest methods of assessing risk is the creation and application of a ranking hierarchy. This is a method of ranking risks in order of their importance. For instance, a firm might decide that the process risk of volume sensitivity is higher than the system risk of inadequate security, or that a lack of training is higher risk than the pace of change. The assessment may be subjective – depending on the experience of the professionals involved, or objective – being supported by historical data, or a combination of both. In either event, the ranking decision depends on two criteria – the likelihood of the risk being realised and the magnitude of the business impact – you can see that here we are back to the topic of impact and probability

Qualitative Risk Assessment

Business Impact	Low	Medium	High
High	C	B	A
Medium	C	B	B
Low	C	C	C

Likelihood

If we refer back to the earlier section on risk status codes, we can see that this diagram has been linked to red, amber and green: Risk A is a high impact and high probability risk that is defined as Red. Risks B covering three different locations on the grid (high likelihood/medium impact, medium likelihood, medium impact and medium likelihood/high impact) and are deemed Amber. The remaining less likely and/or less impact risks are deemed Green. However the Green risks should never be ignored because if they occur in large enough numbers, the impact on the firm could be large. Also the environment could change and this could affect the impact and/or probability which can change the definitions of these risks.

Firms need to decide which staff members should be involved in the risk self assessment process. Employees involved need to have sufficient knowledge in the matters to be discussed in order to ensure the accuracy of the results to management. They need to represent a sufficient cross-section of the firm so that the results obtained will represent an accurate cross-organisational picture, with a blend of understanding of both risk and operational issues.

QUESTION TIME 3

Your manager has asked you to prepare PowerPoint slides on the advantages and disadvantages of ranking.

What factors would you include in your bullet points?

Write your answer here then check with the answer at the back of the book.

5.3 Scenario analysis

This will take the key external loss events and then appraise whether they could happen within the firm. This might, of course, be perfectly possible. Given a proper risk mapping, firms can begin to get a better picture of the rare but high impact risk events that are potentially of such great concern. Earlier in the course, reference was made to the London riots that happened during the summer of 2011. Whilst your organisation may not have been directly affected by this event, it would have been prudent for the business to carry out scenario analysis to determine what the potential impact of such an event could have been on the organisation.

Scenario analysis together with using loss data is a good approach. It is clear from Basel's rules that external loss data needs to be considered. How it can be combined with a firm's own data is always open to interpretation, but there are some solutions available on the market which do assist with scenario analysis. These will take the key external loss events and then see whether they could happen to the firm.

Effective risk identification considers both internal factors (such as the complexity of the firm's structure, the nature of its activities, the quality of personnel, organisational changes and employee turnover) and external factors (such as changes in the industry and technological advances) that could adversely affect the achievement of its objectives. There will be many different scenarios to consider and the more remote the likelihood that is considered, the harder it may be to imagine or evaluate. However, just because something is difficult to imagine or evaluate, it does not mean that the risk goes away. Creating a risk profile where risks are understood, controlled, mitigated or accepted is part of effective and efficient management of the business and its resources.

Basel recognises that banks are beginning to quantify their operational risks and are trying to come up with meaningful measures. What is also clear is that there will need to be an involvement of the operational risk team in the new business committees, to ensure that the impact of any new development on the total operational risk framework is properly considered. However, there are other drivers. Being able to properly measure the additional operational risk applying to a new product will enable appropriate product pricing. There have been many examples of transactions or types of activity that have looked profitable in credit risk or market risk terms, only to incur disproportionate levels of operational risk – perhaps settlement problems and penalties or excessive legal work being required. Involving the operational risk team at an early stage will ensure that matters are properly considered prior to activity being undertaken.

Scenario analysis is normally deemed to be a subjective method of highlighting potential risk issues. It relies upon the experience of seasoned business professionals to capture possible scenarios that have occurred in the past (perhaps externally rather than in-house), or may result in a loss in the future. By investigating these scenarios, preventive measures can be determined to reduce their risk of occurrence. Its advantages are the same as for the ranking method, whilst its main disadvantage is that it depends on the expertise of the managers involved. If there are gaps in knowledge, experience or loss data histories, then the scenarios may lack sufficient rigour.

5.4 Bottom-up analysis

The bottom-up measurement approach seeks to identify and analyse the individual risks and adequacy of controls across the entire business. It is called bottom-up because it builds up a detailed profile of the risks that occur in each area, aggregating them to provide overall measures of exposure for departments, divisions or the firm as a whole. It is the process-centric view and requires a sound foundation of categorisation.

As is the case with ranking self assessment in general, it uses the experience of line managers and staff, coupled with loss data as its source of information so the resultant measures contain both qualitative and quantitative elements. Compiling bottom-up profiles usually involves a combination of these methods to produce a consolidated understanding of the risk exposure. Much of the data will often be collected during a risk review. It is basically using subjective and objective input.

Bottom-up analysis

Both subjective and objective

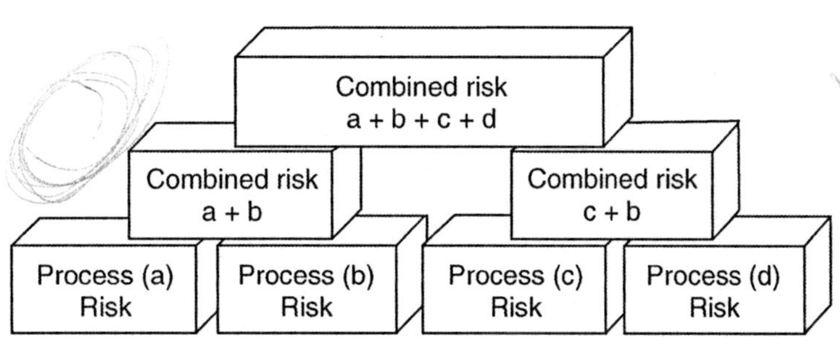

The advantages of bottom-up analysis are that:

- It addresses risk and control issues at the process level, thus complementing the role of line managers.
- Accountability and responsibility for risk management can be clearly defined. The owner or manager of a process is usually made accountable for managing the risks it contains.
- It encourages a risk aware culture and a more transparent environment.
- It encourages a continuous improvement approach to risk management. As risks are identified and assessed, mitigation action can be taken immediately if necessary. This means that improvements to the control environment can be made quickly in the short-term.
- It improves the quality of management information by creating a detailed profile of risks in each business area.
- It allows a cross-section of staff to give a balanced view.

On the other hand, certain disadvantages exist in that:

- Although powerful with respect to detail, it takes time to implement. The assessment of all operational risks requires a detailed understanding of how a firm's processes work and what its weaknesses are. Documenting this can be a lengthy exercise.
- The continuing maintenance of firm risk profiles is often a major undertaking, which would be exacerbated in a high change environment where profiles may change continuously.
- It can be influenced by senior managers if not properly managed.

5.5 Key risk indicators

By identifying and assessing the severity of risks and properly understanding the cause of the chain of events, objective measurement criteria can be chosen to measure ongoing risk status. These measures are called **risk indicators**. They are a health check on the performance of the business and are used by all functions to ensure that risk is satisfactorily controlled. They usually measure the effects (rather than the cause) of risk at set control points in the business and act as early warning signals or forward-looking measures to alert management to problem areas.

Risk indicators are statistics and/or metrics, often financial, which can provide insight into a firm's risk position. These indicators tend to be reviewed on a periodic basis (such as monthly or quarterly) to alert managers to changes that may be indicative of risk concerns. Such indicators may include the number of failed trades, staff turnover rates and/or severity of errors and omissions. They can be applied to a whole variety of things depending upon the firm's level of sophistication and its business mix. In order for this system to work efficiently, it is important that key information is directed to the correct person on a timely basis.

This idea appears in Basel under its sound practices. What this highlights is that the key risk indicator is intended to highlight matters within the risk structure of the firm. These indicators may demonstrate that the risk profile of the company has changed or that there are areas requiring additional investigation.

Thresholds and limits are typically tied to risk indicators (threshold levels) which, when exceeded, alert management to areas of potential problems. Some of the key risk indicators will be a specific limit has been exceeded and as a result action will be required. Of course if the limit is exceeded by a comparatively small amount then one action may be required, whereas another action may result from a greater level of excess. This concept is not dissimilar to triggers that can be set in lending conditions attached to a customer's loan. For example, if shares are held as security and their market value falls below the trigger level, then the bank must make a response based on the higher level of risk that it now faces.

When building a set of performance indicators the starting point must be to decide what the monitoring is for. If it is to ensure that action can be taken long before a loss is taken then one level of indicator may be appropriate, whereas the disaster scenario may be a different level altogether. Some metrics may be efficiency based, for example trades processed per individual, but may not actually be intended to highlight risk. These are normally called key performance indicators (KPIs). A reduction in processing per individual may purely relate to the reduction in general business levels and highlight very little about the control environment.

Key controls must de identified. These are the controls whose failure will significantly impact the risk profile of the firm. Therefore the most significant level of monitoring will be directed towards these controls. However, just having the risk indicators is not sufficient; it is the action taken as a result of the indicator being exceed which is crucial. This serves a number of purposes. First, it reinforces the importance of the indicator level to the management directly involved. Second, the prompt review should reduce the incidence of loss.

QUICK QUESTION

What KPIs have you encountered at work?

Write your answer here before reading on.

Typical KRIs include:

- Total transaction levels
- Error rates or losses
- Staffing levels
- Unreconciled items on cash and customer accounts
- Disputed amounts
- Number of client complaints and levels of claims
- Employee turnover rates
- Confirmations not received
- Systems downtime
- Key transaction types.

These might additionally be tracked according to their characteristics (name of staff member processing the item, severity, age and size etc.). The actual key performance indicator to be chosen in a specific case will depend upon the nature of the risk itself. The main idea is that the risk indicator must be seen to be indicative of a change in the level of the key risk. If the metric is insufficient to do this then it should either be replaced or supplemented by an additional metric.

Just because you are able to think of metrics for everything does not mean that every metric should be calculated and reported, or that the metrics should be provided in the same form to all members of staff. More senior management may, for example, be more interested in the trends in data rather than the actual figures themselves. So a clear insight into what the message is trying to achieve is required. Furthermore, those metrics to be installed will be those that are of greatest use to the firm. As they are installed and reported against the extent of their risk sensitivity can be increasingly assessed, leading to either their amendment or their replacement.

Many of the indicators currently collected by firms are for managing expected rather than unexpected losses. Therefore their contribution to capital measurement under Basel may be limited but the value they add to the business for managing its exposure to a wide range of losses can be enormous.

Setting relevant and reliable indicators is a challenge. They must of course be linked to the causes of operational risk incidents so that managers can monitor the causes of operational risk exposure on an ongoing basis. When the indicators are first designed, it will not be known whether they are going to be successful until they have been refined with experience. Experience will build and may require over two years worth of complete indicator data to be built up. Firms that invest in building such databases will generate a dynamic library of indicators which will be useful to predict and manage their ongoing risk management processes.

The eventual goal for firms would be to have the ability to generate a day-to-day dashboard of operational risk exposures for risk acceptance or control decisions which can be deployed effectively across all core business divisions.

5.6 Historical loss data

Creation of a loss database is crucial to the requirements of both the Basel Accord and to the approach used by regulators such as the PRA. For example, Basel II states that the ability to monitor loss events and effectively gather loss data is a basic step for operational risk measurement and is a pre-requisite for movement to the more advanced regulatory approach.

Consequently firms need to develop an operational loss database. Of course, no amount of internal data will include every type of loss event that can occur, so it will also be necessary to consider purchasing external loss data, or participating in some form of event sharing system.

When developing a loss database it is necessary to consider whether a firm wants to map it initially to the structure proposed by the regulators, whether to include expected and unexpected losses and how to deal with loss mitigants.

Loss data evaluation is important in mapping the actual losses experienced by the firm back to a sensible categorisation system. Once the data has been collected (from either internal or external sources) it can then be used in the measurement process, often using benchmarking or statistical methods. For instance, a loss distribution curve may be created that records the value of all material (direct) losses in a particular risk category over a time period of, say, three years. By analysing this curve using similar VaR techniques to those in market risk, some prediction of future losses can be made within specified confidence limits.

No. of incidents
Expected Losses
Unexpected Losses
Value of Loss (£)

Expected losses are those that occur with reasonable frequency. They represent known weaknesses, or sit within the risk appetite of the firm – these would include items such as small lending losses, or levels of compensation made to complaining customers. They must be managed by good process controls and an effective, continuous risk management process. The unexpected losses are those low-frequency, high-impact events that can create serious problems – for example, the losses incurred by banks as a result of the LIBOR Rate fixing scandal of June 2012. They are much more difficult to manage on a day-to-day level because they don't occur often enough to test the control environment. They are best managed using contingency planning.

The advantage of this measurement method is that it allows the firm to understand the size of losses, in monetary terms, which can be attributed to particular risks. Its main disadvantage is that it does not predict unexpected losses very well, due to the lack of data or imagination in anticipating them. Some firms also don't make allowance for near misses, i.e. potential events that might have caused serious harm but were detected in time – by luck or judgement. As a result, reporting the results of historical loss analysis in a way that makes decision making easier can be difficult. It is also worth noting that often firms do not always include indirect or soft costs, as these are not easily identifiable from the accounting system or general ledger.

KEY WORDS

Key words in this chapter are given below. There is space to write your own revision notes and add any other key words or phrases you want to remember.

- Expected loss
- Statistical loss
- Stress loss
- Cause
- Effect
- Risk Register
- Risk map
- Ranking
- Scenario analysis
- Bottom up analysis
- Key risk indicators
- Historical loss Data.

Adv:
assign risks and losses in monetary terms

Disadv:
Doesn't predict unexpected losses well, due to lack of data or imagination in anticipating them

To make allowances for near-misses huge events that could have had a significant impact but were detected in time.

REVIEW

Now consider the main points that were raised in this chapter. These are listed below. Tick each one as you go through them.

- Risk must be assessed to allow the firm to estimate how likely it is that a risk event may occur and if it does occur, what the likely level of impact will be.
- When assessing risk, an organisation should seek to review the losses that it has incurred, consider how effective its control procedures are, internally assess the risks associated with its operations, consider other risk indicators, consider reported external operational losses and exposures and review changes in its operating environment.
- The Risk Register is an internal document that seeks to list those risks identified by a business under risk categories.
- Risks can be categorised as Red, Amber or Green depending upon their risk profile.
- Techniques for assessing risk include: ranking, scenario analysis, bottom up analysis, key risk indicators and historic loss data.

chapter 4

RISK MITIGATION

Contents

Learning objectives

On completion of this chapter, you should be able to:

- differentiate between a range of risk mitigation techniques
- assess the relevant merits of different approaches to risk mitigation
- identify and describe tactical control measures that could be used to manage risk.

Introduction

We are now about to look at the third phase of the risk management lifecycle – risk mitigation.

The chapter will start by defining what is meant by risk mitigation, before moving on to consider some of the ways by which firms (and individuals) can mitigate risk. The two mitigating controls – preventative controls and detective controls are discussed next, before exploring the ways in which a risk loss can be reduced. The next part of the chapter will discuss ways in which operational risk exposure can be reduced. Probably the most common way by which risk can be transferred is by taking out appropriate insurance, so it is useful to consider the field of insurable risk at the conclusion of this short chapter.

1 Risk mitigation

Having identified and assessed risk, we are now in a position to consider how risk can be mitigated. This stage of the lifecycle addresses actions taken to reduce the probability that the loss represented by the risk will occur. Mitigation recognises that the purpose of an organisation is to deliver goods and services to their respective customers in order to meet business goals. It provides for a cost/benefit analysis of a mitigating action prior to implementation.

Mitigation does not mean removing risk completely (as we discussed earlier, a risk-free world does not exist) but rather to make risk outcomes less intense or severe. Risk mitigation is about controlling risk. The important thing here is to identify the subset of controls that are actually contributing to the mitigation of the risks that the firm has identified and assessed. It is well worth also taking the opportunity of evaluating the cost of the control because at the heart of any operational risk framework is the risk reward relationship. The objective is to increase certainty and efficiency, with also an objective of increased profitability. A risk aware culture is a key necessity which needs to be embedded within a firm. This can be achieved in part by the use of risk awareness training.

A risk mitigation strategy is an organisation's plan for how it will address its identified risks. Creating and implementing mitigation strategies is one of the most effective ways to protect an organisation's assets, and is nearly always more cost effective than repairing the damage after a security incident.

There are many types of risk mitigation that can be applied to certain sorts of risk.

QUICK QUESTION

List some of the ways by which your organisation mitigates risk.

Write your answer here before reading on.

Here are some examples:

- Increased scrutiny
- Four eyes checks – meaning that one member of staff checks the work of another or one group checks the work of another group. This can be as part of the internal audit process or as part of the control procedures established within the firm
- Accounting standards
- Establishing default probabilities on credit risk
- Enhancing the firm's approach to remuneration, with a greater emphasis on risk mitigation
- Close monitoring of external supply contracts
- Managing technology threats against the organisation
- Introducing mandatory training (such as anti-money laundering awareness)
- System enforced rules, such as entries to a general ledger only being allowed if the journal debit and credit amounts balance
- Monitoring the changing situation globally.

We will now move on to consider some of the techniques used to mitigate risk.

1.1 Risk avoidance

It makes sense not to place a business or operation into a risky situation in the first place. Avoiding risk therefore means either withdrawing from a business because of an unacceptable level of risk, or deciding not to take on new business, corporate merger or acquisition for the same reasons. At its simplest level in banking risk avoidance occurs when a bank declines a lending proposition received from a customer as they feel it unlikely that the customer will be able to repay any advance made.

Risk avoidance also includes not performing an activity that could carry risk. An example would be not buying a property or another business or engaging a business activity in order to not take on the legal liability that comes with it. Another would be not to enter a foreign market in order not to avoid material risks that could be present. On a personal level, an example would be not to take part in an Outward Bound development course due to a fear of heights.

Avoidance may seem the answer to all risks, but avoiding risks also means losing out on the potential gain that accepting (retaining) the risk may have allowed. Not entering a business to avoid the risk of loss also avoids the possibility of earning profits. At its ultimate level, should a business embrace a strategy of risk avoidance, it will not do any business at all and as a result, it will not generate any sales and will not make profits.

1.2 Risk sharing

Briefly this may be defined as sharing with another party the burden of loss or the benefit of gain, from a risk, and the measures to reduce a risk.

Risk sharing is the style of a method of risk management in which the costs or consequences of risk is distributed among several stakeholders across an organisation or industry. An example of this would be sharing insurance losses across various insurance syndicates or in the reinsurance industry.

At the level of a single enterprise, for example a small to medium enterprise, it is very common for a particular company to share infrastructure risks with fellow businesses in the same area or in the same building. For example, different business could share the costs of a standby generator to mitigate the risk of loss of central power to the building.

The term risk transfer (see below) is often used in place of risk sharing in the mistaken belief that you can transfer a risk to a third party through insurance or outsourcing a business activity to them. In practice if the insurance company or contractor goes bankrupt or ends up in court, the original risk is likely to still revert to the first party. As such, in the terminology of practitioners and scholars alike, the purchase of an insurance contract is often described as a transfer of risk. However, technically speaking, the buyer of the contract generally retains legal responsibility for the losses transferred, meaning that insurance may be described more accurately as a post-event compensatory mechanism. For example, a personal injuries insurance policy does not transfer the risk of a car accident to the insurance company. The risk still remains with the policy holder (namely the person who has been in the accident). The insurance policy simply provides that if an accident (the event) occurs involving the policy holder then some compensation may be payable to the policy holder that is commensurate to the suffering/damage. But how long might it take for the insurance company to pay out and to what extent of the notional loss(es) after the process of loss adjustment has been completed?

Some ways of managing risk fall into multiple categories. Risk retention pools are technically retaining the risk for the group, but spreading it over the whole group involves transfer among individual members of the group. This is different from traditional insurance, in that no premium is exchanged between members of the group up front, but instead losses are assessed to all members of the group.

1.3 Risk transfer

This refers to changing the nature of the risk by transferring it, perhaps by outsourcing, to another company or transferring the responsibility to an insurance company or by taking out a lien or some other form of financial protection which would invoke should a risk event occur. Credit derivatives transfer credit risk to another counterparty and other derivatives are used to transfer market risk. It is more difficult to transfer operational risk, but not impossible with certain remedies.

1.4 Risk acceptance

The term risk acceptance simply implies that a risk has been examined and assessed and a company decides to accept the level of risk they have assessed and to retain it within their own ownership. Many risks are clearly accepted in business. Some risks that are accepted by companies are systematic and symptoms of the industries that the company operates in: A manufacturing company will have rejected items from time to time even ranging through to total product recalls. A supermarket will have complaints from customers about food and other items purchased which are faulty or past their sell by date or where the packaging is damaged. On the other hand, some risks will be accepted because they occur time to time due to occasional human error. For example, in a bank, there will be single errors made by staff, such as payment errors.. Such risks are fully accepted and priced into the cost of doing business by the bank concerned.

Sometimes a risk has to be accepted because a company has insufficient resources to mitigate or manage the risk. For example, a bank manager may not have budget to chase customers over small unauthorised overdraft breaches.

1.5 Risk retention

If a firm is satisfied that its risk identification and measurement systems are rigorous and effective, and that it has a good understanding of its risks, it may decide to retain a certain level of risk. In other words, a degree of risk appetite is acceptable in return for higher profit.

Risk retention therefore involves accepting the loss, or benefit from a risk when it occurs. Risk retention is a viable strategy for small risks where the cost of insuring against the risk would be greater over time than the total losses sustained. All risks that are not avoided or transferred are retained by default. This would also include the level of excess on an insurance policy. Normally the greater the excess, then the lower the levels of premiums to be paid – therefore the level of risk represented by the excess is the retained risk.

Risk retention will also include those risks that are so large or catastrophic that they either cannot be insured against or the premiums would be infeasible. War is an example since most property and risks are not insured against war, so the loss attributed by war is retained by the insured. This may also be acceptable if the chance of a very large loss is small or if the cost to insure for greater coverage amounts is so great it would hinder the goals of the organisation too greatly. Again, we have returned to the risk/reward continuum!

1.6 Control measures

The cycle of activity in managing operational risk has controls as an important step in the overall loop. Once risks are identified and measured the next job is to control them. Any measure whether organisational, or relating to technology will fall under this heading. Controls are there to be defined and implemented. Beyond that the task is for the controls to be checked and reviewed periodically to see if they are operating effectively and smoothly. This latter task falls to internal audit groups within firms.

When setting up an operational risk programme it is important to remember from earlier that operational risk management exists throughout an organisation, from the Board to the junior staff members – although ultimate responsibility will always remain with the Board. As such it is not sufficient just to identify the owners of the risk and the owners of the controls, but rather there is the need to ensure that risk and risk ownership are monitored as they percolate throughout the business. Each and every member of the staff, including agents and contractors, must be part of this process. This is another example of where sound risk management must become embedded within the practices and culture of the organisation.

Line managers will own risks and some will own the controls which are in place to mitigate those risks. Clearly a signpost that does not tell you where you are or where to go is of no value. Likewise operating a control environment where the controls either are ineffective, cost more than the expected loss or duplicate existing controls is clearly wasteful. One of the problems here can be that vigilant internal auditors have recommended the implementation of additional controls as a result of the identification of a specific event or failure. Such an additional control may itself duplicate a control that should have identified the error, but failed to do so. Rather than implementing an additional control, the effectiveness of the original control should be improved.

If the controls are not achieving any real degree of risk mitigation, then they are probably of limited value. Another result of this part of the work can be that duplicate controls are identified; that is controls which would only identify the same control failures that another control is already identifying. Risk managers are also likely to identify controls which are either inefficient or ineffective.

To do this, measures will be required covering the throughput of the control. Information is also required on contracts corrected and errors that still occur. As a consequence of this analysis, a view can be taken on the effectiveness of the controls and whether they need to be enhanced. Part of this enhancement could be training or reporting, rather than a change to the actual control.

1.7 Types of mitigating controls

QUICK QUESTION

How would you describe a preventative control?

Write your answer here before reading on.

Preventive controlsare those that prevent errors occurring in the first place. They attempt to tackle the fundamental causes of risk at or near to the point of origin and are most effective when incorporated within processes at the outset by anticipating a risky outcome at the risk identification stage of the lifecycle. IT and **systems controls** built in to operational processes are used as a key means of implementing preventive controls. A key preventive control is the **segregation of duties.**This means the separation of trading, operation and control, financial reporting and risk management functions. The aim of segregatingthese functions is to prevent too much responsibility, authority and power being concentrated in the hands of too few individuals. In turn, this prevents the possibility of the internal control structure being compromised and the risk of fraud arising. The lack of appropriate segregation of duties is one of the major process causes of operational risk.

From the transaction processing perspective, another important area is the maintenance of data integrity in systems. For instance, the incorrect capture of a transaction's details in a firm's systems due to errors created through manual input. If the process was designed so that the transaction was captured once at the point of execution and checked and this data then flowed automatically into the downstream systems, the risk of manual errors would disappear (being replaced by system risks, which are generally considered to be smaller). This illustrates the benefit of a straight-through processing (STP) environment, one of the key objectives of many operational process flows within financial firms.

QUICK QUESTION

What other examples of preventative controls can you think of?

Write your answer here before reading on.

Other examples of preventive controls are:

- The setting up and ongoing maintenance of good procedures to prevent unauthorised actions and errors
- The use of training to reduce the likelihood of human error arising from a lack of expertise
- The use of well-designed systems to automate processes and controls to eliminate risk due to human error.

QUICK QUESTION

Now that you understand preventative controls, how would you describe detective controls?

Write your answer here before reading on.

Detective controls detect errors once they have occurred. They can be further split into two sub-categories – internal and external detection.

- **Internal detection controls** are thereto trap errors after they have occurred but before a potential loss is realised in the outside world, i.e. they detect the risk event in order to prevent the effect and avoid escalation of the problem (stopping the rot). Checking and inspection-type activities fall into this category.For instance, checking the content of a legal contract before it is signed is a control that may detect errors in the terms and conditions of that contract. These errors would then be rectified and the contract sent out at no loss to the firm. If the control did not exist, the potential for legal risk to be realised would increase.
- **External detection controls** are those that detect errors and losses once they have been realised, i.e. they detect the effects. Post-settlement checks such as statement-to-ledger reconciliations fall under this category. If a problem is found, for instance, whena counterparty has not been paid on time, loss due to a compensation claim for lost interest will occur. If the detective control is effective, the problem will be resolved quickly and the loss effect limited.External detective controls are important because they can limit the direct and indirect losses to the firm. External detective controls are perhaps more concerned with reducing the impact of loss, rather than reducing the likelihood of loss (because the loss has already occurred). The best example of such controls is the activity of **reconciliation**, which checks the status of information within the firm against externally held records. Examples might be a bank trading foreign exchange which would check its US dollar nostro balances with its correspondent bank in New York or an asset management firm, which would wish to check its stock and cash accounts against records held by its custodian. Reconciliation is a daily discipline and affects all types of products and asset classes.

If a risk does crystallise, there are a number of ways that the resulting loss to the firm can be reduced.Using detective controls is one method. Other strategies are outlined below.

- **Diversification strategies:** an over-reliance on a particular customer, product or market may expose the firm to heavier losses than if it operated a more diverse business. By widening the net, the firm is spreading the risk.
- **Risk sharing:** by collaborating with other firms, or pursuing joint ventures, it is possible to share any potential operational losses, as well as having the potential to share benefits and profits with the other party.
- **Financial reserves:** by having access to emergency funding or borrowing, or capital reserves.

- **Insurance:** having insurance against the financial loss presented by a risk event is valuable. It may take time for the insurance arrangements to take effect and therefore firms need to see this as a contributing but not total remedy for risk mitigation.
- **Business continuity or contingency planning:** in the same way that financial provisioning provides financial continuity, the ability to anticipate and plan for potential operational crises reduces the harm of unexpected losses. Firms should address and decide how best to keep their businesses operating and available (particularly for customers) in case of adverse events. Continuity or contingency planning may take the form of disaster recovery, succession planning or the production of other fall-back procedures to deal with potential crises or threats to the continuity operation of the business. Both business continuity and business availability are important for management to address. This includes emergency response, crisis management and business resumption planning, covering a whole range of scenarios as identified by the business. Businesses need to understand the underlying risks and the potential impact of each type of disaster. A contingency plan needs to be drawn up, maintained, tested and checked regularly. It is also important to consider the magnitude of the risks which could result in these impacts. This will help determine which scenarios are most likely to occur, and to which ones resources should be directed at the planning stage. Analysis of any potential disruption is required, ranging from minor mishaps to major catastrophes.

QUESTION TIME 1

A colleague approaches you and says that they cannot understand the differences between a preventative control and a detective control.

How would you explain this to them?

Write your answer here then check with the answer at the back of the book.

QUICK QUESTION

What types of risk events could lend themselves well to continuity planning?

Write your answer here before reading on.

Typical risks that fall under this heading are:

- Fire
- System failure
- Power failure
- Natural disasters (floods, earthquakes, tsunamis, hurricanes)
- Explosions
- Civil unrest, terrorist actions, police intervention
- Strikes
- Adverse weather (snow, storms, ice, flooding, stifling temperatures).

- **Good communication and reporting:** having high quality, integrated management information systems allows information to be shared globally and efficiently. This means that if a risk is realised, the firm is able to react quickly to reduce its impact.

- **Outsourcing:** is described as entering into a contract with another company for services to provide operational and administrative support and is now commonplace in the financial services industry. The inclusion of outsourcing as a risk mitigation technique is important. Generally a firm needs to build a programme that is capable of being amended to take account of changing circumstances. One of these is the opening, closing, purchasing or selling or a product, division or company. Another is the outsourcing of a division or department to a third party – for example, payroll services that in the past were supplied internally as part of the HR function of a bank are now commonly provided by a third party. It is important to recognise that the third party service provider's operational risk framework will need to be considered as part of the originating firm's operational risk framework. Roles may be delegated to a third party but firms cannot delegate their responsibilities in this respect. Consequently the framework that is developed needs to be capable of dealing with such changing circumstances. It also needs to be able to evaluate the impact on the overall operational risk environment of any such change.

  Basel and the Markets in Financial Services Directive (MiFID) state that banks should establish policies for managing the risks associated with outsourcing activities. Outsourcing of activities can reduce the institution's risk profile by transferring activities to others with greater expertise and scale to manage the risks associated with specialised business activities – possibly at a lower cost. The PRA, from MiFID, insist that firms should not enter into outsourcing arrangements if they increase the amount of operational risk being taken on board. Furthermore, firms must have explicit policies to exit from outsourcing contracts and must reveal evidence of this and all other planning during PRA visits.

  Outsourcing arrangements should be based on robust contracts and/or service level agreements that ensure a clear allocation of responsibilities between external service providers and the outsourcing firm. Furthermore, firms need to manage residual risks associated with outsourcing arrangements, including disruption of services.Depending on the scale and nature of the activity, firms should understand the potential impact on their operations and their customers of any potential deficiencies in services provided by outsource vendors and other third-party or intra-group service providers.

  Another key point to remember about outsourcing is that a firm cannot outsource its duty of regulatory compliance when entering into an outsourcing contract. It remains firmly on the hook to its regulator with respect to its compliance duties.

- **Limit setting:** market and credit risk limits are also relevant management strategies for operational risk as exceeding limits can be the first sign of operational errors. Limits can be used in other ways to reduce the impact of risk, such as setting capital limits on major technology development or using them as early warning signals in process controls (e.g. risk indicators).

- **Risk awareness training:** Employees do not come to work to make mistakes, so one objective of the risk management framework is to increase the likelihood that staff will carry out tasks in the way intended. In particular when the organisation is under stress, perhaps due to an increase in business or an external event, then the operational risk framework needs to provide staff with additional guidance. Such information will enable them to appreciate the importance of individual controls and, if they are to make a decision not to operate a control, the impact of such a decision. This means that the information available to the staff will need to be at both a summary and a detailed level. It also means that training will be required throughout the organisation and that this training will need to be reviewed on a regular basis.

1.8 Methods for reducing operational risk exposure

1.8.1 Reducing the likelihood and the impact

Once risks have been identified and measured, the firm is in a position to take effective action to address them.

QUICK QUESTION

In what form do you think this corrective action could take?

Write your answer here before reading on.

There are **four** potential mitigation methods, these are to:

- **reduce the likelihood** of the risk occurring
- **reduce the impact** of the risk, should it occur
- transfer the risk
- retain and accept the risk.

The likelihood of operational risk exposure can be reduced through the use of **operational risk controls** and therefore the impact of the risks on the firm, should they occur, can hopefully be minimised. Operational risk controls are activities that are inserted into a process to protect it against specific operational risks. Controls do not generally add value to processing in direct terms but they can add value in indirect terms by protecting against error and consequential loss.

Risk awareness training for all relevant staff should be given by the firm to help staff understand the principle of reducing the likelihood of risks occurring and details of such training being given and attendance should be recorded. For instance, a procedural control might be set up to protect against the risk of a member of staff diverting funds to a personal bank account when making a payment (committing fraud). This procedure might ensure that one person prepares the documentation to send a payment and another person physically sends it. This action doesnot directly make the process any quicker or cheaper (in fact in might make it slower and more costly) but it is necessary to protect the firm against fraudulent activity in order to save money in the longer term and offer protection against reputational damage.

There should be an independent control function and/or internal system audit trail in place to prevent this from happening in practice.Potential risks should be anticipated and evaluated when the process is first designed and the necessary controls embedded within it.

As the process of risk mitigation improves and becomes bedded in a move towards a heat map style could be envisaged (this concept was introduced in the last chapter). This would show the varying degrees of risk assessment and could plot risks as they develop from one level of impact and likelihood to another.

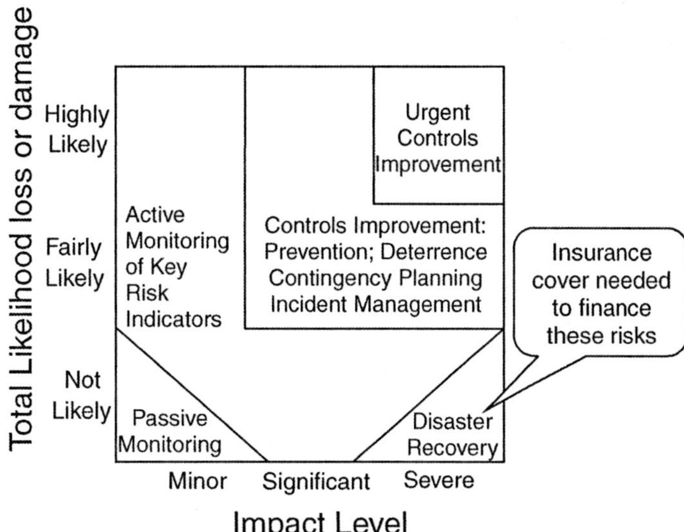

1.9 The cost of controls

Controls for the sake of it may not make sense. Clearly the more money spent on a control will be related to the level of risk perceived in the control. Firms with an effective risk policy and systems will have a better idea as to the actual risk they are running. This is counterbalanced by the level of cost incurred in operating the control. That should not just focus on the people elements, but also the opportunity costs if any such costs exist.

QUICK QUESTION

What is meant by opportunity cost?

Write your answer here before reading on.

Opportunity cost is the consequence of giving up one potential course of action as a result of taking an alternative course of action. For example, on receipt of a bonus payment you may decide that you could either spend this money on a holiday or a new bathroom. If you decide on the bathroom, then the opportunity cost is the holiday – in other words, what you had to give up when you took the decision to invest in the bathroom.

There is always a balance to be drawn. For example, increasing the cost of a control by growing staff numbers will cost say £500k There is the expectation that there will be a reduction in losses and an increase in efficiency of £NN. If £NN is greater that £500k then it is worth making the investment in the improved control. However £500k is a figure that can be estimated with reasonable accuracy, whilst £NN is actually a trend, a distribution that we are trying to evaluate. In other words, why have a control mechanism which costs the firm more than it can possibly save?

The presence of this softer information in the business does not change the need to make decisions like this all of the time. The objective of the modelling system should be to facilitate such decision making and improve the nature of information used.

2 Insurable risk

2.1 Insurable risk

With any business, there are various risks involved that could result in the failure of the firm. It is often possible to take out insurance to mitigate these risks, but not all risks can be insured.

Everyone is familiar with insurance and it is used by individuals and businesses alike. The same holds true for banks as insurance is probably the easiest and most common form of transfer of operational risks to others. If banks understand their risk profile and also possess the ability to put in place effective insurance with clarity as to what that insurance actually offers, then it is a very beneficial business exercise.

There are many types of commercial insurance which cover, amongst other things, property, staff liabilities, key person, public liability, directors' insurance and product liability. The key challenge for firms is to assess whether any particular insurance policy is appropriate and indeed whether the premium represents good value against the impact and probability of the risk event occurring. In the main, insurance addresses operational risk. The key point that follows from this of course is whether the type of operational risk is in fact insurable.

Some risks are plainly uninsurable because of illegality, impossibility or because they extend beyond the financial limits of available insurance. Every insurance company will always wish to assess the total liability for which they might be potentially responsible through the process known as loss adjustment. The essence of having insurance enables a transfer of risk through an insurance mechanism from the bank to the insurance company at a premium (the price at which the insurance cover is procured and provided). An insurance claim is triggered by an event but there will always be an examination of why the event occurred – the cause. For example a policy to protect a building against fire will pay potentially for the damage caused by the fire but not necessarily if the fire was set by an employee of the firm or if the bank concerned had no fire protection mechanisms installed e.g. sprinkler systems. The same thing can apply to theft but not necessarily if the theft was the result of an internal fraud. In the case of banks they normally take out insurance cover through what is called a Bankers Blanket Bond, a type of fidelity bond issued by an insurance company that protects a bank against losses from a variety of criminal acts carried out by its employees. Some nation states require Bankers Blanket Bond coverage as a condition of operating a bank.

2.2 Types of insurance cover

QUICK QUESTION

What types of risk would you expect to be covered by insurance?

Write your answer here before reading on.

The following types of insurance cover are likely to be readily available in the marketplace and will cover either against losses or against particular claims made according to the terms of the policy written by the insurance provider.

Types of policies are as follows.

- Business interruption
- Computer crime
- Commercial liability
- Directors' and officers' liability
- Employment practices liability
- Key person
- Kidnap and ransom
- Motor
- Pension trustees
- Property insurance
- Professional indemnity
- Terrorism
- Unauthorised trading.

An **insurable risk** is a risk that meets the ideal criteria for efficient insurance. The concept of insurable risk underlies nearly all insurance decisions.

For a risk to be insurable, several things need to be true.

- The insurer must be able to charge a premium high enough to cover not only claims expenses, but also to cover the insurer's expenses. In other words, the risk cannot be catastrophic, or so large that no insurer could hope to pay for the loss.
- The nature of the loss must be definite and financially measurable. That is, there should not be room for argument as to whether or not payment is due, or what amount the payment should be.
- The loss should be random in nature, or else the insured may engage in adverse selection (anti-selection).

2.3 Factors determining uninsurable risk

- A risk is uninsurable when an insurance company cannot calculate the probability of the risk and therefore cannot work out a premium that the business must pay. For example, you cannot take out insurance against possible failure of the business itself.
- Risk is too widespread, for example, when there is a war.

- When the loss is incurred due to your own deliberate actions, it cannot be insured. If, for example, you have financial problems in your business and decide to set fire to your premises in order to obtain a cash payout from insurance, this will be a void claim.
- You cannot insure a business for such things as:
  - Price fluctuations from the time the order for goods is placed and the delivery of those goods
  - Different price levels at different places
  - New inventions that replace old technology, e.g. in the IT industry
  - Nuclear weapons
  - Changes in fashions when goods become obsolete.

2.4 Factors determining insurable risk

- If the insurance company has enough statistics to work out the probability of the risk, they will call it an insurable risk.
- Actuaries are highly qualified people working for insurance companies; their role is to work out exactly what risks their company will carry. The degree of the risk will influence the size of the insurance premium.

2.4.1 Some examples of insurable risk

- **Fire insurance**

  A fire insurance contract is a contract of indemnity for losses suffered due to a fire. A building and its contents can be insured against fire, but additional clauses must be added for damage by hail, wind or riot. Fire insurance is expensive – the greater the perceived risk, the higher the premium. The fire insurance may also have a clause sometimes called the iron safe clause, whereby all books and records must be kept in a safe.

  The book value and the market or replacement value of insured property will no doubt be different and this can pose a potential loss for the party taking out the insurance. For example assuming a building is insured for £1,000,000 (book value) and the replacement rebuild value is £3,000,000. Should the building burn down, the insurance company will only pay out a maximum of £1,000,000 and the owner will lose £2,000,000 should it be rebuilt.

- **Fidelity insurance**

  An organisation can take out fidelity insurance to protect its business against dishonest employees.

KEY WORDS

Key words in this chapter are given below. There is space to write your own revision notes and add any other key words or phrases you want to remember.

- Risk avoidance
- Risk sharing
- Risk transfer
- Risk acceptance
- Risk retention
- Preventative controls
- Detective controls
- Opportunity cost
- Insurance risk
- Insurable risk
- Uninsurable risk

REVIEW

Now consider the main points that were introduced in this chapter. These are listed below. Tick each one as you go through them.

- The objective of risk mitigation is not to remove risk, but to reduce the outcome to the firm should the risk event occur.
- Risk mitigation strategies include: risk avoidance, risk sharing, risk transfer, risk acceptance and risk retention.
- Once risks have been identified and measured, the next step is to control them. These controls can either be preventative or detective.
- If a risk event does occur, then the firm should take steps to reduce the effect of the event. For example, through early identification, having robust and tested plans in place to deal with the event, or through arranging appropriate insurance.
- For certain types of risk it is possible to take out an insurance policy to reduce the impact to the firm should the risk event occur.

chapter 5

MONITORING AND REPORTING

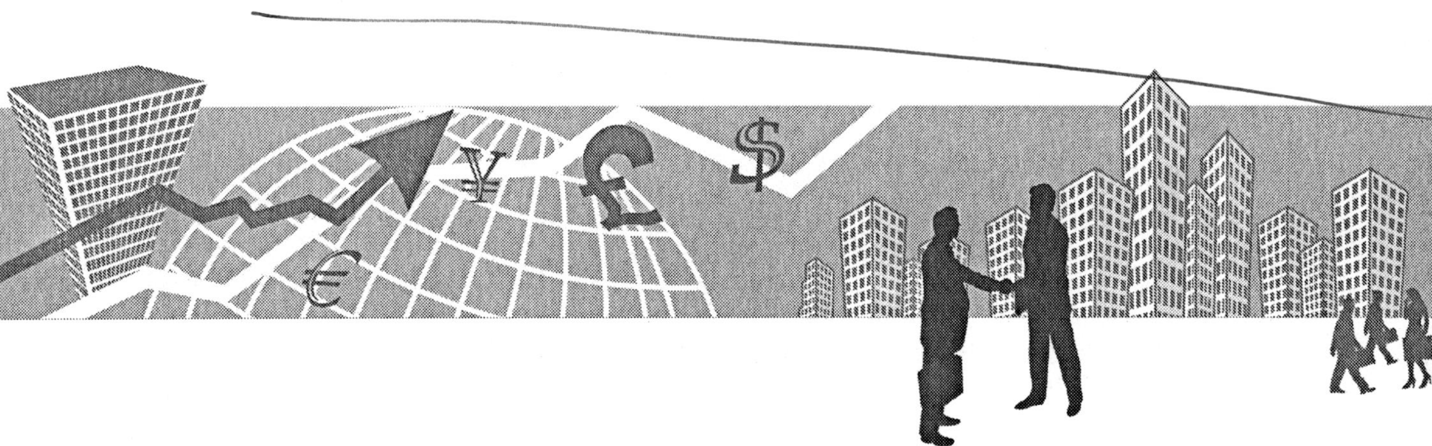

Contents

Learning objectives

On completion of this chapter, you should be able to:

- examine the role of risk monitoring and reporting in the risk management process
- critically review a range of tools and techniques used to monitor and report risk.

Introduction

We are now at the final stage of the risk management lifecycle – monitoring and reporting. This chapter starts with a discussion around the advantages of monitoring and reporting, before moving on to consider to whom the report is being made and what their requirements are, which can influence the style and content of the report. Much of the risk reporting carried out by banks is to meet regulatory requirements, so this topic is introduced next. The second part of this chapter is concerned with loss data analysis. This theme is covered by explaining how historical loss data information is used to measure operational risk, before engaging in a discussion around internal and external loss data.

1 Benefits of monitoring and reporting

The final step in the risk management cycle is that of monitoring and reporting. These are the final stages that follow the identification, assessment and mitigation steps. There is really not much value to be gained in carrying out these processes as part of a risk framework without following it up with good reporting. Reporting leads to informed decision making in connection with the risk management procedures. Without it, poor decisions are far more likely to be made or even no decisions whatsoever to the detriment of everyone.

It is not always straightforward to present good risk reporting as it is more difficult than it at first appears. The activity of reporting will cover all aspects of risk indicators, risk and control assessment and event capture and analysis.

1.1 Recognising different requirements

Risk reports are no different from any other report – they must be written in the right form for the ease and benefit of the reader. These may be heads of business lines, risk committees or the Board itself.

Clear, high quality reports are essential to good operational risk management. Key information must be easily accessible and communicated in such a way as explicitly to be of value. The overall goal is to be able to provide better information in order to make informed decisions on the firm's risk profile. It is far too easy to be overwhelmed by data and information which is not focussed on the needs of the reader. It may be sheer overkill of information, information which is not relevant to the reader or information that may be relevant but is not presented in a way that is intelligible. For operational risk reports, readers can be at every level of the firm so the range of reporting styles will be very wide.

As stressed elsewhere in this course, the importance of communication and understanding are absolutely vital with respect to monitoring reporting activities.

1.2 Reporting styles and techniques

Different styles are useful for different reports and for managing desired outcomes.

QUICK QUESTION

What factors should you keep in mind when considering your reporting style?

Write your answer here before reading on.

Reporting styles can take the form of the following below. Reporting style is dependent on the objective of the report and the target audience:

- Pie and bar charts
- Using 3-D
- Using a 2 dimensional graph
- Using colour
- Using shading
- Using a dashboard approach
- Internal collaborative web-based reports
- Pdf reports
- Audio reports
- High-level reports designed for senior management that only contain key information
- Detailed reports with high volumes of information designed at providing in-depth analysis.

QUICK QUESTION

What do you understand by the term dashboard reporting?

Write your answer here before reading on.

A dashboard report is a visual summary of key data, often presented at a high level with information on a number of Key Performance Indicators (KPIs) beings presented together. Dashboards are of great value because they are able to provide more summarised information drawn from large sets of data focused for the reader's attention and as a result the reader can ask for further supporting detail to address aspects that are conveyed in summary form at the dashboard level. Hence a daily dashboard approach is an effective way to present a concise document to the reader which can then be supported by larger amounts of useful information under the bonnet as it were.

Another attribute of dashboards is that they can be constructed to focus on the most serious risks as recognised by the firm and present highlighted information, again at a summary level, for the benefit of all readers.

1.3 Basic principles of reporting

It is important to remember that presenting complex risk information to a broad and diverse audience is a challenging task. One of the key things that is required for effective risk analysis and reporting would be to answer these three questions that might result from the review of risk results.

- What does this number mean?
- Why is it at that level?
- What should be done about it?

The reporting of risk results is a continuously evolving process.

Reporting should be timely, accurate and complete. It can be difficult to do this all the time as data may be missing. It is better to have accurate reports than no reports at all and, in the absence of any report, risk assumptions should be that we are concerned about everything because nothing is definite.

Risk reporting should enable people to take ownership of the information. Numbers alone are not good enough – they need to be in context. There should be some text and commentary from a named individual to whom the reader can then revert with any subsequent queries. Providing accurate information to the right people on a timely basis is really the key because people will wish to have access to everything they need to know. The information they use needs to be both accurate and timely.. Information requirements are dynamic owing to the changing organisational structure and changing market conditions. It is important that management and staff are trained in the methodologies and language used so that there is little chance of miscommunication or misinterpretation.

When building a reporting structure it is important first to define the boundaries of which type of risk is being addressed and also to recognise and incorporate explicit definitions of the interdependencies of market, credit, operational risk and any other applicable risks.

Following that, it is important to address organisational issues whereby owners of the risk management group and the internal audit group can each contribute to the process.

It is vital that the process is sustainable and improves with time. Improvement comes partly from review and partly from open-mindedness. Everyone can learn; reviews do make sense and standards will rise with experience. The reporting must be deemed to be important and valuable to the business line. It must be flexible and easy to use. It may also be possible to integrate reporting with other processes for example internal audit, planning and budgeting, performance measurement, salary reviews. Much depends upon the exact risk that is being reported.

It is essential to be able to capture the right level of detail from the business and then, within that, with respect to the processes and individual activities that take place. Reporting should demonstrate value and success which will benefit both the business line, the risk management groups and the organisation as a whole.

1.4 Report definitions

A report definition is usually a single sheet of paper for each report and typically might contain:

- Name of report
- Objective(s)
- Distribution list
- Names of fields to be used
- Any calculations required on the fields
- Manual actions to be performed on the fields
- How to use the final report (including typical actions resulting from the final report).

Reports will range from key indicator reports, loss reports and risk performance.

1.5 Regulatory reporting

The Basel Committee requires regular reports from both business units and internal audit. They should address the top level objectives and show the reader the extent to which the risk management system is complying with the controls. They should go on from this to identify and enable the treatment on non-compliant areas where controls are not satisfactory. A good example of this is the use of key risk indicators which, having been set at trigger levels, can then be shown on a simple trend report to see whether mitigating controls are actually working in the business to control the particular risks that the KRI is monitoring.

The PRA has also laid down requirements for explicit identification, measurement and monitoring to be carried out by firms and for reporting measures to be consistent with good standards. The regulator wants to see documented evidence of actions that were taken to control risks and similarly active reporting on exposure thresholds and actual exposures. In particular, the PRA is seeking to make sure that the tools that the company is using for its risk management are indeed effective. The main thrust of the PRA's attention is to satisfy themselves that a firm and its Board are receiving information enabling them to identify, measure, manage and control risk which can be of regulatory concern and are therefore by very definition causing a risk to the PRA in carrying out its own objectives against its own responsibilities and mandate.

The PRA states that the effective management of operational risk depends upon consistent and timely reporting of exposures. They regard it as imperative that business line managers can make the connection between the overall view and what they need to achieve on the ground. Operational management information plays a key role in linking senior management and staff level incentives to deliver against the operational risk strategy.

QUESTION TIME 1

Describe the benefits that you would associate with risk reporting.

Write your answer here then check with the answer at the back of the book.

2 Loss data analysis

2.1 Using historical loss data in measuring operational risk

Creation of a loss database is crucial to the requirements of both the Basel Accord and to the approach used by regulators such as the PRA. For example, The Basel Accord states that it should be noted that the ability to monitor loss events and effectively gather loss data is a basic step for operational risk measurement and management and is a pre-requisite for movement to the more advanced regulatory approach.

Consequently firms need to develop an operational loss database. Of course, no amount of internal data will include every type of loss event that can occur, so it will also be necessary to consider purchasing external loss data, or participating in some form of event sharing system.

When developing a loss database it is necessary to consider whether a firm wants to map it initially to the structure proposed by the regulators, whether to include expected and unexpected losses and how to deal with loss mitigants.

Loss data evaluation is important in mapping the actual losses experienced by the firm back to a sensible categorisation system. Once the data has been collected (from either internal or external sources) it can then be used in the measurement process, often using benchmarking or statistical methods. For instance, a loss distribution curve may be created that records the value of all material (direct) losses in a particular risk category over a time period of, say, three years. By analysing this curve using similar VaR techniques to those in market risk, some prediction of future losses can be made within specified confidence limits.

2.2 Internal loss data

Loss data lies at the heart of everything the Basel Committee is looking at in its Basel II and Basel III Accords. Internal loss data is crucial for tying a bank's risk estimates to its actual loss experience. This can be achieved in a number of ways, including using internal loss data as the foundation of empirical risk estimates, as a means of validating the inputs and outputs of the bank's risk measurement system, or as the link between loss experience and risk management control decisions.

The tracking of internal loss event data is an essential prerequisite to the development and functioning of a credible operational risk management system. The idea is that loss data can be used to validate the material collected through other means perhaps by controlling risk self-assessment and scenario analysis for example. It will allow management to assess whether they need to reassess their assumptions. The second alternative is to go the other way using loss experience to consider the decisions that the bank needs to make regarding the control environment.

Internal loss data is most relevant when it is clearly linked to a bank's current business activities, technological processes and risk management procedures. Therefore a bank must have documented procedures for assessing the ongoing relevance of historical loss data, including those situations in which judgement overrides scaling before other adjustments.

Internally generated operational risk measures used for regulatory capital purposes must be based under Basel on a minimum 5-year observation period of internal loss data, where the internal loss data is used directly to build the loss data or to validate it.

To qualify for regulatory capital purposes a bank's internal loss collection processes must meet the following standards.

- A bank must be able to map its historical internal loss data into the relevant level 1 supervisory categories.
- It must have documented objective criteria for allocating losses to the specific business lines and event types.

So an essential part of operational risk mapping within Basel is to allocate losses against the eight business lines (nine including insurance) and the seven defined operational risk event types. Few banks will have activities in all business lines, however.

A bank's internal loss data must be comprehensive in that it captures all material activities and exposures from all appropriate sub-systems and its geographical locations.

There is a reporting threshold within the Basel rules of 10,000 euros. By using this the Basel rules are saying that the database should not capture losses where the gross amount is below 10,000 euros. There is an acceptance within the rules that this could vary but it should be consistent with other peer banks. It is also necessary under Basel again for banks to keep a report on the level of detail that is commensurate with the size of the loss. Aside from information on gross loss amounts Basel requires that a bank should collect information about the date of the event, any recoveries of gross loss amounts as well as some descriptive information about the drivers or causes of the loss event. So, practically speaking, banks need to be able to explain in sufficient detail a justification for excluding a loss from the summary of loss data. Elements that are excluded will reduce the capital charge in respect of that particular loss.

A bank must develop specific criteria for assigning loss arising from an event in a centralised function (e.g. an information technology department) or an activity that expands more than one business line, as well as from related events over time. This presents real issues as firms must decide how they would choose to split various costs. Sometimes losses need to be allocated to more than one department; sometimes there will be an insurance claim mitigation.

2.3 External loss data

Sometimes external loss databases are available which are useful to benchmark against your own firm. It is helpful to see how your firm might cope with the problems that have been experienced by other people. This is also required by the Basel Committee as part of its Advanced Measurement Approach (AMA) but will only form part of any solution. External loss events are of use in telling a firm about possible losses that are not within their current experience. Hopefully they will remain outside their experience but contemplating the potential impact if they were to occur is valuable as an exercise. Loss databases, although valuable, will not in themselves add value but loss investigation could reduce the risk of recurrence. If it were possible furthermore to benchmark against competitors, that might provide a bank with further useful information. However none of this lies at the heart of a risk management strategy.

QUESTION TIME 2

Describe each stage of the risk management lifecycle and identify the main benefits arising at each of those stages.

Write your answer here then check with the answer at the back of the book.

KEY WORDS

Key words in this chapter are given below. There is space to write your own revision notes and add any other key words or phrases you want to remember.

- Dashboard reporting
- Internal loss data
- External loss data

REVIEW

Now consider the main points that were introduced in this chapter. These are listed below. Tick each one as you go through them.

- Monitoring and reporting makes sense of the risk management lifecycle as there would be little point in carrying out the first three steps if proper reporting is not the outcome.
- The form and content of a risk report must be made with the end user in mind.
- Reporting is required to meet the demands of both the Basel Accord and the PRA. Reports should show the extent to which controls are being complied with as well as highlighting non-compliant areas with a description of what is being done to remedy the situation.
- Firms must maintain a database of loss data to meet regulatory requirements.
- The threshold for reporting losses on the internal database under the Basel Accord is €10,000.
- An external loss database can be used to benchmark losses against a particular firm's performance.

chapter 6

RISK MANAGEMENT FRAMEWORK (PART 1)

Contents

Learning objectives

On completion of this chapter, you should be able to:

- evaluate the credit risk function of a bank's head office and its role within the risk management framework.

Introduction

In the next two chapters we are going to consider the large topic of the Risk Management Framework. The topics that we will discuss in these chapters are:

- The risk management framework
- Credit risk
- Market risk
- Operational risk
- Strategy risk
- Basel II and III
- How risk is managed and overviewed
- Asset and liability risk (including liquidity risk)
- Insurance and investment risk
- Legal, regulatory and external risk
- The Audit Committee

This chapter will cover the risk management framework, how risk is managed and overviewed, credit risk and asset/liability risk With the remaining topics being covered in the next chapter. Throughout the chapter, reference will be made to the 'Group'. This is because the chapter is assessing the Risk Management Framework from the perspective of a generic large banking Group which has a variety of different banking subsidiaries.

The chapter starts with a view of the credit risk management function of a bank. This area of the firm has a key role to play in assessing the financial position of customers and organisations that the bank will do business with. As you will be becoming aware, regulation is never far from our minds in the study of risk, so the Basel Practices for the management of credit risk are introduced next. The management and overview of risk is the next topic to consider – this is done by modelling, stress testing, segmentation, the use of external ratings, the setting of limits, provisioning and the use of Key Performance Indicators (KPIs). The next section of this chapter is devoted to credit risk, which is a fundamental risk to the business of banking. The policies and procedures that banks have in place to manage this risk are described in this section. The chapter then moves on to discuss the topical issues relating to counterparty risk, starting with the due diligence that should be carried out on customers before credit is granted to them. Other risk management techniques include the setting of limits, taking guarantees, netting, taking collateral, diversification and using central counterparties. Once this work has been completed, we will move on to consider setting credit limits for trade book and loan products. One of the ways in which this is done is by setting limits for every customer and counterparty. This risk can also be measured using VaR techniques and by looking at concentration risk. The chapter concludes with an examination of asset and liability risk with the techniques used for this being explained. Derivatives can be used to help mitigate this risk

1 The risk management framework

The responsibility of a credit risk management department within a firm is fundamentally to assess the financial health of the customers and counterparties that the firm is dealing with and provide input into the decision as to whether to lend funds or not.

QUICK QUESTION

In order to meet this responsibility, what actions do you think the credit risk management department should carry out?

Write your answer here before reading on.

Therefore a summary of the actions will include the following.

- Credit risk assessment of counterparties and customers.
- Recommendation of credit limits for counterparties and customers.
- Monitoring, reviewing and reporting credit limits, credit events.
- Carrying out regular reviews of all credit assessments.
- Drawing up the credit risk policy for the board and gaining its agreement.
- Making recommendations to the board of the firm with respect to credit policy.
- Ensuring with the board that the credit risk policy is followed.
- Analysing and managing credit risk exposure.
- Recommending and implementing risk mitigation techniques to reduce and transfer risk.
- Monitoring and making use of external resources such as those of ratings agencies.
- Designing a credit scoring model for the use by the firm in granting credit to clients. This would involve using models which would potentially have both qualitative and quantitative elements to them in order to give a holistic picture of the credit risk assessment. The models should be assessed carefully and be stress tested to ensure that no model risk existed and would address customers' operating experience, expertise and financial strength.
- Using models and ratings agencies to assess the quality, leverage and liquidity ratios of products to avoid issuer risk.
- To provide input and reporting to the firms' credit committee by escalating credit risk issues to senior management.
- To monitor market issues and to address any developing credit or sovereign risk problems.
- To recommend and provide input to the board on the collateral management policy of the firm.
- To monitor and liaise with the board and external agencies with respect to the firms' own credit rating from external agencies.
- Providing information for the assessment of the firm's capital adequacy.

1.1 Reporting and escalation tools of credit risk management

Thinking about the general functions of the credit risk management department, the reporting elements of their activities will be structured according to an individual firm's own organisation and internal structure. Most firms will have an overall risk committee to which the credit risk officers will report along with colleagues from other risk disciplines, for example operational risk.

In any risk discipline the reporting is of utmost importance to the Board with regard to the frequency, style, content, completeness and accuracy of the reports produced. In the case of the credit risk management function the matters should address the potential credit risks affecting the firm's business and this would be described against market sectors, individual clients and counterparties and all products.

The escalation issue is vital in the respect that no time can afford to be lost in the event of any credit event and therefore the escalation step from the credit risk department would be to the chief risk officer of the firm and beyond that to the board.

It is recommended that risk departments report directly to the Board.

1.2 Credit risk policy development, modelling and control

Within a bank, the credit management policy should be dependent upon the following.

1.2.1 Basic structure

Credit assessment and any decision about the granting of credit to clients and counterparties must be independent of the trading division of the firm. The credit policy under which risks are assessed must be integrated within the firm's general policy and strategy towards its overall risk management. Credit policy will start with assessment of counterparties and clients and will also look at non-counterparty factors including markets, countries, sectors and products.

1.2.2 The policy

The firm's Board should approve the policy, which will most probably have been developed by the credit risk management function. The Board should approve the policy as part of its corporate governance oversight. The policy will provide a high level overview of the Group's approach to lending with reference to supporting policies that will underpin lending activities. For example, the Group may target lending to large businesses in Europe and Africa.

The policy is also likely to include references to the culture of the Group, such as a commitment to sustainable and ethical lending practises., as this ensures that the lending policy is consistent with the objectives of the Group. For example, 79 financial institutions have signed up to the Equator Principles, which is a risk management framework for environmental and social risk in projects.

The policy will be implemented and kept under review. The policy should make clear which tools are to be used including customer assessment techniques, stress testing, scenario modelling, limits setting with controls and other measures as outlined later on in this chapter.

As with most risk management, the reporting of feedback into the policy group of the effectiveness of controls will only help to improve the policy going forward. It is an ongoing process.

1.2.3 Customer assessment

A great deal of support can be obtained from other useful sources such as ratings agencies, credit reference agencies, other financial institutions and of course through other firms' annual audited and published reports. The fact that a customer firm is regulated is not in itself enough because capital adequacy is a moveable feast. There may also be some particular risk issues to do with certain types of customers, those that are acting for several funds or those that are a subsidiary of a much larger group.

1.2.4 Reducing the risks

One of the key basic risks is failure to repay and one of the major operational objectives of any firm would be to have a smooth and highly risk-averse settlement structure. Great benefit can be obtained here from central market utilities such as central counterparties, central securities depositories and custodians. The use of Delivery versus Payment (DvP) settlement (sometimes called delivery against cash) and netting offsets are very robust measures with respect to the reduction of risk. Firms may wish to consider the use of credit derivatives and collateral (both of which will be covered later). The standard documentation of ISDA (the International Swaps and Derivatives Association), for example, creates a very powerful platform for limiting credit risk and setting abilities to net and set off amongst the major players within the (Over-the-Counter) OTC derivatives industry.

1.2.5 Exposure monitoring

Monitoring must be conducted every day and the aggregated exposure to a group of related counterparties must be taken into account. Most firms would advocate a daily dashboard system which highlights immediately credit exposures for the firm with any one of their clients or counterparties. A useful addition to dashboards would be the ability to monitor scenarios and therefore to potentially work out the possible escalation of credit risk with respect to other parties in the event of certain market circumstances. These are a form of stress test or scenario test and are very commonly adopted by such organisations as central clearing counterparties which need to assess their exposures against the clearing members to whom they are guaranteeing fulfilment of sets of contracts.

1.2.6 Review

We have already stressed the requirement for review and the frequency of reviews is vital. One of the elements of a credit review would be to address unutilised credit lines. A counterparty might begin to use such a facility with your firm because they may be experiencing a credit situation or squeeze from other creditors.

1.2.7 Potential credit events

There are many signals, both macro and micro, which deliver potential warning of credit risk events.

QUICK QUESTION

What do you think some of these signals might be?

Write your answer here before reading on.

These include slow payment, disputes, risky deals and enquiries from other creditors. Depending upon the type of business and the number of clients involved, a monitoring system will be important to be able to address these in a meaningful way. Most lenders or traders would cut the credit line or begin renegotiation in the event of a credit event.

The major step would be to reduce the exposure by taking security or collateral, or by not extending the size of position and only entering therefore into offsetting trades. This is very much one of the tools that clearing houses use to mitigate their risks against clearing members in market clearing structures.

Should a credit event occur, it is most important to face it and deal with it and make a decision – the worst course of action is for the firm to ignore the situation in the hope that it will resolve itself.

Common methods of credit enhancement and credit risk mitigation techniques are to provide direct credit support through covenants, netting or collateral or indirect credit support (via third parties) which include such things as a third-party guarantee, the use of credit derivatives or even credit insurance from the insurance market. By far and away the most effective way of reducing exposure is to net it down and take collateral against the net balance. This is very much the approach of most derivative structures for example.

It is also necessary to bear in mind the regulatory risk when dealing with other counterparties. Some of the key problems are Conduct of Business Rules and money laundering regulations. Before transacting business with a client, a firm needs to know its customer to demonstrate compliance with the money laundering rules. Similarly the Conduct of Business rules of regulators impose varying requirements as to the precise type of client concerned. The current regime in Europe for example defines three sorts of clients – eligible counterparties, professional clients and retail clients and therefore good risk management involves thorough knowledge of not only the counterparty but also the manner in which different counterparties or customers must be treated under the regulatory structure.

In parallel with explicit counterparty risk there are some other non-credit counterparty risks which include such elements as legal risks and structural risk. A firm should be clear whether a counterparty or agent or client have the necessary legal authority to enter into a transaction - does the individual have the ability to commit on behalf of their firm? There may also be issues surrounding any failure to follow required procedures and when looking further afield at other parts of the world there may be some sovereign immunity issues from time to time. So in this regard, it may be argued that counterparty risk presents other types of risk on top of the fundamental element of credit risk itself.

There are many sorts of markets and clients and in dealing with them different rules will apply: for example charities, market structures, over the counter trades, private companies and registered companies, trustees, domestic firms and foreign firms. Because the mix is complicated firms must consider the different areas of exposure of counterparty risk that they may face and this applies across banking, securities and all investment activity.

QUESTION TIME 1

Why would a bank issue a credit policy?

Write your answer here then check with the answer at the back of the book.

2 The Basel sound practices

The Basel Committee presents ten principles for sound practices with respect to credit risk assessment within firms and by regulators. These are divided under two headings, as follows.

2.1 Supervisory expectations concerning sound credit risk assessment and valuation for loans

- A bank's board of directors and senior management are responsible for ensuring that the bank has appropriate credit risk assessment processes and effective internal controls commensurate with the size, nature and complexity of its lending operations to consistently determine provisions for loan losses in accordance with the bank's stated policies and procedures, the applicable accounting framework and supervisory guidance.
- A bank should have a system in place to reliably classify loans on the basis of credit risk.
- A bank's policies should appropriately address validation of any internal credit risk assessment models.
- A bank should adopt and document a sound loan loss methodology, which addresses credit risk assessment policies, procedures and controls for assessing credit risk, identifying problem loans and determining loan loss provisions in a timely manner.
- A bank's aggregate amount of individual and collectively assessed loan loss provisions should be adequate to absorb estimated credit losses in the loan portfolio.
- A bank's use of experienced credit judgement and reasonable estimates are an essential part of the recognition and measurement of loan losses.
- A bank's credit risk assessment process for loans should provide the bank with the necessary tools, procedures and observable data to use for assessing credit risk, accounting for loan impairment and determining regulatory capital requirements.

2.2 Supervisory evaluation of credit risk assessment for loans, controls and capital adequacy

- Banking supervisors should periodically evaluate the effectiveness of a bank's credit risk policies and practices for assessing loan quality.
- Banking supervisors (i.e. regulators) should be satisfied that the methods employed by a bank to calculate loan loss provisions produce a reasonable and prudent measurement of estimated credit losses in the loan portfolio that are recognised in a timely manner.
- Banking supervisors should consider credit risk assessment and valuation policies and practices when assessing a bank's capital adequacy.

3 How credit risk is managed and overviewed

3.1 Risk modelling in relation to managing credit risk

Many of the world's largest banks have developed sophisticated systems in an attempt to model the credit risk arising from important aspects of their business lines.

Such models are intended to aid banks in quantifying, aggregating and managing risk across geographical and product lines. The outputs of these models also play increasingly important roles in banks' risk management and performance measurement processes, including performance-based compensation, customer profitability analysis, risk-based pricing and active portfolio management and capital structure decisions. Credit risk modelling should result in better internal risk management and may have the potential to be used in the supervisory oversight of banking organisations. Models should be conceptually sound, validated, and produce capital requirements.

Formal risk modelling is required under Basel for all the major international banking institutions by the various national depository institution regulators.

3.1.1 Factor inputs

We will now turn the focus to an area you will have some personal experience of – credit scoring. The factor inputs (or input factors) are those pieces of data which are used to model a credit score. They will contain any information required by models about risk premiums, economic factors and debt histories and so on.

3.1.2 Credit scoring systems

This is perhaps best described by a simple modern-day example with which you will be familiar – applying for credit from banks. When a person applies for a credit card or current account or to borrow money, the lender will usually **credit score** their application. This helps the lender decide whether to accept the application and, where relevant, helps set a credit limit and interest rate.

QUICK QUESTION

Write down a summary of your understanding of credit scoring.

Write your answer here before reading on.

Credit scoring works by awarding points to the information provided on the applicant's application form and to the information recorded on their credit report (held by a credit reference agency). Lenders often use all this information to try to predict the level risk they are taking by allowing a person to borrow money and whether they can afford to repay it. It helps them decide:

- Whether to grant a credit card or loan
- What credit limit to give
- What interest rate to charge (based on the level of risk attached to the credit request).

If the applicant doesn't score enough points to reach the lender's pass mark, the lender may:

- turn down the application
- offer to lend a smaller amount
- charge a higher rate of interest.

Each lender has its own scoring system, but most systems will generally grant a higher score for people whose credit assessment is better – in other words, those who present a lower credit risk to the bank.

QUICK QUESTION

What factors and characteristics would describe a person who is deemed to be a good credit risk?

Write your answer here before reading on.

There are a number of factors to consider here including:

- Is the customer married or in a civil partnership?
- Does the customer own their home?
- How long has the customer resided at the same address?
- Do they have a land telephone line?
- Is the customer in a stable and permanent job?
- Has the customer adequate surplus income to meet the repayment schedule?
- Has the customer a good record of repaying past loans?

The information on a credit report is very important and having a good credit history will improve the chances of getting credit. Someone who has had a credit card and pays all their regular bills on time may score more points than someone who's new to borrowing. On the other hand, it can count against those who may already have several loans and credit cards, or if they have made lots of different applications recently.

Credit scoring is addressed in further detail later.

QUESTION TIME 2

Your line manager has stated that credit scoring has altered the organisational structure of banks over the past 25 years. Why is this the case?

Write your answer here then check with the answer at the back of the book.

3.1.3 Stress testing

Many industries use the practice of stress testing – these include medicine, engineering, IT and, of course, finance. **Stress testing** is a form of testing that is used to determine the stability of a given system, process or entity. It involves testing beyond normal operational capacity, often to a breaking point, in order to observe the results. Stress testing has a more specific meaning in finance where it is used to test scenarios with respect to risk criticality. These may be directed towards credit, market or operational risk. For example:

- What if credit spreads against the UK base rate move up by 20 basis points?
- What if UK mortgage defaults/unemployment/company bankruptcies rises by 50%?
- What if US interest rates rise (or fall) by 150 basis points?
- What if interbank lending liquidity in the UK dries up?
- What if energy market volatility doubles?
- What happens if the domestic settlement system fails for one full week?

The idea of stress testing is that it enables potential losses or gains to be assessed. Difficulties with stress testing include being able to identify the firm's particular sensitivities and choosing the most appropriate stresses to model (models are innately open to flaws – see the quote from Andrew Haldane below).

Scenario analysis is also very often used in conjunction with stress tests. Such tests do not really follow a quantitative approach but are intended to generate critical consideration and a creative approach to high-impact, low-likelihood events. For example what would be the consequences of a major economic event? Which parts of our business would be affected and how? Following this, management could assess what steps could be taken now or later to minimise those effects.

Stress testing and scenario analysis must address:

- Major economic moves e.g. stock market crashes, interest rates spikes
- Changes in liquidity – for example periods of volatility, credit lending squeezes
- Changes in correlations – any observed incidence of factors becoming more correlated or less so and thus impacting the benefits of diversification
- Portfolio-specific characteristics – tests should reflect the actual instruments to which a firm is exposed. For example when selling derivatives, owing to the in-built leverage, only a small market movement might generate large potential losses.

The risks associated with loan portfolios represent the greatest threat to the viability of many banks. Developments in this area are lagging those in the area of market risk. Credit spreads in trading books, such as swap spreads, corporate bond spreads and credit default swap (CDS) spreads present difficulties. Stress testing of loan books and other credit exposures is important. The stress testing of credit spreads in trading portfolios is reasonably straightforward as the availability of the market price means that one variable – the credit spread – can be used to produce a mark to market value. In the separate stress testing of loan books, loan related variables such as the probability of default, recovery rates, collateral values, rating migration probabilities and internal ratings assigned to borrowers are stressed. These scenarios are often underpinned by a shock to a macroeconomic environment.

This type of analysis has become increasingly widespread and has been taken up by various regulatory bodies as a regulatory requirement on certain financial institutions to ensure adequate capital allocation levels to cover potential losses incurred during extreme, but plausible, events. This emphasis on adequate, risk adjusted determination of capital has been further enhanced by modifications to banking regulations such as Basel. Stress testing models typically allow not only the testing of individual stress factors, but also combinations of different events.

The intent that lies behind stress testing and other models is, of course, sensible and good, but as Andrew Haldane, Executive Director for Financial Stability at the Bank of England said in a speech in early 2009 (when looking back at banks' risk management during the credit crisis), 'fortunately, there is a simpler explanation – the model was wrong. Of course, all models are wrong. The only model that is not wrong is reality and reality is not, by definition, a model. But risk management models have during this crisis proved themselves wrong in a more fundamental sense. They failed Keynes' test – that it is better to be roughly right than precisely wrong. With hindsight, these models were both very precise and very wrong'.

3.1.4 Segmentation

The role of segmentation is an attempt to improve the performance of scoring systems. When the credit characteristics and risk characteristics of different groups of clients or counterparties are addressed, by identifying the appropriate sub-groups, the characteristics that are most predictive in isolating risk are optimised for that group. Consider a sub-prime lender and a prime lender, for example. These institutions would target individuals with vastly different risk profiles. From the perspective of a sub-prime lender the number of severely non-performing accounts is a pervasive and defining element of the target population but is not necessarily a good predictor of who would be lower risk. From the perspective of a prime lender the difference in the number of severely delinquent accounts would be a significant factor in ranking risk. In some ways, segmentation is the reverse of diversification whereby a more detailed aspect of real risks is identified by sub-dividing the population of obligors with respect to the credit risk presented.

3.1.5 External ratings

As is covered elsewhere in this chapter, external ratings are the views of specialist independent credit rating agencies (for example, Experien and Equifax) which consider the ability to pay with respect to both corporate and government issuers of securities. You will no doubt be more aware of this when it is applied to the personal credit market – for example, you will have your own credit rating.

3.1.6 Setting limits or caps

Again, as is set out elsewhere in this chapter, both the setting of a credit limit or the capping of a credit exposure are common techniques that are applied by firms. This is arrived at by a process of internal assessment and establishes a limit within the risk appetite of the firm as expressed towards an individual obligor or counterparty. It is the maximum amount that the firm is lending on a particular account.

3.1.7 Internal credit grading

Firms will have their own techniques for deciding their own credit assessment of internal staff and dealing operations together with customers and counterparties. This may result in the credit risk department employing a methodology whereby internal credit assessments are conducted and grading levels accordingly established. This may be supported by external evidence from credit ratings agencies and others (as expressed elsewhere in this chapter). This is the maximum amount that each member of staff who is authorised to sign off a credit proposal is allowed to sanction. It is quite possible that the member of staff (sometimes called a sanctioning officer) will have more than one credit limit.

QUICK QUESTION

What factors do you think would influence these differing credit limits?

Write your answer here before reading on.

The main determining factor would be the availability and quality of security offered by the customer. Therefore, a sanctioning officer may have a lower limit for unsecured loans and a higher limit if the customer has provided good quality security.

QUICK QUESTION

What do you think is the rationale behind these two different levels of limit?

Write your answer here before reading on.

Again, we return to the level of risk. If the customer has provided good quality security, then the risk of a bad debt to the bank is lower, therefore they are happy to have the sanctioning officer signing off on higher levels of loan for this type of customer rather than the riskier, unsecured loan applications.

3.1.8 Provisioning and impairment

Setting aside provisions for future credit issues – **provisioning** – is a straightforward concept for a prudent risk manager to grasp. **Impairment** simply refers to a worsening credit risk situation – for example, more of a firm's mortgage customers progressively failing to pay their monthly instalments in times of general economic downturn and general hardship.

An important element of sound credit risk management is analysing what could potentially go wrong with individual credits and the overall credit portfolio if conditions within the environment in which borrowers operate were to change significantly. The results of this analysis can then be factored into the assessment of the adequacy of making credit provision (setting aside capital) and the overall capital of the institution. Capital provisioning is exactly what has been suggested by many governments and central banks during the credit crisis – making sure that banks are financially strong enough to withstand potential future credit crises by holding enough capital by way of provision.

There is also a link from here back into stress testing; each stress test should be followed by a contingency plan as regards recommended corrective actions. Senior management must regularly review the results of stress tests and contingency plans. The results must serve as an important input into a review of the credit risk management framework, in the setting of limits and provisioning levels.

International accounting standards require that financial institutions should, in addition to individual credit provisioning, assess credit impairment and ensuing provisioning on a credit portfolio basis. Financial institutions must, therefore, establish appropriate systems and processes to identify credits with similar characteristics in order to assess the degree of their recoverability on a portfolio basis.

3.1.9 Key statistics and key performance indicators

Key risk indicators (KRIs) act as early warning signals by providing the capability to indicate changes in an organisation's risk profile. KRIs are a fundamental component of a full featured risk and control framework and sound risk management practice. Whereas they are best known for the role they play in operational risk management, they are also adaptable and therefore perfectly useful in serving requirements to address credit risk issues. Their usefulness stems from potentially helping the business to reduce losses and prevent exposure by proactively dealing with a risk situation before an event actually occurs.

A key risk indicator is a measure used to indicate how risky an activity is. It differs from a key performance indicator (KPI) in that the latter is meant as a measure of how well something is being done while the former is an indicator of the possibility of future adverse impact. KRIs give an early warning to identify potential events that may harm continuity of any activity or project.

4 Credit risk

QUICK QUESTION

This topic was introduced in Chapter 1. Write down a short definition of credit risk.

Write your answer here before reading on.

Credit risk is the risk that a counterparty will fail to perform on an obligation. This is what is meant by **counterparty risk** and is indeed exactly the definition used by the Basel Committee and by the International Organisation of Securities Commissions (IOSCO). It could be extended to address the risk of loss resulting from a counterparty going into default. Credit risk therefore may be described as default risk or any credit exposure or equivalent. It presents itself in settlement risk, pre-settlement risk, delivery risk and payment risk.

QUICK QUESTION

Write down a short definition for each of these risks.

Write your answer here before reading on.

- **Settlement risk** – the risk that the other party does not make payment when due under the terms of the contract.
- **Pre-settlement risk** – the risk that the other party defaults on the contract before settlement is due.
- **Delivery risk** – this can also be called settlement risk and covers the situation where the other party to the contract does not deliver an asset that underlies a contract. An example of this would be where the customer fails to deliver the agreed security to the bank.
- **Payment risk** – the risk that the customer fails to make payments to the bank as agreed in the contract.

Therefore firms must manage the potential of a failure to pay or deliver on time with all customers and counterparties with whom they transact business.

However, not only counterparties are considered under the banner of credit risk; there is also the matter of **issuer risk**, which refers to the risk that an issuer of securities could fail to perform with respect to the duties under its issued securities. An example would be not to pay interest on bonds or to default upon the redemption of bonds or other securities.

4.1 The fundamental importance of credit risk in banking

Credit risk is one of the principal risks facing banks, perhaps for obvious reasons. In many banks its management could be split between wholesale market credit risk and retail credit risk.

As previously discussed, credit risk is the risk of the bank suffering financial loss should any of its customers, clients or market counterparties fail to fulfil their contractual obligations to the bank. This can also arise when an entity's credit rating is downgraded, leading to a fall in the value of the bank's investment in its issued financial instruments. You will have read of this happening as a fallout from the banking crisis. For example, in June 2012 Moody's cut the credit ratings of RBS, Barclays, HSBC and Lloyds.

Typical credit risks that a bank would face would be wholesale and retail loans and advances together with the counterparty credit risks which arise from derivatives contracts entered into by a bank with its clients and counterparties. Other sources of credit risk arise from trading activities which may include debt securities, settlement balances with market counterparties, available-for-sale assets and reverse repurchase agreements. Generally, losses arising exposures held for trading (derivatives and debt securities) are accounted for as trading losses rather than impairment charges even though the fall in value causing the loss may be attributable to credit deterioration.

With banks, the granting of credit is one of the major sources of income and similarly as one of the most significant risks. Accordingly therefore banks will dedicate considerable resources to controlling and mitigating credit risk.

The credit risk management objectives of a typical bank are to:

- establish a framework of controls to ensure credit risk taking is based on sound credit risk management principles
- identify, assess and measure credit risk clearly and accurately across the activities of the bank within each of its separate business from the level of individual facilities up to the total portfolio
- control and plan credit risk taking in line with external stakeholder expectations avoiding undesirable concentrations of risk
- monitor credit risk and adherence to agreed controls and limits
- ensure that risk-reward objectives are met.

4.2 Credit risk exposures on loans and advances

QUICK QUESTION

To what broad areas of the economy would banks typically lend money to?

Write your answer here before reading on.

The areas to think about here include:

- Home loans and mortgages
- Loans to financial institutions
- Credit cards, unsecured loans and personal lending
- Construction and property
- Business and other services
- Wholesale and retail distribution and leisure
- Manufacturing
- Energy and water industries
- Government.

It is likely that the greatest exposure will be in the first two segments covering home loans and advances to financial institutions.

Banks will generally state a level of riskiness against outstanding loan portfolios. This might take a form as follows.

Strong – there is a very high likelihood of the asset being recovered in full.

Satisfactory – whilst there is a high likelihood that the asset will be recovered and therefore be of no real concern to the bank, the asset may not be collateralised (in other words have adequate security underpinning it), or may relate to retail banking facilities such as unsecured loans or credit cards, which are being classified as satisfactory, regardless of the fact that the output of internal grading models may have indicated a higher classification. At the low end of this segment customers would be more carefully monitored. These would include for example corporate customers which are indicating evidence of some deterioration, mortgages with a high loan to value ratio and unsecured retail loans operating outside normal packaged product guidelines.

High risk – in this final category there would be a concern over the borrower's ability to make payments when due. However these may not yet have converted to being delinquent loans. There may also be doubts about the value of collateral or security provided. However, the borrower or counterparty is continuing to make payments when due and is expected to settle all outstanding amounts of both principal and interest to the bank.

4.3 Credit risk levels

Credit risk exposure can be analysed at different levels. The levels that are used will vary from bank to bank, depending on their strategy and lending policies. Typical examples of credit risk levels include:

- **Geographic region** – Asia, Europe, South America etc.
- **Country** – Germany, Turkey, Brazil etc.
- **Local region** – Split by town, county, city etc.
- **Industry** – Retail, oil, construction etc.
- **Size** – Small and medium sized enterprises, large corporates, multinationals etc.
- **Internal division** – Secured loans, structured finance, syndicated loans etc.
- **Internal subsidiary** – Business lending division, personal lending division etc.

Breaking credit risk exposure into these different levels is a very useful management tool, as it highlights where high levels of credit risk are concentrated. If concentration is too high at certain levels, management may take proactive steps to reduce the credit exposure by halting new loans in that area, or selling the existing loans to other banks.

4.4 Credit risk management structure

Many banks structure the responsibilities of credit risk management so that decisions are taken as close as possible to the business, whilst ensuring robust review and challenge of performance, risk infrastructure and strategic plans.

The credit risk management teams in each business would be accountable to the business risk directors in those businesses who, in turn, report to the heads of their businesses and also to the bank's Chief Risk Officer.

There may also be a group risk function whose role is to provide group-wide direction, oversight and challenge of credit risk-taking. This function sets the Credit Risk Control Framework, which provides a structure within which credit risk is managed together with supporting group credit risk policies. Group risk also provides technical support, review and validation of credit risk measurement models across the group.

QUICK QUESTION

What policies does your bank have in place to mitigate credit risk?

Write your answer here before reading on.

Credit risk policies which may be in force include:

- Maximum exposure guidelines to limit the exposures to an individual customer or counterparty.
- Country risk policies to specify risk appetite by country and avoid excessive concentration of credit risk in individual countries.

- An aggregation policy to set out the circumstances in which counterparties should be grouped together for credit risk purposes.
- Expected loss policies to set out the approaches for the calculation of the bank's expected loss, i.e. measure of anticipated loss for exposures.
- Repayment plans policy for setting the standards for repayment plans and restructures within retail portfolios.
- Impairment and provisioning policies to ensure that measurement of impairment accurately reflects incurred losses and that clear governance procedures are in place for the calculation and approval of impairment allowances.

The largest credit exposures would be approved at the Credit Committee at the Group Risk level. This function would also manage and approve the mandates and scale limits and triggers which mitigate concentration risk and define appetite in risk sensitive areas of the portfolio such as commercial property finance.

The principal committees that review credit risk management and which would in most cases approve overall Group credit policy and resolve all significant credit policy issues could be the Board Risk Committee, the Group Risk Oversight Committee, the Wholesale Credit Risk Management Committee and the Retail Credit Risk Management Committee. Senior Group and business risk management would be represented on the Group Risk Oversight Committee, the Wholesale Credit Risk Management Committee and the Retail Credit Risk Management Committee.

The Credit Risk Impairment Committee (if established) would obtain assurance on behalf of the Group that all businesses are recognising impairment in their portfolios accurately, promptly and in accordance with policy, accounting standards and established governance.

This committee would be chaired by the Credit Risk Director and will review the movements in impairment, including those already agreed at Credit Committee, as well as potential credit risk loans, loan loss rates, asset quality metrics and impairment coverage ratios.

This committee would make recommendations to the Board Audit Committee on the adequacy of Group impairment allowances. Impairment allowances will be reviewed relative to the risk in the portfolio, business and economic trends, current policies and methodologies, and the Group's position relative to peer banks.

5 Issues relating to counterparty credit risk

5.1 Areas of exposure of counterparty and issuer risk within banking

Perhaps the most obvious and basic point about counterparty risk is that credit risk management begins with making basic checks on your customer or the counterparty with whom you are dealing. You may have also heard about this described as due diligence. It is necessary to understand the counterparty's ability to pay. The due diligence requirements will vary based on the type of counterparty: individual retail customers, companies and governments

Basic controls to be established for individual retail customers include:

- Credit scoring
- Using credit reference agencies
- Analysis of recent bank statements
- References from other banks.

Basic controls to be established for individual retail customers include:

- Collateral available
- Source of wealth checks
- Liquidity checks.

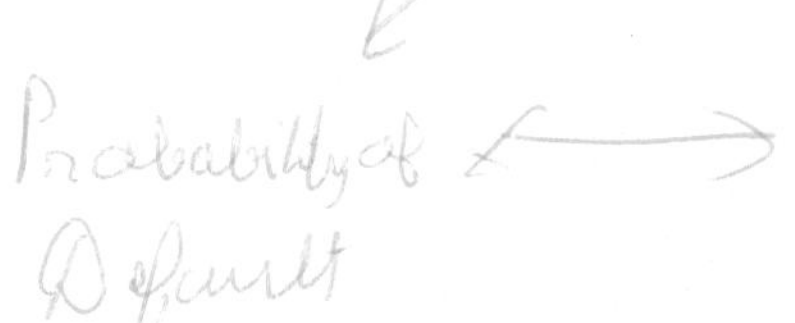

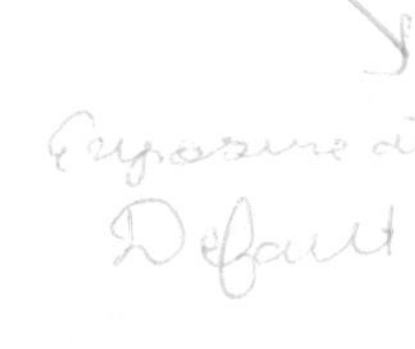

Basic controls to be established for companies include:

- Checking public information about the counterparty including all aspects of their financial position
- Checking the strategic objectives of the client or counterparty and their attitude to risk
- Knowing the quality of management of the counterparty
- Assessing the experience and degree of profitability of the previous trading of the counterparty
- Making some assessment or check on the counterparty's standing amongst its business creditors
- Checking the size of the exposure by way of the counterparty positions compared with other market users of a similar scale.

Basic controls to be established for governments include:

- Checking current account and reserve account balances
- Checking currency reserves
- Analysis of sovereign credit reports from credit ratings agencies
- Analysis of past and projected tax receipts
- Analysis of government monetary and fiscal policy
- Analysis of key government policies.

Such counterparty checks are all part of due diligence before commencing a business arrangement with anybody else in the marketplace. Everyone is a counterparty to somebody else therefore every firm must have a meaningful credit risk assessment policy which assesses the strength of counterparties. Some firms, for example major banks, will have millions of customers. Others may be conducting transactions with relatively few wholesale counterparties. Every business is different and must plan its credit risk policy accordingly.

The other exposure is to the markets and products within which the counterparties are trading with the counterparties concerned. Here also occurs the point about issuer risk where securities have been issued by another institution in the marketplace and the credit quality of the issuer is called into question. This will particularly affect the value of bonds and the perceived credit risk of the issuer, perhaps as stated by credit ratings agencies.

An important element of the risk management approach will be to keep all the matters that were highlighted above under regular review. It is no good opening a line of credit today for a new client and not reviewing it in the light of ongoing changing circumstances both in the market and with the respective client. Remember that risk is a dynamic area and therefore should be subject to ongoing review in light of changing circumstances.

5.2 Credit risk boundary issues

The phrase boundary issue simply means the potential problems which arise in the definition and treatment of one risk against another where risk types touch each other or overlap. One of the issues pointed out by the Basel Committee in its papers is the incidence of boundaries between credit risk and other risk types. The most important one of these highlighted is the boundary between operational risk and credit risk.

Firms should track operational failures that result in credit losses, even though for the purpose of calculating the Basel capital requirement they should continue to treat them as credit losses. This is because credit risk capital requirements have been calibrated on the basis of all credit-related losses, including 'operational' credit losses.

Another boundary issue is the treatment of different products as part of the overall credit risk assessment process. This means that risk managers must be alive to the need for separate and different treatment between for example the credit assessment of straight bonds against more complex securitised debt products and asset backed securities.

5.3 Underwriting standards

The term underwriting standards describes the standards that financial institutions apply to borrowers in order to evaluate their creditworthiness and therefore to provide some sort of mitigation against the risk of default. Evaluation of this kind requires particular knowledge about the counterparty's or customers specific knowledge of their business and will include various due diligence checks, some of which are as follows.

QUESTION TIME 3

Imagine that you have been asked to assess a credit proposal from a corporate customer. What checks would you want to carry out regarding this proposal?

Write your answer here then check with the answer at the back of the book.

5.4 Guarantees

Third party guarantees, (for example a parent company guaranteeing its subsidiary or a bank issuing a bank guarantee for one of its customers), come in various forms.

Guarantees will always have a legal edge to them with respect to:

- The triggers under which the guarantee will be invoked
- The degree of benefit that the guarantee provides and whether there will be any capping or conditionality about this
- The form of guarantee and the evidence presented in writing signed by the guarantor
- Any special legal defences
- The right of the guarantor to seek indemnity and reimbursement
- Whether the guarantee is full or only partial – the guarantee of part of a debt might apply to a second tranche of a debt rather like an excess on an insurance policy.

5.5 Instruments with inbuilt guarantees

Various forms of instruments exist which have guarantee-like attributes. These include letters of credit, performance bonds, options and credit derivatives. All of these may behave like guarantees and therefore need very careful documentary provisions to be in place.

In essence however, the idea of a guarantee is to limit credit risk because effectively some or all of it is being transferred or the nature of it is being changed by the existence of a guarantee. Remember however that the guarantee itself is yet another form of credit risk that may not deliver and hence the legal aspects of guarantees are so vital to get right in their drafting and in the enforceability of the documents. We will only ever know the real value of a guarantee when we call it up.

5.6 Credit limits

Elsewhere in this study text we discuss credit limits in more detail but at this point it will suffice to understand that credit limits are ways of establishing maximum levels of indebtedness for all aspects of customers or counterparties presenting credit exposure to a firm. This typically applies to lending by any financial institution as well as exposure with respect to any sort of product or contract that is being entered into with another counterparty. Clearly no firm will want the concentration risk of too much credit risk residing with one counterparty (or a small number of counterparties) and thus credit limits are there to prevent this. Credit limits can also be applied against whole sectors or indeed whole sovereign risks for firms. All financial institutions will set credit limits with respect to their customers and counterparties and the degree of sophistication will vary from firm to firm. Any loan to another firm or person will not be unlimited and will always be with relation to a specific limit.

5.7 Netting

Netting describes the practice whereby two firms would execute multiple transactions during a particular period and there would be the ability to set off the liabilities arising from these in terms of the net amounts owing one against the other.

Netting is normally described as existing in two forms – either bilateral netting between two counterparties directly or multilateral netting which involves any number of counterparties together using the services of a central clearing house (central counterparty) against which everyone has a position. This is described a little further on.

5.8 Collateral

Collateral is a big subject. First however, we should define what is meant by collateral. The objective of taking collateral from another party is to convert credit risk (the concern about the right to receive money) into market risk (the right to sell property). Thus, collateral arrangements are commonly encountered in banking; they include such things as a security against a house under a mortgage, a cash payment against a margin requirement, a parent company guarantee to cover a loan to a subsidiary company from a lending institution, a negotiable security to cover a short options position or a bond taken in a stock lending transaction.

The big issue with collateral, apart from its very availability, is whether the value of the collateral offsets the basic credit risk it is there to cover. Thus collateral must be re-valued in line with changing market rates. Most forms of collateral will be discounted by the lender. Therefore if you offer a lender an asset in security for an advance, with a market value of, say, £1M, the lender may choose to reduce its value to, say, £800,000. The amount of this discount will vary with the type of security offered – a security with the potential for volatile fluctuations – for example, stocks and shares – will be discounted to a lower value then a more stable asset – such as a cash deposit.

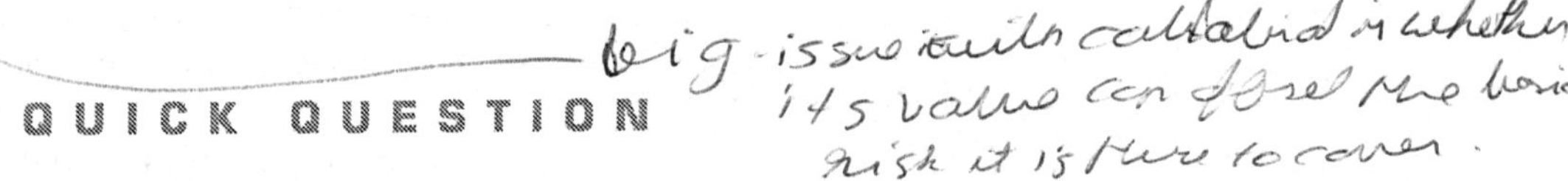

QUICK QUESTION

Why do you think lenders choose to discount the value of some assets pledged as security?

Write your answer here before reading on.

There are a number of reasons for this, including:

- to build a cushion for potential falls in the market value of the asset
- to cover the situation where, if the firm comes to realise the security, the account in above its upper credit limit
- to allow for the expenses of realisation
- to build in a cushion for debit interest and charges to be applied to the loan.

QUESTION TIME 4

What are the discount rates currently in force in your bank?

Write your answer here then check with the answer at the back of the book.

Collateral may also be substituted from time to time at the wish of the parties.

There are various techniques for establishing rights over collateral depending upon assets. The objective of taking collateral is to mitigate a credit risk into the right to own a charge over property which can be turned into liquid funds in the market.

The various forms of collateral include the following:

- Charges or mortgages – a transfer of title ownership to the collateral taker. Charges can be floating or fixed. Floating charges are over a class of assets and are distinguished from a fixed charge in that the collateral provider is permitted to deal with the collateral. The collateral taker cannot keep the collateral after an enforcement event but must sell it to satisfy his claim.
- Lien – the right to retain possession of the collateral, sometimes known as charges.
- Pledge – whereby security interest is provided to another party. In this case the collateral taker cannot keep the collateral after an enforcement event but must sell it to satisfy his claim.
- Transfer and set-off – under which the collateral ownership absolutely is transferred to the collateral taker.

There are various methods of presenting collateral and various securities and forms of collateral which are typically observed in the market. Clearly cash is the most common and indeed is the most popular. Normally cash is acceptable to a receiver of collateral in the major currencies but of course in domestic jurisdictions domestic currency will be king. Other forms of acceptable collateral will be government securities, guarantees from prime banks, negotiable money market instruments such as certificates of deposit (CDs) and any other near-cash securities which can readily be turned into liquid funds.

Collateral therefore is used to mitigate credit risk for a variety of transactions and is commonly seen in foreign exchange transactions, securities lending, and many forms of derivatives.

Typically collateral arrangements between firms can be unilateral, bilateral or netted:

- A unilateral agreement means that one party gives collateral to the other.
- A bilateral agreement allows for double-sided obligations (for example with swaps or foreign exchange transactions) to be catered for. Under such an arrangement, both parties must post collateral for the value of their total obligation to the other.

- Netted – this is an arrangement whereby the net obligations between two parties may be collateralised so that at any point in time the party who is the net obligor posts collateral to the other for the value of the net obligation outstanding.

Collateral is increasingly used as the preferred credit enhancement technique and has many advantages. For example in lending stock, a UK equity would be collateralised by a UK government gilt for example, which is innately stronger than an equity in terms of credit risk. Therefore collateral presents advantages when doing business with customers and counterparties who do not have high levels of creditworthiness, provided that the collateral itself is of high quality that will reduce the credit risk to a more tolerable level.

The act of collateralisation will clearly have no effect on your counterparty's propensity to default nor will it improve the counterparty's credit rating and may or may not reduce the credit exposure. Collateral is also entity-specific and refers to the legal entity that supplied the collateral and to no other. Cross-collateralisation between firms, even within the same group, adds a high degree of additional complexity.

Collateral will normally be marked to market and re-valued. It is important to know what the present value is at all times and therefore the exercise will be conducted on a daily basis. Should the collateral reduce in value, it will be necessary for the obligor to present additional collateral and the reverse will be true when the collateral is surplus to requirements. This is very much the case with margining on futures markets, for example, when marking to market positions each day derives a flow of profit or loss between the client and their broker or between the clearing member and the clearing house as positions are revalued on a daily basis.

5.9 Diversification

This is a fundamental rule in investment whereby risks should be diversified and it has its application therefore in the realms of credit risk; for example lenders will diversify credit risk by taking guarantees and taking collateral.

Another level of diversification is the manner to which it is used to offset risk across a portfolio by spreading it across borrowers or across investments. This has the effect of creating a different set of non-correlating risks and avoids unwanted concentrations of credit risk.

For example, a mortgage-providing institution will have thousands of customers. Some of those will have better credit ratings than others and have the ability to repay their mortgage instalments regularly and on time. By diversifying its mortgage book across thousands of clients without over-extending and developing concentration risks into the particular sector of sub-prime borrowers a bank should be able to diversify its credit risk. This example proved not to be the case in the experience of the United States which demonstrated clearly that one of the root causes of the credit crunch was indeed the over-zealous lending to sub-prime borrowers. However, the bigger factor was the subsequent on-selling of securitised products across the financial markets themselves based upon the questionable asset of overly high rated tranches of securitised debt secured by sub-prime mortgages.

5.10 Central counterparties

Since around the turn of the 21st century, the adoption of a central counterparty has greatly accelerated across many markets and is now commonplace in most market segments at the wholesale level. Listed futures and options markets have always had central clearing houses whereby all the members of an exchange would trade happily with each other knowing that every trade that was conducted between them would be transferred by a legal process known as novation. The process of novation involves a central counterparty clearing house becoming the buyer to every seller and the seller to every buyer. In this way the central counterparty presented a single point of relationship and a single credit risk to every individual member of the exchange rather than the exchange members having risks with each other.

CASE STUDY

Lehman Brothers

When Lehman Brothers went bankrupt in September 2008 all the central counterparty structures in the world were able to return value to the administrators of the collapsed bank and to protect all other non-defaulting clearing members from financial compromise because they were controlling the credit risk of one of their clearing members going into default. The successful outturn at that time led the case for further adoption of the central counterparty model into other markets; in the summer of 2009 we have seen particularly the credit default swap market adopting central counterparties on both sides of the Atlantic. There has almost been a race to adopt the central counterparty model to mitigate the perceived risks of the credit default swap market. Other markets that use a central counterparty model are cash equities, some swaps, energy markets, base metal markets, repos and, as stated earlier, a wide variety of futures and options markets from all parts of the world.

Some of the best known central counterparties are the Options Clearing Corporation (the OCC) and the CME Group's clearing house in the United States, together with LCH.Clearnet and Eurex Clearing in Europe. Most exchange structures across the world utilise central counterparty clearing models. Many new ones have been formed in the past few years.

As indicated above, the central counterparties (CCPs) themselves present a credit risk to the firms with whom they have a relationship and in most cases these firms are larger financial entities than the central counterparties themselves. Hence the financial backing and management strength of the central counterparties is vitally important. Typically, this is provided not only by shareholder funds but also a sizeable fund in cash provided by the clearing members of the CCP and possibly by other resources. But before this financial strength kicks into play the key risk mitigants in the CCP model are the quality of the clearing members and the criteria upon which they are judged before they are permitted to become members and also the margining disciplines together with the risk management strength of the CCP management that are put in place. The risk management element of the central counterparty model is the most important of the services that it provides to the exchanges that they support and the members thereof.

5.11 Loss given default (LGD)

Under the Basel rules, **loss given default** (LGD) is the magnitude of likely loss of the exposure; it is expressed as a percentage of the exposure.

This is the loss that actually occurs when the default event occurs. As such it does take account of risk mitigation strategies including collateral. There should be data available to support this analysis.

Loss given default is facility-specific because such losses are generally understood to be influenced by key transaction characteristics such as the presence of collateral and the degree of subordination.

The factor is determined in one of two ways. Under the foundation methodology, LGD is estimated through the application of standard supervisory rules, which differentiate the level of loss given default based upon the characteristics of the underlying transaction, including the presence and type of collateral. The supervisory rules and treatments were chosen to be conservative. The starting point proposed by the committee is the use of a 50% LGD value for most unsecured transactions, with a higher LGD (75%) applied to subordinated exposures. For transactions with qualifying financial collateral, the LGD is scaled to the degree to which the transaction is secured, using a haircut methodology adapted from that described for the standardised approach. For transactions with qualifying commercial or residential real estate collateral, a separate set of supervisory LGD values and recognition rules are applied. All other transactions are viewed as unsecured for this regulatory purpose.

In Basel's advanced methodology, the bank itself determines the appropriate loss given default to be applied to each exposure, on the basis of robust data and analysis which is capable of being validated both internally and by supervisors. Thus, a bank using internal loss given default estimates for capital purposes might be able to differentiate LGD values on the basis of a wider set of transaction characteristics (e.g. product type, wider range of collateral types) as well as borrower characteristics. As with probability of default (PD) estimates (see below), these values would be expected to represent a conservative view of long-run averages, although banks are free to use more conservative estimates. A bank wishing to use its own estimates of LGD will need to demonstrate to its supervisor that it can meet additional minimum requirements pertinent to the integrity and reliability of these estimates.

5.12 Probability of default (PD)

This is the likelihood that a specific asset will go into default. It is a percentage. This is based on the historic loss experience of the institution.

The **probability of default** (PD) of a borrower or group of borrowers is the central measurable concept on which Basel's internal ratings based (IRB) approach is built.

The probability of default of a borrower does not, however, provide the complete picture of the potential credit loss. Banks also seek to measure how much they will lose should a borrower default on an obligation.

This is contingent upon two elements. First, the magnitude of the likely loss on the exposure, which is termed the loss given default (LGD, as defined above), and is expressed as a percentage of the exposure. Secondly, the loss is contingent upon the amount to which the bank was exposed to the borrower at the time of default, commonly expressed as exposure at default (EAD).

These three components (PD, LGD, EAD) combine to provide a measure of expected intrinsic, or economic, loss.

All banks, whether using the foundation or advanced methodologies, must provide supervisors with an internal estimate of the probability of default associated with borrowers in each borrower grade. Each estimate of probability of default must represent a conservative view of a long-run average PD for the grade in question and thus must be grounded in historical experience and empirical evidence. Preparation of the estimates, and the risk management processes and rating assignments that stand behind them, must reflect full compliance with supervisory minimum requirements (including internal use and disclosure requirements associated with the estimates) to qualify for Basel's IRB recognition.

5.13 Exposure at default (EAD)

This is the gross amount of the exposure at the time that the default actually occurs. This will be a combination of the various exposures to the specific counterparty. The calculation at this stage ignores collateral. Firms should forget who the counterparty actually is and just view the total exposures at a point in time.

If an asset suffers from a lower valuation or a loan defaults, the **exposure at default** figure shows how much the firm will lose as a result of the default. The loss is contingent upon the amount to which the bank was exposed to the borrower at the time of default, commonly expressed as exposure at default (EAD).

Exposure at default (EAD) is a measure of potential exposure (in currency) as calculated by a Basel credit risk model for the period of 1 year or until maturity whichever is soonest.

A bank must provide an estimate of the exposure amount for each transaction (commonly referred to as exposure at default (EAD) in banks' internal systems). All these loss estimates should seek to fully capture the risks of an underlying exposure.

5.14 Recovery rates

When companies are computing their loss given default (LGD) factors they can only do this provided they have some experience of the incidence of losses and the degree to which they recover money that is due to them. The **recovery rate** is a factor which can be proved by diligent record keeping over time and is used to create discount rates in order to arrive at the LGD figures. Measures of recovery rates can be computed in several different ways. One method is to discount the stream of recoveries and the stream of work-out costs (costs of recovery) by a risk-adjusted discounted rate which is the sum of the risk-free rate adjusted by a spread appropriate for the risk of the recovery and the work-out cost cash flows. Another technique is to convert the stream of recoveries and the stream of work-out costs into certainty-equivalent cash flows and to discount these by the risk-free rate. A third technique is to set a combination of adjustments to the discount rate and adjustments to the recovery stream and work-out costs that are consistent with the firm's practices.

It is important that within a firm the process for arriving at a discount rate should be consistent for all exposures of the same kind. Firms should take care to justify this point clearly to insure the absence of any arbitrage caused by manipulating discount factors. Whenever they apply a risk-free rate, they should demonstrate to their supervisors that any remaining risk is covered elsewhere in the calculation.

5.15 Credit events

A **credit event** is the financial term used to describe a general default event related to a legal entity's previously agreed financial obligation. In this case, a legal entity fails to meet its obligation on any significant financial transaction (a coupon on a bond it issued or interest rate payment on a swap for example). The marketplace will recognise this as an event related to the legal entity's credit worthiness. Or it may be a financial event related to a legal entity which triggers specific protection provided by a credit derivative (e.g. credit default swap, credit default swap index, or a credit default swap index tranche).

The events triggering a credit derivative default event are defined in a bilateral swap confirmation which is a transactional document that typically refers to an ISDA master agreement previously executed between the two swap counterparties. There are several standard credit events which are typically referred to in credit derivative transactions, which are embodies within the ISDA practices.

- Bankruptcy
- Failure to pay
- Restructuring
- Repudiation/Moratorium
- Obligation acceleration
- Obligation default.

Typically therefore, these types of credit event will be the trigger for a credit derivative to be invoked (e.g. a credit default swap).

5.16 Maturity

Maturity is the life of a security. It may also refer to the final payment date of a loan or other financial instrument, at which point all remaining interest and principal is due to be paid. Thus this applies to many types of security. For example, bonds, pensions, insurance products and many derivatives will refer to the maturity date. This will be a specific date and usually at a specific time on that date.

Maturity date is a financial term referring to the date when a principal amount of a debt instrument becomes due or payable. It is also a termination or due date on which an instalment loan must be paid in full. For example, a bond due to mature on January 1, 2012, will return the bondholder's principal and final interest payment when it reaches that maturity date.

5.17 Weighted average

The **weighted average cost of capital** (WACC) is the rate (expressed as a percentage, as with interest) that a company is expected to pay to bondholders (cost of debt) and shareholders (cost of equity) to finance its assets.

WACC is the minimum return that a company must earn on its existing asset base to satisfy its creditors, owners, and other providers of capital. Companies raise money from a number of sources including common equity, preferred equity, straight debt, convertible debt, exchangeable debt, warrants, options, pension liabilities, executive stock options and governmental subsidies.

Different securities are expected to generate different returns. WACC is calculated taking into account the relative weights of each component of the capital structure - debt and equity, and is used to see if the investment is worthwhile to undertake.

6 Setting credit limits for trade book and loan products

6.1 The trading book and banking book

The trading book is the portfolio of financial instruments held by a firm. The financial instruments in the trading book are purchased or sold to facilitate trading for their customers and counterparties, to profit from spreads between the bid/ask spread, to generate profits by buying and selling or to hedge against various types of risk.

On the other hand, the banking book is an accounting set of records that includes all securities that are not actively traded by the institution, that are meant to be held until they mature. These securities are accounted for in a different way than those in the trading book, which are traded on the market and valued by the performance of the market.

Loan products is a phrase used to describe any lending business including bank loans and mortgage lending activity.

6.2 Credit limits

Most institutions will have a number of relationships. Each will need to have agreements in place and credit limits by product. Credit risk is one of the largest risks run by a firm.

Every time that a firm decides to enter into a relationship with another financial institution there will be a range of matters that it will need to take into account. Prior to taking on a new counterparty, due diligence should include a review of the service quality and backup systems, the ownership and controls within the counterparty, its management and credit ratings, any known information about it and the reason why the additional counterparty is to be considered. The firm should raise issues on the nature of the product and the market in which the counterparty is to be used. They will also wish to consider the size of the limit(s) to be imposed upon the customer or counterparty. These will generally be set according to the experience that the firm has of dealing with the customer, its financial strength and size of proposed activity or loan. Limits may be set taking into account industry norms, or what best suits your firm, and also, what best suits the customer's basic needs. A key consideration will always be the perceived ability of the customer to repay.

Banks, for example, work with banking counterparties in every area from cash placement through every part of the treasury instrument cycle. Each of these maintains a level of credit risk, even if some of that is at best indirect. External credit ratings (Fitch, Moody's Standard & Poor's) can be used to enable a bank to manage these counterparty limits. This would result in a reduction in limits were a counterparty to have their credit rating reduced, for example – you will recall that this reduction in credit ratings was discussed earlier in this chapter. Such a system can easily be implemented.

The advantage of having limits in place is to control exposure and to present warning signs against which to manage changing counterparty risk. Firms will need to consider also the process that should be adopted for setting and revising the limits. Similarly they will have to address the process for the approval of excesses and the importance of making sure that the limits are actually relied upon and complied with inside the business – so they do not end up in disrepute.

The monitoring should be by way of limits and excesses – and these should be evidenced that they have been regularly monitored – so an audit of this work is relatively straightforward. The management will need to see that this is evidenced and acted upon – there is no point in having limits that nobody takes any real notice of. Management need to enforce these limits (whether hard or soft) in accordance with clear documented policies.

An additional point affecting firms would be the ability to set limits on the firm's own traders and dealing desks. The ability to control the trader within the firm is clearly of vital importance and although this might be deemed to be more of a market risk limit, it does have a boundary with credit risk issues at the same time.

Additional considerations with respect to limits occur when dealing with derivative transactions or more complex transactions, which by their very nature may be highly leveraged; therefore the understanding of risk and the potential speed of escalation required due to leverage must be more closely monitored. This may interface also with the firm's hedging programme. In any event, derivatives limits are fundamentally important and will interface into escalation policies for the firm.

It is vital that all the limits described in this section are regularly monitored.

6.3 Controlling trading book risk

We need to examine value at risk and confidence levels as both play a large part in the management of credit risk (and other risks). This is particularly relevant with the Basel Committee approaches.

6.3.1 Value at Risk (VaR)

In the mathematics and risk management activities of finance, Value at Risk (VaR) is a widely used measure of the risk of loss on a specific portfolio of financial assets. For a given portfolio, probability and time horizon, VaR is defined as a threshold value such that the probability that the mark-to-market loss on the portfolio over the given time horizon exceeds this value (assuming normal markets and no trading in the portfolio) is the given probability level.

It is mainly used in measuring market risk but may also be deployed in the direction of credit and operational risk. For example, if a portfolio of stocks has a one-day 5% VaR of $1 million, there is a 5% probability that the portfolio will fall in value by more than $1 million over a one day period, assuming markets are normal and there is no trading. Informally, a loss of $1 million or more on this portfolio is expected on 1 day in 20. A loss which exceeds the VaR threshold is termed a VaR break.

VaR has five main uses in finance – risk management, risk measurement, financial control, financial reporting and computing regulatory capital. VaR is sometimes used in non-financial applications as well.

6.3.2 Confidence levels

In statistics, a confidence interval (CI) is a particular kind of interval estimate of a population parameter. Instead of estimating the parameter by a single value, an interval likely to include the parameter is given. Thus, confidence intervals are used to indicate the reliability of an estimate. How likely the interval is to contain the parameter is determined by the confidence level or confidence coefficient. Increasing the desired confidence level will widen the confidence interval.

A confidence interval is always qualified by a particular confidence level, usually expressed as a percentage; thus one speaks of a 95% confidence interval. The end points of the confidence interval are referred to as confidence limits. For a given estimation procedure in a given situation, the higher the confidence level, the wider the confidence interval will be.

The calculation of a confidence interval generally requires assumptions about the nature of the estimation process – it is primarily a parametric method – for example, it may depend on an assumption that the distribution of the population from which the sample came is normal. As such, confidence intervals are not robust statistics, though modifications can be made to add robustness.

6.4 Controlling concentration risk

Concentration risk in finance and banking is a term denoting the overall spread of a firm's outstanding accounts over the number or variety of debtors to whom the firm has credit risk. With banks and the loans they construct, this risk is calculated using a concentration ratio which explains what percentage of the outstanding accounts each bank loan represents.

QUICK QUESTION

If a bank has five outstanding loans of equal value each loan would have a concentration ratio of 0.2, what would the concentration ratio be if it had three equal value loans?

Write your answer here before reading on.

In this case the concentration ratio would be 0.333.

Various other factors enter into this equation in real-world applications, where loans are not evenly distributed or are heavily concentrated in certain economic sectors. A bank with ten loans, valued at 1,000 dollars each would have a concentration ratio of 0.10; but if nine of the loans were for 1,000 dollars, and the last was for 500,000 dollars, the concentration risk would be considerably higher. Also, loans weighted towards a specific economic sector would create a higher ratio than a set of evenly distributed loans because the evenly spread loans would serve to offset the risk of economic downturn and default in any one specific industry damaging the bank's outstanding accounts.

Risk of default is an important factor in concentration risk. The basic issue raised by the concept of default risk is: does the risk of default on a bank's outstanding loans match the overall risk posed by the entire economy or are the bank's loans concentrated in areas of higher or lower than average risk based on their volume, type, amount, and industry?

From time to time firms will notice a shift in the potential credit risk accruing from one customer, for example a major bank (for example, consider Lehman Brothers in the run-up to its collapse). Again, a concentration risk trend may be detected into one market sector such as mining or oil production. Banks might suffer from an overdependence upon loans to sub-prime borrowers (the credit crunch again). All of these are examples of concentration risk.

Therefore an analysis of where the risk lies with respect to the concentration of risk against a single name or group is of significant importance as is the exposure towards a single country, region, industry or economic sector. All of these exposures can be modelled and assessments made upon the risk profiles generated by this exercise.

6.5 Limitations of credit risk measurement

There are several areas where it could be argued that credit risk management has its limitations as clearly it is not going to be possible to do everything completely accurately. There will always be many unknowns and changing circumstances.

One limitation concerns the application of limits themselves; placing limits on the amount of risk which a firm is willing to contemplate is self-explanatory. If a risk is difficult to measure it may be hard to quantify that and a numerical limit may in fact be meaningless. But nevertheless a qualitative limit may still be achievable.

Many of the applications for measuring credit risk depend upon the use of models. Models are only as good as the data that is fed into them and the assumptions upon which the models themselves are based. There is therefore an innate limitation in this and indeed a source of risk – model risk itself is presented.

It has been highlighted that credit ratings are a particularly useful external source of value in measuring credit risk but again it should be remembered that these are limited and the quality of credit ratings are only really as good as the date they were published and the data and opinion upon which they were based at the date they were published. The passage of time will affect the veracity and accuracy of the ratings. Therefore it is very common to find an unexpected ratings change to be announced in the market by one of the leading ratings agencies. It is impossible for ratings agencies to keep all of their rated securities and entities under review at all times. Owing to limited resources they must review them regularly but not at all times. So therefore there is an innate inability to have a real time measure here.

7 Asset and liability risk

7.1 What is asset liability management?

Asset liability management (ALM) can be defined as a mechanism to address the risk faced by a bank due to a mismatch between assets and liabilities either due to liquidity or changes in interest rates. Liquidity is an institution's ability to meet its liabilities either by borrowing or converting assets. Apart from liquidity, a bank may also have a mismatch due to changes in interest rates as banks typically tend to borrow short term (fixed or floating loans/facilities) and lend long term (fixed or floating).

In banking, asset and liability management is the practice of managing risks that arise due to mismatches between the assets and liabilities (debts and assets) of the bank. This can also be seen in insurance.

Banks face several risks such as liquidity risk, interest rate risk, credit risk and operational risk. Asset liability management (ALM) is a strategic management tool to manage interest rate risk and liquidity risk faced by banks, other financial services companies and corporations.

Banks manage the risks of asset liability mismatch by matching the assets and liabilities according to the maturity pattern or matching the duration, by hedging and by securitisation. Many of the techniques for hedging stem from the delta hedging concepts introduced in the Black–Scholes model and in the work of Robert C. Merton and Robert A. Jarrow. The early origins of asset and liability management date back to the high interest rate periods of 1975-6, the late 1970s and early 1980s in the United States.

7.2 Development of modern ALM techniques

Modern risk management now takes place from an integrated approach to enterprise risk management that reflects the fact that interest rate risk, credit risk, market risk, and liquidity risk are all interrelated. The Jarrow-Turnbull model is an example of a risk management methodology that integrates default and random interest rates. The earliest work in this regard was done by Robert C. Merton. Increasing integrated risk management is done on a full mark to market basis rather than the accounting basis that was at the heart of the first interest rate sensitivity gap and duration calculations.

A comprehensive ALM policy framework focuses on bank profitability and long-term viability by targeting the net interest margin ratio and net economic value subject to balance sheet constraints. Significant among these constraints are maintaining credit quality, meeting liquidity needs and obtaining sufficient capital.

A discerning view of ALM is that it simply combines portfolio management techniques (that is, asset, liability and spread management) into a coordinated process. Thus, the central theme of ALM is the coordinated – and not piecemeal – management of a bank's entire balance sheet.

ALM is a systematic approach that attempts to provide a degree of protection to the risk arising out of asset/liability mismatches.

Although ALM is not a relatively new planning tool, it has evolved from the simple idea of maturity-matching of assets and liabilities across various time horizons into a framework that includes sophisticated concepts such as duration matching, variable rate pricing, and the use of static and dynamic simulation.

As the landscape of the financial services industry becomes increasingly competitive, with rising costs of intermediation due to higher capital requirements and deposit insurance, financial institutions face a loss of spread income. In order to enhance the loss in profitability due to such developments, financial institutions may be forced deliberately to mismatch asset/liability maturities in order to generate higher spreads.

ALM is a systematic approach that attempts to provide a degree of protection to the risk arising out of the asset/liability mismatch. ALM consists of a framework to define, measure, monitor, modify and manage liquidity and interest rate risk. It is not always possible for financial institutions to restructure the asset and liability mix directly to manage asset/liability gaps. Hence, off-balance sheet strategies such as interest rate swaps, options, futures, caps, floors, forward rate agreements, swaptions, and so on, can be used to create synthetic hedges to manage asset/liability gaps.

7.3 The enemy – interest rate risk

The function of ALM is not just protection from risk. The safety achieved through ALM also opens up opportunities for enhancing net worth. Interest rate risk (IRR) largely poses a problem to a bank's net interest income and hence profitability.

Changes in interest rates can significantly alter a bank's net interest income (or NII), depending on the extent of the mismatch between the asset and liability interest rate reset times. Changes in interest rates also affect the market value of a bank's equity.

Methods of managing interest rate risk first require a bank to specify goals for either the book value or the market value of NII. In the case of the former, the focus will be on the current value of NII and in the latter, the focus will be on the market value of equity. In either case, though, the bank has to measure the risk exposure and formulate strategies to minimise or mitigate risk.

The immediate focus of ALM is interest-rate risk and return as measured by a bank's net interest margin.

7.4 Measuring and managing interest rate risk

One of the chief areas of concern with asset and liability management is interest rates. The primary forms of interest rate risk include re-pricing risk, changes in the yield curve (yield curve risk), basis risk and optionality. Changes in interest rates can have adverse effects upon both a bank's earnings and its economic value. From the earnings perspective, the focus is upon the impact of changes in interest rates on accruals or reported earnings. Any variation to earnings is an important focal point for analysis because reduced interest earnings will threaten the financial performance of a financial institution. There is also an economic value perspective. Variation in market interest rates can also affect the economic value of a bank's assets, its liabilities and any off-balance sheet positions. Since the economic value perspective considers the potential impact of interest rate changes on the present value of all future cash flows, it provides a more comprehensive view of the potential long-term effects of changes in interest rates than is offered by the earnings perspective.

A model that is commonly adopted for asset and liability management measures the extent and the direction of mismatches between assets and liabilities through different maturities. It identifies the maturity gaps where these mismatches occur. A gap of zero is the optimum outcome because, with a zero gap, the bank will be fully protected against both increases and decreases in interest rates as its net interest earnings will not change in either case. However, it is very difficult for banks to manage these gaps successfully because, in the normal course of events, no financial institution is capable of predicting the markets and thus protecting against the possibility of gaps existing. These models also assume that banks can adjust their assets and liabilities flexibly to attain the desired gap outcome and this may not be possible. Similarly, these approaches focus only on the current interest sensitivity of assets and liabilities and may ignore the effects of movements of interest rates on the value of those assets and liabilities.

Basic gap modelling can be extended into cumulative gap models and duration gap models. The former of these two techniques would sum the various gaps at different maturities whereas the latter, using duration, would calculate the average life of a financial instrument. It would give an approximate market value of every asset and liability on the bank's balance sheet to obtain the combined asset and liability duration. The result of this would deliver the bank with a mechanism of discovering the effect of interest rate changes on the net worth of the bank.

It is also possible to move on to simulation analyses at a higher level to construct the risk return profile of the banking portfolio. Using scenario analysis these simulations would address the issue of uncertainty associated with the future direction taken by interest rates by applying **what if** simulations.

Depending upon the risk tolerance of an institution, risk can be controlled using a variety of techniques using either direct or synthetic models. The direct approach would involve restructuring the balance sheet by changing the contractual characteristics of assets and liabilities to achieve a desired duration or maturity gap. By contrast, the synthetic method would rely on the use of financial instruments, mainly derivatives, such as interest rate swaps, futures and options and other customised OTC derivatives to alter the balance sheet risk exposure. Additionally, the process of securitisation and financial engineering can be used to create assets with wide investor appeal in order to adjust asset liability gaps.

7.5 Using derivatives to mitigate interest rate risk

7.5.1 Interest rate swaps

Interest rate swaps (IRS) represent a contractual agreement between a financial institution and a counterparty to exchange cash flows at periodic intervals, based upon a notional amount. The purpose of such an instrument is to hedge interest rate risk. By arranging for another party to assume its interest payments, a bank can put in place such a hedge. Financial institutions can use such swaps synthetically to convert floating rate liabilities into fixed rate ones. The arbitrage potential associated with different comparative financing advantages (spreads) enables both parties to benefit through lower borrowing costs.

Financial institutions can also use options on swaps (known as swaptions) to provide additional flexibility.

7.5.2 Exchange-traded futures

As an alternative to using OTC derivatives, exchange-listed futures contracts can also be used. These can be applied either at the macro level of the entire balance sheet or at a micro level. A micro hedge would be applied to individual assets or individual transactions. A buyer with a long futures position would have purchased a futures contract when interest rates were expected to fall. The seller of a futures contract on the other hand would take a short position in anticipation of rising prices. The protection provided by financial futures instruments is symmetrical in that losses (or gains) in the value of the cash position are offset by gains (or losses) in the value of the futures position. It is also possible to use OTC forward foreign exchange contracts to hedge against exchange rate risks. These have the same economic fundamentals as futures contracts but are not exchange-listed products.

Futures contracts are not without their own risks. Among the most important is basis risk which represents the manner in which the forward price moves against the spot cash price. Basis can widen or narrow. Being standardised products, exchange traded derivatives come in standard shapes and therefore banks must pay close attention to the hedging ratio. Financial managers must be careful to follow any regulatory or accounting regulations which govern the use of futures contracts.

7.5.3 Using options – exchange-traded or OTC

Another derivative technique available is to use options to hedge against interest rate risk. Options are far more flexible than other derivatives and can create a very wide range of potential hedging outcomes. Call option strategies are profitable in bullish interest rate scenarios. Put options can be used to provide insurance against price declines with limited risk if the opposite occurs. Similarly, call options can be used to enhance profits if the market rallies with the maximum loss on any option purchased always restricted to the amount paid as the upfront premium. OTC option products can also be used to customise interest rate exposure and create such things as caps and floors and also collars which restrict potential interest rate exposures to set levels.

Customised interest rate agreements is the general term used to classify instruments such as interest rate caps and floors, which are constructed by using options. In return for the protection against rising liability costs, the cap buyer pays a premium to the cap seller. The pay-off profile of the cap buyer is asymmetric in nature, in that if interest rates do not rise, the maximum loss is restricted to the cap premium. Since the cap buyer gains when interest rates rise, the purchase of a cap is comparable to buying a strip of put options. Similarly, in return for the protection against falling asset returns, the floor buyer pays a premium to the seller of the floor. The pay-off profile of the floor buyer is also asymmetric in nature since the maximum loss is restricted to the floor premium. As interest rates fall, the pay-off to the buyer of the floor increases in proportion to the fall in rates. In this respect, the purchase of a floor is comparable to the purchase of a strip of call options.

By buying an interest rate cap and selling an interest rate floor to offset the cap premium, financial institutions can also limit the cost of liabilities to a band of interest rate constraints. This strategy, known as an interest rate collar has the effect of capping liability costs in rising rate scenarios.

7.6 Securitisation

By using securitisation, financial institutions can create securities suitable for resale in capital markets from assets which otherwise would have been held to maturity.

In addition to providing an alternative route for asset/liability restructuring, securitisation may also be regarded as a form of direct financing in which savers are directly lending to borrowers. Securitisation also provides the additional advantage of cleansing the balance sheet of complex and highly illiquid assets as long as the transformations required to enhance marketability are available on a cost-effective basis. Securitisation transfers risks such as interest rate risk, credit risk (unless the loans are securitised with full or partial recourse to the originator) and pre-payment risk to the ultimate investors of the securitised assets.

Besides increasing the liquidity and diversification of the loans portfolio, securitisation allows a financial institution to recapture some part of the profits of lending and permits reduction in the cost of intermediation.

KEY WORDS

Key words in this chapter are given below. There is space to write your own revision notes and add any other key words or phrases you want to remember.

- Credit risk committee
- Credit policy
- Modelling
- Credit scoring
- Stress testing
- Segmentation
- External ratings
- Credit limits
- Provisioning
- Impairment
- Counterparty risk
- Due diligence
- Boundary risk
- Netting
- Collateral
- Central counterparty
- Loss given default
- Probability of default
- Exposure at default
- Credit event
- Maturity
- Trading book
- Concentration risk
- Asset liability management

REVIEW

Now consider the main points that were introduced in this chapter. These are listed below. Tick each one as you go through them.

- The credit risk management function of a firm is responsible for assessing the financial state of customers and other organisations that it will lend funds to. In the normal course, the firm will have a Risk Committee to whom the credit risk staff report.
- Each firm will have a Credit Policy that will inform credit decisions within the business.
- Banks are required to follow the Basel principles for credit risk assessment. These fall under the headings of supervisory expectations for concerning sound credit risk assessment and valuation for loans; and supervisory evaluation of credit risk assessment for loans, controls and capital adequacy.
- A variety of tools and techniques are used to manage credit risk – including modelling, stress testing (including scenario analysis), segmentation, external ratings, setting credit limits, internal credit gradings, provisioning and impairment and key statistics and KPIs.
- Credit risk is the risk that a customer or counterparty may fail to make repayment – this is a key risk in the banking industry, so banks must invest a significant amount of time and effort into controlling and mitigating this risk.
- Counterparty risk can be managed through carrying out due diligence, taking appropriate guarantees, setting the correct credit limits, netting, using collateral, diversification, and the use of central counterparties.
- Credit limits will always be put in place for each customer and counterparty to control trading book risk, as well as using VaR and considering current levels of concentration risk.
- Asset Liability Management is used to manage risks brought about by either liquidity problems or changes in interest rates.

chapter7

RISK MANAGEMENT FRAMEWORK (PART 2)

Contents

Learning objectives

On completion of this chapter, you should be able to:

- evaluate the concepts of liquidity risk, market risk, insurance and reinvestment risk, legal risk and strategy risk with the risk management framework
- evaluate the role of the audit committee and the part they play in corporate governance and risk management.

Introduction

This chapter starts with a comprehensive explanation of liquidity risk. This is the risk that a firm cannot meet their financial obligations as they fall due. The banking crisis which began in 2007 was essentially a liquidity crisis so it is important that you have a clear understanding of this topic. The Basel Committee has set out 17 Liquidity Principles which are set out at the start of this chapter before we move on to consider a primary technique used to manage this risk - the maturity ladder. The concept of liquidity risk is further developed with an explanation of some of the causes of this risk, including asset liquidity risk, and funding liquidity risk. The steps taken by both the regulators and the Basel Committee to address liquidity risk since the banking crisis are outlined next. Having laid this foundation, we can then consider some other tools and techniques used to manage liquidity risk – including stress testing, being able to accurately estimate future funding requirements, having access to a range of sources of funds, liquidity limits, scenario analysis, Liquidity at Risk techniques, examining the accessibility of funding, diversification, behavioural analysis, netting and an awareness of market dislocation.

Having fully discussed liquidity risk, the chapter then moves on to the topic of market risk, starting with a definition of the types of market risk. Systematic risk is introduced next – this describes the situation where investments in a market fall due to conditions that affect the whole of the market, for example, a change of government. By this stage, you will have a good understanding of what market risk is, so we can move on to think about ways in which this risk can be managed –including hedging, market risk limits, diversification and stress testing.

Insurance and investment risk is the next topic to be covered. The types of risk in this category are explored – currency risk, interest rate risk, bond risk, equity risk, commodity risk, and property risk. The rate of return available from differing asset classes varies – the chapter will discuss return opportunities from cash deposits, fixed interest securities, equities, commodities, and alternative investments such as antiques and paintings. The next topic for discussion is the identification and measurement of investment risk – examples of this are market neutral arbitrage and market neutral securities hedging. Those assets that are not readily saleable due to doubts about value or the existence of a market are referred to as illiquid assets and the come under the microscope next, with the examples of venture capital, private equity and property being looked at. After a short discussion on tracking error, the text moves on to consider investment mandates, which set out the rules under which a collective investment scheme is to be conducted. Whilst on the subject of collective investments, we will then turn our attention to the mitigation of investment portfolio risk. Risk transfer instruments are up for discussion next, before this section concludes with a discussion on the monitoring, management and reporting of investments.

As we begin to approach the end of the chapter, legal risk is introduced. Legal risk depends upon legal uncertainty and it can also rear its head when there are legislative or regulatory changes to the environment that the firm is operating in. In order to manage legal risk the firm must have a clear understanding of the legal and regulatory environment that it operates in. In addition to this, there must be an effective legal risk management function in the organisation. The penultimate section of this chapter considers strategy risk and strategic risk. All strategic initiatives will involve an element of risk – the importance of exploiting risk is explored, along with a description of some examples of where taking on too much risk has resulted in strategic errors. The final section of this chapter describes the role and work of the Audit Committee.

1 Liquidity risk

QUICK QUESTION

Reflecting on the earlier parts of this course, write down your definition of liquidity risk.

Write your answer here before reading on.

Liquidity risk is the risk that a firm or bank is unable to meet its obligations as they fall due resulting in: an inability to support normal business activity; failing to meet liquidity regulatory requirements or rating agency concerns. As the success of the banking industry is based on trust, this will be severely undermined if depositors are not able to access their funds. You only need think of the queues of customers outside branches of Northern Rock in 2007 when they realised that the bank had a liquidity crisis to realise the powerful impact such a crisis can have.

As a result of sudden, large and potentially protractedincreases in cash outflows, the cash resources of the firm could be severely depleted. These outflows couldbe principally through customer withdrawals, wholesalecounterparties removing financing, ratings downgrades or loan drawdowns.

This could result in:

- Limited ability to support client lending, trading activities and investments
- Forced reduction in balance sheet and sales of assets
- Inability to fulfil lending obligations
- Regulatory breaches under the liquidity standardsintroduced by the FSA on 1st December 2009.

These outflows could be the result of general marketdislocations or specific concerns about the firm.

1.1 The Basel Committee

In September 2008, the Basel Committee published its *Principles for Sound Liquidity Risk Management and Supervision,* a revised version of a set of 17 guidelines first written in 2000. While the Committee expected banks and supervisors to implement the revised guidelinesthoroughly, it offered no binding quantitative metrics for liquidity buffers or structural funding. This has now been addressed as part of Basel III (see later).

However a set of rules drawn up for consultation in summer 2009 by the committee's working group on liquidity created a liquidity coverage ratio as well as quantitative funding requirements. The liquidity coverage ratio uses a risk-sensitive approach, based on a short period of acute liquidity stress, to calculate a requirement for a pool of high-quality assets that banks would be required to hold in as a liquidity buffer. The supplementary funding requirements would encourage banks to put greater reliance on stable long-term funding for long-term assets, with quantitative constraints on banks' structural funding to be calculated in due course.

The intention behind the new rules is to have a harmonised common standard that allows individual regulatory authorities to implement certain assumptions appropriate to their particular jurisdiction.

The Basel rules define liquidity risk. They refer to liquidity as being the ability of a bank to fund increases in assets and meet obligations as they come due, without incurring unacceptable losses. Basel also defines two types of liquidity risk. **Funding liquidity risk** is the risk that the firm will not be able to meet efficiently both expected and unexpected current and future cash flow and collateral needs without affecting either daily operations or the financial condition of the firm. **Market liquidity risk** is the risk that a firm cannot easily offset or eliminate a position at the market price because of inadequate market depth or market disruption.

The fundamental role of banks in the maturity transformation of short-term deposits into long-term loans makes them inherently vulnerable to liquidity risk, both of an institution-specific nature and that which affects markets as a whole. Virtually every financial transaction or commitment has implications for a bank's liquidity. Effective liquidity risk management helps ensure a bank's ability to meet cash flow obligations, which are uncertain as they are affected by external events and the behaviour of other parties. Liquidity risk management is of paramount importance because a liquidity shortfall at a single institution can have system-wide repercussions – for example, consider the reputational damage caused to the whole of the banking industry triggered by the Northern Rock crisis. Financial market developments in the past decade have increased the complexity of liquidity risk and its management.

1.2 The Basel liquidity principles

For completeness, the headline description of all 17 principles is reproduced below. They are grouped under sub-headings as shown.

1.2.1 Fundamental principle for the management and supervision of liquidity risk

Principle 1: A bank is responsible for the sound management of liquidity risk. A bank should establish a robust liquidity risk management framework that ensures it maintains sufficient liquidity, including a cushion of unencumbered, high quality liquid assets, to withstand a range of stress events, including those involving the loss or impairment of both unsecured and secured funding sources. Supervisors should assess the adequacy of both a bank's liquidity risk management framework and its liquidity position and should take prompt action if a bank is deficient in either area in order to protect depositors and to limit potential damage to the financial system.

1.2.2 Governance of liquidity risk management

Principle 2: A bank should clearly articulate a liquidity risk tolerance that is appropriate for its business strategy and its role in the financial system.

Principle 3: Senior management should develop a strategy, policies and practices to manage liquidity risk in accordance with the risk tolerance and to ensure that the bank maintains sufficient liquidity. Senior management should continuously review information on the bank's liquidity developments and report to the board of directors on a regular basis. A bank's board of directors should review and approve the strategy, policies and practices related to the management of liquidity at least annually and ensure that senior management manages liquidity risk effectively.

Principle 4: A bank should incorporate liquidity costs, benefits and risks in the product pricing, performance measurement and new product approval process for all significant business activities (both on- and off-balance sheet), thereby aligning the risk-taking incentives of individual business lines with the liquidity risk exposures their activities create for the bank as a whole.

1.2.3 Measurement and management of liquidity risk

Principle 5: A bank should have a sound process for identifying, measuring, monitoring and controlling liquidity risk. This process should include a robust framework for comprehensively projecting cash flows arising from assets, liabilities and off-balance sheet items over an appropriate set of time horizons.

Principle 6: A bank should actively manage liquidity risk exposures and funding needs within and across legal entities, business lines and currencies, taking into account legal, regulatory and operational limitations to the transferability of liquidity.

Principle 7: A bank should establish a funding strategy that provides effective diversification in the sources and tenor of funding. It should maintain an ongoing presence in its chosen funding markets and strong relationships with funds providers to promote effective diversification of funding sources. A bank should regularly gauge its capacity to raise funds quickly from each source. It should identify the main factors that affect its ability to raise funds and monitor those factors closely to ensure that estimates of fund raising capacity remain valid.

Principle 8: A bank should actively manage its intraday liquidity positions and risks to meet payment and settlement obligations on a timely basis under both normal and stressed conditions and thus contribute to the smooth functioning of payment and settlement systems.

Principle 9: A bank should actively manage its collateral positions, differentiating between encumbered and unencumbered assets. A bank should monitor the legal entity and physical location where collateral is held and how it may be mobilised in a timely manner.

Principle 10: A bank should conduct stress tests on a regular basis for a variety of institution-specific and market-wide stress scenarios (individually and in combination) to identify sources of potential liquidity strain and to ensure that current exposures remain in accordance with a bank's established liquidity risk tolerance. A bank should use stress test outcomes to adjust its liquidity risk management strategies, policies, and positions and to develop effective contingency plans.

Principle 11: A bank should have a formal contingency funding plan (CFP) that clearly sets out the strategies for addressing liquidity shortfalls in emergency situations. A CFP should outline policies to manage a range of stress environments, establish clear lines of responsibility, include clear invocation and escalation procedures and be regularly tested and updated to ensure that it is operationally robust.

Principle 12: A bank should maintain a cushion of unencumbered, high quality liquid assets to be held as insurance against a range of liquidity stress scenarios, including those that involve the loss or impairment of unsecured and typically available secured funding sources. There should be no legal, regulatory or operational impediment to using these assets to obtain funding.

1.2.4 Public disclosure

Principle 13: A bank should publicly disclose information on a regular basis that enables market participants to make an informed judgement about the soundness of its liquidity risk management framework and liquidity position.

1.2.5 The role of supervisors

Principle 14: Supervisors should regularly perform a comprehensive assessment of a bank's overall liquidity risk management framework and liquidity position to determine whether they deliver an adequate level of resilience to liquidity stress given the bank's role in the financial system.

Principle 15: Supervisors should supplement their regular assessments of a bank's liquidity risk management framework and liquidity position by monitoring a combination of internal reports, prudential reports and market information.

Principle 16: Supervisors should intervene to require effective and timely remedial action by a bank to address deficiencies in its liquidity risk management processes or liquidity position.

Principle 17: Supervisors should communicate with other supervisors and public authorities, such as central banks, both within and across national borders, to facilitate effective cooperation regarding the supervision and oversight of liquidity risk management. Communication should occur regularly during normal times, with the nature and frequency of the information sharing increasing as appropriate during times of stress.

The principles underscore the importance of establishing a robust liquidity risk management framework that is well integrated into the firm-wide risk management process. The primary objective of this guidance is to raise banks' resilience to liquidity stress. Among other things, the principles seek to raise standards in the following areas.

- Governance and the articulation of a firm-wide liquidity risk tolerance.
- Liquidity risk measurement, including the capture of off-balance sheet exposures, securitisation activities, and other contingent liquidity risks that were not well managed during the financial market turmoil.
- Aligning the risk-taking incentives of individual business units with the liquidity risk exposures their activities create for the bank.
- Stress tests that cover a variety of institution-specific and market-wide scenarios, with a link to the development of effective contingency funding plans.
- Strong management of intraday liquidity risks and collateral positions.
- Maintenance of a robust cushion of unencumbered, high quality liquid assets to be in a position to survive protracted periods of liquidity stress.
- Regular public disclosures, both quantitative and qualitative, of a bank's liquidity risk profile and management.

The principles also strengthen expectations about the role of supervisors, including the need to intervene in a timely manner to address deficiencies and the importance of communication with other supervisors and public authorities, both within and across national borders.

The guidance focuses on liquidity risk management at medium and large complex banks, but the sound principles have broad applicability to all types of banks and financial institutions. Basel notes that implementation of the sound principles by both banks and supervisors should be tailored to the size, nature of business and complexity of a bank's activities. Other factors that a bank and its supervisors should consider include the bank's role and its systemic importance in the financial sectors of the jurisdictions in which it operates.

1.3 Steps being taken internationally to address liquidity risk

The events of 2008 in particular showed all observers how the financial world was rocked to its core by essentially a liquidity risk problem. As a result of this, much debate has gone on globally involving politicians, central banks and regulators. The collapse of institutions within the market and the removal of liquidity resulted in deep concern about excessive leverage and these indeed almost brought down the global financial system. There was great panic which damaged economies across the world and wiped out jobs and trillions of dollars in savings and investments. Governments have recognised that financial breakdowns have devastating effects and have consequently put in place various safety nets and new plans to limit the disruption resulting from instability.

Such safety measures come at a cost because they have the tendency to insulate financial institutions from the full consequences of their actions and reduce market discipline. For example, since many of the UK High Street banks were bailed out by the public purse, there has been much debate as to whether this would have happened in any other economic sector and has the effect of this action by the government been to remove bankers from the consequences of their actions. Regulatory approaches have been suggested to contain this moral hazard. Governments have also suggested severe curtailment on financial firms to maintain reserves and capital buffers in proportion to their risks, so that they can absorb losses at their own expense rather than be bailed out by tax payers, which has been evident in many countries.

The regulatory framework globally was seen to be insufficient. In particular the UK model came under severe criticism. Even despite the efforts of the Basel approaches under Basel II, major global financial institutions maintained their capital at too low a level and relied too heavily on unstable short-term funding (Northern Rock and HBOS are prime examples of this). A major point that has attracted a lot of public debate has been the bonus culture and reward packages for financial executives which rewarded excessive risk taking. Large banks often held less capital relative to their risks and used greater leverage than smaller banks (note Lehman, UBS and Merrill Lynch as examples). The resulting market distortion made the global financial system dangerously fragile. The interconnectivity and contagion risks have been evident for all to see. Many products were complex in nature (credit derivatives and securitised products being good examples).

Even well into 2009, governments and regulators were seeking approaches to combat the liquidity risk problem. This was addressed by a number of headline approaches. The headline techniques that have been formulated at inter-government level involve the following.

(1) More substantial capital requirements for banks. Systemically important banks will be required to be better supported than others. The notion of globally significant international financial institutions (or GSIFIs) is now commonplace.

(2) Regulators want to have higher quality forms of collateral to enable a greater ability by financial firmsto absorb losses. This will require increase to equity shareholdings.

(3) More forward-looking capital requirement and accounting rules. This is to save capital in good times, setting it aside for more difficult periods in the economic cycle.

(4) Liquidity standards are to be explicit and stronger to improve resilience of firms with respect to combating liquidity risk in the overall financial system.

(5) Improvement in risk management practices and rules to be embedded in the financial marketplace across banks and other financial institutions. This will also address the ability to combat the use of leverage and to be able to withstand market volatility.

1.4 Basel Committee activities

The Basel committee issued guidelines earlier in the 21st century on how banks should handle their liquidity needs. Until the summer of 2008 these principles attracted far less attention in the financial world than other aspects of banking supervision, such as capital adequacy rules, since most banks and some regulators believed the growth of capital markets had reduced the chance of liquidity crises at banks.

The events of that year shattered that assumption and left regulators determined to tighten liquidity rules. In the summer of 2009, the Basel committee issued a discussion document which suggested that global banks should adopt 17 principles for liquidity management – as reproduced earlier. For the first time these included a demand that banks should maintain a robust cushion of unencumbered, high quality liquid assets to be in a position to survive protracted periods of liquidity stress, and that they pay far greater attention to the risk that off-balance sheet vehicles could trigger liquidity shocks.

The Basel committee did not define what a robust cushion of assets might mean in practice, since regulators would prefer to leave this to policymakers in each country and economic area, and this may create strong debate around the world. The banks are likely to resist the introduction of tough measures and could be aggressive in exploiting any future differences between national regimes. However, the goal in developing these global standards is to raise the bar significantly for the management and supervision of liquidity risk at banks.

1.5 Managing liquidity risk

The ability to predict and plan for bad days can be a powerful weapon in the financial manager's arsenal. But whilst managers typically have a feel and sense what is right or wrong in terms of amounts, prices and access to funds, this may ignore other events that might have an influence on the cost or the ability to fund a certain position in a certain currency in the short term. What is needed is a more coherent framework for measuring liquidity at risk.

So, how can liquidity risk be measured? As you know, liquidity risk is the risk that a financial institution has an unexpected short-term cash flow gap at the end of a value day. Almost independent of the cause, measuring this risk requires an understanding of incoming and outgoing cash flows and how they are generated. As a result, the net funding requirement at the end of the value day is the variable that has to be determined in order to gain a feeling for the magnitude of the liquidity risk.

1.5.1 Maturity ladders

Cash is the lifeblood of any business, a fact that has been brought into sharp focus by the global economic climate. Should a firm not have sufficient cash resources available to meet its obligations as they fall due, then the results for that business can be catastrophic. This applies just as much to a corner shop as it does to a global bank. Cash flow forecasting is therefore a vital role of the treasury function – by being able to map accurately incoming and outgoing cash flows through collecting as much relevant information as possible, treasurers and money managers can ensure that their firm is operating at maximum efficiency by putting in place the necessary short-term funding measures. This will always be a difficult balancing act. If the firm has too many assets in liquid form, then these funds are not working hard enough and are getting a lower return than they could get if they were invested and used elsewhere. However, as we have discussed, if we do not have enough liquid funds available when required, then the results can be catastrophic.

In securities settlement for example, once the settlement instructions have been sent out, both parties have to ensure that they will have the cash available to pay for their purchases, and the stock available to deliver for their sales. Therefore, most settlement systems incorporate a cash flow projection module. Sometimes this module is referred to as a **maturity ladder**.

The same approach can be applied to any cash flow projection model to whatever the type of business relates.

QUICK QUESTION

What are the main cash inflows and outflows for a bank?

Write your answer here before reading on.

Basel recommends that a maturity ladder should be used to compare a firm's future cash inflows to its future cash outflows over a series of specified time periods. Cash inflows arise from maturing assets, saleable non-maturing assets and established credit lines that can be tapped. Cash outflows include liabilities falling due and contingent liabilities, especially committed lines of credit that can be drawn down. In the table on the following page, the maturity ladder is represented by placing sources and amounts of cash inflows on one side of the page and sources and amounts of outflows on the other.

In constructing the maturity ladder, a firm has to allocate each cash inflow or outflow to a given calendar date from a starting point, usually the next day. (A firm must be clear about the clearing and settlement conventions it is using to determine its initial point).

As a preliminary step to constructing the maturity ladder, cash inflows can be ranked by the date on which assets mature or a conservative estimate of when credit lines can be drawn down. Similarly, cash outflows can be ranked by the date on which liabilities fall due, the earliest date a liability holder could exercise an early repayment option, or the earliest date contingencies can be called. Significant interest and other cash flows should also be included.

The difference between cash inflows and cash outflows in each period, the excess or deficit of funds, becomes a starting-point for a measure of a firm's future liquidity excess or shortfall at a series of points in time.

It is this net funding requirement that requires management. Typically, a firm may find substantial funding gaps in distant periods and will endeavour to fill these gaps by influencing the maturity of transactions so as to offset the gap. For example, if there is a significant funding requirement 30 days hence, it may choose to acquire an asset maturing on that day, or seek to renew or roll over a liability. The closer a large gap becomes, the more difficult it is to offset. Thus, firms will typically collect data on relatively distant periods so as to maximise the opportunities to close the gap before it gets too close – and too costly. Most would regard it as important that any remaining borrowing requirement should be limited to an amount which experience suggests is comfortably within the firm's capacity to fund in the market – remember, having more liquid assets than necessary means a missed opportunity for the firm to utilise these funds more profitably.

As already indicated, net funding requirements can be calculated from the cash in and outflows for every value date.

In this respect, the use of a value ladder or maturity ladder is useful, because it helps us understand trends in cash flows. Many financial institutions use these ladders in order to manage the day-to-day business. The diagram below shows such a maturity ladder for a hypothetical financial institution based on the total inflows and outflows for the end of the value day.

Incoming flows are marked by grey shaded areas above the centre line and out-flows are marked by the heavier shaded areas below the line. The net funding requirements are represented by the black line. Left from the vertical value date line are historic cash flows and right from the line are projected cash flows based on known maturities. The latter contain a certain element of uncertainty, which becomes greater the further into the future the cash flows are projected.

Cash flow maturity ladder

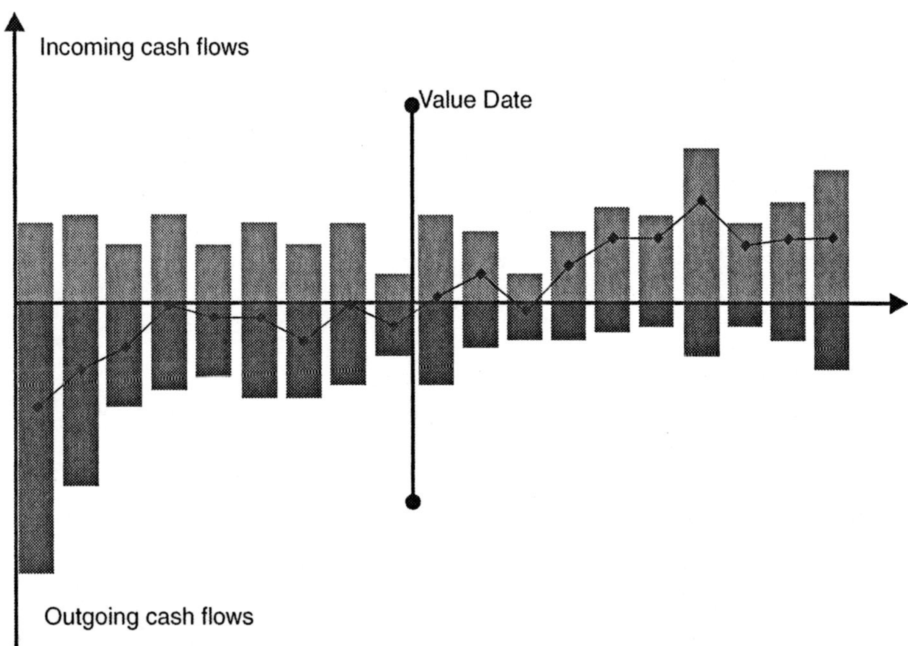

The net funding requirements for the next couple of value dates can be determined accurately by looking at the maturity ladder. Hence the potential liquidity risk can also be calculated accurately assuming that the liquidity resources are known.

This approach gives financial institutions an effective tool to monitor the liquidity risk continuously and anticipate potential liquidity risk in advance.

Incorporating the cash flows for future value dates can however become quite involved. A whole spectrum of products and their behaviour at value date has to be taken into account as well as the deposit and other products. One of the biggest issues for example is the group of financial products that have built-in triggers based on credit ratings. If those triggers become effective, then in a relatively short timescale quite huge amounts of liquidity have to be moved.

Nevertheless, the fact that a treasurer already has some understanding of future trends (as opposed to a portfolio manager managing market risk) should basically help to determine the net funding requirements at a fairly accurate level for the future value dates.

1.5.2 Actual and contractual cash receipts

The cash receipts and disbursements method of accounting (the cash method) is based on the theory of actual receipts and actual payments. Accordingly, under the cash method, income is recognised generally at the time it is actually received into the business.

On the other hand, contractual cash receipts are those which arise as an agreement under a contract where cash is credited/ debited at a date as agreed contractually despite the cash not actually having been paid.

It is easy to see the risk here with respect to liquidity concerns. What if an entity goes bust under a contractual arrangement before the actual cash movement have been executed?

1.5.3 Asset liquidity risk

QUICK QUESTION

A liquid asset has a number of features. What do you think they are?

Write your answer here before reading on.

These features include:

- It can be sold rapidly, with minimal loss of value, any time within market hours.
- There are ready and willing buyers and sellers at all times.
- The probability is that the next trade is executed at a price equal to the last one in a liquid marketplace.
- There are ready and willing buyers and sellers in large quantities. This is related to the concept of market depth that can be measured as the units that can be sold or bought for a given price impact. The opposite concept is that of market breadth measured as the price impact per unit of liquidity.

An illiquid asset is an asset which is not readily saleable due to uncertainty about its value or lacking a market in which it is regularly traded. The mortgage related assets which resulted in the subprime mortgage crisis are examples of illiquid assets as their value is not readily determinable despite being secured by real property. Another example is an asset such as large block of stock, the sale of which will affect the market value.

Asset liquidity risk describes the phenomenon that risk is attached to any asset that cannot be sold due to a lack of liquidity in the market where the sellers and buyers for that asset meet. In some ways it is a subset of market risk and it is characterised by the following:

- A widening of the bid offer spread
- Setting aside explicit liquidity reserves
- Lengthening the holding period for VaR calculations.

This aspect of liquidity risk arises where a party interested in trading an asset cannot do so because nobody else in the market wants to trade in that asset. Liquidity risk therefore becomes particularly important to those parties who are about to hold or currently do hold an asset since it affects their ability to trade. It is not the same phenomenon as a dip in the price of an asset – that is market risk. If market value drops to zero, an asset would be worthless. However if one party cannot find another counterparty interested in trading the asset, this potentially is a problem for them both – one of illiquidity in the market. This is commonly demonstrated in thinly traded markets, perhaps those of emerging markets or ones here there is low volume activity.

QUESTION TIME 1

What assets are particularly liquid and particularly illiquid?

Write your answer here then check with the answer at the back of the book.

Liquidity risk tends to compound other risks. If a trading organisation has a position in an illiquid asset, its limited liability to liquidate that position at short notice will compound its market risk. This is often demonstrated in securities markets where a firm has offsetting cash flows with different counterparties on a given day. If a counterparty that owes another firm a payment defaults on that payment the firm will have to raise cash from other sources to make its own payment in turn. Should it be unable to do so, it too will default. This is an example of liquidity risk compounding the fundamental credit risk (or counterparty risk).

1.5.4 Funding liquidity risk

This development of liquidity risk refers to the risk that liabilities present liquidity risk in so far as they:

- Cannot be met when they fall due
- Can only be met at an uneconomic price – for example shares in RBS when they were in free fall
- Can be name-specific or systemic.

The materialearlier concerning maturity ladders and liquidity at risk address this aspect of funding liquidity risk. It will be necessary for any market participant to be able to have the ability to borrow funds or to borrow assets to meet funding liquidity risks in order to meet their commitments to others in the marketplace. This is a normal element of securities settlement fails management.

It was demonstrated in 2008 that a committed available line from an illiquid bank or insolvent bank may prove unavailable, as was seen by companies with facilities from Icelandic banks and Lehman Brothers.

Even if a company had own funds available, the expected liquidity of those funds during the period under consideration is important. Funds deposited with Lehman Brothers or Icelandic banks became unavailable and other institutions threatened to follow suit. This experience shows therefore that holdings of securities may become illiquid or immediately realisable only at a material discount.

Examples of collapses resulting from liquidity risk

There are some other powerful examples of films collapsing under the weight of liquidity issues. The three which follow below are presented in chronological sequence.

CASE STUDY

Long Term Capital Management

A US hedge fund, Long-Term Capital Management (LTCM), was bailed out by a consortium of 14 banks in 1998 after being caught in a cash flow crisis when economic shocks resulted in excessive mark-to-market losses and margin calls. The loss was finally stated to be $4.6bn. The flaws in its trading strategies were finally triggered by the Russian financial crisis during August and September 1998 and the resulting flight to liquidity. The fund suffered from a combination of funding and asset liquidity. Asset liquidity arose from LTCM's failure to account for liquidity becoming more valuable (as it did following the crisis). Since much of its balance sheet was exposed to liquidity risk premium its short positions would increase in price relative to its long positions, which worked greatly to its detriment as it was forced to close out positions at increasingly more severe levels of loss. This was essentially a massive, unhedged exposure to a single risk factor. LTCM had been aware of funding liquidity risk. Indeed, they estimated that in times of severe stress, haircuts on AAA-rated commercial mortgages would increase from 2% to 10%, and similarly for other securities. In response to this, LTCM had negotiated long-term financing with margins fixed for several weeks on many of their collateralised loans. Due to an escalating liquidity spiral, LTCM could ultimately not fund its positions in spite of its numerous measures to control funding risk.

CASE STUDY

Amaranth Advisors

Amaranth Advisors, another US hedge fund, lost roughly $6bn in the natural gas futures market in September 2006. Part of the story is attributable to liquidity issues. Amaranth had a concentrated, undiversified position in natural gas futures contracts spreads. Brian Hunter, the Canadian trader behind the fund's strategy, had used leverage to build a very large position, representing around 10% of the global market in natural gas futures. The inability to sell a futures contract at or near the latest quoted price is related to a firm's concentration in the product. In Amaranth's case, the concentration was far too high and there were no natural counterparties when they needed to unwind the positions. As indicated, they owned a sizeable portion of the open interest (the outstanding contracts on the market), and as such were greatly exposed to illiquidity when they least wanted it. Their other error was the lack of diversifying strategies in their overall investment portfolio (everything depended on natural gas). They also had incorrectly read the gas market, for in the previous year they had been highly successful in a similar gas related strategy but the market prices at that time were hugely boosted by the effect of Hurricane Katrina and the price behaviour did not perform in the repeat fashion twelve months on.

The Amaranth losses were not as threatening to the financial system as had been the losses of Long-Term Capital Management, but it has led to increased pressure on the SEC (the US Securities and Exchange Commission) to regulate hedge funds.

CASE STUDY

Northern Rock

As outlined earlier in this section, in the UK, Northern Rock, a building society which had been demutualised into a bank, suffered from funding liquidity risk, which culminated in September 2007 due to the onset of the subprime crisis. The firm was over-exposed to the sub-prime mortgage sector and suffered from short-term liquidity issues despite being solvent at the time. It had famously depended on strong liquidity in the interbank market, which dissipated as the credit crisis took hold. In response the PRA now places greater supervisory focus on liquidity risk especially with regard to high-impact retail firms.

1.6 The potential impact of liquidity risk

Liquidity risk has to be managed in addition to market, credit and other risks. Owing to its tendency to compound other risks, it is difficult or impossible to isolate liquidity risk alone. In all but the most simple of circumstances, comprehensive metrics of liquidity risk do not exist. A simple technique, already described, is that of the maturity ladder which shows future cash flows on a day-by-day basis going forward. This approach will highlight any day that has a sizeable negative net cash flow that is of concern. Such an analysis can be supplemented with stress testing. Cash flows can be examined on a day-to-day basis with the assumption that a particularly large counterparty might default. It is easy to understand how the market defaults and liquidity issues of the market in 2008 have changed firms' approaches to the management of liquidity risk in current times.

Another aspect to be considered is contingent cash flows, such as cash flows which occur with respect to derivatives or mortgage-backed securities. If a firm's cash flows are largely contingent, liquidity risk may be assessed using some form of scenario analysis. A general approach utilising scenario analysis might involve the following steps:

- construct multiple scenarios for market movements and defaults over a given period of time
- assess day-to-day cash flows under each scenario.

There is also a systemic risk level to these liquidity concerns and this is what occupies the attention of financial regulatory authorities across the world.

1.7 Liquidity gap analysis

Gap analysis is a technique of assessing a future scenario of excepted activities and highlighting the potential risks as gaps. It might refer to a project or business case or equally validly to a set of cash flows. Hence the name - liquidity gap analysis.

The use of gap analysis for assessing liquidity risk involves the bucketing of cash flows. Fixed amount cash flows will be straightforward to plot. The cash flows from floating rate instruments are bucketed according to their maturity. The actual values of floating rate cash flows will not be known but estimated values may be used. The idea of liquidity gap analysis is to anticipate periods when a portfolio will have large cash outflows. Such buckets are called **liquidity gaps**.

A shortcoming of gap analysisis the fact that it does not identify mismatches within buckets. An even more significant shortcoming is the fact that it cannot handle options in a meaningful way. In today's markets, options and optionality proliferate. Fixed income portfolios routinely hold caps, floors, swaptions, mortgage-backed securities and callable bonds for example. Options have cash flows whose magnitudes – and sometimes timing – is highly uncertain. Those uncertain cash flows cannot be bucketed. For this reason, gap analysis has largely fallen out of use. Today, gap analysis is most useful as a theoretical tool for communicating issues related to interest rate and liquidity risk.

1.8 Stress testing

Any risk modelling approach needs to be stress tested to show that the model stands up under various scenarios and to assess and qualify the predicted outcome and in order to make judgments as to mitigation strategies. One of the main drivers for effective liquidity risk management is to employ stress tests, which consist of performing scenario analyses with regard to market conditions, business strategies and client behaviour.

For testing their liquidity contingency,banks willrun stress tests on market, credit and funding liquidity risks under static and dynamic analyses combined with going concern scenarios. It will be necessary to be flexible enough in its approach to address all types of scenarios for testing the firm's liquidity risk contingency under stress conditions.

QUESTION TIME 2

Using your newly acquired knowledge of stress testing gained earlier on in this course, produce a list of scenarios that a bank might use to test liquidity risk.

Write your answer here then check with the answer at the back of the book.

1.9 Expected future funding requirement

As with any business activity – be it a start up, takeover or project of any kind the key question will be the ability to obtain the cash funding necessary to complete the exercise successfully without difficulty. Clearly, all funding plans need to be managed as with any other enterprise. With respect to normal day-to-day transactions and liquidity planning, the task of providing ongoing funding falls to the company treasurer and the finance department.

The major issue here is one of confidence that liquidity management is being conducted with respect to risk contingency planning. Consider the fact that Bear Stearns had more than $12 billion of available collateral the day before it failed and more than $2 billion when it failed. Confidence not cash was king in March 2008. However that is not to say that cash is not king in other circumstances and traditionally it always has been.

Liquidity risk managers need to forecast future cash flows. Part of that exercise requires forecasting potential liability losses across different scenarios and at different stress levels. Another method is to estimate how stable the liabilities and cash resources are. The word stickiness has been used within Basel thinking for defining the tendency of funding not to run off quickly under stress conditions.

There are eight identified characteristics that individually, and certainly in combination, determine this concept of stickiness with respect to firms.

(1) Is the liability an insured deposit? Government-insured deposits are not what they used to be, as the case of some federal owned mortgage and home-loan structures attests (Countrywide, a US mortgage lender for example).

(2) Is the liability secured? This implies that it is backed by some quality collateral.

(3) Are the funds controlled by the owner? This refers to the fact that the funds are unencumbered.

(4) Does the depositor or liability counterparty have other relationships with the bank, such as loans? If the depositor does have such a relationship then it is more unlikely that they will want to move all their deposits elsewhere.

(5) Is the depositor or liability counterparty a net borrower? If so, they might take comfort in their right of offsetting their deposits and advances.

(6) Does the funds provider lack internet access to the funds? This refers to the ability for customers with online relationships being able easily to move funds electronically and therefore move deposits to other firms to obtain better interest rates.

(7) Is the depositor or liability counterparty financially unsophisticated? This refers to the phenomenon whereby those who don't follow financial news closely are unlikely to remove their funds quickly.

(8) Did the bank obtain the deposits directly rather than through a third-party deposit broker? Brokered deposits are more likely to be volatile. Brokers may be bound by mandates, perhaps by dint of the law, only to place deposits with strong banks and so, given a confidence issue with the bank, they are likely to withdraw their deposits.

In times of great stress in the marketplace, when customers are seeking to remove funds from a financial institution (think of Northern Rock), banks in particular must be prepared to increase the physical cash levels that are available in their ATMs. In the modern world customers from other banks are able to withdraw cash from any other bank's ATMs and an issue of confidence might result if a bank's ATMs run out of cash. Similarly banks must be prepared to raise the amount of cash kept in their branches and to extend their operating hours, as evidenced with Northern Rock and the problems suffered by RBS in June 2012 when a software upgrade resulted in customer's salary credits being delayed. In line with this, again addressing modern business delivery mechanisms, firms must make sure that their websites have greater bandwidth in times of stress than is needed in normal market situations. The capacity should be increased to be at least twice the recent maximum level of activity.

1.10 Diversification of funding sources

Firms will be well advised to limit holdings of assets with no reasonably objective second means of valuation even if they are highly liquid today. This was made very evident in the economic crisis period.

The same thing holds true with sources of funding. A business cannot run out of cash and must manage its cash requirements daily. This will lead to the need for funding facilities. These may be standby credit lines or borrowing facilities. If several liquidity providers are on call then if any of those providers increases its costs of supplying liquidity, the impact of this will be felt. While a company is in good financial shape, it may wish to establish durable, ever-green (i.e. always available) and liquid lines of credit. The credit issuer should have an appropriately high credit rating to increase the chances that the resources will be there when needed.

Diversification is just as important with respect to liquidity provision as it is with respect to investment portfolio cover.

1.11 Employing liquidity limits

When firms are addressing their liquidity contingency planning there are a number of indicators that can be built into the risk management system in order to present control over and warnings with respect to potential limit breaches. These will address the following:

- Regulatory limits
- Prudential limits
- Primary liquidity (with respect breaching prudential limits)
- Movements in the ratings from any of the credit ratings agencies
- Wholesale funding profile
- Foreign exchange maturity profile
- Credit spread alterations
- Wholesale finding costs.

Bank liquidity was brought sharply into focus in the UK when the collapse of Northern Rock was revealed in 2007. Resulting from this many observers said that banks and building societies should have quantitative liquidity limits built in respect to their risk management practices. These will be particularly valuable for short-term measurement.

1.11.1 Counterparty credit limits

Credit risk limits are part of a well-designed limit system. They should be established for all counterparties (including all clients) with whom an institution conducts business, and no dealings may begin before the counterparty's credit limit is approved – as would be the case with an overdraft limit arranged for a business or personal customer. The credit limits for each counterparty must be aggregated globally and across all products (i.e. loans, securities, derivatives) so that a firm is aware of its aggregate exposure to each counterparty. Procedures for authorising credit limit excesses must be established and serious breaches reported to the supervisory board. These limits should be reviewed and revised regularly. Credit officers should also monitor the degree of credit risk utilisation by each counterparty against its limits. Researching the identity and legal status of a new client should be part and parcel of any credit assessment of new counterparties. Staff should be encouraged to put a face to all counterparties and should not take for granted a client's reputation into authorising unjustified credit lines. Explicit research and verification should be fulfilled in every case.

1.12 Scenario analysis

As you now know, scenario analysis is a process of analysing possible future events by considering alternative possible outcomes. The analysis which results is designed to enable improved decision-making in risk management to be achieved because it allows consideration of outcomes and their implications. In financial markets, a firm might attempt to forecast all possible scenarios with respect to market conditions, market returns and even whole economy events. These can be broken down into various subsets of information addressing different asset classes and the liquidity operating within each of these. Computer models can be employed to calculate the resulting outcomes using statistical analysis (typically standard deviation) to reveal normal and extreme scenarios. In essence the key lies in the ability to be able to assign probabilities to different scenarios. Other references in this course refer to scenario analysis which can be applied to various aspects of risk management.

1.13 Liquidity at risk

Another question we might attempt to answer is,how much does a financial institution have to fund on a bad day? As an additional constraint to this question, the answer should be applicable to situations that have not previously arisen. This is the start of liquidity at risk (LaR). It is akin to Value at Risk (VaR) where we wish to establish the worst case scenario with respect to market risk exposure.

We have already established a basic understanding of liquidity risk and the exposure a financial institution incurs. Applying the concept of the maturity ladder can create a very detailed picture about the liquidity risk in the present, but does it make any statement about the likelihood that this risk will crystallise in reality?

The following is proposed to determine the likelihood of such an event to occur:

$$\text{LaR} = \text{p(liquidity)} - \text{CaR}$$

Where LaR is Liquidity at Risk, p (liquidity) is the probability to access a certain amount of liquidity and CaR is Cash Flow at Risk.

In order to rationalise the concept of LaR we must take a more detailed look at the net funding requirements and the ability to raise liquidity when needed.

1.13.1 Cash flow at risk

Net funding requirements can be represented in a very different way than described above to create a powerful metric.

Imagine first a series of buckets that represent intervals of amounts, i.e. one bucket might represent the funding requirement between -10million to -8million currency units, another one from -8million to -6million currency units and so forth. The buckets will also include long amounts in order to create a comprehensive picture of the net funding requirements.

Now the actual net funding amounts over a defined time interval are counted and put into the corresponding buckets. Amounts between -10million and -8million might be counted 12 times, whereas those between -8million and -6million might be counted 16 times.

What is created at the end of this exercise is a frequency analysis similar to the diagram below. This represents how often certain amounts fall into given amount intervals (buckets).

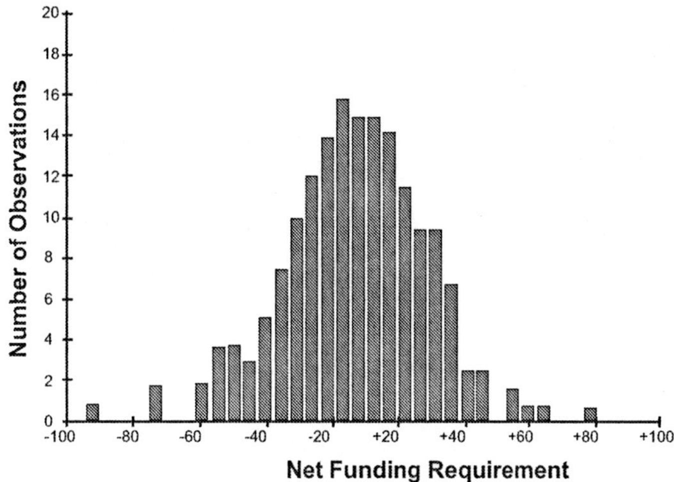

This frequency analysis basically tells the treasurer how often the financial institution is long or short in a particular amount as well as the average amount that the financial institution is long or short.

However, the diagram holds even more interesting information than the calculation of an average could ever give. Looking at the lower number of occurrences on the left half of the curve reveals that the hypothetical financial institution was once almost 100million currency units short and twice almost 80million currency units short. On the other side, the financial institution was once 80million currency units long.

Assuming a distribution can be fitted to the frequency analysis, presents the probability that these extreme short positions will occur. In other words, if a bad day, in the definition of the treasurer, means having to fund 60million currency units, then a probability can be attached to how likely this will happen.

This representation helps the treasurer to prepare for unforeseen events because statements can be made about the probability of certain events, even though they have never previously arisen. For example, with the fitted distribution it can be determined that there is a 1.5% probability that the treasurer will have to fund 60million currency units. We can assert that this will happen three times within 200 business days but it is still unknown whether it will happen within three consecutive days or once a month or with some other completely random pattern.

However, since it is known that it will happen, appropriate measures can be taken to mitigate these events.Be aware however of the fact that these analyses are related to a single currency framework.

Once a financial institution has more than one single currency in which to manage cash flows, other currencies may be used as a provider of liquidity.

You should note the similarity of this approach to VaR models. Liquidity at risk is basically an extension of liquidity risk into the techniques that are applicable to the modelling of market risk exposure under the description of value-at-risk or VaR. This is an attempt therefore to quantify the actual amount of liquidity risk according to specific parameters, just as is performed under VaR.

1.13.2 Accessing liquidity

The second variable in LaR refers to the probability of access to liquidity, i.e. can the required amount be accessed at reasonable cost?

It is clear that certain products are more liquid than others. It is therefore helpful to tier the available assets with regard to their liquidity and distinguish between those which are very easily liquidated and those that are illiquid. It is also assumed that a so-called fire sale can be accomplished within a few days, i.e. that there are no operational constraints that prohibit a rapid conversion of assets into necessary liquidity.

Depending on whether the liquidity risk manager is managing LaR in a single or in a multiple currency framework, the range of products to liquidate is different.

In a single currency framework, a liquidity risk manager aims to liquidise money market instruments with the highest liquidity first, then bonds, equities, etc. according to his or her evaluation of which can be most efficiently liquidated. Depending on the amount of financial assets to be sold, market liquidity, depth of the market as well as the time horizon in which liquidity has to be provided, may each have an impact on the price, which has to be taken. Only once all financial assets have been sold will the institution start liquefying tangible assets and intangible assets.

In multiple currency frameworks, a liquidity risk manager may sell the cash amount held in other currencies before accessing other liquidity sources to cover shortfalls in currencies with negative liquidity. Such a decision, however, may be overlaid by a strategic currency allocation depending on the liquidity risk manager's expectations of future currency exchange rates. Depending on his or her expectation either the sale of another currency's cash position or the sale of money market instruments in the same currency are reasonable ways of accessing liquidity.

QUESTION TIME 3

You have guaranteed a loan for a friend and they have defaulted on payment. As a result, their lender has called up the guarantee, which you now need to honour. The amount is £15,000.

In what order would you liquidate your assets to make this payment?

Write your answer here then check with the answer at the back of the book.

1.13.3 Why liquidity at risk is useful

Treasurers have, of course, a feel and sense what is right or wrong in terms of amounts, prices and access.

However this view negates or ignores all other events that might have an influence on the cost or the ability to fund a certain position in a certain currency for the next couple of days.

LaR is a measurement that can tell the treasury that there is a 95% probability, for example, that it will have to fund an extraordinary amount at least once a year. This should help to prepare for those cases and as a result keep at least funding costs down. If it is included in a sound risk management policy it should help the treasurer to cover his positions even if the market is turbulent.

The beauty of LaR is that it summarises this particular risk in a single number and can be held against the risk management policy. LaR also recognises and summarises future outcomes even though they are not known. This is the real strength of LaR.

1.14 Diversification

In the same way that market risk and investment risk can be mitigated by diversification, the same thing applies to liquidity risk in markets – **market liquidity risk.**

In financial markets, diversification is an accepted fundamental technique for risk management similar to hedging and requires the spreading of activity and exposure in order to reduce overall risk. It is an avoidance of concentration risk or the dependence upon one asset, one process or one marketplace. When applied to markets and liquidity within those markets the fluctuation of any single market, its dislocation or higher volatility will have less impact upon a diversified portfolio hence diversification of market activity across different markets will minimise the risk that accrues from any one individually. However should markets correlate and impact upon each other the degree of diversification offset may well be diminished.

There are three levels of diversification which could be used with respect to the strategy to be adopted. The first of these could be to spread activity across multiple investments or markets. The second approach is to vary the risk in any one individual market and the third is to vary the exposure by a geographical split.

QUICK QUESTION

Can you identify a weakness associated with the geographical spilt technique?

Write your answer here before reading on.

Financial markets are global and therefore the contagion risk of liquidity or volatility sharply moving from one market to another across the globe is only to be expected and this may militate against the benefits of the third strategy outlined above. However the more that diversification horizontally across markets and vertically within them can be secured the greater will be the capacity for reducing liquidity risk.

1.15 Behavioural analysis

Analysis of market behaviour is the central component with respect to making intrinsic decisions about calculating the fundamental value of assets in markets and the risk management component at the end of the cycle (see diagram below).

The fundamental value is a function of the cash flows that an asset would generate for its owners subject to any appropriate discount rate. This discount rate will be impacted by the risk-free rate of return, inflation and risk premium.

Market behaviour analysis addresses the understanding that the market environment where prices are not reflecting intrinsic value. The third segment of risk management is a disciplined process of capturing investment opportunities in the right relationship to their significance and the risk which attaches to any particular investment.

Market behaviour analysis is the name given to the understanding of the prevailing state where there are discrepancies between price and value as demonstrated in a market. In order to manage this element, investment managers will concern themselves with the timing and magnitude of any strategic change to actively managed portfolios. The requirement is to be able to make investment decisions but to recognise potential deviations due to market liquidity and the length of time that fundamental mis-valuation could persist. This is achieved by a process-driven approach rather than a reactive or ad hoc one. It will enable investment managers to be able to understand market price discrepancies which move away from the stated intrinsic value. For example why is the market falling? Why is the market too far away from intrinsic value?

The job of market behaviour analysis therefore is correctly to identify market movements, liquidity shifts and dislocations and to factor them into effective decisions to modify the forms of investment strategy. This may address the ability to use leverage and the ability to identify any bias in attitudes to risk in response to market information.

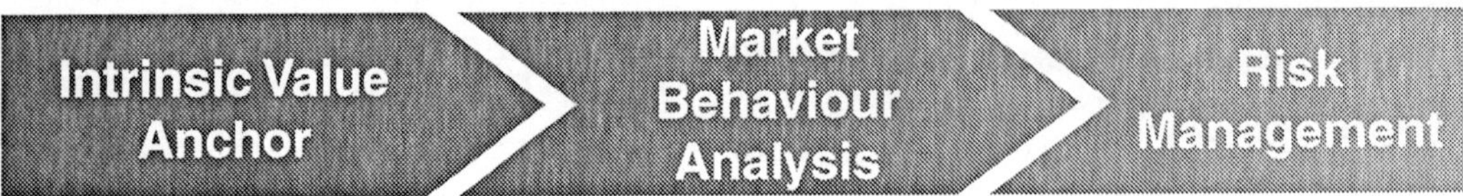

1.16 Netting

Netting is defined as the set-off of two or more cash flows, assets, or liabilities. The types of netting used are payments or settlement, close-out, bilateral or multilateral. Firms establish their netting rights through various means including legally binding set-off agreements, collateral agreements, facility agreements, security agreements and the terms and conditions of trading (including ISDA Master Agreements when considered appropriate). Where documented rights to net have been established a net limit may be used for exposure assessment and monitoring.

Netting of cash flows or obligations is a means of reducing credit exposure to counterparties. Two forms of netting are widely employed in derivatives and other markets – these are payment and closeout netting.

Payment netting reduces settlement risk. If counterparties are to exchange multiple cash flows during a given day, they can agree to net those cash flows to one payment per currency. Not only does such payment netting reduce settlement risk, it also streamlines processing.

Closeout netting reduces pre-settlement risk. If counterparties have multiple offsetting obligations to one another – for example, multiple interest rate swaps or foreign exchange forward contracts – they can agree to net those obligations. In the event that a counterparty defaults, or some other termination event occurs, the outstanding contracts are all terminated. They are marked to market and settled with a net payment. This technique eliminates cherry picking whereby a defaulting counterparty fails to make payment on its obligations, but is legally entitled to collect on the obligations owed to it.

With **bilateral netting**, two counterparties agree to net with one another. They sign a master agreement specifying the types of netting to be performed as well as the existing and future contracts which will be affected. Bilateral netting is common in the OTC derivatives markets.

Multilateral netting occurs between multiple counterparties. Typically, it is facilitated through a membership organisation such as an exchange. Multilateral netting has the advantage that it reduces credit exposure even more than does bilateral netting. It has the disadvantage that it tends to mutualise credit risk. Because credit exposure to each counterparty is spread across all participants, there is less incentive for each participant to scrutinise the creditworthiness of each other counterparty.

With multilateral netting, all parties' obligations are netted. Specific rules are adopted for allocating residual obligations to the non-defaulting parties.

While netting can be an effective means of reducing credit exposures, it can raise legal issues. Many jurisdictions do not recognise the enforceability of closeout bilateral netting agreements, arguing that such agreements undermine the interests of third-party creditors. Responsible legal counsel should be consulted before entering into any netting arrangement.

1.17 Market dislocation

During 2008 in particular there were was great evidence of global dislocation in financial markets. The term dislocation refers to markets which are erratic and highly volatile and have moved from stable conditions to erratic scenarios. The resulting instability and volatility created huge impact upon market and investor confidence and this is very explicitly characterised by a marked reduction in liquidity. Around September and October 2008 at the time of the Lehman Brothers collapse and many other linked events it was greatly evident how the benchmark interest rates, particularly those represented by the UK Libor benchmark, were spiking greatly above normal levels. The same thing was happening in credit spreads comparing the pricing of corporate and even investment grade debt securities against government risk-free benchmarks.

One of the principal consequences in the UK and beyond of the crisis in the financial markets was the steps taken by central governments to inject liquidity into the financial systems and to require (and participate in) the recapitalisation of the banking sector to restore confidence to the market. In the UK this was demonstrated most obviously by the intervention with respect to RBS and Lloyds Banking Group.

Following the market dislocation as described there has been even more rigorous focus on the governments, accountabilities and execution capabilities to ensure adherence to an even lower risk profile. Major banking groups in particular (including the British banks referred to above) have learned lessons from the credit crisis and the risk culture of those firms has been reappraised with respect to improving their ability to limit ongoing exposure.

As has been made evident to banking institutions throughout the world, the market dislocation necessitated improvement and further development of credit, liquidity and market risk control frameworks. Credit spreads and the ability to stress test and model them has been of particular significance. Liquidity control frameworks have needed to be improved and these map across to oversight of funding, capital and asset liability management issues.

2 Market risk

2.1 The nature of market risk

Market risk is the risk that the value of a market position or investment portfolio will decrease due to the change in value of the market risk factors.

Market risk is managed with a short-term focus. Long-term losses are avoided by avoiding losses from one day to the next. On a tactical level, traders and portfolio managers employ a variety of risk metrics – such as duration and convexity. A common market risk methodology that is used is referred to as 'the Greeks'. The Greeks are a series of derivatives risk measures with different names (such as delta and vega) that measure the sensitivity of the value of an asset or portfolio to a change in an underlying parameter. For example, vega measures the sensitivity to volatility. There will be specific Greek limits in place to ensure that risk taking is limited to within the risk appetite of the organisation. On a more strategic level, organisations manage market risk by applying general risk limits to traders' or portfolio managers' activities, such as counterparty and country limits. Increasingly, value-at-risk is being used to define and monitor these limits. Some organisations also apply stress testing to their portfolios.

2.2 Different types of market risk

Many types exist, which are described below.

2.2.1 Price level risk

With respect to market risk, the fundamental axiom with respect to markets is that prices move all the time. This is **price level risk**. The price of every tradable asset is effectively moving every minute of the trading day as a result of supply and demand factors, economic developments and other events. It is the changing price level which presents market risk to anybody who is running a position in the market. This will affect farmers with the price of agricultural commodities; similarly it will affect treasurers and financiers with respect to the cost of money through interest rates and energy and power traders as the price of electricity is priced minute by minute throughout the day.

2.2.2 Volatility risk

In addition to the price level changing, the speed of that change and its magnitude, both up and down – the volatility – represents what is known as **volatility risk**. Flat markets are one thing but markets that spike, swing and plunge are entirely different and volatility risk therefore is the descriptor for the additional risk that not only do prices move but also the speed at which they move and the degree to which they move.

2.2.3 Liquidity risk

Much is presented elsewhere in this course with respect to liquidity risk. There are three variants – asset liquidity risk, financial liquidity risk and market liquidity risk. In this section let us just concentrateon market liquidity risk, which isthe risk that a firm cannot easily offset or eliminate a position at the market price because of inadequate market depth or market disruption. It is an extension of asset liquidity risk.

2.2.4 Currency risk

When trading any asset from another part of the world the base currency of that tradable asset will be different from the home currency and therefore the ability to switch and convert from one currency to another opens the trader to an additional risk which is known as currency risk. For example, if we are dealing in copper on the global market the price will be quoted in US dollars. However we may be a German company where our activities are fundamentally linked to the euro. Therefore the issue of the performance of the dollar against the euro will have a bearing upon any investment, trading or hedging strategy that we might put in place.

2.2.5 Basis risk

Basis risk is encountered when hedging positions using futures contracts. Itrepresents the difference between prices in the spot market and the cash market, i.e. the price right now as against the future or forward price when looking ahead into the cost of carry going forward. It is therefore a familiar concept with forwards and futures markets.

Hedging is not an exact science – there is no such thing as a perfect hedge This means that it is not always be possible to eliminate risk altogether. This difference is known as the basis risk.

If the basis between the future and the underlying price remained constant, then it would be possible to have a perfect hedge. Factors which affect the basis risk are easily visible. For example in commodity markets, products such as crude oil have many different qualities or grades. The oil which is being hedged may be of a different quality, and may be being delivered to a different location, to the oil as defined in the futures contract specification. This causes fluctuation in the basis risk. It is very important when hedging that this basis risk is measured constantly.

Basis can change as a result of:

- Changes in supply and demand
- Changes to the cost of carry, e.g. interest rates, insurance costs, dividend yields
- Changes in time remaining to expiry (convergence).

2.2.6 Interest rate risk

All trading and investment is subject to the value of money and the price at which it can be obtained. This presents the phenomenon of interest rate risk. With interest rates at fixed levels there is little volatility and therefore plans can be made by anyone who is wishing to borrow or lend money. However should the Federal Reserve in New York or the European Central Bank change interest rates then everything that is geared to those interest rates with respect to the US dollar and the euro will be altered. The relationship and differentials will be reset. Should interest rate change announcements be unexpected, they will have a greater effect upon the reaction in the market and therefore present a greater market risk.

2.2.7 Commodity risk

Commodity risk represents the shortage of supply, which is a phenomenon quite commonly experienced in commodity markets. For example there is little crude oil available or there is a squeeze in the supply of aluminium or perhaps there is little available coffee owing to a poor harvest in the main coffee growing countries of the world. So the availability therefore for consumers and traders to plan with respect to availability of commodities which are linked to commercial industrial programmes presents an additional risk of the availability and with it the freedom of supply of the commodity concerned. Clearly the price of the commodity will also be presenting an issue but this is covered in the concept, which we have already established, of price level risk.

2.3 Boundaries between different types of market risk

There are three other sorts of risks connected with market risks which present obvious boundary issues. By boundary issues we mean whether this is pure market risk or another sort of risk(s) resulting from a situation.

For example a trader with a position in equities markets will be affected by the very price of the equities or the index of the equities market in which they are trading and that is quite simply market risk. At the same time however, that trader will also be faced with the counterparty risk or the credit risk of those counterparties with whom he is trading being able to deliver with respect to the securities that he has purchased or has sold to others in the marketplace. In this way therefore there is a clear boundary between credit risk and market risk and this occurs in every conceivable type of asset trading.

Another boundary issue is that of concentration risk which also interfaces directly with market risk. In this context we are considering a concentration of activity in one particular asset or market. Let's consider for example a particular financial setback in a particular country such as happened in Russia in August 1998. If a trader was heavily exposed to the price of fixed income securities in Russia then not only would there be a market risk with respect to the prices and their volatility but there would also be the concentration risk boundary issue as to the fact that the trader's positions were heavily concentrated upon the Russian marketplace in particular. Thus concentration risk maps across as a boundary issue to market risk itself.

2.4 Systematic risk (market risk)

Systematic risk – another phrase relating to market risk – is the risk that markets generally will fall, for example because of a sudden switch in market sentiment, or a major change in the economy or in government policy. In 1987, major world stock markets fell by 20% in two days. This illustrates the sometimes dramatic effects of systematic risk, when the whole market can be affected.

Suppose that the economy generally is performing poorly. Consumer demand may be weak, affecting companies generally. The international political situation may be seen as fragile. Such factors can affect market confidence and investment values generally. If share prices generally are falling and returns are declining, then a wide and diversified portfolio of shares is very likely to fall in line with the wider market. The risk of this happening affects the whole system – the market. Systematic or market risk cannot be diversified away by holding a range of investments in that particular market.

Research has shown that almost all the investment-specific risk is eliminated in a portfolio of as few as 15 to 20 securities. What remains in such a portfolio is market risk. The diagram below illustrates the components of risk and the decline of risk as the number of investments increases.

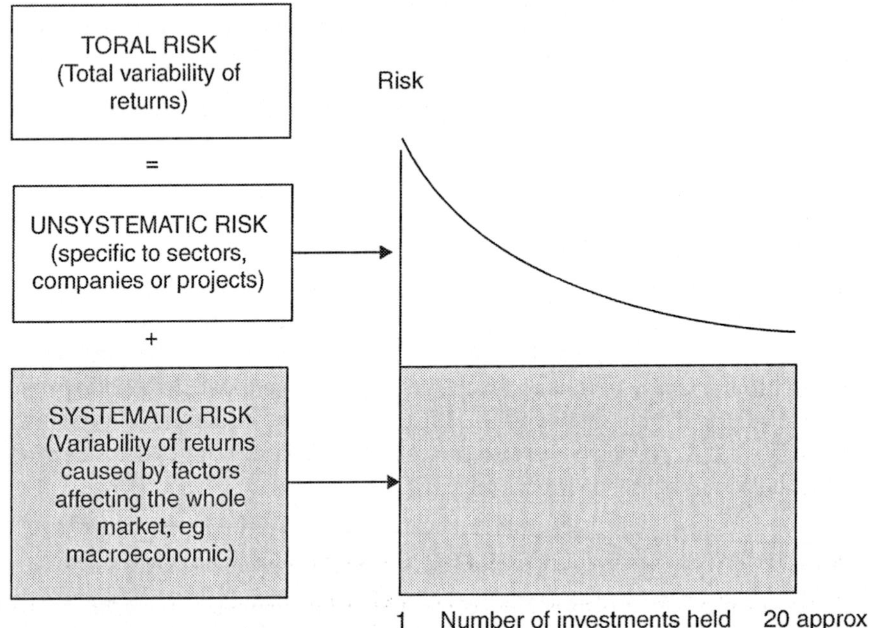

Once a portfolio contains about 20 shares in different companies in different sectors, most (but not all) of the unsystematic risk is diversified away. However, systematic risk is not affected by diversification.

Market risk is characterised by a number of subsets as follows:

- Price level risk – this is due to the potential for adverse movement in the price of any instrument or asset and will include exposure to foreign exchange or currency risk, interest rates, equity prices, commodity prices, energy prices, etc.
- Volatility risk – this is the risk of price movements that are more uncertain than usual affecting the price of assets.

- Liquidity risk – or to be more precise market liquidity risk, which is the risk of loss through not being able to trade in the market or obtain a price on an asset when it is required.
- Basis risk – this occurs when one kind of risk exposure is offset with another exposure (through hedging) in an instrument or by an instrument that behaves in a similar but not identical manner. It reflects the uncertainty of the difference in the impact of the market factors on the prices of the two instruments.

Consider the following examples.

- On Black Monday October 19th 1987, stock markets around the world crashed shedding 20% of their value in a very short time. Starting in Hong Kong the market phenomenon spread west across all international time zones. There is some uncertainty as to the reasons why the phenomenon occurred and indeed it has been labelled as a hard to predict high-impact event – (sometimes known as a Black Swan event) being a rare event beyond normal expectations.
- Also consider the phenomenon of the commodity prices, for example for copper and aluminium, as the huge economic engine of China was consuming all the raw materials it could lay its hands on in the period through 2006-7 yet once the credit crunch began to take effect the demand for copper decelerated fairly rapidly and this had a direct effect upon the copper price which went into decline. This was magnified further by the removal from commodity investment of many hedge funds (indeed hedge funds were greatly affected and were reined back hugely by the credit crunch events) and this had a further dampening effect upon copper prices.

QUESTION TIME 4

What other Black Swan event can you think of?

Write your answer here then check with the answer at the back of the book.

Both these examples illustrate that markets are affected by economic fundamentals and this includes market confidence. Thus lying at the heart of any market risk issue will be concerns about understanding what information is available about a market, what factors are impacting upon a market and the prices within it and the relationship between market prices and boundary risks involving credit limits and general information.

2.5 Mitigation and management of market risk

2.5.1 Hedging

QUICK QUESTION

Hedging is an oft-quoted word in financial services. What is your understanding of it?

Write your answer here before reading on.

Hedging is the word used to describe any activity which offsets or mitigates a risk in taking a position in a market. Hedging one's bets, is a phrase associated with offsetting the chances, say in betting on a horse race, by diversifying or laying off risk elsewhere. Hedging is a common practice amongst bookmakers who place alternative bets to cover any potential losses from their own book.

Hedging in financial markets is a position established in one market in an attempt to offset exposure to price fluctuations in some opposite position in another market with the goal of minimizing one's exposure to unwanted market risk. There are many specific financial vehicles to accomplish this, including insurance policies, forward contracts, swaps, options, many types of over-the-counter and derivative products, and perhaps most commonly, futures contracts. In essence, derivatives are used to hedge risk and there are many types of derivative product. Although there were some earlier examples, organised futures markets were established in the mid-1800s in Chicago to allow transparent, standardised products, which could deliver an efficient hedging mechanism for agricultural commodity prices in the burgeoning agricultural markets of the American Mid-West at that time. Those early steps led the way in establishing the very wide variety of exchanges of today offering futures contracts for hedging the values of energy, base and precious metals, foreign currency, equity market and interest rate fluctuations.

A good example of hedging in action might be provided by considering a fund manager who is controlling a portfolio of equity investments in UK stocks, all of which appear in the FTSE 100. If the fund manager feels that the value of the level of the FTSE 100 (a benchmark index for the value of leading UK shares) was likely to fall, then clearly they will be exposed to a fall in the value of the investment portfolio. In order to mitigate this, the manager could hedge this exposure by selling futures contracts to the same contract value on the FTSE 100 index (such a product is listed by NYSE Liffe). If the FTSE 100 level does fall, the short futures position will gain in value thus offsetting the falling value of the portfolio. Thus the fund manager will have entered into a 'short hedge', by selling futures. Long hedges (the reverse) are similarly possible and work in the opposite manner to militate against the cost of underlying instruments rising. So buyers of underlying assets use long hedges and sellers use short hedges, because the former is exposed to market prices rising and the latter is exposed to prices in the underlying (FTSE 100 in the earlier example) falling.

2.5.2 Market risk limits

Risk limits (or simply limits) are a device for authorising specific forms of risk taking.For example, abank hires a group of traders to deal on its behalf in the foreign exchange and money markets. The bank wants to make profits and knows that risks will need to be taken, but it needs to have some specific controls over the level of its risk in the market. The headline policy will therefore establish limits on the overall sizes of market position that any individual trader can run in the market. These will be aggregated across products and across different dealing desks, each of which will have a limit. There will be a daylight limit and an overnight limit beyond which the traders may not deal. It will also preclude products or markets in which it does not permit its traders to trade. Alongside these measures there will also be a set of credit risk controls against counterparties and customers, which may also be subject to position limits.

Hence the system of limits, as defined is intended to control the exposure. Limits will be kept under review in line with changing market circumstances and will be amended as and when necessary.

There are many sorts of limits which can be applied. Here are some suggestions:

- Positions (foreign exchange and interest rates)
- Diversification – by currency and maturity band to avoid over-concentration of risk
- Spreads – control risk that related products may behave inconsistently
- Permitted instruments
- Optionality – option values do not move in straight lines
- Maximum loss limit
- Mark-to-market referral limit for accrual book positions
- VAR – aggregate exposures in terms of potential loss (at branch level only).

A bank or other financial institution might have thousands of limits in place; so the task of controlling them is not insignificant. Consider the number of dealers and traders working across the world's markets for a single major international bank. Different time zones, different products, different currencies would all come into play.

The limits must be embedded into the company and the resultant shape might look like the following:

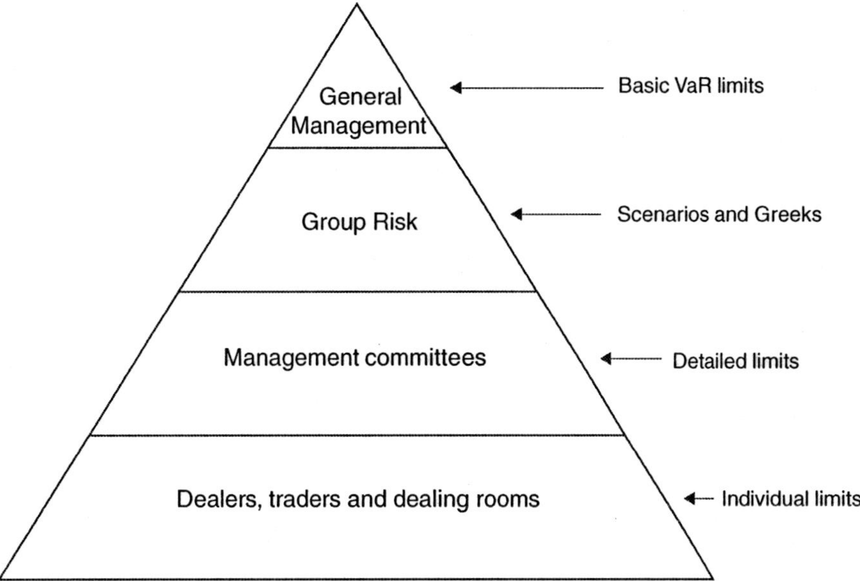

Limits are set using a top-down process. There must be a daily control of all risks against their limits. Daily reporting and aggregation will be addressed at a higher level within the firm.

Market risk limits should be reviewed at the end of each year by the operating divisions (trading or treasuries) according to the business plan for the following year. Changes during the year are possible but will need justification. Limit requests are submitted by the risk manager to the market risk committee (or equivalent), which authorises the limits after presenting them to the general group executive committee (or such similar body). Only major changes need to be escalated to that level; the market risk group would have the authority to approve minor changes.

Once approved, the risk manager allocates the limits to profit centres and dealers according to the business needs, as well as considerations about dealers' experience, markets' fluctuations and budgets. Financial control will be responsible for implementing the limits in the relevant systems and for monitoring overnight exposures against limits. Intraday limits are monitored by the risk manager. Limits therefore are:

- Requested by the business units
- Approved by the board in accordance with policy and structures
- Approved by the risk management group
- Delegated to desk heads and dealers by the risk manager
- Implemented in relevant systems and monitored as at the close of business by the financial control group
- Monitored intraday by the risk manager.

Basel requires that a firm implements exception based reporting. This requires reporting of authorised and unauthorised deviations.

2.5.3 Diversification

Diversification strives to smooth out risk events in a portfolio so that the positive performance of some investments will neutralise the negative performance of others. Therefore the market risk exposure of one asset, be it a bond, share or commodity, is offset by other uncorrelated assets; the benefits of diversification will hold only if the securities in the portfolio are not perfectly correlated.

The goal of diversification is to reduce the risk in a portfolio. Volatility is limited by the fact that not all asset classes, commodities, industries or individual companies move up and down in value at the same time or at the same rate. Diversification reduces both the upside and downside potential and allows for more consistent performance under a wide range of economic conditions.

2.6 Market risk management

An effective market risk management function must operate alongside other risk management activities within a firm. The particular focus of attention of the market risk group will be with respect to managing the trading activities of a firm and managing the positions and exposures taken in the markets in which the firm is trading or making markets.

The most fundamental aspect should be that the firm should not trade in markets and take risks in assets that it does not understand

The principle techniques to manage market risk are to use market risk limits, to operate a diversified trading policy and to hedge market risks in an effective manner. This last point, of course, normally requires the use of financial derivatives.

Although these processes are well understood the market risk management function should also have systems for evaluating the risk of markets particularly through VaR models and have the ability to model or mark-to-market their risk at all times. Ideally the ability should exist in real-time but certainly should be done no less frequently than daily. Modelling requires the use of assumptions and data and the sources and origins of each of these inputs must be reviewed.

2.6.1 Controls on traders

The trader will have a series of positions that arise as a result of the instruments entered into and any risk passed to them to trade out. Since positions are all available for sale they should be marked to market intraday and also at end of day. Limits need to be applied at both stages.

Mark to market provides the snapshot of the value of positions held. If the market is sufficiently liquid then these prices will be reliable. If not then the default is to mark to model. There is a need to have two pricing feeds to ensure that inconsistencies are identified.

When a firm is unable to mark to market it needs to mark to model. There is still a need for independent valuation to be applied. So that probably means that two models will be required. The pricing must be independent from any interest in the price.

The market price volatility of any instrument can be measured and tracked. Interest rates and yield curves can be measured and predicted.

The dealers will generally dislike all of the controls that the firm will be seeking to employ and it is not uncommon to find that they take steps to avoid them. However, some trading desks are intrinsically risk averse and see themselves as part of the risk management function, reducing the risk in the institution. Others take a different viewpoint and seek to earn income for the firm through market manipulation of varying forms.

The consequences of not having adequate controls on traders can be severe, as shown by the collapse of Barings Bank in 1995. Nick Leeson was the general manager of Baring's Singapore futures market operation. However, he was making profits by executing unauthorised speculative trades. While his unauthorised trading was successful at first, he soon began to lose money, which he managed to hide in Baring's error accounts. His losses totalled £827 million, which led to Baring's being declared insolvent and Leeson fleeing to Singapore.

Despite this scandal, similar large scale unauthorised trading events have occurred in recent years: Jerome Kerviel was a trader at Societe Generale who used his knowledge of the bank's computer systems to execute trades that exceeded his trading limits. When his fraudulent trades were eventually discovered in 2008, his losses totalled €4.9 billion. In 2011, Kweku Adoboli, a trader at UBS was arrested on fraud charges for unauthorised trades that caused losses of $2.3 billion.

Risk managers must ensure that traders understand what they are responsible for. They should understand what the procedures are and understand the supervisory structures.

2.7 Stress testing

Stress testing is performed in order to test the reliability of a system or component to carry out a designated task for a particular period in a specific environment.

Reliability is a probability. A model will normally take a level of stress that is reasonably possible, although unlikely. Sensitivity deals with the expected level of an event. It shows a unitary movement in a key variable and is therefore looking at what is expected. The stress test takes a series of these consecutive sensitivity analyses and comes up with a result for something that is possible. The firm wants to know what would be the impact of this actually happened – say interest rates moved by 20 basis points (a common stress test), or a major flood occurred (a scenario example).

2.7.1 Benefits of stress testing

Stress testing enables an organisation to assess the impact on its business of significant but likely changes to its business. This can lead to some form of risk mitigation strategy, which will enable the board to understand the risks they are running and take action if necessary. Such mitigation strategies will relate to the type of risk being stress tested; for market risk there is hedging to consider. Positions could be closed out if their uncertainty causes a problem; derivatives can transform the exposure.For credit risk there is the use of credit derivatives; additional collateral can be taken to change a risk profile, or loans can be called in, repaid or replaced/rescheduled.For operational risk there are remedies like better controls, better trained staff and insurance.

2.7.2 The approach to stress testing

Here some basic high-level ideas to apply to planning a stress testing exercise:

- first understand your business
- then identify key elements that vary
- then work out the distribution that fits the data

- then vary the data by unitary amounts
- then evaluate the differentials.

That is what firms should be doing, using a systematic approach. The big question is, what are they actually doing? The failure to do this analysis properly leaves boards in a difficult position – they do not really know the full impact upon their business of unitary changes of key variables.

2.7.3 A framework for stress testing

It is recommended to start with understanding the risks that exist within thefirm. Then decide upon the key variable that you are seeking to stress. Next, decide which stress tests you intend to address. Finally, decide upon the level of stress testing that is appropriate

There are four main areas where stress testing tends to be used – market risk, credit risk, treasury and operational risk. To some extent treasury should be treated separately since this will cover the banking book as opposed to the trading book. In all cases it is important to start by thinking through the risks of the different areas and then consider the stress test that could be applied. However, in most actual cases companies are really doing scenario tests looking at actual events and judging what are the key lessons that come from them.

Firms will need to decide how much they want to do and how much is it realistic to conduct. As indicated previously, they must consider which risks are suitable for stress testing and this will start with those where sensitivity analysis can be applied. The tests can then take that to an extreme in the stress environment.

Firms are under stress in various parts of their activities, they originate from varying causes. Firms need to decide for themselves which types of stress could affect their business and plan accordingly. These might originated from operational events, credit issues and liquidity shortages or from others. The implications of operational failures for example need to be thought through.

2.7.4 Market risk stress testing

With market risk stress testing, the firm should have a clear idea of what constitutes normal market conditions. From this foundation, it will be easier to determine and identify when there are abnormal market conditions. The next question will be to decide whether the firm can use standard approaches toits market stress testing and from that to go on to decide what are likely to be the key market risk stress tests that they will employ. Some of the issues surrounding the planning of the market risk stress tests will be:

- What stress tests are suitable for the firm?
- What level of stress testing will we want to do?
- How often will we conduct your stress tests?
- How will we report our stress tests?

2.7.5 The problems with market risk stress tests

There are inevitably some drawbacks and obstacles:

- Stress tests are mostly used in market risk.
- Market risk modelling makes assumptions.
- If considering a single variable is this realistic?
- Is varying more than one variable too hard?
- How good is the modelling in the first place?

2.7.6 Real event models

Here are some real-life events which can be used as comparators or examples in planning stress test scenarios:

- Black Monday (18 – 20 October 1987)
- Bond market crash (18 – 21 February 1994)

- Emerging market crisis (24 – 28 October 1997)
- Financial market crisis (July – October 1998)
- Czech' scenario (May 1997)
- Credit crunch (pre-2007 to 2008)
- Lehman Brothers collapse (September 2008)
- Oil prices hikes
- 1973-1974 oil price movement
- Both Gulf wars
- Property price volatility.

In addition to modelling the normal VaR calculations, one can also carry out a subjective test to attempt to establish what the risk positions might possibly lose given a worst case scenario.Remember that a normal VaR is a figure that is unlikely to be exceeded more than the confidence level would indicate in normal trading circumstances.

There will be times when your positions get caught up with significant market moves, outside the normal expectations. So that we can get a feel of what the potential worst case down side may be, applying the worst cases that you can conceive will arrive at the stress test figure. In terms of an equity position you may emulate the 1929 crash or the 1987 market turmoil. For emerging markets, you might use the 1989 tiger economy crash. For foreign exchange you might use the EMU crisis. In addition to emulating the worst cases that you can imagine, you would remove all correlation.

Some stress tests produce figures showing market movements of in excess of 15 standard deviations in movement.

3 Insurance and investment risk

3.1 Insurance risk

Banks tend to make economic capital provision for insurance risk as part of a general pool of other risks. As many banks typically offer insurance products to customers which include wealth management, term assurance, annuities, property and payment protection insurance products, they therefore face insurance risk with respect to the potential of claims resulting under the insurance policies under which they are obligated.

Other contracts that do not contain significant insurance risk are generally classified as investment contracts, which thus face investment risk. Within this group would be financial assets and liabilities relating to investment contracts and asset-backed insurance contracts which may be treated under a different international accounting standard.

Premiums are recognised as revenue proportionally over the period of the insurance coverage. Claims and claims handling costs would be charged to income as incurred based on the estimated liability for compensation owed to policy holders arising from events that have occurred. These would be based on assessments of individual cases reported to the bank together with supporting statistical analysis of the claims incurred but not reported. Also typically liabilities under unit-linked life insurance contracts (such as endowment policies) would reflect the value of the assets held within discrete investment pools.

3.2 Investment risk

The Basel Committee issued the text of its Basel III rules in December 2010. The chief element of this textis to include many controls with respect to managing liquidity risk within banks because the committee felt that this was the risk element that had been overlooked and poorly managed during the credit crisis. The Committee believes that the higher levels of capital required under Basel III combined with a global liquidity framework will significantly reduce the probability and severity of banking crises in the future. The Basel III thinking is in line with the G20 agenda set in place by the G20 members in September 2009.

The new Basel set of rules incorporates measures to promote the build up of capital that can be drawn down in periods of stress together with the introduction of two global liquidity standards. These are known as the Liquidity Recovery Ratio (LCR) and the Net Stable Funding Ratio (NSFR). This is a long-term commitment and the Basel Committee recognise that there will be a transition period in order to assess whether the proposed design and calibration of the new measures will operate satisfactorily across a full credit cycle and for different types of banking business models. Therefore there will be a period of migration up to the beginning of 2018 before implementation will be final. Banks will have until 2015 to meet the LCR standard and until 2018 to meet the NSFR standard.

The goal of the Committee is that the increased capital and liquidity standards contained within Basel III will gradually raise the level of high quality capital in the banking system, increase liquidity buffers and reduce unstable funding structures. Banks have been given ample time to move to these new standards alongside a backdrop of a drive for economic recovery across the world's markets.

3.3 The measurement of investment returns

3.3.1 Currency risk

This describes the risk that the value of an asset or the income from it may vary with exchange rate movements. **Currency risk**is the risk arising from fluctuations in the value of currencies against each other. A UK resident (that is, someone whose home currency is sterling) who buys stocks or bonds in other currencies, for example the euro or the US dollar, faces currency risk.

As we discussed earlier in this chapter, suppose that a UK investor buys shares in a US company which does most of its trading in the US. The share price in US dollars fluctuates on the US stock market. Additionally, the value of sterling fluctuates against the US dollar. Therefore, the sterling value of the investment will fluctuate in time as a result of twoeffects: the changing dollar share price, and the changing US dollar/sterling exchange rate.

QUICK QUESTION

Currency risk can be removed by investing only within the UK. Do you agree or disagree with this statement and why?

Write your answer here before reading on.

Exposure to currency risk is not totally avoided by investing within the UK due to globalisation and the traditional overseas looking nature of UK businesses. Many UK companies do much of their business abroad. This means that their earnings will be affected by exchange rate fluctuations. If a UK company manufactures goods in the UK using domestically sourced raw materials, and exports much of its products to the European Eurozone countries, then it is exposed to a rise in the value of sterling against the euro. If sterling rises in value, the euro-priced receipts from the company's Eurozone sales will buy fewer pounds sterling than before.

Some companies hedge their foreign exchange earnings or their foreign raw materials costs, to give them greater certainty about future earnings and to reduce currency risks. This may be done, for example, by entering into forward currency contracts, fixing the value of future transactions of the company in advance.

Some larger multinational companies have costs and revenues in many different countries, and they may also have shareholders in many different countries. Since shareholders will be based in various currency areas, there may be no currency hedging strategy that serves all shareholders equally. In general, a company may seek to hedge currency exposures in such a way that currency risks between input (raw materials) costs and the income from that production are hedged. Then, each production unit should have a chance of meeting its profit targets without being affected too much by exchange rate fluctuations.

For any investor purchasing overseas or international bonds, there is obviously also the risk of currency movements.

3.3.2 Interest rate risk

The possible future movement of interest rates affects borrowers and savers in conversely different ways.

QUICK QUESTION

In what ways will this risk be different for borrowers and savers?

Write your answer here before reading on.

The following examples of interest rate risk help illustrate this point.

(a) A rise in interest rates is a risk for a borrower who is borrowing at a variable rate.
(b) A saver with a variable rate account faces the risk that interest rates will fall in the future.

A borrower who locks into a fixed rate mortgage rate is protected against a rise in rates of interest for the fixed period. However, the possibility that the fixed rate he locks into could be higher than prevailing variable rates, if rates fall in the future, could be seen as a risk he takes on if he locks into the fixed rate deal.

Conversely, a saver who locks into a fixed rate account without instant access, or carrying penalties for withdrawals, may be worse off than he might have been with a variable rate account, if interest rates rise during the period of the investment. The term income risk can be used to refer to the possibility that the income from a fund will fluctuate due to changes in interest rates. Another use of this term concerns the risk carried by individuals that their salary or wages will fall.

3.3.3 Bond risk

The income (coupon)from a bond remains the same through its life. However, during the life of the bond, there are factors that can make the bond more or less attractive to investors. These factors lead to the price of bondschanging. Investments are subject to systematic risksarising from general market conditions and changes, such as:

- Economic prospects
- Government policy decisions
- Changes in inflation
- Changes in interest rates generally.

If interest rates rise, the prices of bonds will generally fall.The reason for this can be seen if we appreciate that investors will require a particular level of return, depending upon rates of interest generally. If interest rates rise, investors' required rate of return rises. That means that they will be prepared to pay less for a particular bond with a fixed rate of interest than they were prepared to pay previously. If interest rates generally fall, then investors will be prepared to pay more for a fixed-rate bond than previously, and bond prices will tend rise.

QUESTION TIME 5

To illustrate this point, calculate the actual return on 10.5% Treasury stock if the price for £100 of this stock is:

- £115
- £103

Write your answer here then check with the answer at the back of the book.

This mechanism can be appreciated more clearly by thinking of investors' required return determining the yield they expect from bonds. Yield is a measure of the rate of income paid out as a proportion of the bond price. The rate of income does not change, but the bond price changes, and thus the yield changes.

Investors will generally require a higher return if the expected rate of inflation rises. Therefore, prices of fixed-rate bonds will tend to fall with rising expectations of inflation. However, index-linked bonds have a coupon that is linked to the inflation rate, with the result that the price of index-linked stock will tend to rise as higher inflation is expected.

Macro-economic factors can lead to changes in interest rates and therefore to changes in bond prices, particularly changes in inflation rates or in real rates of return.

Another fundamental risk with bonds is issuer quality and the risk that a bond may neither be redeemed nor the coupon interest serviced throughout its life by the issuer. Such credit issues were addressed in the discussion on credit risk.

3.3.4 Equity risk

This describes the risk that an investor's or a fund's equity investments will depreciate because of stock market dynamics causing a loss. **Equity risk** is, as with most investments, linked to risk and reward. The measure of risk used in the equity markets is typically the standard deviation of a security's price over a number of periods. The standard deviation will delineate the normal fluctuations one can expect in that particular security above and below the mean, or average. Movements above the mean are profitable and would not constitute risk per se.

When owning equity investments, an investor may receive dividends – which are profit distributions payable at the discretion of the firm – and may enjoy capital appreciation in the form of a rising share price; but whether the payment of dividends is an option for management is directly dependent on the company's performance (its profitability); and a rising share price depends on the market's assessment of the company's performance.

In other words, the value of an equity investment rides on the company's ability to be successful and profitable at whatever it does in the economic environment and the market's ability to recognise that success. Therefore it is an example of investment risk.

The market perception part of this riskiness is a more tricky issue than the hard facts of whether a company is actually likely to be successful and profitable.There are companies with a strong track record which the market consistently fails to value as such; and, even more unbelievably, companies with no track record at all, upon which the market places a very high value.

Capital risk is the possibility of loss of some or all of the original capital invested.This can be a very significant form of risk, with potentially devastating results to the unwary investor. Holding equities (shares) presents a capital risk. With purchases of individual shares, there is the risk that the value of the investment will fall, and it could be totally wiped out. This can be particularly so for shares in newer smaller companies without a track record and without a full stock exchange listing. A company might be set up to develop a new product, such as a new type of hydraulic pump, with no revenues expected for four to five years after the company is set up. If revenues fail to materialise and the company is liquidated, all of the investors' capital could be lost. If an investor had invested half of his savings in the company, the personal effect on that investor would be dramatic. Real-life events as examples include Enron, Refco Woolworth's and RBS.

Especially for derivative investments, such as futures contracts, options or contracts for differences (CFDs), it is possible to lose more than the original capital invested. Such investments can be geared so that they offer the prospect of magnified gains, but also the risk of magnified losses.

3.3.5 Commodity risk

Commodities as an asset class present many un-correlated opportunities when compared against other asset classes because of a lack of price correlation. **Commodity risk**principally refers to the uncertainties of future market values and of the size of the future income, caused by fluctuation in the prices of commodities. Commodities are very diverse in terms of usage, origin, attributes, quality and delivery/storage mechanisms. As a group, they include grains (wheat. corn, rice), soft commodities (coffee, cocoa and sugar, for example), metals, oil, gas and electricity.Investors first will need to consider price risk (arising out of adverse movements in world prices, exchange rates, the basis between local and world prices). A commodity enterprise needs to deal with the following kinds of risks:

Producers (farmers, plantation companies, and mining companies) face price risk, cost risk (on the prices of their inputs) and quantity risk. Buyers (consumers, commercial traders and processors) face price risk between the time of original purchase and subsequent sale, typically at the port, to an exporter. Exporters face the same risk between purchase at the port and sale in the destination market and may also face political risks with regard to export licenses or foreign exchange conversion. Governments face price and quantity risk with regard to tax revenues, particularly where tax rates rise as commodity prices rise (generally the case with metals and energy exports) or if support or other payments depend on the level of commodity prices.

3.3.6 Property risk

An investor may suffer from **property risk** associated with illiquidity. A sale can only be made if a buyer can be found and this can prove a great problem. During the early 1990s, with a stagnant housing and property market few buyers of residential property could be found and prices fell. Many homeowners had negative equity: the value of their house fell to below the value of their debt (mortgage). If a client invests in property via the medium of a Real Estate Investment Trust (REIT), property unit trust or investment bond he may suffer similar, although not such acute, illiquidity. Under the terms of these investments the proceeds of a sale may be delayed for up to six months to allow the managers to realise assets to pay the investor.

QUESTION TIME 6

Categorise commonly encountered investments under the following headings:

- Negligible risk
- Low risk
- Low/medium risk
- Medium risk
- Medium/high risk
- High risk

Write your answer here then check with the answer at the back of the book.

3.4 Rates of return from the main asset classes vary

The rate of return (ROR), also known as the return on investment (ROI), rate of profit or sometimes just return, is the ratio of money gained or lost (whether realised or unrealised) on an investment relative to the amount of money invested. The rates of return on certain asset classes will be greater than others. For example, bond returns are linked to the yields offered by fixed interest investments whereas equity returns are linked to the performance of companies in the global economy and will normally demonstrate greater returns over bonds, particularly over the longer term.

Returns on cash investments however depend upon interest rates (set even lower than with bonds as they are a shorter form of investment) and will be poorer than bonds and equities.

3.4.1 Cash deposits

These come in many forms and include bank and building society accounts plus national savings vehicles and income bonds.

The key reasons for holding money as **cash deposits**are security and liquidity.Accounts for holding cash deposits are generally characterised by a high level of security.Capital is very unlikely to be lost, at least in money terms. The purchasing power of capital held on deposit will, however, be eroded by inflation. Against this, there is the reward of any interest receivable, and the rate of interest may exceed inflation, resulting in a real rate of return for the investor.

An important advantage of cash deposits held in instant access accounts is their liquidity. Every investor could have a need for cash at short notice, and so should plan to hold some cash on deposit to meet possible needs and emergencies.

Most people would be best advised to hold some cash deposits before they consider more risky investments.A cash deposit account can serve as a vehicle for reaching a savings target, for example when saving for the cost of a major purchase, or for the deposit (part payment) on a house purchase.

Cash deposits generally earn for the investor a return in the form of interest paid regularly, but no capital growth. Interest is normally paid at a percentage rate on the capital invested, at rates of interest prevailing from day to day, or alternatively at rates fixed over certain periods.The performance of cash deposits as an investment can be measured as a 'real' rate of return by comparing the interest rate with the rate of inflation.

Approximately:

Rate of interest – Rate of inflation = Real rate of return

For example, if annual interest is paid at 5%, and the rate of inflation is 2%, then the real rate of return is 3%.The purchasing power of the cash investment is increasing at 3% per year.

QUICK QUESTION

What risks does a cash depositor face?

Write your answer here before reading on.

From the point of view of risk, cash deposits involve:

(a) Very low capital risk, since capital will be lost only if the deposit taker defaults and is not covered by a government depositor compensation scheme.

(b) Inflation risk, since inflation could exceed the interest payable. While an investor is locked in at fixed interest rates, inflation might race ahead due to unforeseen economic conditions, and the purchasing power of the investor's capital could fall.

(c) Interest risk, if the rate of interest paid is less than could otherwise be obtained on other low-risk investment products or the investor is locked in at a fixed rate for fixed terms, when he might otherwise have been able to take advantage of rising interest rates available in the market.

With a deposit investment, the capital is secure in that the original capital is returned when the deposit is withdrawn, or the account matures, subject to any penalties which will have been made explicit in the terms and conditions of the account. Some degree of capital risk does however exist for the depositor. This is because there is a chance that the deposit taking institution fails, and therefore defaults and will not repay depositors' capital. This happened with the Bank of Credit and Commerce International, which collapsed in 1991.

If a UK deposit taker fails, the depositor will have recourse to the Financial Services Compensation Scheme (FSCS).

3.4.2 Fixed interest securities

This segment contains all corporate and government bond products plus variants of these (convertibles, index linked, treasury bills, zero coupon bonds, local authority bonds, junk bonds and many others).

Fixed interest securities carry more risk than holding money in a deposit account because their capital value varies but the rates of interest payable are normally higher than for cash deposits. Changes in interest rates and other economic factors can affect bond prices. The return on these investments is dependent upon the yield to maturity, which is shown by the shape of the yield curve showing the yields on bonds having different periods to maturity. Bonds from lower quality issuers (companies with poor credit ratings) will have higher yields than higher quality issuers (such as governments), reflecting the different levels of default risk. If held to redemption, the investment cash flows of fixed interest securities are known, assuming that the bond issuer does not default.

3.4.3 Equity investment

Equities are bought and sold by private investors, by large institutions such as life assurance companies and pension funds, and by foreign investors. The investor buys ordinary shares for two main reasons:

- to receive dividends from the company's earnings stream (income)
- to gain from increases in the price of the share (capital gain).

Share prices are influenced by wider factors such as economic conditions and general investor sentiment as well as by specific factors relating to the particular company.Fundamental analysis is concerned with identifying underlying factors that indicate the strength of performance by a company. Investment ratios help in understanding and evaluating a company's shares as an investment.Ratios for similar companies can be compared and it may be possible to identify shares that are currently under-valued. Ratios can also help in identifying trends in a company's performance through time.

Investors in equities usually hope for capital growth in the value of their shares and may also receive income in the form of dividends.There are risks in holding shares: much or even all of the investor's capital might be lost. Diversification can help to reduce the risk, but equities are not suitable for all investors.

The real (inflation-adjusted) returns achieved by equities over the long term can seem impressive. £100 invested in 1899 in a broad portfolio of equities, with income reinvested, would have grown to £815,000 by the end of 2002 (as shown in Barclays Capital studies). Over the long term, global equity returns can be expected to be in the order of 5-6% above the rate of inflation. The ability of equities to produce these returns above inflation reflects the fact that economic growth produces growth in companies' earnings, which benefits shareholders.

Consider also though, that the same £100 from 1899 mentioned above would have grown to £1,200,000 when stock markets peaked at the end of 1999. The risk of equity investment is highlighted if we note that an investment of £10,000 made at the market peak in 1999 would have lost about 33% of its value by the end of 2003, over the space of four years. The value would have fallen to approximately £6,700. That investment then needs to grow by 50% for the investor to get back to their starting position of £10,000: this could take many years.

This illustration underlines the possible downside effects on an investor's capital from the volatility of share prices. There have been periods in which sharp falls in stock markets have occurred – for example, in the USA in 1929, in the UK in 1973-74, globally in 1987, in Japan after 1989 and more recently as a result of economic recession, the banking crisis and the Eurozone crisis.

3.4.4 Commodities

Investment in commodities can be done directly in the commoditiesthemselves or in the shares or bonds of companies who are themselves engaged in the commodities business. There is also the ability to invest in negotiable securities which are directly supported by a commodity as an underlying asset. This is particularly true in the case of precious metals such as gold.

Investing in commodities is complex but can derive quite significant returns and as such is regarded by many investors as a useful adjunct in an overall diversified investment portfolio as an asset class in its own right.

There are three sources of commodity returns. The first of these is the spot price, which is the market price of the commodity concerned. If the spot price moves up after the investor has bought the commodity it can then be resold at a greater price. As much commodity investment can be conducted through derivatives in the form of commodity futures.There is also the ability to generate profit because of the concept of initial margin as commodity futures are leveraged products and the investor is only required to put down a margin amount (let's say 10-20% of the overall value). The balance of the purchase price will be held as collateral in another form and commodity index funds and exchange-traded funds (ETFs) will invest this collateral in a safe asset which delivers a cash yield. A third element of commodity returns is known as the roll yield and this is linked to the fact that futures contracts, because they have the finite expiries, need either to be closed or rolled forward. When rolling the open positions forward and extending the exposure there is a differential between the original investment and the next available forward date. Where the prices for forward dates are lower than the earlier ones the roll yield will be positive and deliver a benefit to the investor. The other, more normal, case is where the roll yield is negative because the forward futures price is greater than the nearby.

There are also some global indices which relate to commodity indices. A good example is the Goldman Sachs Commodity Index (GSCI) which has about three quarters of its value linked to the energy sector.

3.4.5 Alternative investments

There are a number of asset types which are alternative forms of investment, some of which are collectable – fine wines, antiques, stamps and coins, for example. Collectables generally produce no income and can be difficult to value and realise, particularly for unique items. The investment opportunity is for the value to increase but values can change as fashion changes or in cases of changing inflations. Collectables can also be expensive to keep or to store because they are vulnerable to atmospheric change, burglary and other risks. The cost of buying and selling them can be high and they may have low marketability. There is also always a high requirement for specialist expertise and knowledge and investors generally will be vulnerable to unscrupulous operators.

All the various forms of investment discussed in this section also need to be considered with respect to the cost of making the investments and the cost of holding them together with the outturn which is always subject to tax. Therefore issues such as the investor's domicile, withholding tax, the notice period to withdraw funds and the tax exempt structures of certain products (such as ISAs) will have an impact upon investment outcomes. Similarly, hedge fund investment, which is not available to all investors but only to wealthier investors, may have access to structures and techniques not available to everybody in the investment marketplace. Hedge funds, for example, can produce absolute returns of great attraction in certain market conditions but also can be poorly managed and deliver no real value. The notice period with hedge funds is significant (perhaps up to six months) and the fees charged by hedge fund managers will include a profit share fee based on their performance as well as a standard management fee.

On balance therefore, there are several disadvantages to investment in collectable assets.

3.5 Identification andmeasurement of investment risk

A number of different coefficients are used for different situations. The best known is the Pearson product-moment correlation coefficient, which is obtained by dividing the covariance of the two variables by the product of their standard deviations.

Intuitively, covariance is the measure of how much two random variables vary together (as distinct from variance, which measures how much a single variable varies). If two variables tend to vary together (that is, when one of them is above its expected value, then the other variable tends to be above its expected value too), then the covariance between the two variables will be positive.On the other hand, if when one of them is above its expected value, the other variable tends to be **below** its expected value, then the covariance between the two variables will be negative.

Increasingly, many asset managers are relying upon more sophisticated option-adjusted simulation methods, such as Monte Carlo simulation, to account for correlations and non-linear return profiles.

Banks that choose not to implement such models, at the very least, should model user-defined interest rate and volatility scenarios. Such market value stress tests should include horizon re-pricing under various scenarios to capture the effects of variable relationships among key markets, changes in the shape and slope of the yield curve, and changes in liquidity and optionality characteristics.

These are some examples of techniques used to offset investment risk:

Market neutral – arbitrage – Attempts to hedge out almost all market risk by taking offsetting positions, often in different securities of the same company. For example, the fund can be long convertible bonds and short the underlying shares of the company. These funds may also use futures to hedge out interest rate risk. The focuses of these funds is on generating returns with low or no correlation to both the equity and bond markets. These relative value strategies include fixed income arbitrage, mortgage backed securities, capital structure arbitrage, and closed-end fund arbitrage. Typical risk islow.

Market neutral – securities hedging – Invests equally in long and short equity portfolios generally in the same sectors of the market. The aim is to reduce market risk and to generate a return from relative mispricing between the stocks. One technique is **pairs trading** which can be used for pairs of stocks whose prices are closely correlated and tend to move together. If the historical price relationship between them is ever breaks down, a long-short position is established in the two stocks in anticipation of the relationship being re-established. These funds usually have low or no correlation to the market and may uses market index futures to hedge out any residual market (systematic) risk. Typical risk is low.

3.5.1 Alpha and beta factors

Alpha is a measure of the risk-adjusted return of a security or of a fund.Alpha measures the difference between the actual return and its expected performance, given its level of risk as measured by beta.

A positive alpha indicates the investment has performed better than expected, given its level of risk (beta).

A negative alpha indicates the investment has underperformed for a security or fund with its level of risk.

In practice, for funds, a negative alpha is more likely because of the effect of fund management charges in reducing the overall return.

Investment-specific (non-systematic) risk can be reduced by diversification, but market (systematic) risk still remains.The **beta** factor measures the volatility of a security relative to the market as a whole. The higher the value of beta for a security, the greater the movement will be in its return relative to the market.

(a) A security with a beta factor of 1 moves in line with the market. If the market (for example, as indicated by a share price index such as the FTSE-100) moves up 5%, the price of this security is likely to move up 5%.

(b) A security with a beta factor greater than 1 varies more widely than the market. If the market moves up 5%, the price of a security with a beta of 2 is likely to move up 10%.

(c) A security with a beta factor of less than 1 fluctuates less than the wider market. If the market moves up or down 10%, the price of a security with a beta of 0.5 is likely to move up or down respectively by 5%.

Beta shows the measure of a company's common stock price volatility relative to the overall market, i.e. the sensitivity of the stock to general market movements. Thomson Reuter's beta measure, for example, compares the 60-month percentage price change of the stock relative with the percentage price change of a designated local market index.

Beta factors are calculated for collective funds as well as for individual securities. The beta factors forfunds measure the fund's volatility against a benchmark such as the FT-SE All-Share Index, or some otherbenchmark appropriate to the fund.

Betas for funds are generally calculated over a 36-month period, from monthly data.

- A fund with a beta factor of 1 moves in line with its benchmark.
- A fund with a beta factor greater than 1 is more volatile than its benchmark.
- A fund with a beta factor of less than 1 is less volatile than its benchmark.

As with standard deviations, the beta factors are calculated from historical data. Changes in the strategy ofa fund, or changes resulting from a change in manager, may mean that future performance and volatilitydiffer from the past.

3.6 Illiquid assets in relation to investment risk

The liquidity of a product can be measured as how often it is bought and sold; this is known as volume.

A liquid asset has some or more of the following features. It can be sold rapidly, with minimal loss of value, any time within market hours. The essential characteristic of a liquid market is that there are ready and willing buyers and sellers at all times. Another good definition of liquidity is the probability that the next trade is executed at a price equal to the last one. A market may be considered deeply liquid if there are ready and willing buyers and sellers in large quantities. This is related to the concept of market depth that can be measured as the units that can be sold or bought for a given price impact. The opposite concept is that of market breadth measured as the price impact per unit of liquidity.

An illiquid asset is an asset which is not readily saleable due to uncertainty about its value or lacking a market in which it is regularly traded. The mortgage-related assets which resulted in the subprime mortgage crisis are examples of illiquid assets as their value is not readily determinable despite being secured by real property. Another example is an asset such as large block of stock, the sale of which affects the market value.

Such assets demonstrate a form of liquidity risk.

3.6.1 Venture capital

Venture capital (also known as VC) is a type of private equity capital typically provided to early-stage, high-potential, growth companies in the interest of generating a return through an eventual realization event such as an Initial Public Offering (IPO) or trade sale of the company. Venture capital investments are generally made in cash in exchange for shares in the invested company. It is typical for venture capital investors to identify and back companies in high technology industries such as biotechnology and information and communication technology.

Venture capital typically comes from institutional investors and high net worth individuals and is pooled together by dedicated investment firms.

Venture capital firms typically comprise small teams with technology backgrounds (scientists, researchers) or those with business training or deep industry experience. VC has a reputation of being a particularly impenetrable career path, employing only those who bring expert value.

A core skill within VC is the ability to identify novel technologies that have the potential to generate high commercial returns at an early stage. By definition, VCs also take a role in managing entrepreneurial companies at an early stage, thus adding skills as well as capital (thereby differentiating VC from buy out private equity which typically invest in companies with proven revenue), and thereby potentially realizing much higher rates of returns.

A venture capitalist is a person or investment firm that makes venture investments, and these venture capitalists are expected to bring managerial and technical expertise as well as capital to their investments. A venture capital fund refers to a pooled investment vehicle that primarily invests the financial capital of third-party investors in enterprises that are too risky for the standard capital markets or bank loans.

3.6.2 Private equity

In finance, private equity is an asset class consisting of equity securities in operating companies that are not publicly traded on a stock exchange. Investments in private equity most often involve either an investment of capital into an operating company or the acquisition of an operating company. Capital for private equity is raised primarily from institutional investors. There is a wide array of types and styles of private equity and the term private equity has different connotations in different countries.

Among the most common investment strategies in private equity include leveraged buyouts, venture capital, growth capital, distressed investments and mezzanine capital. In a typical leveraged buyout transaction, the private equity firm buys majority control of an existing or mature firm. This is distinct from a venture capital or growth capital investment, in which the private equity firm typically invests in young or emerging companies, and rarely obtain majority control.

There are a number of risks to the performance of privately owned companies. Such entities are, like all companies, vulnerable to macroeconomic shocks such as deep recessions, to sector cycles, to poor strategy and to weak management etc. All of these factors can obviously damage a company's trading performance and profitability. The leveraged nature of private equity backed companies means that they have less of a cushion should costs rise or revenues fall.

By far the most significant perceived risk for private equity owned companies is, however, a sudden increase in the cost or decrease in the availability of debt capital, particularly if this comes against a backdrop of a rapid economic downturn. This could be triggered by a sudden and unexpected material increase in interest rates or a dislocation in the debt market. Such events could cause significant losses for companies and investors alike.

3.6.3 Property

Wealth – the amount in assets that people have – is also related to social structure. In the UK, a large proportion of wealth is held as property, and so increases or falls in property prices can affect wealth significantly. In 1971, 26% of personal sector wealth was in dwellings. By 1991 this had risen to 36%, before falling to 26% in 1995 as a result of declining house prices. Since then, house prices have risen again very significantly before losing value in the recession.

Property has very many similar characteristics to shares as an investment class. Over the long term the value of property tends to rise and the income an investor could derive from it (rent) also rises, just like the capital value and income from shares. There are, however, a number of distinguishing characteristics of property that impact on their suitability as an investment vehicle.

Given their substantial size and the fact that a lender can usually be given security in the form of a legal charge/standard security on the property, property investments are often made with help from borrowed funds. That is, the investment is geared. The gearing effect of borrowing for property purchase can be severe if prices start to fall, and negative equity can even result in some cases where the loan is a high percentage of the property value.

Research shows that, over the long run, investment in property has provided real returns ahead of the returns on cash and gilts and slightly below that of equities. The annualised return for commercial property was 11.6% over the 30-year period to the end of 2001 (Investment Property Databank, IPD estimates). Returns from equities were 13.5% over the same period. The commercial property market has undergone 'crashes' from time to time: between 1989 and 1992, following a period of significant levels of speculative development in London, some office rent levels halved. Property yields are currently looking attractive on income grounds relative to the low yields from government bonds.

3.7 Correlation of performance between asset classes

Correlation is a measure of how the movement of one instrument impacts another. In probability theory and statistics, correlation, also called correlation coefficient, indicates the strength and direction of a linear relationship between two random variables. In general statistical usage, correlation or co-relation refers to the departure of two variables from independence, although correlation does not imply causation. In this broad sense there are several coefficients, measuring the degree of correlation, adapted to the nature of data.

How much will diversification reduce risk in a portfolio? This depends on the degree to which the prices of the different investments chosen move in line with each other – that is, the degree of correlationbetween their prices. If two companies are in the same sector and are relatively similar, then their share prices may move closely in line with each other. If two companies have activities that are complementary in some way, there may be a high degree of correlation resulting from that. For example, personal computer (PC) manufacturers and retailers, as well as micro-chip manufacturing companies, should stand to gain from a surge in demand for PCs.

There is positive correlation between investments, such as the share prices of two companies, if their prices move up and down together. There is negative correlation if the prices tend to move in opposite directions to each other. If prices bear no relationship to each other, then there is no correlation between them.

Diversification is most effective when the investments combined are negatively correlated. The fluctuations or volatility in the price of each investment will then tend to cancel each other out.

Correlations do change over time. This can only happen if the average correlation between domestic and international assets decreases for longer time horizons. Economically speaking, the differences between the domestic and the global market become more important with longer time horizons. If, for instance, the business cycle of the UK economy lags behind the global business cycle by a few months or years – as is often the case – this lag will not manifest itself in lower year one or year three correlations. Except when the business cycle is turning, the economic trend in the UK will be the same as the economic trend all over the world when averaged over three years. When correlations are averaged over longer intervals, there will be periods of co-movement as well as times when the UK economy is still growing while the global economy is already turning. This effect will tend to decrease the correlation between UK and global equity markets, for instance, and hence increase the attractiveness of international assets.

3.8 Tracking error

Passive management involves the establishing of a strategy with the intention of achieving the overall objectives of the fund. A passive fund manager believes that markets are efficient and that no mispricing exists. Once established, this strategy should require little active intervention, being largely self-maintaining.The simplest strategy is to buy and hold. However, perhaps the most common form of passive management is indexation.

With indexation, the fund manager selects an appropriate index quoted in the market place. Having established the index, the fund manager builds a portfolio that mimics the index, the belief being that this portfolio will then perform in line with the index numbers. Such funds are known as index or tracker funds.

Overall, the likelihood is that the fund will underperform the index for a number of reasons. Firstly, there is the cost of creating the portfolio in the first place. However, and perhaps more importantly, all index funds tend to be based on a sampling approach and consequently exhibit a degree of **tracking error**.

It should be noted that indexation itself is not a totally passive form of investment management, since the constitution of each index will, over time, change and as such, the portfolio will also be required to change.Tracker funds will, however, incurlower transaction costs as a result of the lower levels of turnover, an advantage over actively managed funds.

In finance, tracking error is a measure of how closely a portfolio follows the index to which it is benchmarked. The most common measure is the root-mean-square of the difference between the portfolio and index returns. The term refers to a divergence between the price behaviour of a position or a portfolio and the price behaviour of a benchmark. This is often in the context of a hedge or mutual fund that did not work as effectively as intended, thus creating an unexpected profit or loss instead. Tracking errors are reported as a 'standard deviation percentage' difference. This measure reports the difference between the return received and that of the benchmark upon which it was modelled.

Many portfolios are managed to a benchmark, normally an index. Some portfolios are expected to replicate, before trading and other costs, the returns of an index exactly (an index fund), while others are expected to 'actively manage' the portfolio by deviating slightly from the index in order to generate active returns or to lower transaction costs. Tracking error (also called active risk) is a measure of the deviation from the benchmark; an index fund would have a tracking error close to zero, while an actively managed portfolio would normally have a higher tracking error. Dividing portfolio active return by portfolio tracking error gives the information ratio, which is a risk adjusted performance metric.

3.9 Investment mandates

An investment mandate will set out the effective rules under which a portfolio or fund or investment arrangement will be conducted. Inter alia, it will state all the assumptions, objectives and conditions that will affect the conduct of the investment approach. These will include:

- asset classes in which to invest, their origins and styles
- the investment strategy – long, long/short, use of derivatives and the parameters attached
- any other linked investment strategies
- the mix or balance between growth, income and maximising returns
- whether short selling or writing covered derivatives will be permitted
- the style of analysis and research before investments are made with respect to earnings prospects, cost, debt and market liquidity.

The mandate will also link into the corporate governance issues which surround the proper conduct of an investment programme. It will define the history and conduct of the management, the directors and the dominant shareholders and will comment on the treatment of minority shareholders.

It will define the methods of reporting, valuation and transparency connected with the transactions carried out and the manner in which the fund is valued.

The mandate will also need to define its long-term view with regard to market trends with respect to the chosen investment strategy. It is expected that the style of investment may well vary over time and therefore the policy towards valuations and rebalancing of portfolios will need to be addressed as part of the mandate.

The mandate will address the approach to the management of risk within the investment portfolio and in this connection the mandate will need to state the risk management assumptions and policy and thereby define the manner by which various risks will be addressed and managed. It will need to comment on the controls that will be put in place and this will address the general methodology towards risk management. Detailed areas to be considered under this part will define information security, sovereign risk, market and credit risk, the reputational risk of the firm and the general risk tolerance as part of the overall policy under the corporate governance oversight.

The mandate should:

- define the long-term goals and objectives
- identify risks associated with those objectives
- prioritise risks by likelihood and potential impact
- define mitigation strategies for the principal risks
- define the committed resources for implementing risk management strategies
- define the mechanism(s) for continuous monitoring of the effectiveness of mitigation controls in the overall changing risk landscape.

3.10 Mitigating investment portfolio risk

3.10.1 Systematic and non-systematic risk

Systematic risk, as discussed earlier in this chapter, is also sometimes called market risk, aggregate risk, or undiversifiable risk. It is the risk associated with aggregate market returns. Systematic risk is a risk of security that cannot be reduced through diversification. It should not be confused with systemic risk, which is the risk that the entire financial system will collapse as a result of some catastrophic event.

In the capital asset pricing model, the rate of return required for an asset in market equilibrium depends on the systematic risk associated with returns on the asset, that is, on the covariance of the returns on the asset and the aggregate returns to the market. Risk in asset returns that is uncorrelated with aggregate market returns is called specific risk, diversifiable risk, or idiosyncratic risk. Given diversified holdings of assets, each individual investors exposure to idiosyncratic risk associated with any particular asset is small and uncorrelated with the rest of their portfolio. Hence, the contribution of idiosyncratic risk to the riskiness of the portfolio as a whole is negligible. It follows that only systematic risk needs to be taken into account.

Systematic riskor market risk, as previously discussed,is the risk that markets generally will fall, for example because of a sudden switch in market sentiment, or a major change in the economy or in government policy. As you know, in 1987, major world stock markets fell by 20% in two days. This illustrates the sometimes dramatic effects of systematic risk, when the whole market can be affected. The risk that a particular company share will fall in price, irrespective of the overall performance of the market is known as **unsystematic risk**or investment-specific risk.

Diversifying across individual shares (that is, holding a number of different shares) can reduce unsystematic risk of a portfolio of shares.

3.10.2 Optimisation and diversification

The first step every investor should take is to assess his or her individual financial goals and needs. There should also be an assessment of their ability and preparedness to take on risks. Riskier assets like equities in general provide higher returns in the long run but they may also incur significant losses for extended periods. How much risk can be taken on board depends upon various factors such as the starting wealth of the investor, the need to access investment to cover expenses and the timescale of the target investment horizon.

The establishment of a diversified portfolio requires strategic asset allocation which will define the long-term allocation to different asset classes. The number of asset classes invested in should not be too large so as to incur excessive administrative costs. At the same time there are certain asset classes that diversify risks more efficiently than others. The exact allocation per asset class depends on the risk profile. Nevertheless the asset mix and allocation is the most important determinant of the overall risk of the portfolio. Asset allocation risk vastly surpasses risks of market timing, individual security selection and others.

Financial markets are not always fully efficient and this means therefore that investors and fund managers must exploit tactical opportunities to add value by exploiting short-term market deviations. This is an example of optimisation.

Successful active managers will also not only try to exploit short-term opportunities but will also try to select the best stocks, bonds, structured products and other instruments in order to construct the best portfolio. Diversification is of paramount importance. The old adage is don't put all your eggs in one basket to avoid concentration risk. This applies within asset classes and also across asset classes.

Many investors typically are not sufficiently well diversified within different asset classes with concentrated portfolios in just a few investments. Experience has shown that investors in such companies as Enron, WorldCom or Swissair learned the hard way that a concentrated portfolio may suffer much bigger losses than a well diversified one. This also may well have applied to investors in British banking stocks in 2008, which in many cases became distressed very rapidly.

Any portfolio has to be continuously monitored and reviewed. Rebalancing is crucial to ensure that the risk profile of the implemented portfolio always matches the intended risk profile based upon the original strategic and tactical asset allocation. Every professionally managed portfolio is rebalanced to its benchmark weights from time to time. This might be an annual procedure or it could occur more frequently. This is an appropriate method to control the risks of a diversified portfolio. Since portfolio rebalancing implies selling previously successful stocks and buying previously losing stocks it can also be seen as a kind of diversification technique. Rebalancing will tend to generate additional small returns when compared to a portfolio that has not been rebalanced.

Different assets display different returns over time, thus if a portfolio has not been rebalanced due to these return differentials the portfolio composition will deviate from the benchmark.

3.10.3 Portfolio hedging using derivatives

Hedging is generally approached by using derivatives and many product choices exist. Investors sometimes shy away from using derivatives to manage portfolio risk because of the sophistication needed to understand these instruments and the potentially significant losses if derivatives are not used properly. However, derivatives offer unique opportunities to investors who do understand their risks and have concentrated positions in publicly traded securities.

There are a number of strategies that can be used in order to hedge the portfolio position or to enhance the income of the portfolio. All of these techniques are of value to the fund manager. These techniques include selling covered call options where income enhancement can be achieved by selling call options backed by the securities within the portfolio. Another technique is to buy protected put options.

Such products allow an investor to sell stocks at a fixed price until the option expires and this is a hedging strategy that protects the investor against the loss of value if the stock price should drop below a certain threshold. The price of establishing an option position requires the payment of a premium much like an insurance policy. There are also derivative strategies such as collars which by using a combination of options, which can be structured in such a way that the value of the position is limited into a concentrated range. Such a strategy can be achieved at low cost because the purchased options are offset by the proceeds of the sold options in establishing the position.

Equity swaps are another derivative strategy applicable to liquid stock positions. Using such a technique, the fund or investor agrees to give up the cash flows of the stock position and in return receives the cash flows of a diversified index such as the S&P 500 or even the cash flows of a fixed income investment based for example on government bonds or a bond index. The advantage of this approach is that the cash flows are netted regularly so that the behaviour of the concentrated position is effectively exchanged for a more diversified position. On the other hand, one disadvantage of the technique is that typically the stocks given into an equity swap cannot be voted on by the owner of the portfolio but such strictures can often be avoided by careful swap construction. The other significant risk in a swap is the counterparty risk introduced by the counterparty with which one sets up the swap. Should the counterparty default the investor may be exposed to financial losses because there is no central counterparty or intermediary exchange that may cover any losses.

A simple hedge is a portfolio consisting of a long position in the stock and a long position in the put option on the stock, so as to be riskless and produce a return that equals the risk-free interest rate.

3.10.4 Short selling

Short selling (also known as shorting or going short) is the practice of selling assets, usually securities, which have been borrowed from a third party with the intention of buying identical assets back at a later date to return to the lender. The short seller hopes to profit from a decline in the value of the assets between the sale and the repurchase, as he will pay less to buy the assets than he received on selling them. Conversely, the short seller will make a loss if the price of the assets rises. Other costs of shorting may include a fee for borrowing the assets and payment of any dividends paid on the borrowed assets. Shorting and going short also refer to entering into derivative contracts with an equivalent economic effect.

Going short can be contrasted with the more conventional practice of going long, whereby an investor profits from any increase in the price of the asset.

Buying an asset and then selling it later to benefit from a rise in market price is universally an acceptable trade but selling an asset which one does not own but has merely borrowed seems to some observers to be anathema and in 2008 the practice was indeed temporarily stopped using special short selling rules by regulators in the UK and elsewhere, fearing that the act of short selling was driving down market prices.

Short selling is only made possible where securities can readily be borrowed and, to this extent, the lenders of securities, who earn money from their lending activity, are culpable with respect to short selling. Some official investigations (for example the one conducted by the authorities in Hong Kong) into short selling practices found that they were not responsible for depressing the levels of financial and banking stocks during the market volatility in 2008.

3.11 Risk transfer

Financial firms take on risk to make money, for example by granting a loan. If the return drops or the concentration of risk becomes too high, firms may want to reduce the amount of risk they hold. Risk transfer instruments are a wide group of financial products used to transfer risk to another party. This could be the risk of a borrower not repaying (credit risk) or the risk of a catastrophe occurring. The former risk could be transferred using credit derivatives, the latter by using catastrophe bonds.

Credit default swaps are the most common type of credit derivative. They are contracts which allow one party (the protection buyer) to buy protection from another party (the protection seller) in case a reference obligation from a legal entity defaults. That entity could be a firm or a state. The protection buyer will pay a fee or premium either until maturity of the contract or until a default or other event occurs. If such an event occurs, then the protection buyer will receive compensation from the protection seller. Other ways to transfer risk include securitising assets using special purpose vehicles.

Risk transfer also takes place via insurance policies; but transferring risk should be about much more than buying an insurance policy; the assessment of risk appetite and allocation of capital to risk can create valuable upside and significant opportunities to companies. In order to do this, companies need to develop the right strategies for financing risk. It is essential for companies to follow a robust process when determining how to strike the right balance between risk and reward. Companies that follow such a process can realise a number of benefits that can include reducing exposure to the volatility of the insurance market cycle and delivering a sustainable and lower total cost of risk.

Transferring risk to different parts of the financial services industry generally requires complicated legal structures. This complexity means that poor management of risk transfer instruments could expose firms to significant risk. However, risk transfer instruments could reduce the impact of economic downturns as they allow firms to diversify their risks more widely than they were able to previously.

Research has shown that the most important driving force behind the transfers of risk across sectors of the financial market has become the different risk appetites of the firms involved, rather than regulatory arbitrage (trying to exploit differences in regulatory regimes). A noteworthy trend of the risk transfer market was the transfer of risk from banks to global reinsurance companies and specialist monoline insurers, based primarily outside the United Kingdom. The very large American monoline insurers, including Ambac and MBIA, became severely compromised during the credit crisis and had to be rescued by federal intervention.

3.12 Monitoring, management and reporting of investments

As has been explained earlier in this chapter and consistently with all risk management policies, timely and accurate monitoring and feedback reporting will enhance the management of risk.

Where investments in a portfolio are constantly being measured and reviewed it will be possible to provide the fund managers with constant feedback and effectively an audit that their investment decisions make sense and are continuing to perform in line with the original objectives. Thus the virtuous circle of risk management activity should be to monitor risk to the portfolio, then to perform controls consistent with the management of the investments and then to report how well the investments and the controls are working together. This reporting is a means of communication which effectively completes the loop back into the policy to show the degree of success or lack of it and from which management decisions can rapidly be taken where an adjustment or improvement is required.

Reporting is an example of escalation whereby market issues and problems are quickly realised and fed back to the investment managers who can then proceed to adjust their portfolios in the light of the information received about increasing risks. Thus fund managers can maintain within their desired guideline limits the degree of exposure and risk that they are seeking to be exposed to in the market.

4 Legal risk

This is normally regarded as a subset of operational risk.

The Basel II Accord defines legal risk as follows:

Legal risk includes, but is not limited to, exposure to fines, penalties, or punitive damages resulting from supervisory actions, as well as private settlements.

This sort of definition links legal risk to legal uncertainty. Other definitions of legal risk might also refer to uncertainty about factual elements.The definition of legal risk should distinguish it from other types of risk. It is necessary therefore to categorise the different forms in which legal risk materialises.

Legal risk exists with respect to contracts and ownership or entitlement to assets, software licences, intellectual property and actual property.

If a bank considers the risk of exposure to a fine for particular breaches of regulation it needs to consider a number of uncertain aspects. The risk of censure by a regulator resulting in a fine can also be regarded as a form of regulatory risk.

4.1 Legal uncertainty

Essentially legal risk depends upon legal uncertainty. This is the sort of risk that any unexpected interpretation of law which presents legal uncertainty will leave the bank exposed. This might for example occur in respect of payments with unforeseen financial exposures and possible losses. Hence legal risk addresses both legal and factual uncertainties.

A good example of this in the banking world is trading OTC derivatives or any kind of contract with another bank where explicit agreements need to be made as a formal legal contract between the two counterparties to a transaction. In an exchange environment where banks are trading with others under the terms of a central exchange's rulebook or perhaps via a clearing house the essential aspect of legal risk is similarly that there may be the risk of some uncertain result with respect to contracts entered into under the exchange's standard rules.

4.2 Changes to the environment

Legal risk can also manifest itself when there is a change in the legal environment or the regulatory environment. Consider whether a change of law that has been introduced into market practice delivers a legal risk to banks' trading positions. Clearly one good example is when a bank or a trading company enters into insolvency or goes bust. The cases of Lehman Brothers or MF Global are good examples where any other bank dealing with them as an external counterparty would have had the legal certainty of its contracts with the defunct entity called into question. This presented a legal risk which essentially is addressing the lack of clarity over the counterparty risk issue of the collapsed bank. Thus, as with many other risks, boundaries and overlaps exist between legal risk and other forms of risk.

Although a subset of operational risk its definitions may differ widely as there may not be in fact a generally accepted definition of the term.

4.2.1 Examples of legal risk areas

These are types of legal risk to which financial institutions can be open:

- Customer failure
- Supplier failure
- Product/service failure
- Personal data abuse or loss
- Employment (discrimination) claim

- Health and safety investigation
- Competition investigation
- Infringement of intellectual property rights
- Environment pollution incident
- Impact of new regulation.

4.3 Managing legal risk

In managing legal risk a bank will need to assess the full picture of regulatory compliance and make sure that it has an effective legal risk management function overlapping or perhaps also empowered with its regulatory compliance function.

The ability to put in place an effective legal risk management process has to be led by the senior management, (sometimesthe Board of a company). It has to keep a close eye on what its peers in the market are doing and has to have full support and positive leadership from the board.

There will need to be some internal legal resource in the form of in-house counsel who will lead on identifying the priority areas of legal risks and establishing processes for mitigating those risks. There will also need to be a well-established secure process for drawing up contracts and contracting with third-parties and suppliers.

As with so many operational risks the assessment of legal risks can be done by a number of means. The primary one would be to analyse probability and impact from a risk control assessment point of view. This could be supplemented by carrying out a full legal review and possibly by benchmarking against other practice(s) outside the company. As with all risk issues, it is important to carry out a review on a regular basis and therefore there will be the requirement for internal audit to cross-check that legal risk is being managed efficiently.

The entire organisation will need to be kept on a sound legal footing. This will depend extensively on the business culture, the overall environment and the tone from the top provided by the board. It is necessary to improve the legal awareness of line managers and also to increase the commercial awareness of internal lawyers plus those providing the company with legal advice from outside the firm.

Legal issues will very often end up in some sort of dispute resolution process. This may be with respect to the bank's own employees and it will be necessary for the organisation to keep track of trends in dispute resolution in the industry. Firms will need to recognise threats and implications which may also present themselves from a regulatory origin and address and respond to such events once identified.

The legal costs for any bank, and certainly one of a substantial size, would be considerable because, at every step of its operation, it has to be sure that it is carrying out its responsibilities as part of the overall economic community. This is partly because it is a regulated entity and also because it is providing services to members of the general public and business community. Thereforethe responsibility that is carried is very substantial. Attention to formulation of new contracts with respect to supplies, outsourcing, software development and marketing all will take up considerable resource for which there will be a sizeable cost, particularly if the expertise is sourced from outside the company.

4.4 Risk from litigation

Litigation risk can be described as an organisation's likelihood of being taken to court. In a litigious society, all members are at risk of some litigation. Large firms with deep pockets can be especially prone to litigation risk since the rewards for any plaintiffs can be considerable. These might be members of staff, journalists, suppliers, customers or competitors. Banks typically have measures in place to identify and reduce these types of risks, such as ensuring product safety and following all pertinent laws and regulations.

There is always the possibility that legal action might be taken because of a bank's actions (or inactions), products, services or other events. Banks would generally employ some type of litigation risk analysis and controls management to identify key areas where the litigation risk is high, and thereby take appropriate measures to limit or eliminate those risks., preferably before they strike.

The very process of going to court to pursue or defend a litigation action is fraught with its own additional risks. Cost will be a major consideration together with the time taken, the quality of evidence and the choice of expert witnesses and advisors. Non-financial costs need to be considered as well. Of these, reputational risk impacts directly as any court ruling will be public and reported widely in the media. For this reason so many actions never reach open court but settle out of court. There is after all nothing wrong with reaching a settlement. Settlement, whether by alternative dispute resolution or more traditional without prejudice negotiations, is not a dirty word. It is often far better to negotiate a settlement that all parties are reasonably happy with than to hold out for your day in court, with its associated risks.

QUESTION TIME 7

Describe how your firm manages legal risk.

Write your answer here then check with the answer at the back of the book.

5 Strategy risk and strategic risk

Why would risk-averse individuals and entities ever expose themselves intentionally to risk and increase that exposure over time? One reason is that they believe that they can exploit these risks to advantage and generate value. How else can one explain why companies embark into emerging markets that have substantial political and economic risk or into technologies where the ground rules change on a day-to-day basis?

By the same token, the most successful companies in every sector and in each generation – General Motors in the 1920s, IBM in the 1950s and 1960s, Microsoft and Intel in the 1980s and 1990s and Google more recently- share a common characteristic. They achieved their success not by avoiding risk but by seeking it out.

There are some who would attribute the success of these companies and others like them to luck, but that can explain businesses that are one-time wonders – a single successful product or service. Successful companies are able to replicate this success again and again, in new products and in new markets. To do so, they must have a template for dealing with risk that gives them an advantage over the competition.

Firms will use their information advantage and also the speed advantage to provide them with an edge in the marketplace. A further advantage is the ability to exert their experience or knowledge over their competitors. Other companies will have a resource advantage giving them the ability to deal with market developments, particularly crises, as they occur to give them a significant advantage over their competitors. There is also the ability to be more flexible than competitors and hence to remain more resilient in a competitive marketplace.

5.1 Gaining an edge

Firms that gain a competitive advantage from risk taking do not do so by accident. In fact,there are key elements that successful risk-taking organisations have in common. First,they succeed in aligning the interests of their decision makers (the executive management) with theowners of the business (the shareholders) so that firms expose themselves to the right risksand for the right reasons. Second, they choose the right people for the task; someindividuals respond to risk better than others. Third, the reward and punishmentmechanisms in these firms are designed to punish bad risk taking and encourage goodrisk taking. Finally, the culture of the organisations is conducive to sensible risk takingand it is structured accordingly.

If there is a key to successful risk taking, it is to ensure that those who expose a business to risk or respond to risk make their decisions with a common purpose in mind – to increase the value of their businesses. If the interests of the decision makers are not aligned with those of those who own the business, it is inevitable that the business will be exposed to some risks that it should be not be exposed to and not exposed to other risks that it should exploit. In large publicly traded firms, this can be a difficult task. The interests of top management can diverge from those of middle management and both may operate with objectives that deviate significantly from the shareholders and also to the lenders to the corporation.

In recent years, we have seen a spirited debate about corporate governance and why it is important for the future of business. In particular, proponents of strong corporate governance argued that strengthening the oversight that shareholders and directors have over managers allows for change in badly managed firms and thus performs a social good. There is also a risk-related dimension to this discussion of corporate governance. At one end of the spectrum are firms where managers own little or no stake in the equity and make decisions to further their own interests. In such firms, there will be too little risk taking because the decision makers gain little of the upside from risk (because of their limited or non-existent equity stakes) and too much of the downside (they get fired if the risk does not pay off). A comparison of shareholder controlled and management controlled banks would find that shareholder controlled banks were more likely to take risk. In general, managers with limited equity stakes in firms not only invest more conservatively but are also more likely to borrow less and hold on to more cash. At the other end of the spectrum are firms where the incumbent managers and key decision makers have too much of their wealth tied up in the firm. These insider-dominated firms, where managers are entrenched, tend take less risk than they should for three reasons:

- The key decision makers have more of their own wealth tied up in the firm than diversified investors. Therefore, they worry far more about the consequences of big decisions and tend to be more wary of risk taking; the problem is accentuated when voting rights are disproportionately in incumbent managers' hands.
- Insiders who redirect a company's resources into their own pockets behave like lenders and are thus less inclined to take risk. In other words, they are reluctant to take on risks that may put their benefits at peril.
- Firms in countries where investors do not have much power also tend to rely on banks for financing instead of capital markets (stock or bonds), and banks restrict risk taking.

5.2 Exploiting risk

The essence of risk management is not avoiding or eliminating risk but decidingwhich risks to exploit, which ones to let pass through to investors and which ones toavoid or hedge. While there is evidence that higher risk taking, in theaggregate, leads to higher returns, there is also enough evidence to the contrary (i.e. thatrisk taking can be destructive) to suggest that firms should be careful about which riskthey expose themselves to.

To exploit risk, a firm needs an edge over its competitors who are also exposed to that same risk, and there are five possible sources. One is having more timely and reliable information when confronted with a crisis, allowing the firm to map out a superior plan of action in response. A second is the speed of the response to the risk, since not all firms, even when provided with the same information, are equally effective at acting quickly and appropriately. A third advantage may arise from possessing experience in weathering similar crises in the past. The institutional memories as well as the individual experiences of how the crises unfolded may provide an advantage over competitors who are new to the risk. A fourth advantage is grounded in resources, since firms with access to capital markets or large cash balances, superior technology and better trained personnel can survive risks better than their competitors. Finally, firms that have more operating, production or financial flexibility built into their responses, as a result of choices made in earlier periods, will be able to adjust better than their more rigid compatriots.

5.3 Strategic errors

Banks similarly take strategic risks in shaping their business objectives across the opportunities that present themselves. Some famous cases in recent years such as the insurance company AIG in the Unites States and RBS in the UK banking sector showed how strategic desire to grow the business into new areas (credit default swaps in the case of AIG and overzealous expansion in the case of RBS) led strategically to the situation where both institutions had to be rescued by public funds. In the RBS example, it has been widely discussed in the press that Fred Goodwin as the then Chief Executive and his Board committed themselves to the financial uncertainties of the takeover of Dutch bank ABN Amro such that the toxic debts that they then owned proved the last straw in the weakening of a very large global bank as the financial crisis unfolded. Goodwin was committed to growing the bank at too rapid a pace and embarked upon a series of acquisitions of different types of businesses (many indeed being non-banking activities) which subsequently were wound by the next RBS management group led by Stephen Hester.

So, strategic risk runs across corporate governance. Sensible decision making at the top of a bank. Wise investment in markets and products, sensible utilisation of technology and great care in committing the bank to new operations without proper review of the potential outcome of that course of action.

6 Audit committee

In recent years the audit committee has become one of the main pillars of the corporate governance system in British public companies, including banks and other financial institutions (or BOFIs, as the 2009 Walker Report calls them).

QUICK QUESTION

What is the purpose of the audit committee?

Write your answer here before reading on.

The audit committee is created with the aim of enhancing confidence in the integrity of an organisation's processes and procedures relating to internal control and corporate reporting. Boards rely on audit committees, among other things, to review financial reporting and to appoint and provide oversight of the work of the external auditor. Audit committees can also play a key role in providing oversight of risk management.

The Financial Reporting Council (FRC) is the UK's independent regulator responsible for promoting confidence in corporate governance and reporting. It promotes high standards of corporate governance through the Combined Code (see below), but does not monitor or enforce its implementation by individual boards. Itsets standards for corporate reporting and actuarial practice and monitors and enforces accounting and auditing standards. Also,it oversees the regulatory activities of the professional accountancy bodies and operates independent disciplinary arrangements for public interest cases involving accountants and actuaries.

The Combined Code contains broad principles and more specific provisions. Listed companies are required to report on how they have applied the main principles of the Code, and either to confirm that they have complied with the Code's provisions or – where they have not – to provide an explanation. Note that although it strictly applies only to listed companies, firms of any size may (and do) use it as a set of standards upon which to base their approach to good corporate governance.

Under the Combined Code, a bank's Board should establish formal and transparent arrangements for considering how they should apply the financial reporting and internal control principles and for maintaining an appropriate relationship with the company's auditors.

This is achieved in the main through the audit committee, which will monitor and review theformal arrangementsestablished by the Board inrespect of the financialstatements and reporting ofthe bank; internal controlsand the risk managementframework; internal audit;and the bank's relationshipwith its external auditors.

The effectiveness of the internal control system should reviewed regularly by both the Board and the Audit Committee, which also will receive reports ofreviews undertaken around the bank via its group risk and group audit functions. The Audit Committee receives reports from the external auditors (which include details of significant internal control matters that they have identified), and should conduct a discussion with the external auditors at least once a year without executives present, to ensure that there are no unresolved issues of concern.

There should be an ongoing process for identifying, evaluating and managing the significant risks faced by the firm. The Audit Committee plays an important part in achieving this.

6.1 Auditor independence and remuneration

Both the Board and the external auditors must have safeguards in place to protect the independence and objectivity of the external auditors. The auditcommittee will need a comprehensive policy to regulate the use of external auditors for non-audit services. This policy will set out the nature of work the externalauditors may not undertake, which includes work which will ultimately be subject to external audit, internal audit services and secondments to seniormanagement positions in the bank that involve decision-making. It will also include the bank's policy on hiring former external audit staff. For thoseservices that are deemed appropriate for the external auditors to carry out, the policy should state the approval process that must be followed for each type ofassignment. The Chairman of the Audit Committee must be consulted regarding potential instructions in respect of allowable non-audit services witha value above defined fee limits.

Each year the Audit Committee will establish a limit on the fees that can be paid to the external auditors in respect of non-audit services and will monitor, say quarterly, the amounts paid to the auditors in this regard. The external auditors will in their turn also report regularly to the Audit Committee on the actions that theyhave taken to comply with professional and regulatory requirements and current best practice in order to maintain their independence. This includesthe rotation of key members of the audit team.

The Audit Committee will evaluate the performance of the external auditors during the year and will periodically repeat this exercise. The AuditCommittee might from time to time suggest to the Board that an independent tender process be undertaken.

It is important for a bank to have procedures that are designed to ensure auditor independence, including a check that fees for audit and non-audit services are approved inadvance. This approval can be obtained either on an individual engagement basis or, for certain types of non-audit services, particularly those of arecurring nature, through the approval of a fee cap covering all engagements of that type provided the fee is below that cap. All statutory audit workas well as non-audit assignments where the fee is expected to exceed the relevant fee cap must be pre-approved by the Audit Committee on anindividual engagement basis. On a quarterly basis, the Audit Committee might receive a report detailing all pre-approved services and amounts paid tothe external auditors for such pre-approved services.

QUICK QUESTION

What tasks do you think would be carried out by the audit committee?

Write your answer here before reading on.

The duties of the audit committee will therefore address the following:

- review the financial statementspublished in the name of theBoard and the quality andacceptability of the relatedaccounting policies, practicesand financial reporting disclosures
- review the scope of the workof the group audit department,reports from that department and the adequacy of its resources
- review the effectiveness of thesystems for internal control, riskmanagement and compliancewith financial services legislation and regulations
- approve the external auditors'terms of engagement and remuneration
- assess the external auditors' independence and objectivity
- recommend the externalauditors' appointment, re-appointment and removal
- review the results of theexternal audit and its cost effectiveness
- review reports from the auditorson audit planning and theirfindings on accounting and internal control systems
- review procedures forhandling complaints regardingaccounting, internal accountingcontrols or auditing mattersand for staff to raise concerns inconfidence.

KEY WORDS

Key words in this chapter are given below. There is space to write your own revision notes and add any other key words or phrases you want to remember.

- Funding liquidity risk
- Market liquidity risk
- Maturity ladder
- Value ladder
- Asset liquidity risk
- Funding liquidity risk
- Diversification
- Netting
- Price level risk
- Volatility risk
- Currency risk
- Basis risk
- Interest rate risk
- Commodity risk
- Systematic risk
- Hedging
- Market risk limits
- Bond risk
- Equity risk
- Capital risk
- Property risk
- Alternative investments
- Market neutral arbitrage
- Market neutral securities hedging
- Illiquid assets
- Venture capital
- Private equity
- Investment mandates
- Unsystematic risk
- Short selling

REVIEW

Now consider the main points that were introduced in this chapter. These are listed below. Tick each one as you go through them.

- Liquidity risk is the risk that financial commitments cannot be paid as they fall due. Liquidity principles have been set out by the Basel Committee and compliance with these should ensure that a bank has an embedded liquidity risk management process.
- Liquidity risk can be managed using maturity ladders.
- Causes of liquidity risk include asset liquidity risk and funding liquidity risk.
- Both the Regulator and the Basel Committee have put measures in place to manage liquidity risk since the banking crisis which started in 2007.
- Other tools used to manage liquidity risk include – stress testing, the accurate estimation of future funding requirements, having a range of sources of funds, liquidity limits, scenario analysis, Liquidity at Risk techniques, examining the firm's access to liquid funds, diversification, behavioural analysis, netting as well as an awareness of market dislocation.
- Market risk can be price level risk, volatility risk, liquidity risk, currency risk, basis risk, interest rate risk, and commodity risk.
- Investments will always be subject to systematic risk – where the market falls due to underlying conditions affecting all of the market, for example political or economic situations.
- Market risk is managed through hedging, market risk limits, diversification and stress testing.
- Insurance and investment risk includes currency risk, interest rate risk, bond risk, equity risk, commodity risk, and property risk.
- The returns available to savers and investors will vary depending upon the type of asset invested in.
- Illiquid assets are those not readily tradable as there is a doubt as to their value or the existence of a market.
- An investment mandate sets out the rules by which a collective investment scheme is run.
- Legal risk can manifest itself in a number of areas, including customer failure, the loss of personal data and health and safety investigations. It is managed by the firm having a clear understanding of the legal and regulatory landscape that it finds itself in and must have a strong legal risk management function.
- The implementation of any strategic initiative will involve an element of risk and this is necessary in order for forms to gain a competitive advantage. However if too much risk is taken on, then there is the possibility of strategic errors occurring.
- The Audit Committee will review financial reporting as well as appoint and overview the work of the external auditors.

chapter 8

APPLYING CREDIT RISK PRACTICES

Contents

Learning objectives

On completion of this chapter, you should be able to:

- assess credit risk and apply credit risk practices
- critically review the role of credit scoring as a credit risk practice and assess the implications of recent developments in this field
- describe how you would use the 5 Ps of lending to analyse a credit risk.

Introduction

This chapter starts with a discussion around what is meant by credit scoring – a system of credit assessment that you will probably have some first-hand experience of. We consider what credit scoring is before listing the benefits of this procedure. The chapter then looks at different forms of credit scoring – the judgemental scoring model and the statistical scoring model. The work of credit scoring companies is described next, along with the factors that are taken into account when assessing a credit application, before this introductory section is concluded by examining the types of organisation that use credit scoring.

Next, the chapter moves to the analysis of credit risk – a topic that you will now be aware of. One of the ways we can mitigate this is through the use of due diligence which has been discussed earlier in the course and is a theme that we return to at this point. We develop credit scoring further by explaining that credit exposure, credit risk premium and credit ratings can all be used to measure credit risk.

The work of the credit ratings agencies is considered now – these are the firms that rate the creditworthiness of organisations and countries. You will have heard of these on news broadcasts when they change their assessments of countries. This section concludes with a discussion on the pros and cons of these agencies.

The final major topic to discuss in this chapter is pricing risk. This can manifest itself when using models, when quoting for sales, when receiving quotes for purchases, or if errors made pricing loans.

The chapter moves onto the subject of credit risk mitigation – although most of this was covered when studying Group Credit Risk Practices. The final area covered in this chapter is the description of a structured approach to assessing credit requests – this is done through the 5Ps of credit.

1 Credit scoring

You will be aware from your experience as a bank customer that when banks lend money to clients one of the fundamental methodologies that they follow is that of credit scoring. This provides an accurate model for making sensible and prompt lending decisions. The key challenge to the bank or loan-making institution is to be able to perform a detailed and consistent analysis to avoid unnecessary credit risk. Credit scoring helps with this.

QUICK QUESTION

No doubt you have had your own credit requests processed through a credit scoring system. How would you describe credit scoring?

Write your answer here before reading on.

Credit scoring is a method of evaluating the creditworthiness of customers by using a standard formula or standard set of rules. Depending upon the make-up of the customer-base, credit scoring can normally be engineered to present considerable benefits to banks.

Scoring models are the prime indicator of an applicants' credit strength, with variation by product in the reliance on models. Unsecured lending relies heavily on credit scoring models for underwriting, pricing, and line assignment. Secured lending supplements scores with information on down payments, ability to service debt for underwriting and pricing decisions.

The degree of judgment varies across products with credit card lending being most automated and property secured lending being less automated. In addition to the refreshed applicant credit scores, lenders also rely on updated behaviour scores (based on borrower payment behaviour) for various decisions, including change in credit line and loan pricing.

1.1 The benefits of credit scoring

QUICK QUESTION

In the past, credit applications were scrutinised by lending officials and either signed off or declined, whereas now many are credit scored using an automated process. What do you think are the benefits of this approach for banks?

Write your answer here before reading on.

Using a standardised approach, lenders are able to benefit in a number of ways. These are summarised as follows.

- **Speed** – when used with an automated software system, each customer is evaluated or scored very quickly. Customer applications are processed without undue delay. Also automated data feeds can speed up data entry of financial data, ratings, account status and exposure, and other key data points.
- **Consistency and accuracy** – all factors involved in the credit score are considered and used in the same way. Since credit scoring analyses each customer using a similar set of rules, there is consistency in the evaluation process by the entire staff at all locations. Human error is also eliminated. In the past, when applications were scrutinized manually (called manual underwriting) it would be possible for two different lending officials in the same organisation coming to a different decision on the same application. Therefore, if your loan request was declined at one branch of the bank, it could be possible to re-apply at a different branch and this time have your request approved. This would give the customer a poor perception of the decision making process within the organisation. This manual underwriting is the judgmental scoring model described below.
- **Reduction in bad debts** – when approving new customers, all of the necessary factors involved in the credit decision process are received and scored. High-risk customers are identified as exceptions and can be reviewed by a credit analyst.
- **Reduced personnel costs** – particularly with firms having many thousands of customers, the impact of credit scoring, combined with the use of an automated software system, can significantly reduce personnel costs. Each activity in a credit department has personnel cost

associated with it. With automated credit scoring, far fewer people are needed to research customers, check references and make decisions.

- **Collection activities are prioritised** – credit scores enable the credit executive to have different collection strategies for low risk, medium risk and high risk customers. When credit risk scores are coupled with amounts owed, collection activity is prioritised.
- **Decision support and planning tools** – credit scoring enables the credit executive to prepare reports that accurately reflect the quality of the total accounts receivable portfolio, and other reports that will reveal if certain groups of customers carry more risk. Additional reports will focus attention on the amount of bad debts for each risk category, pricing strategies, overly rigid or liberal applications of credit policy, credit department staffing and expenses, and other issues vital to a firm's future.
- **Compliance with audit mandates** – due to regulatory requirements such as the Sarbanes-Oxley Act in the United States, auditors are more likely to require supporting materials on the collectability of receivables and class of receivable. Expert reviews can reveal inadequate bad debt reserve and overlooked significant write-offs from prior periods. This failure could result in material errors in past and current financial statements. Credit scoring enables firms to support decisions by tracking data evaluated and how decisions were made. Furthermore, they can credit score to re-evaluate their portfolios regularly. In this way, decisions will be more reliable and supportable for financial reporting.

1.2 The different types of credit scoring

Credit scoring is based on the assumption that past experience can be used as a guide in predicting creditworthiness. There are two types of credit scoring models. Both can be statistically validated.

1.2.1 Judgmental scoring model

A judgmental scoring model is based on traditional standards of credit analysis. Factors such as payment history, bank and trade references, credit agency ratings and financial statement ratios are scored and weighted to produce an overall credit score.

The determination of which factors to use, and how each will be scored and weighted, is generally based on the credit executive's past experience with their company, the products or services they sell, and the industry they are in. Judgmental models are enhanced by comparing industry financial profiles using peer groups. Including scoring factors that reflect the individual characteristics and policies of their own firm further enhances the judgmental model.

Judgmental scoring is the most straightforward to implement because it uses a firm's own credit policies and decision processes, the number of rules are easily set, and the grading scale can be simple or complex. Therefore, it is easier to understand and augment.

1.2.2 Statistical scoring model

Statistical models function in much the same way as judgmental models. However, in choosing the factors to be scored and weighted they rely on statistical methods rather than the experience and judgment of a credit manager.

Statistical models consider many factors simultaneously, a process that calculates and analyses the correlation between different factors to identify the relevant tradeoffs amongst them, and assigns statistically derived weightings used in the model. The key factors are generally captured from credit agency reports and the credit files of the client.

Statistical models are often described as a scorecard, a pooled scorecard or a custom scorecard. A scorecard uses data from one firm. A pooled scorecard uses data from many firms. A custom scorecard blends a statistical model with some of the factors used in a judgmental model.

1.3 Credit scoring companies

In the UK the best known credit scoring company using automated credit scoring and reporting is Experian. Experian is used by thousands of clients in order to evaluate the risk of extending loans, credit cards and other financial products to members of the public. Lenders use the information on a credit report together with information they receive from their customers when they apply for credit (either online or in some other form of application) in order to derive a credit score. The lender then uses the credit score to assess the risk of offering credit to the client.

Different organisations may take different data elements into account when they compute a credit score and may use different formulas for different products. This means that individual members of the public can receive different scores even from the same lending bank in certain circumstances. Banks do not have to disclose exactly how they work out credit scores but they should present a succinct and clear explanation of how their scoring system works and inform customers whether their applications have been refused because of the credit score or because of other information held on a credit report about an individual. The bank would not want to be too specific about how this scoring works as, if this information got into the public domain, then it would be much easier for unscrupulous individuals to present false applications that they know would pass the credit score.

In an age of easy credit, it is very common for members of the public to have a number of loans, credit cards and other borrowings each of which would be included within an overall credit scoring system.

QUICK QUESTION

Think about your experience of credit scoring either as a customer or as an employee and list the factors that are taken into account in order to assess a credit application.

Write your answer here before reading on.

Fundamental data elements about individuals which are typically contained within credit scoring systems are as follows:

- Information about the individual as contained on the electoral roll
- Names and other aliases
- Associations – to show whether financial links exist with other persons
- Records of court judgements, bankruptcies and voluntary arrangements
- Credit account information
- Personal information such as owner/tenant of property, length of time at current address, length of time with current employer, use of land telephone line, etc.

In the UK major lenders have agreed to share details of their customers' credit agreements. This is achieved by storing the details with one or more of the credit reference agencies, e.g. Experian. When customers apply for credit they have to grant permission to the lender to enable them to check the individual status with other lenders over the past few years. This helps banks and finance companies to decide whether individuals can afford to take on new borrowing and whether they are likely to keep up to date on a schedule of repayments. It is customary for status codes to be generated. Such codes show whether the individual has met credit repayments over the past period (say for the last months or three years). Lenders will be looking for evidence of default where the repayment terms have not been met or delays of payment have occurred so an aggregated scale could be drawn up. At best this would mean that all payments are always made on time and the account is up to date. On the other hand the account could be in default, there might have been other payment delays or the account could now have been closed and there is nothing outstanding. The record on file would contain the amount of credit limit granted by each individual lender, the amount of money outstanding on any loan and the history of repayment against the loan.

A typical credit scoring table ***Source - Experian***

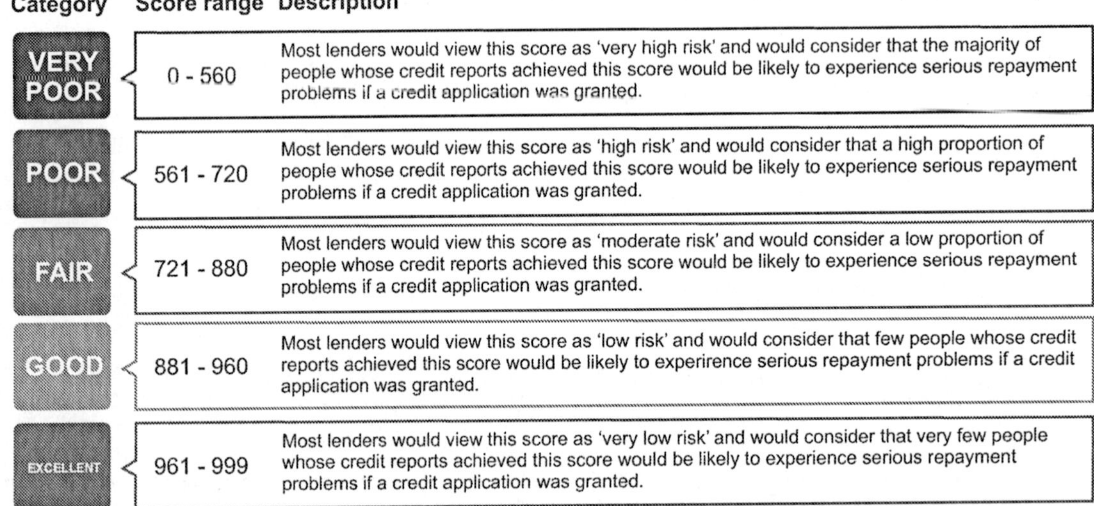

Category	Score range	Description
VERY POOR	0 - 560	Most lenders would view this score as 'very high risk' and would consider that the majority of people whose credit reports achieved this score would be likely to experience serious repayment problems if a credit application was granted.
POOR	561 - 720	Most lenders would view this score as 'high risk' and would consider that a high proportion of people whose credit reports achieved this score would be likely to experience serious repayment problems if a credit application was granted.
FAIR	721 - 880	Most lenders would view this score as 'moderate risk' and would consider a low proportion of people whose credit reports achieved this score would be likely to experience serious repayment problems if a credit application was granted.
GOOD	881 - 960	Most lenders would view this score as 'low risk' and would consider that few people whose credit reports achieved this score would be likely to experirence serious repayment problems if a credit application was granted.
EXCELLENT	961 - 999	Most lenders would view this score as 'very low risk' and would consider that very few people whose credit reports achieved this score would be likely to experience serious repayment problems if a credit application was granted.

One of the features of the UK system is that individuals are permitted to review their own credit score by approaching a credit agency and this can be done at very little charge or even free. In line with the levels of protection provided by the Data Protection Acts, firms keep records of:

- linked addresses; and
- evidence of borrowers with debts who have moved home without giving a new address (this is known in the UK as the GAIN database).

When reviewing the status of an individual it might be easy to draw the wrong conclusion from the bare facts that are contained there. Therefore there is always provision for what is known as a 'notice of correction' to enable a short additional entry to be included on the credit report to explain circumstances relating to an individual. This is there for anyone who inspects the credit record to be able to view a more complete explanation enabling them to arrive at their lending decision more accurately.

Not only is credit scoring used to enable banks to decide whether to offer credit to customers but it is also used to decide what interest rate to charge – as mentioned earlier on the course, the higher the risk, then the higher the potential reward the lender is hoping to get. If the credit score infers a higher risk, then the lender may charge a higher rate of interest to compensate for this. These processes are usually automated. In general a higher credit score suggests the customer is less likely to experience problems repaying credit. Different lenders use different ways of working out their credit scores. Customers should also realise their credit score may change over time as their financial circumstances change. For example, paying off a loan or a debt could improve an individual's credit score whereas the emergence of a County Court Judgment on the record would certainly reduce the credit score.

Credit scores do not take account of an individual's gender, religion, race or ethnic origin. The score is based entirely upon the credit report. Note that lenders will use other information in parallel with a credit report to make decisions about extending credit - the information that the customer presents when they first make their application for credit.

One of the modern problems in the financial marketplace has been caused by internet technology and the manner in which criminals can seek to steal identities from other people and therefore apply for credit effectively masquerading as being somebody else.

QUICK QUESTION

What can banks do with their customers to discourage this practice occurring?

Write your answer here before reading on.

Banks will counsel clients to reduce the risk of their customers' details being used fraudulently. This includes:

- Never responding to emails asking for personal information – banks will never operate in this way but criminals will.
- Do not give personal information to people who say they are calling from organisations you have not dealt with before. Insist on calling them back.
- Always destroy any paper work and waste that contains personal information including cheque stubs, receipts and bank statements. Never throw away anything with your name and address on it even an envelope without shredding it first. Shredding all such documents is a very sensible move.
- If your postal mail suddenly stops arriving contact the Post Office immediately to make sure it is not being redirected.
- Be vigilant when using the internet and never disclose personal information.
- Make sure that your computer protection software is up to date and is of reasonable quality to prevent cyber-attacks or malware entering your system.

QUESTION TIME 1

Consider the following attributes and attribute one of the following to each one.

- High value
- Medium value
- Low value

Age 18-21

Age 50-60

Living with parents

Living in rented property

Homeowner

Less than 2 years at this address

More than 10 years at this address

No credit searches in past 3 months

4 credit searches in past 3 months

1 credit search in past 3 months

Has landline phone

Less than 2 years in current employment

2-5 years in current employment

More than 5 years in current employment

Write your answer here then check with the answer at the back of the book.

1.4 Who uses credit scoring and what do they have in common?

The first firms to use credit scoring were catalogue companies followed by credit card companies and the consumer lending divisions of commercial banks. The huge number of transactions involved in consumer credit necessitated a computer-generated score to approve and service their customers in a cost effective and timely fashion.

Fortunately, the credit information they needed for their statistical scorecards was readily available, much of it free. Their credit application provided data concerning employment, annual salary, home value, mortgage and other obligations. Additional data was available in consumer credit reports that were usually very comprehensive.

The information required to conduct a credit appraisal for a consumer is far less than that of a business. A salary of £50,000 can be measured easier than a bank reference or a financial statement.

Finally, the cash amount of each consumer credit transaction is usually low, so that a single scorecard rejection of a sale will have little impact on overall sales revenue.

All of the above factors contributed to making credit scoring quite successful for those firms in the high volume consumer credit business.

The second group to use credit scoring was banks, leasing companies and finance companies lending to small business firms. Similar to the credit card businesses, the numbers of transactions were high and the financial amount on each relatively low. Since they could not afford to spend hours gathering and analysing credit information on each transaction they turned to statistical scorecards.

Today, credit scoring is being used by business credit providers of all types.

2 Analysing credit risk

As you know, credit risk is the risk that a counterparty will fail to perform on an obligation. This is what is meant by **counterparty risk** and is indeed exactly the definition used by the Basel Committee and by The International Organization of Securities Commissions (IOSCO). It could be extended to address the risk of loss resulting from a counterparty going into default. Credit risk therefore may be described as default risk or any credit exposure or equivalent. It presents itself in settlement risk, pre-settlement risk, delivery risk and payment risk.

Therefore firms must manage the potential of a failure to pay or deliver on time or even at all with customers and counterparties with whom they transact business.

However, not only counterparties are considered under the banner of credit risk; there is also the matter of **issuer risk**, which refers to the risk that an issuer of securities could fail to perform with respect to the duties under its issued securities. An example would be not to pay interest on bonds or to default upon the redemption of bonds or other securities.

An associated point is that market risk can in fact turn into credit risk should a counterparty or customer default. A profitable in-the-money position would represent a potential gain if the counterparty performs in accordance with the contract and an in-the-money hedge would represent a replacement cost if the counterparty did not perform as it should. In either of these situations, if the counterparty defaults, the value is lost although the amount at stake is the replacement cost of the trade. If the counterparty should default at the settlement date the amount at stake could be much worse – the whole principal value of the transaction in fact, since the non-defaulting party may have paid in full before receiving anything by return.

Similarly credit risk can become market risk. Consider the case of a central counterparty clearing organisation which guarantees its clearing members. In the event of a default of one of the clearing members the CCP takes over the positions of the defaulting company and is immediately thereafter exposed to the market risk of those positions.

2.1 Counterparty and issuer risk within banking

Perhaps the most obvious and basic point about counterparty risk is that credit risk management begins with making basic checks on your customer or the counterparty with whom you are dealing – this is the due diligence that we carry out before a penny is advanced to the customer. It is necessary to understand the counterparty's ability to pay. Many lenders will argue persuasively that if we have doubts about the customer's ability to repay, then there is no point in taking the credit assessment any further as in there is no point lending money that we are not going to get back.

QUICK QUESTION

What basic controls would you carry out when approached by a business customer for credit?

Write your answer here before reading on.

The basic controls to be established will therefore include the following:

- checking public information about the counterparty including all aspects of their financial position
- checking the strategic objectives of the client or counterparty and their attitude to risk
- knowing the management quality of the counterparty
- assessing the experience and degree of profitability of the previous trading of the counterparty
- making some assessment or check on the counterparty's standing amongst its business creditors
- checking the size of the exposure by way of the counterparty positions compared with other market users of a similar scale.

Such counterparty checks are all part of due diligence before commencing a business arrangement with anybody else in the marketplace. Everyone is a counterparty to somebody else therefore every firm must have a meaningful credit risk assessment policy which assesses the strength of counterparties. Some firms, for example major banks, will have millions of customers. Others may be conducting transactions with relatively few wholesale counterparties. Every business is different and must plan its credit risk policy accordingly.

The other exposure is to the markets and products within which the counterparties are trading with the firm concerned. Here also occurs the point about issuer risk where securities have been issued by another institution in the marketplace and the credit quality of the issuer is called into question. This will particularly affect the value of bonds and the perceived credit risk of the issuer, perhaps as stated by credit ratings agencies.

An important element of the risk management approach will be to keep all the matters that were highlighted above under regular review. It is no good opening a line of credit today for a new client and not reviewing it in the light of ongoing changing circumstances both in the market and with the respective client. Once a facility has been signed off, it can be tempting to put it to the back of your mind until the renewal date of the loan. However, it is imperative that control of lending starts with as soon as the original loan has been sanctioned.

3 Credit risk assessment

All of the three methodologies described here are seeking to measure the degree of credit risk that exists when addressing specific credit exposures with other parties.

3.1 Credit exposure

Although credit exposure is really a synonym for credit risk, many firms have a specific way of defining their credit exposure.

QUICK QUESTION

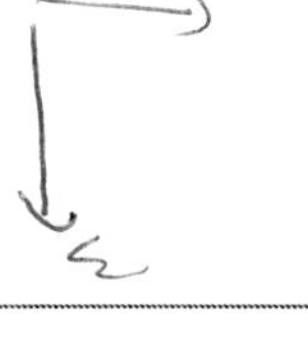

How would you define credit exposure?

Write your answer here before reading on.

A bank might define its credit exposure as meaning all transactions where losses might occur due to the fact that counterparties may not fulfil their contractual payment obligations to them. They might calculate the gross amount of the exposure without taking into account any collateral, other credit enhancement or credit risk mitigating transactions. Their main credit exposures categories are likely to be loans, contingent liabilities, over-the-counter (OTC) derivatives and tradable assets.

Loans would mean net loans as reported on the bank's balance sheet but before deduction of any allowances for loan losses. Contingent liabilities will consist of financial and performance guarantees, standby letters of credit and indemnity agreements as issued by the bank to third parties. OTC derivatives will refer to the bank's credit exposures from over-the-counter derivative transactions that they have entered into. On the balance sheet, these will be included under trading assets and, for derivatives entered into for non-trading purposes, under other assets. The tradable assets category will include bonds, loans and other fixed-income products that are registered under trading assets as well as in securities available for sale.

A bank will assess every element of its credit exposure to others in the marketplace. Thus for major universal banks the spread of these activities will be very wide indeed with perhaps a matrix of potential risks being assessed across clients and counterparties across every product and asset class of the bank's operation.

3.2 Credit risk premium

The concept of **credit risk premium** is simply the addition of a premium over the fair value being paid by the market for the credit risk of the product.

Consider, for example, the bond market. The United States government, being triple-A rated (AAA), represents the best quality credit risk available in the market to investors in its paper (its issued securities). Thus the interest paid upon its bonds would be set at the lowest fair value. It demonstrates the effective risk-free rate paid by the market at the time of issuance, being the best available credit risk but paying the lowest interest therefore. Other borrowers, being less creditworthy than the US government, would only be able to borrow if they paid a greater interest rate. The premium between the risk-free rate and the actual interest rate paid by them is the credit risk premium.

Thus the credit risk premium is an additional amount included in a security's yield which reflects what could be lost if the issuer were to default. A company or government rated AAA would not pay a risk premium when issuing securities; a company rated BB or less would.

Moving on from this, the whole world of credit spreads comes into play which follows the differentials in credit risk of instruments bearing different levels of credit rating. As the ratings weaken, so the credit spread widens against the strongest benchmark rate with the weakest credits having to pay higher levels of interest. In times of market uncertainty these spreads can widen enormously (as was seen in the period around September 2008 at the time of the Lehman Brothers collapse).

CASE STUDY

At the height of the credit crunch in September 2008 when Lehman Brothers went bankrupt the jump in credit spreads between Libor, as a benchmark rate, against Fed funds, representing the best quality risk available jumped by two full percentage points. Indeed, at that time investors were more concerned about leaving money with banks than with anybody else as they were asking themselves which bank was about to collapse next. So therefore investors and institutions and indeed banks were happy only to invest money with sovereign risk attached, i.e. to deposit their money with governments. This was done despite the fact that government interest rates were maybe giving them even a negative return at that very volatile time in the marketplace. This demonstrates that credit risk premiums between the finest available credit (that of high quality sovereign debt) against any other credit risk can move around in an extremely volatile manner. Only in the summer of 2009 did we see credit risks back to where they stood two years ago before the onset of the credit crunch at the beginning of August 2007 prior to the Northern Rock collapse.

3.3 Credit ratings

A credit rating estimates the creditworthiness of an individual, corporation, or even a country (this is called sovereign risk). It is an evaluation made by credit assessment officers of a borrower's overall credit history. Credit ratings are calculated from financial history and current assets and liabilities. Typically, a credit rating tells a lender or investor the probability of the subject being able to pay back a loan. However, in recent years, credit ratings have also been used to adjust insurance premiums, determine employment eligibility, and establish the amount of a utility or leasing deposit. Every would-be home owner who makes a mortgage application or any individual who applies for a credit card or loan will be aware of the credit assessment procedures which are typically followed by lenders.

A poor credit rating indicates a high risk of defaulting on a loan, and thus leads to the imposition of higher interest rates or the refusal of a loan by the creditor as previously discussed.

4 Credit ratings agencies

A **credit rating agency** is a company that assigns credit ratings for issuers of certain types of debt obligations as well as the debt instruments themselves. Although there are over thirty such specialist firms active in the world, the three best known internationally are Standard & Poor's, Moody's and Fitch. In some cases, the servicers of the underlying debt are also given ratings. In most cases, the issuers of securities are companies, special purpose entities, state and local governments, non-profit organizations, or national governments issuing debt-like securities (i.e. bonds) that can be traded on a secondary market. A credit rating for an issuer takes into consideration the issuer's creditworthiness (i.e. its ability to pay back a loan), and it affects the interest rate applied to the particular security being issued.

The chart shows the ratings used by the principal players:

	Moody's	S & P	Fitch
Best quality investment Very well protected	Aaa Aa A	AAA AA A	AAA AA A
Medium grade not highly protected not poorly secured	Baa Ba B	BBB BB B	BBB BB B
Bonds of poor standing Some threat to security	Caa Ca	CCC CC	CCC CC
Lowest grade Poor prospects	C	C D	DDD DD D

Everything down to the S&P's BBB- level (or equivalent with the other agencies) is known as investment grade and further down as non-investment grade or below investment grade.

Credit rating agencies publish default probabilities, expected recovery statistics and rating migration probabilities. Their ratings from AAA to D concern the payment of interest and principal on issued securities and determine the cost of borrowing. The following chart might have been produced in early 2008 before the financial crisis.

S+P	Moody	Fitch	Comment	Example
AAA	Aaa	AAA	Prime quality	USA, Germany, Rabobank
AA	Aa	AA	High quality	BNP Paribas, China, HSBC, Wal-Mart
A	A	A	Good quality	RBS, Citibank, Goldman Sachs, McDonald's
BBB	Baa	BBB	Investment Grade	Bank of America, Brazil, Marks & Spencer
BB	Ba	BB	Speculative	Turkey, General Motors
B	B	B	Very speculative	Ukraine
C	C	C	Extremely speculative	
D		D	Default	

4.1 The credit rating business model

An interesting point to remember with ratings agencies is that they are paid by the issuers whose security and creditworthiness they measure rather than by the users of the ratings (i.e. the investor community). Neither is an agency an independent body operated as such by a government. They themselves are private, non-governmental, commercial organisations. Thus there is the potential charge of vested interests. Nevertheless, this is the model that has operated successfully in the market for such a long time. The events of 2007 onwards brought this criticism to the surface.

The value of such ratings has been widely questioned after the financial crisis when the Securities and Exchange Commission submitted a report to the US Congress detailing plans to launch an investigation into the anti-competitive practices of credit rating agencies and issues including conflicts of interest. This led to the US Justice Department issuing S&P with a lawsuit, accusing them of knowingly inflating its ratings of risky mortgage investments. The Justice Department is demanding $5 billion in penalties.

Issuers rely on credit ratings as an independent verification of their own credit-worthiness and the resultant value of the instruments they issue. In most cases, a significant bond issuance must have at least one rating from a respected agency for the issuance to be successful (without such a rating, the issuance may be undersubscribed or the price offered by investors too low for the issuer's purposes). Studies by the Bond Market Association note that many institutional investors now prefer that a debt issuance have at least three ratings.

Issuers also use credit ratings in certain structured finance transactions. For example, a company with a very high credit rating wishing to undertake a particularly risky research project could create a legally separate entity with certain assets that would own and conduct the research work. This special purpose vehicle or special purpose entity (SPV or SPE) would then assume all of the research risk and issue its own debt securities to finance the research. The SPE's credit rating would likely be very low, and the issuer would have to pay a high rate of return on the bonds issued. However, this risk would not lower the parent company's overall credit rating because the SPE would be a legally separate entity. Conversely, a company with a low credit rating might be able to borrow on better terms if it were to form a SPE and transfer significant assets to that subsidiary and issue secured debt securities. That way, if the venture were to fail, the lenders would have recourse to the assets owned by the SPE. This would lower the interest rate the SPE would need to pay as part of the debt offering.

The same issuer also may have different credit ratings for different bonds. This difference results from the bond's structure, how it is secured, and the degree to which the bond is subordinated to other debt. Many larger ratings agencies offer credit rating advisory services that essentially advise an issuer on how to structure its bond offerings and SPEs so as to achieve a given credit rating for a certain debt tranche. This creates a potential conflict of interest: of course, as the agency may feel obliged to provide the issuer with that given rating if the issuer followed its advice on structuring the offering. Some ratings agencies avoid this conflict by refusing to rate debt offerings for which its advisory services were sought.

Credit ratings are used by bond issuers in assigning credit standards to their securities. Ratings are also used by investment banks and broker dealers with respect to their own risk portfolios. Government regulators also may use ratings in order to achieve credit assessment on their securities such as government bonds or bills. In recent years the role of ratings has escalated greatly into their use in structured finance where ratings agencies play a key role in allocating separate ratings to the different tranches of debt in a securitisation exercise under a special purpose vehicle. It was this type of ratings activity and the associated part played in the collateralised debt obligations (CDOs) and similar products that led the ratings agencies into disrepute during the credit crisis. In those types of structure the issuers were seeking to achieve the highest possible credit rating to each of their different segments or tranches of securities and consulted with ratings agencies in order to achieve the most satisfactory outcome for themselves.

The agencies are resisting bans on the issuer-pays model, in spite of the perverse incentives that model presents as long as issuers have a greater need for good ratings than for accurate ones.

4.2 Using credit ratings

There are some limitations of using ratings agencies as well as benefits. This section will examine these in more detail.

Issuers pay fees for their credit ratings and a consequence in 2009 has been that the business of the major credit ratings agencies has been booming. Fundamentally the business model of the ratings agencies remains intact despite the claims that they exacerbated the economic crisis due to the credit crunch. The criticism centred on the fact that the major agencies gave triple-A ratings to hundreds of billions of dollars worth of bonds all of which were backed by risky mortgages. These securities have since been downgraded and indeed many are now worthless. Ratings are also very important to investors because the ratings govern what forms of debt they are permitted or otherwise to buy. This is often governed by the investment mandates under which they operate. For example, most pension funds are mandated to hold a large proportion of high quality government bonds. Therefore the services of ratings agencies remain central to risk assessments by investors and regulators too.

The work of the ratings agencies depends largely upon confidence and transparency. Clearly the more complex securities such as securitised debt obligations and structured investment vehicles are not as straightforward as outright bonds. It may emerge later that regulators do take some action to address this within the regulation. In the United States, the SEC has created special Examiners to oversee ratings agencies and has introduced rules prohibiting executives from providing both ratings and advice on how to structure securities.

It is clear that ratings agencies play a far from passive role in the market and are central to so much pricing and credit quality assessment in the debt markets. They are still an integral element within the debt markets, despite the fact that some observers may have felt that ratings were inaccurate or unreasonably high against securities which later were proved to be almost worthless.

5 Pricing risk

Pricing risk manifests itself in various ways in a bank's business. One of the key areas will be to achieve the correct price for an instrument. This relates directly into market risk. What is the correct price for a bond? How much should the bank be paying for the foreign exchange options it is buying? What should the bank be charging the counterparty for a commodity swap?

In answering some of these questions the approach of the bank will fall into the categories of who does the pricing and how it is done. Clearly if an error is made by the individual who is calculating the price or the system that he or she is using then this is a direct component of operational risk losses that might manifest themselves as a result of mispricing.

5.1 Model risk

Often computer models are used to generate prices. A good example would be in option pricing when a modelling technique such as Black-Scholes would be commonly used to generate the fair value premium (or price) of an option. If the model has a flaw of any sort the answer generated will of course be incorrect and this will manifest itself in losses due to pricing risk. A good example of this was with NatWest Markets in 1997 where a mispricing by an individual option trader cost the firm 90 million sterling and ultimately triggered the sale of the subsidiary by NatWest.

5.2 Other pricing risks

Another manifestation of pricing risk is where the bank is quoting prices for services rendered or is paying for services delivered to it by an external supplier. Is there sufficient clarity in the pricing structure? What is agreed with respect to price increases in the future in line with support, licences, price escalators or volume discounts? The only way to mitigate these types of price risks are to carry out sufficient due diligence in the first place and to agree the terms precisely in any contract. Note the link to legal risk in that context.

5.3 Pricing the trading book

The trading book is normally marked to market using an external pricing feed. If no reliable pricing feed is available then instead the positions are marked to model. This means that some form of internal model is used to create the market price. We will now discuss this in more detail.

5.3.1 Marking to market

A control discipline to control price risk falls within a daily mechanism of marking positions to market. This utilises pricing benchmarks drawn from the marketplace to ensure prices are correctly captured, set up and recorded. Reconciliation and role segregation are also essential.

In order to price positions correctly at least two feeds of the price information will be required so that the failure of a single feed would not prevent the bank from having a viable source of pricing information upon which to carry out its mark to market calculations.

Those who calculate the price should be independent from those who have an interest in what the price actually represents. This is effectively a form of segregation of duties where the correct level of price will be independently set with respect to managing market risk and pricing risk effectively rather than incentivising a salesman or a trader from booking a transaction at a price that is not correctly arrived at.

5.3.2 Mark to model

Mark to model refers to the practice of pricing a position or portfolio at prices determined by financial models, in contrast to allowing the market to determine the price. Often the use of models is necessary where a market for the financial product is not available, such as with complex financial instruments. One shortcoming of mark to model is that it gives an artificial illusion of liquidity, and the actual price of the product depends on the accuracy of the financial models used to estimate the price. On the other hand, it is argued that asset managers and custodians have a real problem valuing illiquid assets in their portfolios even though many of these assets are perfectly sound and the asset manager has no intention of selling them.

Assets should be valued at mark to market prices as required by the Basel rules. However, mark to market prices should not be used in isolation, but rather compared to model prices to test their validity. Models should be improved to take into account the greater amount of market data available. New methods and new data are available to help improve models and these should be used. In the end all prices start off from a model.

Another shortcoming of mark-to-model is that even if the pricing models are accurate during typical market conditions there can be periods of market stress and illiquidity where the price of less liquid securities declines significantly, for instance through the widening of their bid-ask spread.

Hedge funds may use mark-to-model for the illiquid portion of their book. The failure of Long-Term Capital Management, in 1998, is a well-known example where the markets were shaken by the Russian financial crisis, causing the price of corporate bonds and treasury bonds to get out of line for a period longer than expected by LTCM's models. This situation caused the hedge fund to melt down, and required a Federal Reserve bailout to prevent the toxicity from spilling into other financial markets.

The collapse of Enron is a well-known example of the risks and abuses of mark to model pricing of derivative contracts. Many of Enron's contracts were difficult to value since these products were not publicly traded, thus computer models were used to generate prices. When Enron's profits began to fall with increased competition, accounts manipulated the mark to market models to put a positive spin on Enron's earnings.

5.4 Transfer pricing

The transfer price is the price at which divisions of a company transact with each other. Transactions may also include the trade of supplies or labour between departments. Transfer prices are used when individual entities of a larger multi-entity firm are treated and measured as separately run entities.

In management accounting, when different divisions of a multi-entity company are in charge of their own profits, they are also responsible for their own return on invested capital. Therefore, when divisions are required to transact with each other, a transfer price is used to determine costs. Transfer prices tend not to differ much from the price in the market because one of the entities in such a transaction will lose out: they will either be buying for more than the prevailing market price or selling below the market price, and this will affect their performance.

5.4.1 Tax considerations

Another area for attention involving pricing risk occurs with transfer pricing is that inter-company transactions of significant size should be screened carefully for any instances of attracting the attention of tax authorities. In the case of global companies there is a growing set of new risks resulting from tax regimes around the world that can generate tax problems for globally active banks. Since every cross-border inter-company transactions potentially requires dealing with at least two different tax authorities each of which might look at the same transaction in its own different way it is impossible to eliminate transfer pricing risks entirely.

5.4.2 Transfer pricing: risk assessment – HMRC's general overview

The following is taken from HMRC, which explains the principles of how risk should be assessed in applying transfer pricing rules, including when HMRC consider initiating transfer pricing enquiries into tax returns made by businesses or exercising its reserve power for adjusting the results of medium-sized enterprises.

Transfer pricing rules apply, broadly speaking, where a business has transactions with a business to which it is related. In some circumstances, the rules require the actual results of those transactions to be adjusted to arm's length results for the purpose of calculating taxable profits or losses.

A transfer pricing enquiry can be complex and costly both for HMRC and for the business. It should not be undertaken lightly without due regard to the nature of this complexity or a fully considered assessment of the amount of tax that is likely to be at risk. The establishment of an appropriate arm's length result requires judgment as well as knowledge on the part of a business when making its tax return. The same principle applies to HMRC when deciding whether to make an enquiry into that aspect of a return. That is one of the reasons why a detailed business case has to be submitted to the relevant Transfer Pricing Panel whenever a transfer pricing enquiry is considered appropriate.

Where two businesses are related with each other, the amount of the taxable profit of each can be significantly affected by the results of the transactions between them. There is scope, either through manipulation or insufficient attention to the arm's length principle, for the taxable profit of a business to be significantly depressed. The same applies where persons who collectively control a business act together. A decision by HMRC whether to make an enquiry into a particular tax return needs to take account of this possibility.

As far as transfer pricing is concerned, it is generally more likely that the cases where significant amounts of tax are at stake are those that result from manipulation rather than insufficient attention to the arm's length principle. In deciding whether to make a transfer pricing enquiry into the tax return of a business which has transactions with a business to which it is related, HMRC will pay particular attention to the potential opportunities for securing a tax advantage through manipulation. This opportunity will depend to a large extent, on the tax position of the related business. Where the marginal tax rate borne by that other business is the same as, or similar to, the rate borne by the business in question, that opportunity will, in most cases, be lower than when the marginal tax rate of the related business differs to a material extent.

For example, where a UK business has taxable profits on which it pays tax at 25 per cent, and has transactions with a related business (whether or not a UK business) which pays tax at 25 per cent or thereabouts, the tax at risk in relation to such transactions is less likely to be significant than in cases where the related business pays tax at a low rate (including cases where the marginal effective tax rate is zero because of losses).

Having said that, tax can still be at stake where the marginal tax rate is the same or similar and there can be justification in taking up a transfer pricing enquiry in such circumstances.

The amount of tax at risk in respect of transactions between businesses that are related to each other should be judged by reference to the tax to which the business whose tax return is being considered is liable. The tax to which the related business is liable is not directly relevant. It is, however, **indirectly** relevant in a very important sense since, as already explained, there is more opportunity to secure a tax advantage through manipulation where there is a significant difference between the marginal tax rates.

Where there is no, or minimal, opportunity to secure a tax advantage through manipulation, and the business has clearly taken some steps to apply transfer pricing rules, there is less likely to be a need for HMRC to initiate a transfer pricing enquiry.

5.4.3 Indicators of high risk

The following are possible indicators that a high level of risk might be present in a particular case:

- A taxpaying UK business has a commercial relationship with a related party with a low marginal tax rate and receives income from that other business that appears to be small by reference to that relationship, or makes payments to that business that appear to be large by reference to that relationship.
- A loss-making UK business has a commercial relationship with a related party with a higher marginal tax rate and the loss appears to be the result of payments to that business.
- A UK business, whether taxpaying or loss making, has a commercial relationship with a related party and there are non-tax factors that might provide an incentive for manipulation, such as regulatory requirements involving customs valuations, anti-dumping duties, currency exchange or price controls, or cash flow incentives within a group affecting where profit is reported or how dividends are financed.
- A UK company that is a member of a group enters into a cost-sharing arrangement with other group members with no clear expectation of a future income stream commensurate with its obligation to share costs.
- A UK company that is a member of a group has acquired, created or enhanced an asset that is used by other group members, perhaps by incurring expenditure on research and development leading to the creation or enhancement of intellectual property.

5.4.4 Indicators of low risk

The following are possible indicators that a low level of risk might be present in a particular case:

- A UK business has transactions with a related party with a marginal tax rate equivalent to, or more especially greater than, its own.
- A UK business has a low marginal tax rate and the disallowance of a cost, or the attribution of income, as the result of a transfer pricing adjustment would not be immediately effective for tax purposes.
- A UK business enters into transactions with unrelated parties on similar terms to those it enters into in equivalent transactions with related parties.
- A UK company is a member of a group within which there are significant minority shareholders whose interests would be prejudiced by the diversion of profits to a majority shareholder.

6 Credit risk mitigation

6.1 Examples of credit risk protection and mitigation

There are some established techniques for mitigating credit risk. These are the principal ones:

- Underwriting standards
- Guarantees

- Credit limits
- Netting
- Collateral
- Diversification
- Central counterparties
- Margin or collateral adequacy calculations
- Collateral
- Credit default swaps
- The credit risk management function
- Reporting and escalation tools of credit risk management
- Basel II credit risk policy development, modelling and control
- The Basel sound practices
- Credit risk modelling
- Factor inputs
- Credit scoring systems
- Stress testing
- Segmentation
- External ratings
- Setting limits or caps
- Internal credit grading
- Provisioning and impairment
- Key statistics and key performance indicators
- Controlling concentration risk
- Controlling trading book risk.

With the exception of credit default swaps, these were explained in detail during your study of Group Credit Risk Practices. You may wish to refresh your understanding of these techniques before reading more about credit default swaps.

6.2 Credit default swaps

These instruments were introduced in the previous chapter and we will explore them further now. **Credit default swaps** (CDS) are a form of financial instrument for swapping the risk of debt default inherent in debt securities (i.e. issuer risk). They are normally applied to secure bonds and therefore are associated with the risks of holding emerging market bonds, mortgage backed securities, corporate bonds and local government bonds.

Consider an example, say an investment institution wishes to lend money to an issuer by buying its bond, they may well be constrained by the credit rating of the issuer, as provided by a ratings agency in as much as an institution or fund (a pension fund perhaps) is only permitted under its investment mandate to invest in investment grade securities. By definition, these will be bonds carrying a rating of BBB or above. A bond is considered investment grade if its credit rating is BBB- or higher by Standard & Poor's or Baa3 or higher by Moody's. Generally they are bonds that are judged by the rating agency as likely enough to meet payment obligations so that banks and other institutions are allowed to invest in them. Investment grade confers the expectation of being good credit quality. BBB ratings indicate that there are currently expectations of low credit risk. The capacity for payment of financial commitments is considered adequate but adverse changes in circumstances and economic conditions are more likely to impair this capacity.

Now the credit default swap comes into play. You might think of it as credit default insurance but it is not a way to get rid of bad debts. The products are used to offset and pass on credit risk just as firms use interest rate derivatives to hedge rate movements. It is concerned with credit portfolio management. They are not really swaps but more like options, where paying a premium grants the protection buyer some rights.

So, in the example above, the lender may well be able to lend to the lower rated institution (i.e. buy its bonds) because it is able to gain protection from a higher rated seller of CDSs, which is effectively insuring the lender against credit events affecting its investment.

Note however that the capacity to write CDS protection was found to be a major factor in the credit crunch where over-zealous underwriting and poor ratings formed a toxic mix whereby the capacity to pay when the reference credits were called was found to be wanting to a huge degree. Good examples of these events were shown by AIG, Washington Mutual and others. Some observers have suggested that credit default swaps exacerbated the financial crisis of 2008. For example, when Lehman Brothers collapsed, it followed that many credit default guarantees failed. Washington Mutual was one of the parties which had bought corporate bonds in 2005 and hedged their exposure by buying CDS protection from Lehman Brothers. With their bankruptcy this CDS protection was lost.

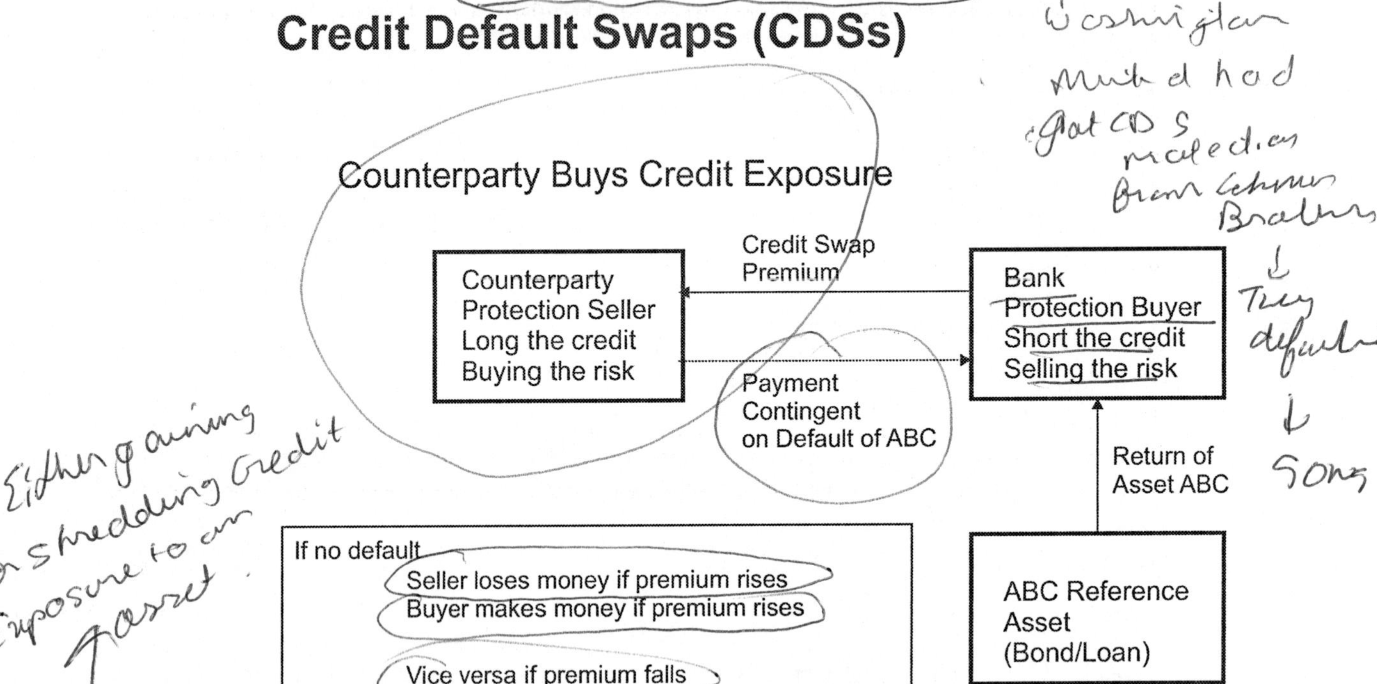

Although others do exist, default swaps are the most common form of credit derivative and are used for either gaining credit exposure to an asset, or shedding credit exposure to an asset. In a default swap, one counterparty agrees to make a periodic payment, (credit swap premium), and in return the other counterparty agrees to make a payment contingent upon the default of an underlying name or asset as explained in the diagram above.

The usual pay-out on a credit derivative is because of an extreme event unlike, for example, financial derivatives which have a pay-out based on a move in interest or foreign exchange rates. Periodic payments are usually made quarterly although any periods can be structured. When an event of default occurs, the protection buyer ceases its premium payment and delivers an acceptable reference obligation in return for the par value of that obligation from the protection seller.

What defaults constitute credit events? We call these credit default swaps, but not every legal default allows one to claim compensation under a CDS. Only certain types of defaults, called credit events, allow a protection buyer to claim compensation. In the US, credit events are typically linked to the reference entity, and include:

- Bankruptcy – filing of a bankruptcy petition by the reference entity (85% defaults)
- Failure to pay – the issuer's failure to make material payment with respect to senior unsecured debt of the reference entity (minimum $1m normally)
- Obligation acceleration
- Modified restructuring – debt restructuring involving, for example, reduction in interest rate and/or loan principal or the extension of final maturity.

Note that a credit event is not:

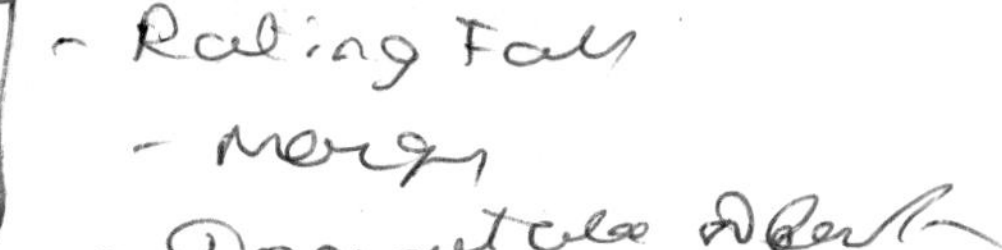

- A downgrade by a rating agency
- The merger of the reference entity with another company
- A documentation default.

7 The five Ps of credit risk

The principles of lending that we are about to look at in this section can be applied at any time when we are assessing credit risk. So, whether a friend asks you to lend them £25 to tide them over until payday, or whether you are dealing with a commercial lending application for £25m, the principles that you will apply to assess the proposition should be the same – it is just the context that will be different.

Following the general principles of lending, will enable you to take a consistent and structured approach to the assessment of credit thus leading to a balanced decision being reached. You will also have added confidence in your decision – if challenged either by a colleague or by the customer – as you will have to hand full justification for the decision you have made.

QUESTION TIME 2

If an existing customer approaches you for a lending facility, what information will you have that can be of use to you as a lending banker?

Write your answer here then check with the answer at the back of the book.

So what are the 5Ps of credit risk?

The 5 Ps are:

- Person
- Purpose
- Payment
- Protection
- Premium.

This section will look at each of these in turn. Whilst this course focuses on commercial propositions, in this section, much of the narrative will look at personal lending. The rationale behind this is that you are likely to have direct experience of this type of lending as a customer and so you should be able to relate more easily to this material. You should also keep in mind that the principles of assessing credit risk are similar no matter the situation.

7.1 The person

The fundamental element that we are looking at here is the trustworthiness of the customer. The banking system is based on trust and if you feel that the customer cannot be trusted, then you should not lend to them. Having said that, if you feel that the customer is trustworthy, that in itself is not sufficient reason to lend. The proposal that the customer is making to us must be viable – and this can only be deemed by carrying out a full analysis. Whilst in the past, some bankers may have been willing to lend solely on the strength of the customer's character, this is no longer the case.

However, when carrying out any analysis of a proposal, the first area we must satisfy ourselves with is the customer's character.

We will start by looking at the sub-headings of:

- Character
- Capacity
- Commitment/capital.

7.2 Character

The integrity of the borrower is paramount, otherwise interviews and discussions would be futile. Many questions will be raised by the banker throughout the course of negotiations and honest, reliable answers must be sought and, on occasion, validated. If the customer promises certain action, then the banker ought to be assured that this action will be carried out.

If you are dealing with a customer who is new to your bank, then you must follow your bank's procedures for recording and verifying the customer's identity – this is to comply with the current anti-money laundering procedures and to ensure that the person we are dealing with is, indeed, who they claim to be. Each bank will also have regulations regarding the validation of identity of existing customers who are opening new accounts, obtaining loans, etc.

Once we have this information on file that is not an end to the story. Customer information is dynamic and changes with time and circumstances. It is vital that the information we hold about the customer is accurate and up to date. It is important to review this information on a regular basis – this can be when we meet the customer and update our records, or if we find out that there has been a significant event in the life of the customer – for example, a change of career.

QUICK QUESTION

What characteristics would you look to be demonstrated by a customer who has asked the bank to lend them money?

Write your answer here before reading on.

You would look for the following characteristics to be demonstrated:

- Respectable and trustworthy
- Honest
- Dependable
- Of high integrity.

It is only when we are happy in this regard that we should further our analysis.

7.3 Capacity

The will to take action is not necessarily the same as ability to see the action through, so you must be assured as to the customer's good health, drive and energy.

Equally, you should not let enthusiasm mask weaknesses in capability. Often, customers who retire early, or are made redundant, tackle new ventures of which they have had no previous experience, such as ex-footballers wishing to run a pub. Another example would be a customer with no experience of house building and having undertaken inadequate research wanting to borrow money from the bank for a self-build on the strength of watching some episodes of Grand Designs on Channel 4.

QUICK QUESTION

What factors would you look for under the heading of capacity?

Write your answer here before reading on.

The factors you would consider here include:

- The age of the customer – for example, will they be able to repay the borrowing before retirement/would repayment be made before their current contract expires?
- What sector is the customer employed in/does their business operate in? Is it stable, expanding or declining? How vulnerable would it be to changes in general economic conditions?
- Experience – does the customer have experience in the field that they are looking to get involved in? The examples of the ex-footballer and the self-build are relevant here.
- Reputation – have we lent to this customer before? If so, what was their repayment record like? Did they adhere to the commitments and promises that they made to us?

7.4 Commitment/Capital

The amount of capital or finance provided by the customer may indicate the customer's commitment to the purpose of the advance. For example, a couple of disillusioned teachers wishing to purchase a property and start trading as a nursery may feel it reasonable to ask the bank for 100% funding as their commitment to the proposal would be their expertise and energy in running the business – but it is highly unlikely that the bank would agree with this lack of financial commitment to the proposal.

For a personal lending proposition, if the customer is looking to use the advance to purchase an asset, how big a contribution are they making towards the overall cost? Also, if the customer has approached you for a mortgage, what percentage of the total cost of the house are they looking for the bank to provide?

With asset acquisition, you may find that the customer's contribution comes by way of the sale of an existing asset. You have probably done this yourself when looking to finance the purchase of a new car, where your contribution towards the cost of the new car is the trade in of your existing vehicle. Therefore, rather than making a physical cash deposit towards the total cost, you are still contributing financially by deducting the value of your trade in from the total cost of the new car.

Generally, the more of their own resources the customer has committed to the project, the greater their commitment to its success is felt to be.

QUICK QUESTION

Can you think of other ways in which a customer's commitment to a proposition can be gauged?

Write your answer here before reading on.

Another way in which you may consider commitment is through any assets that the customer owns and is willing to pledge to the bank as security for the advance.

7.5 Other personal factors

We will now move on to look at some of the other information about the customer that we will need to analyse before coming to a decision.

Firstly, we need to determine the customer's personal circumstances, as these are going to affect the decision about the lending application. Some of these factors we have already discussed – for example, the customer's age.

QUICK QUESTION

What other personal factors do you think should be considered here?

Write your answer here before reading on.

The other factors that should be looked at are:

- Marital status
- Employment
- Previous connections with your organisation – for example, other accounts/products that this customer uses.

QUICK QUESTION

Look at the personal factors that are listed in the table below and complete the table to state why we would look for this information.

Factor	Reason(s)
Marital status	
Dependents	
Employment	
Connections with your organisation	

Write your answer here before reading on.

Here are the reasons why we are interested in this information.

Factor	Reason(s)
Marital status 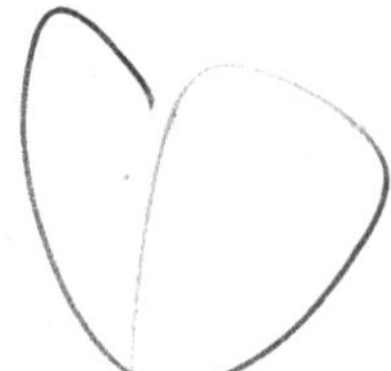	The customers marital status can affect their ability to repay the borrowing – for example, with a couple, they have the potential to both be earning and so increase the amount of free funds that they have available to repay the loan. This additional income may also mean that the borrowing can be repaid quicker than it would have been done has the applicant only had a sole income.
Dependents	Again, this is something that we look at when considering payment. A couple may have a joint income, but by having a family, their monthly outgoings will be far greater than if there were no dependants. If they have a young family, then that may explain the lack of elasticity in surplus of income over expenditure. Due to the ageing population, you should also strive to find out if the applicant has parents or parents-in-law who are dependant (or will shortly become dependent) on them – again, this could increase their monthly outgoings and/or reduce their monthly income and so have an effect on their repayment ability. Later on, when we look at payment, we need to establish the customer's regular income and outgoings. When you get to this stage of the application, you should cross-refer to this information to check that the income and outgoings are realistic for a customer in this given set of circumstances. Again, if you are dealing with an existing customer you can compare how the information given at this stage matches with the conduct of their account.
Employment	The customer's employment will also have a great bearing when we come to look at payment as employment will have a direct effect on the customer's income. When the customer talks to you about their employment, then what arrangement are they specifically referring to? Are they in permanent, full time employment, are they employed on a contractual basis or are they self-employed? The answers that you get to these questions may well trigger further questions. For example, if they are employed on short-term contracts, then when do the current contracts expire/what further contracts do they have lined up/how likely are current contracts to be seen through to fruition/what are the cancellation arrangements. If they are self-employed what exactly do they do/who do they provide goods and services to/what prospects does the business have/who are their accountants/is their tax paid up to date/can we have sight of at least three years audited accounts?

Factor	Reason(s)
	The type of employment may also indicate whether the customer is paid: ▪ Weekly ▪ Fortnightly ▪ Monthly. This information is important when you come to look at the best type of product for the customer so that you can structure the repayment schedule to tie in to when they receive their income – either by way of salary from employment, drawings from a partnership or dividends (and small salary) from a limited company. The customer's employment can also give you an indication of how their salary is broken down between an annual salary and bonuses. If your customer is a sales representative, you will need to determine what their basic salary is as well as how their bonus scheme operates. If they have a low basic salary, this may cause you concern as they may not always earn enough by way of bonus to keep up the proposed repayment. On the other hand, if the customer is a teacher, then you will ascertain that they receive a monthly salary and do not have the opportunity to earn bonuses – although perhaps they could supplement their income by private tutoring or running training commercial courses during the school holidays. These examples are also relevant when you come to decide what the most appropriate product is – for the salesperson, you may wish to structure the borrowing so that, along with the regular monthly repayments they make, you may also want them to be able to make one off payments in reduction of the debt as and when they earn bonuses. For the teacher, you are more likely to be looking for a facility that will allow them to make level monthly repayments until the advance is cleared. The customer's employment details will also give you an insight into their future earning potential – are they employed with an established employer in a sector of the economy that is growing, or are they working for an unknown organisation in an economic sector that you know is in decline? As mentioned earlier, you also need to consider how the industry sector they are involved in is likely to be affected by changes in the economic cycle. For example, a business associated with the building trade is usually amongst the first of businesses to be affected by an economic downturn and amongst the last to see their business pick up as a result of an economic recovery.

Factor	Reason(s)
	Your local knowledge (and that of your colleagues) will also be of use here – it could be that the customer is employed by a company that you know is making a number of redundancies, or is about to relocate to another part of the country. Finally, the customer's employment details will let you know whether they are self-employed or not. You should always remember that even if the customer is receiving a monthly salary from a limited company – they may still be self-employed as the company could be their own, with them the only employee.
Connections with your organisation	If the customer has a connection with your bank, then there is lots of information about them that you will be able to source – for example, by examining the entries that have been both debited and credited to their account over a period of time together with reviewing their automated payments, you will be able to verify that the income and expenditure that they state they have is realistic. Additionally, you may also be able to see other commitments they have – for example, an obligation to an outside party such as Capital One. Also, if the customer has had borrowing with your organisation in the past, you will be able to check to see if these were repaid as agreed at the outset. On the other hand, if the customer has savings products with your bank, then these will give an indication of how well they save – if they have been saving regularly each month, then this should give you confidence that they will be disciplined enough to make the relative repayments. Also, if the customer has savings with you, it may be that they wish to use these, or some of these, as part of their contribution to the cost of the asset being purchased. Alternatively, they may wish the balance of the savings account to be offset against the borrowing to reduce the interest charge. Again, bear in mind that assumptions should never be made about the circumstances surrounding an existing customer and their details and information should always be verified.

7.6 The customer's assets and liabilities

We will now look at the information that we need to record about the customer's assets and liabilities. Whilst the specific documentation that is used to record this information will vary from bank to bank, you will find that the type of information that is recorded will be very similar. This information is normally recorded on a document known as a statement of means.

QUICK QUESTION

Why do you think that we need to consider the customer's assets and liabilities when assessing a lending application?

Write your answer here before reading on.

The need to consider this information is to help allow us to have as full a picture as possible of the customer – so this must include what assets the customer owns as well as looking at what financial obligations they have as well.

An added advantage to looking at the customer's means is that later on in our credit assessment, we may decide that it will be necessary to ask the customer for security before authorising the advance. There are some types of security that are of more value to the lending banker than others. However, if we know what assets the customer has, we can make an informed decision about the type(s) of security that we wish to ask the customer for. As well as knowing what potential security items the customer has, we also need to know if the customer has any debts attached to particular items of security as that would affect the attractiveness of the security to the banker – for example, if the customer owns property, that may be a suitable item of security for our purposes, however, if the customer also has an outstanding mortgage on this property, then this will reduce the attractiveness of this particular item of security to us.

Returning to the examination of the customer's assets and liabilities, we will now look in more detail at what we need to consider here.

QUICK QUESTION

Make a list of the types of asset that a customer may have.

Write your answer here before reading on.

Typically, a customer could have some, or if they are lucky, all of the following assets:

- Property – as well as their main property, the customer may also own a holiday house, property that they let out to tenants, or even property that other members of their family use. This last point would cover the situation where the customer has children studying at university and they have purchased a flat for them to live in for the duration of their studies.
- Stocks and shares. These could be ordinary or preference shares. It is also possible that the customer may have lent money to a business by way of a debenture or bond.
- Government securities – for example, Treasury Stock.
- Life assurance policies.
- Bank/building society accounts.
- Others – for example, antiques, paintings, cars.

The most current value for each of these assets should be recorded – for example, for a life assurance policy, a current surrender value would give the most accurate description of the value of the policy.

QUICK QUESTION

Now make a list of the common types of liability that a customer could have.

Write your answer here before reading on.

Typically, a customer could have the following liabilities:

- An outstanding mortgage(s) on their property
- Loans/credit card debts
- Guarantees.

Again, the most up to date figures should be recorded against these items.

Having looked at a high level at the customer's assets and liabilities, it is a straightforward task to sum up their asset value and deduct from this the total of their liabilities. The resulting figure is often referred to as the customer's net means.

We now have an overall picture of the customer's assets, liabilities and net means. However, as the purpose of credit assessment is to make an informed decision on the request that the customer is making, we need to drill down on these figures to look in more detail at the customer's assets and liabilities.

QUICK QUESTION

Refer back to the list of the customer's assets above.

What other information would you like to have on these assets to inform your lending decision?

Write your answer here before reading on.

Looking at each item in turn:

Property	Where the property is, type of property, valuation, date of the valuation.
Stocks and shares	In what companies the shares are in, amount of shares held in each company, type of shares (for example, ordinary, preference) current stock exchange valuation.
Government securities	Types of stock, coupon rate, redemption date, current Stock Exchange valuation.
Life policies	Name of assurance company, current surrender value, maturity date of policy.
Bank/building society accounts	Name(s) of bank/building society, type of account (for example, instant access, notice), term of notice (if any), balances.
Others	Depends on type of asset held – but generally, you are looking for a description of each asset, a note of the most recent valuation, the basis of the valuation and the date of the valuation.

QUICK QUESTION

You should always exercise care with the reliance you place on any of the assets listed in the section above – why?

Write your answer here before reading on.

It is easy to place a value on a building society account, because the value of the asset will remain constant and it is easy to realise this asset. However the same cannot be said for an original painting. Firstly, it can be difficult to place a value on this type of asset, secondly, the value of the painting may fluctuate widely based on the demand for a particular type of art at any time, and finally, if the customer wishes to sell the painting, it may take some time to find a suitable buyer with both the desire and the means to buy the painting.

As a result of these points, you should exercise great caution when dealing with this type of asset and it is wise not to place too much reliance on them.

QUICK QUESTION

Now look at the liabilities that were listed earlier.

Again, make a note of the addition information you would like to have on these to enable you to make an informed lending decision.

Write your answer here before reading on.

Looking at each item in turn:

Mortgage(s)	The amount outstanding, the property that the mortgage refers to, the type of mortgage (e.g. capital and interest, interest only, current account mortgage), the date of the final payment.
Loans/Credit Cards	The amount outstanding, the name of the lender, the type of debt (e.g. loan, card), the date of the final payment.
Guarantees	Details of the guarantee – the amount, the name of the debtor, the name of the lender, the date of anticipated repayment of the loan.

To conclude this section on the person, we need to ensure that the profile of the customer is consistent with any guidelines that appear as part of the banks strategic and marketing objectives.

7.7 The purpose

We are now ready to move onto the next stage of our analysis – the purpose.

When we start to consider the purpose of an advance, you must firstly look to the credit policy and determine if what you are being asked to fund falls within the parameters of the policy. Keep in mind that you need to consider both the general credit policy that governs the entire organisation and any specific credit policy that applies to the particular area that you are currently working in.

Tied into this point is a consideration that the purpose of the borrowing is legal. When considering legal risk, you need to ensure that the documentation that you use for the facilities – for example, an Offer Letter – provides a legal and binding contract. This would also be the case for any security documentation that is used. However, by using the standard documentation used by your organisation, you will have the comfort of knowing that you are being compliant in this regard. If for any reason the customer wishes to depart from this standard documentation, then you would need to refer this matter to your Legal Department.

This is the point in the application process where we need to be absolutely clear as to what it is that we are being asked to fund. It may well be that you will require the customer to provide you with authenticated documentation to verify and validate what it is that they are looking to have funded. If you do not do this, then you will not know if what you are funding is, indeed within the bank's credit policy.

As well as being satisfied as to what it is that we are funding, we also need to determine at this stage exactly how much it is that the customer is looking to borrow.

QUICK QUESTION

What problems might arise if the customer is borrowing too little money?

Write your answer here before reading on.

If the customer is asking for too little, then they will not be able to see the proposed project to a successful conclusion as they will run out of funds. As a result, they will either have to use more of their own funds or come back to you to request additional funding. In the latter situation, you are placed in a very difficult situation – you may feel that you need to advance this additional request and thus be lending at a level that you are uncomfortable with. On the other hand, if you refuse the request for additional support, then you are putting the future of the customer's project in jeopardy and this may affect the ability of the customer to effect repayment to the bank.

The other side of this funding coin is the situation where the customer is asking for too much money. If this is the case, and unless they are borrowing on overdraft, then they are going to incur higher interest charges than they would have needed to.

The amount that the customer is contributing to the project is also important here – the less the financial commitment the customer is making, then the greater the risk is to the bank as we are being asked to fund a disproportionate amount. This type of situation may affect the level of pricing as the greater the risk the bank is taking then the greater reward the bank will look to secure from the deal. Therefore, if the bank is being asked to make a higher level of contribution, then although the advance may be sanctioned (if it is viable at that level), the level of interest charged may also be greater.

You will also need to be happy that the customer is able to afford the proposed repayments.

QUICK QUESTION

How can you establish that the customer is looking for the correct amount?

Write your answer here before reading on.

The specific steps that you take will vary with each lending proposition. For example, if a personal customer is looking to take out an advance to help with home improvements, you might ask to see estimates for the proposed work. There are a number of advantages to both you and the customer in taking this approach:

- You will be able to ascertain quickly that the customer is looking for the right amount.
- Bearing in mind that you will probably have been presented with this type of request before, you will be able to determine if the estimates are reasonable for the work being proposed.
- If you have asked the customer to obtain more than one estimate, you will be able to compare these.

QUICK QUESTION

You are interviewing a customer for an advance and when you ask them about the purpose of the borrowing, they respond by saying that provided they meet the required repayment schedule, the purpose of the advance should be of no consequence to the bank.

How should you respond?

Write your answer here before reading on.

At the initial stage, you would require details of the purpose of the advance. In the past there have been fiscal or government directives in force which prohibit such lending, or the Credit Policy may have laid down certain restrictions on types of lending. This could be to restrict the bank's exposure to lending in certain fields or sectors. This is commonly known as portfolio limits.

We also need to know the purpose of the borrowing to ensure that it is consistent with all other aspects of the Credit Policy – as lending for some specific purposes may potentially fall outside the Policy guidelines. An example of this may be advances in respect of debt consolidation.

Finally, as mentioned earlier in this section you must be satisfied that you are lending money for a legal purpose that fits with the overall credit strategy. It is also important to consider if the purpose of the borrowing is consistent with the past behaviour and actions of the customer and they there are no suspicions that the bank may have concerning the current anti-money laundering procedures.

7.8 Loan to value

Another aspect to consider under the heading of amount is loan to value.

QUICK QUESTION

What is your understanding of the term loan to value?

Write your answer here before reading on.

Loan to value (or LTV as it is abbreviated), is the ratio of the size of the borrowing compared to the value of the asset being purchased/held as security.

So, if a customer is looking for an advance to purchase property, valued at £250,000, and the mortgage is for £200,000, then the LTV is 80%. You should note that when calculating LTV, the figure taken for the asset should be the lower of the cost or the realisable value of the asset.

LTV is one of the measures of risk for a lender – higher LTV advances are viewed as having a higher risk and to compensate for this, a lending banker will charge a higher rate of interest on the borrowing.

When looking at the amount and purpose, you should also give consideration to the term of the borrowing.

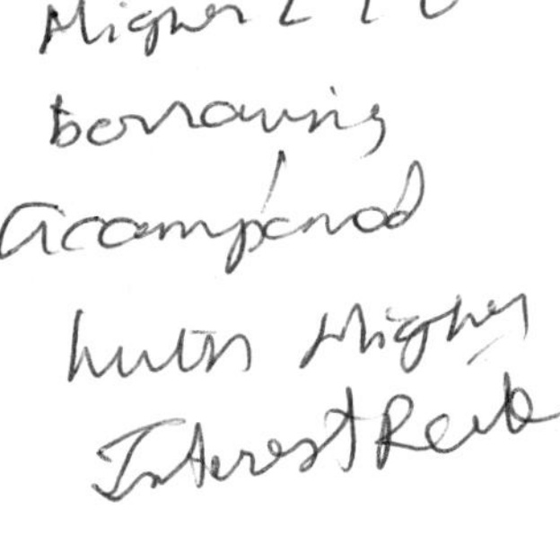

QUICK QUESTION

What is the significance of the term of the borrowing?

Write your answer here before reading on.

There are a number of factors that can be influenced by the term of the borrowing.

Firstly, once we know what the term of the borrowing is, we will know whether we are dealing with short-term, medium-term or long-term borrowing. Secondly, the term of the borrowing will affect the repayment amount – the longer the period the advance is being repaid over, then the lower the monthly repayments will be, all other factors being equal.

QUICK QUESTION

What other figure do you think will be affected by the term of the advance?

Write your answer here before reading on.

The other figure affected by the term of the borrowing is the total amount of interest paid over the life of the advance. Assuming all other things are equal, the longer the term of the borrowing, the higher the total amount of interest that the customer will have paid. If you think about the advertisements seen from providers such as Ocean Finance, you will see that they make claims about how much they can reduce monthly repayments made by borrowers. This is done (in part) by expending the term of the customer's borrowing. As a result of this, the monthly repayment will fall but the term of the borrowing can be increased dramatically. The end result is that the total amount repaid by the customer is far in excess of their original undertaking.

The bank will also want to compare the term of the borrowing with the anticipated life of the asset that the advance is financing. For example, if a customer approaches you looking to borrow money to part finance the purchase of a car, then you would look for the borrowing to be repaid during the lifetime of the car – this is why you will not see a car loan with a term of 10 years.

Whilst we will consider payment in the next section, this is an appropriate point to consider if there is a logical fit between the asset we are being asked to finance and the source of repayment.

QUICK QUESTION

If a customer is asking for assistance from the bank to purchase investment property, what would you expect the repayment source to be?

Write your answer here before reading on.

In this example, the logical source of repayment would be rental income from the property. On the other hand, in this example, if you were being asked to fund investment property, but the repayment source was dividend income, then this is an illogical repayment source and you would wish to ask the customer why you were not being offered rental income as your repayment source.

There could also be a situation where you are being asked to grant facilities for what seems to be a short-term purpose, but repayment seems to be coming from a longer term asset source. For example, the customer may be looking for help to meet the costs of the Christmas season, but is proposing repayment from a life policy that will mature in 6 months' time. This could still be an acceptable situation if the policy has sufficient free funds to cover both principal and interest. Ideally you would hold the policy and have the life policy remit the cheque direct to the bank – thus reducing the risk of repayment being delayed.

Finally, if you sanction facilities and the customer agrees that they will dispose of assets to repay the debt in the event that reduction is proving difficult, then you should not only put this agreement in writing, but you would also wish to have the customer acknowledge this by signing and returning a copy of this letter to you.

7.9 Payment

QUICK QUESTION

It is sometimes said that payment is the most important aspect of the principles of lending. Why do you think that this is so?

Write your answer here before reading on.

Those who argue that payment is the most important will state that there is no point in lending anyone money if you are not going to get it back.

You could, at times, come across a customer who states that provided you have enough good quality security in place, then repayment is guaranteed, so why is the bank so concerned with repayment? However, as a professional and ethical banker should lend against the viability of the proposal – not the quality of the security. After all, we are bankers, not pawnbrokers!

The conditions of the advance concerning repayment and interest need to be clearly established at an early stage. These conditions vary, depending on the nature of the advance; for example, bridging loans are normally for large amounts but repaid very quickly.

Flexibility is necessary and repayment arrangements should be based on fair reflections of profit/surplus income and/or liquid flows, with customer consultation where appropriate. It is important that the customer is happy that they can meet the proposed repayment schedule. It is often necessary to emphasise to the customer the commitment that they are undertaking. Often, when a customer approaches the bank, their focus of attention is on whether or not we are going to lend them the money. It is not until they have the funds and are then faced with meeting the repayment schedule, that their minds turn to this.

When discussing payment, attention should be given to primary, secondary and tertiary sources of payment.

QUICK QUESTION

What is your understanding of primary, secondary and tertiary sources of payment?

Write your answer here before reading on.

A customer's primary source of servicing and meeting loan payments is the surplus of total income less total expenditure. However, always keep in mind that the proposal that the customer is looking for our assistance with will impact on their income and expenditure – the asset may in some cases generate additional income and/or the asset being financed may well involve additional expenditure for the customer. Therefore when we reach this stage of our analysis, we need to take into account:

- The impact of the borrowing on the customer – for example, meeting interest and capital repayments.
- The increased expenditure caused as a result of owning the new asset. For example, if we are being asked to help fund a second home, then there are additional costs by way of insurance, council tax, utilities and so on to be met.
- Owning the asset may generate additional income. In the last example, if the second home is located in the Lake District, then the customer may generate additional income by letting the property out at times as a holiday home.

The secondary source of payment is them realising or liquidating assets that are no longer required and using these funds to reduce their debt.

The tertiary source of payment is the realisation of assets held by the bank as security or the calling up of a guarantee.

As mentioned above, bankers look to future income or earnings to provide the source of repayment, not the realisation of security. This point cannot be emphasised too much. Therefore we are looking for primary payment.

QUICK QUESTION

You could have a situation where the customer can make the scheduled repayments at the time the advance is agreed.

What other factors could come into play that would affect their ability to maintain these repayments in the future?

Write your answer here before reading on.

There are a couple of factors to look at here. These include:

- For borrowing with a variable interest rate, what would happen if interest rates were to increase? Could the customer still make the required repayments?
- How stable is the customer's employment/income source? What would happen if they were to lose their job – there are protection products that the customer could take out to mitigate this risk.

It is possible that the banker can carry out a sensitivity analysis at this point to forecast the effect of changing circumstances during the life of the advance. For example, if the interest rate on the facility will be variable, we can determine what the effect would be of say a 1% increase in rates.

QUICK QUESTION

If you are dealing with a personal customer, how can you ascertain whether or not they will be able to meet the proposed repayments?

Write your answer here before reading on.

Most banks will have some kind of Income and Expenditure Statement that they will ask a prospective borrower to complete in order to assess whether or not they will be able to service the borrowing.

QUICK QUESTION

What main piece of information would you look to have recorded on the income side of an income and expenditure statement?

Write your answer here before reading on.

The main piece of information recorded for income is fairly straightforward. You would look to see the salary details of the borrower(s).

QUICK QUESTION

When looking at the borrowers salary details, do you think that this should be quoted as gross or net of tax?

Write your answer here before reading on.

It is better to record these figures as net of salary – as this is the amount of income that the customer will receive.

QUICK QUESTION

It is normal on this type of document to see a heading for Other Income. What items do you think could be covered here?

Write your answer here before reading on.

The other types of income that could be shown include:

- Child benefit.
- Rental income – the customer could be letting either part of their property or an entire property on a commercial basis.
- Dividends/interest income. In this case, you would want to find out information about the investments that the customer holds that is yielding this income. It may be that you are able to verify this information by looking at the record that you have of the customer's assets and liabilities which we looked at in the person section of this chapter.
- Bonus – remember to keep in mind the points we looked at earlier regarding any bonus that a customer may earn. It is also important to keep in mind that a bonus will not be guaranteed and should not be looked to as a primary source of repayment for the loan.
- Income from a second job – perhaps the customer does part time work in the evenings or weekends to supplement their income. If this is the case, you should find out how regular this income is and for how long it is reasonable to expect this income to continue for.

If you are dealing with an existing customer, you will be able to verify much of this information by looking at the conduct of their account – but remember that you would still want to confirm this understanding with the customer in case their circumstances have changed recently.

QUICK QUESTION

It is also useful to be able to look at the customer's pay slips/salary advice.

What information could you glean from this?

Write your answer here before reading on.

The advantage to be gained from looking at these documents is that you will not only be able to verify that the salary information is correct, but you will also be able to see what the breakdown of the salary is – for example, how much of the salary comprises bonus or overtime payments? If overtime has come into the equation, again you need to find out how often the customer works overtime and how guaranteed this overtime is. Like a bonus, it is unlikely that the bank would want to rely on overtime payments as a primary source of repayment for the loan.

To get a clear picture of the customer's salary it is normal practice to ask to see salary advices for the past three months – this will allow you to see if the customer has a regular level of income, or whether there are wide fluctuations in their income levels.

If the person does not bank with you, it is also possible to verify the applicant's wage/salary by scrutinising pay slips/salary advices. Again, you would be looking for at least the last three months slips.

QUICK QUESTION

List what your regular monthly financial outgoings are.

Write your answer here before reading on.

Whilst there may be some slight variations if you compare your list to someone else's, the major items will almost certainly be the same.

The types of heading that you should have will be:

- Mortgage/rent
- Council tax
- Insurance/assurance
- Telephone
- Electricity/gas
- Travel expenses
- Mobile phone
- Car repayments
- Car running costs
- Food
- Clothing
- Hobbies/interests
- Holidays
- Loan repayments (other than those covered earlier in the list)
- Credit card/store card repayments.

Again, if the customer already banks with you, you will be able to verify much of the information supplied by looking at their account as well as their automated payments.

It can also be worthwhile carrying out, for example, an Experian check at this stage to determine if the customer has any other obligations that we have not been made aware of, or if there are any payments arrears associated with the customer.

It is important that you don't just accept everything that the customer states when looking at their income and expenditure – if a figure seems to be out of line you must challenge this with the customer. Remember that this assessment is vital when looking at the customer's ability to repay the borrowing; therefore, you want to be happy in your mind that you are making an assessment based on realistic and well thought out figures.

When looking at how realistic the information you have gathered in here you should compare the customer's figures with:

- Your personal experience – do these figures seem realistic compared to your outgoings?
- The information that is held on record from other customers' in similar circumstances.

It is also normal practice when looking at the customer's income and expenditure to look at other borrowing that they have outstanding, either with your bank, or with other organisations. One reason for doing this is to ensure that the customer is not becoming financially overcommitted.

The information you gather here should be cross referred to the information that you already hold regarding the customer's expenditure. You must be happy that the monthly loan/credit card repayments detailed under monthly expenditure relates to the loans and credit cards that are listed as loans outstanding.

QUICK QUESTION

If you are collecting information about the obligations that a customer has outstanding, what specific information would you like to have?

Write your answer here before reading on.

You should attempt to organise this information under the following headings:

- Source of loan – is the customer borrowing from another bank, a finance company, a credit union, credit cards or store cards?
- Lending institutions – under the headings listed in the preceding point, you would want to know what organisations the customer has been dealing with. It may be that the customer has already approached one of these companies for the loan and their application has been rejected – you would want to know the reason(s) behind this rejection.
- You would also like to have information on the original amount of each loan, how much is currently outstanding, what the monthly commitment for each loan is and when will each loan be repaid.

Having identified and interpreted all of the information under the heading of Payment you will now be in a position to make an informed decision about whether or not the customer can afford the borrowing.

Earlier in the course we discussed the concept of due diligence and a practical application of this would occur at this stage in the assessment of credit risk when we carry it out on a prospective borrower.

In the context of credit risk, we carry out due diligence in the following ways:

- Completion/validation of the Statement of Means/Income and Expenditure statements
- Property valuations
- Use of credit reference agencies
- Credit searches
- Other relevant internet searches – for example nethouseprice.com.

In order to act in a professional and ethical manner, it is important that we carry out the appropriate levels of due diligence for the proposal that we are currently assessing. The level and type of due diligence can therefore vary according to the particular proposals, but there are certain guiding principles that inform the level of due diligence required.

QUICK QUESTION

What factors do you think would influence the level of due diligence carried out?

Write your answer here before reading on.

The influencing factors include:

- The level of customer background information and financial information that we currently hold and are able to verify independently
- Whether it is a new or an existing customer
- The purpose of the loan
- The amount of borrowing requested
- The complexity of the proposal
- The structure of the proposal
- The amount and type of security being offered

- The repayment source
- For a new connection, the source of the introduction
- The customer's financial track record.

7.10 Statement of Means (SoM)/Statement of income and expenditure

When we encounter a new customer, a SoM would be completed at the time of an initial borrowing request. In the case of an existing customer, we would look to have a SoM completed if they request additional funding, and as a general rule for a borrowing customer we would look to have a fresh SoM completed on an annual basis.

QUICK QUESTION

What actions would you take on receipt of a SoM?

Write your answer here before reading on.

As a minimum the following actions should be taken to validate the authenticity of the information on the SoM:

- Check that the information accurately reflects the profile of the customer and their family history. In many cases this will be possible by referring to existing records.
- Ensure that the picture presented by the SoM reflects the customer's known financial background
- Carry out any investigatory actions as required to validate the authenticity of the information captured.

At the end of this exercise we want to be sure that the SoM gives a true reflection of the customer's current financial position.

QUICK QUESTION

What activities could you carry out to validate the information contained in the SoM?

Write your answer here before reading on.

Investigatory actions would include:

- Scrutinising the account of an existing customer for salary, SO/DD details
- Validate the accuracy of recording of cash deposits – for example, from the maturity of a fixed rate bond
- Check records for any arrears in mortgage and/or credit card
- Validate any property values
- Refer to security records to validate guarantees, etc.
- If the customer has a business connection with your bank adequate liaison should be maintained with the appropriate relationship manager
- Review of payslips and/or P60 document. You will recall from earlier that we would look for at least three payslips
- Validation of the last three months' bank statements
- Seeking independent validation of one off payments – for example, maturity of a life policy, bonus payments, dividends received, etc.
- Obtain documentary evidence of substantial deposits held with another organisation
- Seek conformation, as appropriate, of material obligations
- Ensure that asset ownership is clearly identified
- Seek independent share portfolio, property, life policy, pension valuation, etc.
- For a self-employed customer seek independent validation (from accountants) regarding recent earnings and business performance
- Undertake personal and business Experian/Equifax searches to ascertain financial profile, current outstanding obligations and any potential arrears etc.

7.11 Valuations

Whether dealing with domestic or commercial property, it is vital that if this is being used either as security or as a repayment source that we should have the value of the property validated.

7.12 Personal credit search

For any new customer a personal credit search should be undertaken and the results of this should be maintained in the customer's file. A credit search would be carried out as part of an account opening process, so if there is a credit request at the time of account opening, then it may be that there is no requirement to carry out a more extensive search. However, the sanctioning officer would need to be happy that the level of information obtained from this automatic search is adequate for the amount involved and if not, then a more detailed search would be required.

With an existing customer, a credit search would be carried out if new borrowing is requested, and this would certainly be the case if the customer is requesting a material increase in their borrowing, or if the request concerns debt consolidation or refinancing.

7.13 Business Experian search

If a customer is closely connected to either a limited company or to a Limited Liability Partnership, then consideration should be given to undertaking a Business Experian Search. This will provide information such as:

- Full company profile
- Company net worth/value of share capital. This information can be cross referenced against the individual customer's shareholdings

- Annual accounts. This will include key financial ratio breakdowns. However, when dealing with financial accounts you should always bear in mind that you can be dealing with information that is fast becoming out of date
- Industry performance trend analysis and business benchmarking information
- Records of any court judgements against the business
- Details of unpaid creditors
- Profiles of key personnel – this will include previous directorships and business interests
- Principal shareholder profiles
- Details of previous business trading names – if appropriate.

7.14 Other forms of due diligence

There are other forms of due diligence that can be undertaken – for example, completing the Know Your Customer/Know Your Business requirements will form part of the due diligence process. Also conducting an internet search may yield useful information on the background of a customer and/or their business connections. The information obtained here may spark further investigations that you would wish to carry out.

7.15 Overall viability

What we have been doing so far in our examination of the principles of lending is looking at the **viability** of the proposal. The remainder of this section on the 5ps of credit risk will look at other factors that we should consider as part of a fuller assessment. If by this stage in the assessment we find that the proposal is not viable, then we can stop the assessment now and convey our decision to the customer. After all, if the proposal is not viable, then there is no point in looking at security, or thinking about the level of fees that we might charge, as we will not be granting the facility.

Before moving on to consider these other aspects of the principles of lending, it is worthwhile to reflect back on the work we have done so far on viability.

QUESTION TIME 3

You are working in the credit assessment team of a bank and a new member of staff has joined the team today.

As part of their induction to the team, your manager has asked you to chat through a number of lending applications with them, to let them see how a lending proposal is assessed.

You start by explaining to this person that in order to proceed with any application, the lending banker must be able to assess the viability of the proposal. This is a new term to this person and they ask you to explain it.

How would you respond?

Write your answer here then check with the answer at the back of the book.

7.16 Protection

In the first instance, the proposition should be basically solid and, as you know payment should come from normal sources such as income, sale of an asset, etc. However, all lending bears some element of risk, as we have mentioned on a number of occasions, from the banker's viewpoint, repayment happens in the future and the future is uncertain. Therefore, no matter how attractive and realistic the proposition may be, there is always a risk that what was anticipated does not materialise and payment becomes in doubt.

The ultimate risk which the banker must guard against is the borrower's bankruptcy and, should the banker consider that the advance is more than the unsupported credit justifies, security should be taken.

At this stage in the process, we need to identify the credit risk associated with the proposal and, having done this, can then determine if there are suitable mitigants – for example, security or covenants – and these should be put in place.

We will now move on to consider what factors make for a good security.

7.16.1 Attributes of a good security

If you know the attributes of a good security and you have some appreciation of what each type of security is, then it is much easier to make an assessment of what the advantages and disadvantages are in taking security over each of these assets.

QUICK QUESTION

If you were about to take an asset as security from a customer, what would you look for in that asset to make it a good security?

Write your answer here before reading on.

There are three things that a banker would look for in a security:

- Simplicity of title
- Stability of value
- Realisability.

Most forms of security do not exclusively fall within the plus side of each attribute – they have negative aspects as well. So, arguably, there are few assets that constitute the perfect banking security.

We will now look at each of these attributes in turn.

7.17 Simplicity of title

QUICK QUESTION

What do you think we mean by simplicity of title?

Write your answer here before reading on.

It is an important consideration both to the banker and the borrower that the security can be completed easily, quickly and cheaply – this is equally important to the discharge, realisation or release of the security.

This attribute can be found in most types of security taken by banks with the notable exception of security over property. In the case of this type of security it can be both time consuming and costly for investigation of title and for the formalities of completion of the security to be carried out.

Ideally, we must look for the title to the subject of the security to be free from all liabilities or incumbrances of any nature which might prevent any future action that the bank may want to take with the security. An example of this would be if the customer offered the bank security over their property, but they already had an outstanding mortgage against the property. In this situation, if the customer defaulted on the loan and after following all of the recovery procedures the bank felt that they had no option but to realise the security, they may find this difficult as they would need to obtain the agreement of the first security holder.

7.18 Stability of value

QUICK QUESTION

What do you understand by the term stability of value and why is it important to the lending banker when looking at security?

Write your answer here before reading on.

It is also important that a banker can rely on the value placed on a security. You know what you want the security to be worth when you take it but you also wish to be as sure as you can be that it will be worth the amount you need when you need it. Different types of security vary in this regard with some retaining their value well, others appreciating in value, and some have a value which is more volatile; it can rise or fall over time and with limited predictability.

The overriding rule here is that you ensure that the margin, or the difference between the borrowing you grant and the value of the security is sufficient to allow for a fall in value. It is vital, of course that the value of the asset does not fall below the amount of the borrowing. Be particularly aware of security which may be subject to sudden and wide fluctuations in value, such as some kinds of stocks and shares. Furthermore, when considering the matter of value, you must also take into account whether or not the value, at any time during the lifetime of the security, is easily ascertainable.

QUICK QUESTION

What types of security do you think would be easy to value and what would be more difficult?

Write your answer here before reading on.

The easiest types of security to value are:

- Cash lodgements
- Assignations of life policies
- Quoted stocks, shares and gilts.

It is more difficult to be able to value:

- Specialised or commercial property
- Unquoted shares.

7.19 Realisability

You must bear in mind that repayment of borrowing may not follow the agreed course and the banker may have to seek to realise security held. To do so, the security ideally must be capable of quick realisation without undue formality. Any delay in the procedures for realisation can increase the possible loss of principal debt and interest.

If we have taken a security which has a value that cannot readily be realised, such as a house subject to a tenant's rights or shares in a private company, then this may result in the debt not being extinguished at short notice.

It is worth re-emphasising that we should always look to the viability of the proposal for repayment – not for security. As the name would suggest, security is there as a backup to guard against any unforeseen events that may occur during the life of the loan that will prevent the customer from making the promised repayments. As such, we should never look to security as the primary means of repaying an advance – it is the tertiary source.

It is better to think of security in the same way that a trapeze artist looks at their safely net. The trapeze artist will have prepared for their act with the intention of completing it as planned – not by plunging into the net. However, the fact that the net is there will give the trapeze artist peace of mind. So it is with security – the banker will expect the borrowing to be repaid as agreed as at the outset – but if there are any mishaps along the way, then the security will give them peace of mind.

As discussed earlier in the course, it is normal practice for a bank to discount the value of the security.

It may also be the case that we need to build conditions (or as they are sometimes referred to as covenants) into the borrowing around security and its value. For example, if you are being asked to fund a project and you take shares as security, a condition may be built in to say that if the value of the shares held in security falls below a specified value then either the customer is required to provide additional security or the terms and conditions of the facility will need to be renegotiated. The reason for this is that if the value of the security falls below a certain level, then the credit risk to the bank has increased and as a result, the bank will be looking for a greater reward. As a result of this increased risk the bank may well want to increase the rate of interest changed to the customer.

7.20 Premium

A bank is no different to any other business – it needs to make a profit. In order to make this profit, its income comes from a number of sources, for example:

- The difference in the interest rates that it charges to customers who borrow and the interest rates that it pays to customers who deposit funds
- Arrangement fees in respect of lending facilities
- Charges for services that the bank provides directly – for example, safe custody services, night safe facilities
- The commission and payments it receives from other institutions for business they have passed to them – for example, insurance commission.

QUICK QUESTION

Looking at the above, how will a bank make profits from a lending proposition?

Write your answer here before reading on.

The two ways in which a bank will make profits from lending propositions are:

- The arrangement fees that they charge to set up advances
- The interest rates that they charge for facilities.

It is important that we charge the correct amount for the services that we provide to customers – if we don't get this right, then the profitability of the bank will be undermined.

We will now look at these items in turn.

Arrangement fees

When a customer gets an advance from a bank there are costs that the bank will incur.

QUICK QUESTION

What costs can you think of that fall into this category?

Write your answer here before reading on.

There are a number of costs to look at here. These include:

- If there is an interview with the customer, there will be the cost of staff time in preparing for and carrying out this interview.
- The cost of assessing the application – either by manually underwriting the proposal or putting it through a credit scoring procedure.
- The cost of processing the borrowing on the bank's computer system – setting the account up, setting up the automated payment for the repayments, arranging the drawdown for the customer, etc.
- The cost of preparing the documentation for the borrowing – the offer letter and other supporting documentation.
- The costs of arranging any security associated with the deal.
- If there are review dates set up for the facility, then there will be the cost of reviewing the borrowing at this time.

In order to cover these types of cost, a bank will charge an arrangement fee to a customer to be paid at the time that the borrowing is agreed. This fee may either be added to the borrowing or may be paid separately by the customer. Normally an arrangement fee will be lower when we are looking at the renewal of an existing facility as opposed to the setting up of a completely new advance. The simple reason for this is that it is less time consuming to review an existing facility than it is to set up a completely new facility. The amount of the arrangement fee will be negotiated between the bank and the customer at the time the borrowing is agreed. Whilst there will be some discussion between the bank and the customer as to the level of the arrangement fee, there are some parameters around which the banker will wish to operate.

7.21 Interest rates

Whilst some customers may express surprise from time to time regarding the need to pay an arrangement fee, they should all expect to pay interest on the borrowing. However, how does the lending banker decide on what level of interest rate to apply? For some products the rate of interest will be fixed at the start of the lending and will remain fixed for the duration. The simplest example that comes to mind here is the personal loan. Here the bank will have decided on the pricing of the loan based on interest rates and market conditions at the time the loan is taken out, along with the amount and term of the loan.

For example, if a customer is planning to borrow £7,500 to finance the purchase of a car over 3 years, with an interest rate of 7%, the interest calculation will be:

$$£7,500 \times 7\% \times 3 \text{ years} = £1,575$$

Therefore the total repayment (excluding the arrangement fee) would be:

$$£7,500 + £1,575 = £9,075$$

So this represents a simple situation for the banker – the bank has decided on the interest rate, so all we need do is apply the rate.

However, for other types of borrowing, the banker must negotiate with the customer what the rate of interest will be. This rate of interest will be related to the bank's base rate. The interest rate will be expressed in terms of base rate and so the amount of interest charged will fluctuate with base rate – the interest rate could be quoted as 3/BR. This means that the interest charged is at 3% over the current base rate. Therefore, if at the time the advance is agreed, the bank's base rate is 1%, then the interest rate at the start of the loan will be 4%. Say two months after the borrowing is agreed, the bank's base rate is increased to 1.5%, then the interest on the borrowing will be increased to 4.5%.

So what do we base our decision of what rate to charge on?

The fundamental way in which banks decide on rates of interest for lending is by comparing credit risk to reward. Basically, this means that the more risk is involved for the bank, then the higher the rate of interest that will be charged. The idea behind this is that the higher the likelihood that the bank may lose its money, then the more interest they will charge the customer to compensate for this.

QUICK QUESTION

What factors within a lending transaction would constitute risk?

Write your answer here before reading on.

There are a number of factors that we could look at here. For example, the purpose of the lending may present risk, or alternatively the previous borrowing record of the customer. As you have seen, one way in which the credit risk to the bank can be mitigated is by the customer providing security. Therefore, with all other things being equal, if a customer offers suitable and adequate security, the rate of interest charged by the bank should be lower.

It is important that when agreeing a rate of interest with the customer thought is given as to what the risk to the bank is and the rate of interest should be charged accordingly. This will help to ensure that you are consistent in your approach to customers. You must always be able to justify why you are charging a particular rate of interest – rather than it appearing to be an arbitrary decision. If there is not this consistency and the customer subsequently becomes aware that you are charging different interest rates for very similar types of borrowing, then this will have an adverse effect on the image and professionalism of both you and your bank.

You may find that your bank has a pricing model that allows you to determine what hurdle rate of interest you should charge for a particular facility. It is normal practice for banks to set these guidelines for staff regarding the rates of interest that they should be charging and you should use this information to help with your decision. You will usually find that these figures are not set down in tablets of stone – rather staff are advised of the range of rates that they should be operating within.

You should also keep in mind that no two lending decisions are the same, so there will always be a degree of scope to move on interest rates to accommodate these differences.

8 Other lending considerations

The 5Ps provide a decision-making framework that underpins all general lending. However, there are lending scenarios where using the 5Ps alone does not provide sufficient information to allow a balanced decision to be made. Such instances include lending to wealthy individuals, corporate and commercial customers. This section evaluates what techniques are often used to assessing the lending decision making process to these customers.

8.1 Lending to wealthy individuals

Wealthy individuals (or High Net Worth (HNW) individuals as they are sometimes called) have unique borrowing requirements. These needs can be split into three categories: borrowing to diversify concentrated stock, borrowing to diversify investment portfolios and borrowing for tax and inheritance planning purposes.

8.1.1 Borrowing to diversify concentrated stock

Some wealthy customers will have accumulated their wealth by establishing and running a successful business. If this is the case, it is likely that a large portion of their wealth is tied up in the business. If the majority of the profit generated by the business is reinvested to aid further expansion and development, the owner may have limited cash on hand to fund their personal endeavours (buying a house, living expenses, children's education etc.). Therefore they may wish to borrow some funds, using the shares in their business as collateral. This process is known as diversifying concentrated stock.

The main challenge for the lending banker in this situation is deciding on the value of the collateral. In most cases, the shares in the business will be privately held (they are not listed on a stock exchange). Therefore, detailed analysis will need to be undertaken of the business to derive a fair value of the business. This is a specialist activity that usually needs to be referred to an expert

8.1.2 Borrowing to diversify investment portfolios

Many wealthy individuals have large investment portfolios. To balance the risk and return trade off of their portfolios, it will be necessary to diversify their portfolios into different asset classes. For example, an investor whose portfolio has a large concentration of stocks and bonds may look to buy commercial property or invest in a commodities hedge fund. They may wish to borrow money against their current portfolio in order to finance diversification.

8.1.3 Borrowing for tax and inheritance planning purposes

Wealthy individuals typically have a high tax burden due to their high levels of income. Therefore they use borrowed funds to reduce their tax liabilities. Take for example a a wealthy individual in the UK who wishes to buy a new but-to-let property. While they may have sufficient cash to buy the property without borrowing any funds, they may choose to take out a mortgage on the property. They would take out the mortgage because the interest element of the mortgage payments are tax deductible and will reduce their tax payments.

Inheritance planning is another area where wealthy individuals require customised lending solutions. When a wealthy individual dies, their estate is likely to be liable for inheritance tax. To reduce the inheritance tax liability, the wealthy individual could use a lifetime mortgage scheme on their home. This involves borrowing money against the value of the home, so that when the wealthy individual dies, the value of the estate for tax purposes is reduced by the value of the lifetime mortgage debt.

8.1.4 Collateral used by wealthy individuals

QUICK QUESTION

List what types of collateral a wealthy individual is likely to pledge as security

Write your answer here before reading on.

Special consideration must be given to some unique collateral classes that may be pledged by wealthy individuals, such as:

- Private aircraft
- Yachts
- Rare and classic cars
- Rare art collections
- Fine wine and jewellery.

Valuing this collateral is usually the job of a specialist. Due to the very subjective nature of the value of these assets, the lender may wish to have the collateral valued by more than one specialist.

8.2 Lending to corporate and commercial customers

Consider a dairy farmer submitting a lending application to facilitate expanding production. Now consider a property development business submitting a lending application requesting funds in order to build a shopping centre. Because the dairy famer and the property developer's businesses are so different, specialist analysis will have to undertaken before making the lending decision. Further information in addition to the underlying 5Ps will be required in order to make the lending decision. The crux of this analysis will be centred around financial analysis (based around the financial statements of the business) of the business and non-financial analysis (based around industry and environmental analysis)

8.2.1 Financial analysis

Financial analysis involves evaluating the key financial statements of a company: The profit and loss account, the balance sheet and the cash flow statement. These three statements allow the lender to consider the following:

- Is the business profitable and do trends suggest that it will continue to be profitable for the duration of the lending period? This will be analysed by looking at the current and prior years profit and loss statements.
- What is the financial position of the company and how is the company currently financed? This will be analysed by looking at the current and prior years balance sheets.

- Does the company have sufficient cash to enable it to carry trading as a gong concern? This will be analysed by looking at the current and prior years cash flow statements.

A key technique used to analyse these financial statements is ratio analysis. A ratio used in isolation is of little use. However, when used as a comparative measure against prior year ratios and against the ratios of competitors, they can offer a variety of insights. Ratios typically used by lenders include:

- **Profitability ratios** – the ability of the company to cover its direct and indirect costs and generate sustainable profits.
- **Liquidity ratios** – the ability of the company to have adequate liquid assets available to pay liabilities as they fall due.
- **Cash flow ratios** – the ability of the company to generate enough cash in order to remain solvent.
- **Capital structure ratios** – a breakdown of how the company is financed, broken down into debt and equity components.
- **Serviceability and repayment ratios** – the ability of the company to repay interest and capital to lenders.
- **Breakeven ratios** – operating analysis of the company to ascertain how much a company needs to sell in order the cover its fixed and variable costs.

8.2.2 Non-financial analysis

For the lender to assess whether a company will be able to pay back any borrowings, the lender must also consider the economic, business and operating environment of the company. They must decide if the company has a strategy that will enable it to succeed and generate enough cash to repay its borrowings. A number of established techniques can be utilised to carry out this analysis.

8.2.3 Porter's three generic strategies

A lender will need to look at the overall business strategy of the company and decide if the strategy is coherent and likely to result in the business being successful. Porter's generic strategy framework suggests that three different generic strategies can create competitive advantage:

- Cost leadership strategy – Having the lowest selling price in the target market segment. In order to achieve this and still remain profitable, the company must have a lower cost structure than its rivals.
- Differentiation strategy – Offering customers a unique product/service that is difficult to imitate. This allows the company to charge a premium price and helps to create brand loyalty.
- Focus cost leadership – Once a company has decided upon either a cost leadership or differentiation strategy, they must the decide whether to focus their efforts on specific market segments (narrow focus) or the mass market (broad focus).

8.2.4 PESTEL analysis

The PESTEL framework is used to consider a series of macro-economic factors that can affect a business and its ability to be successful. The factors are:

- **Political** – Government policies affect the economy, such as trade tariffs, quotas, trade laws and tax policies.
- **Economic** – Interest rates, inflation, economic growth rates and foreign exchange rates.
- **Social** – Demographics and social trends.
- **Technological** – innovation, research and development and the rate of technological change.
- **Environmental** – weather and climate change.
- **Legal** – employment law, business law and health and safety laws.

8.2.5 SWOT analysis

SWOT analysis is often used in conjunction with PESTEL analysis. SWOT is a planning tool that evaluates the strengths, weaknesses, opportunities and threats relating to a company.

- **Strengths** (internal factor) – what the company does well. Strengths can be a source of competitive advantage.
- **Weaknesses** (internal factor) – factors that put the company at a disadvantage to competitors, such as poor processes or weak marketing in certain segments.
- **Opportunities** (external factor) – specific areas where the company could exploit its advantages.
- **Threats** (external factor) – factors that could cause problems for the company.

8.2.6 Porter's five forces

Porter's five forces is a tool used to analyse the attractiveness of an industry. By analysing the five forces a company can decide whether entering the industry is likely to result in profits and the competitive make-up of the industry. The five forces are:

- **Existing rivalry** – the intensity of competition that currently exists in the industry.
- **Threat of new entrants** – the barriers to entry of entering for new firms wishing to enter the industry. Is it easy or difficulty to enter the industry?
- **Threat of substitute products/services** – are alternative products available or in development that could damage profits in the industry?
- **Bargaining power of suppliers** – do suppliers to the industry have strong bargaining power? If so, this could reduce profit margins in the industry.
- **Bargaining power of buyers** – do customers have the ability to put company's under pressure (e.g. by switching to a competitor's product or buying in smaller quantities) to reduce selling prices?

8.2.7 The balanced scorecard

The balanced scorecard was pioneered by Kaplan and Norton. The purpose of the balanced scorecard is to enable a company to identify a number of key financial and non-financial measures with associated targets attached to them. If the company is achieving the targets set within the balanced scorecard, they are on course to deliver their strategic objectives.

QUICK QUESTION

Think of the financial and non-financial targets within your organisation.

Write your answer here before reading on.

Designing a balanced scorecard involves the following four steps:

- Translating the strategic vision into specific operational goals.
- Communicating the strategic vision across the organisation linking it to individual performance.
- Business planning.
- Feedback and learning leading to adjustments in strategy (if necessary).

KEY WORDS

Key words in this chapter are given below. There is space to write your own revision notes and add any other key words or phrases you want to remember.

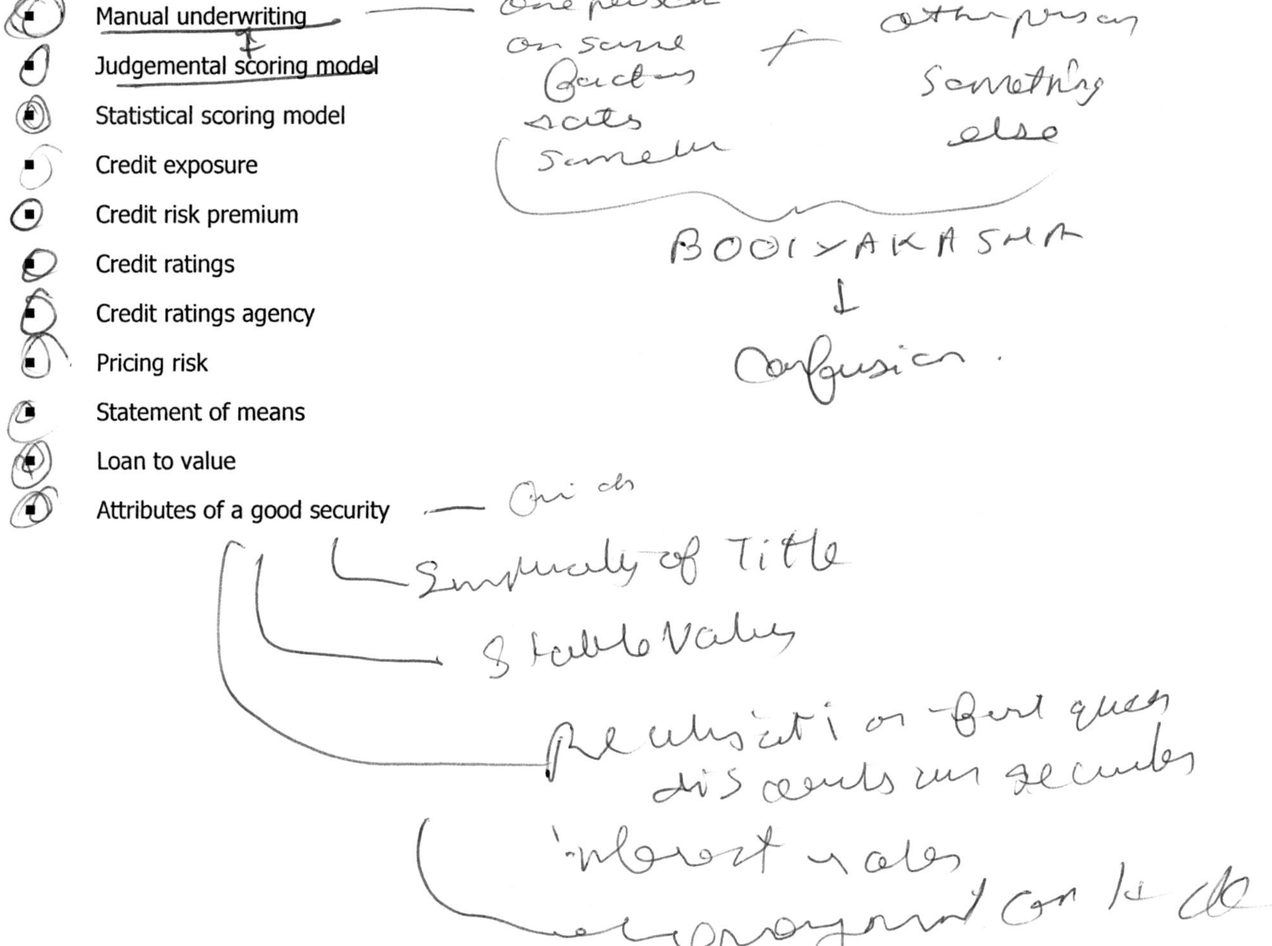

- Manual underwriting
- Judgemental scoring model
- Statistical scoring model
- Credit exposure
- Credit risk premium
- Credit ratings
- Credit ratings agency
- Pricing risk
- Statement of means
- Loan to value
- Attributes of a good security

REVIEW

Now consider the main points that were introduced in the chapter. These are listed below. Tick each one as you go through them.

- Credit scoring is a system for assessing credit applications using a set formula or rules. Normally this process will be automated.
- Credit scoring can be used not only to assess credit, but also to determine the level of interest to be charged for a loan.
- Credit risk can be mitigated through the application of robust due diligence processes.
- Credit risk is measured through credit exposure, credit risk premium and credit ratings.
- A credit ratings agency will give a rating reflecting the creditworthiness of organisations and countries.
- Pricing risk is the risk that an organisation runs should it get its pricing wrong. It can be encountered when using models, when getting the price wrong either in the purchase or sale of products/services, or getting the price of loans wrong.
- The assessment of credit is structured around the 5 Ps model – Person, Purpose, Payment, Protection and Premium.
- When assessing the person we start by considering character, capacity and commitment. Other personal factors to be considered are marital status/dependants, employment and previous connections with the organisation.
- A customer's assets and liabilities are recorded in a Statement of Means.
- It is vital to establish that the customer is looking to borrow the right amount.
- There should be a logical fit between any asset being financed and the repayment source.
- The customer's ability to repay credit is a fundamental aspect of credit assessment.
- An Income and Expenditure Statement is used to assess a customer's ability to repay.
- Security is taken as protection against risk associated with a credit proposal.
- The attributes of a good security are – simplicity of title, stability of value and realisability.
- A bank makes profits when lending through charging fees and interest.
- Any credit assessment involves the identification of the risks associated with the proposal and determining what mitigants can be put in place to reduce the risk.

chapter 9

DEFINING OPERATIONAL RISK

Contents

Learning objectives

On completion of this chapter, you should be able to:

- critically analyse the ways in which a bank assesses and manages operational risks
- analyse the key components of an operational risk framework and evaluate the benefits of effective operational risk management
- examine who in a bank is responsible for managing operational risk and what their respective responsibilities are
- explain the concept of business continuity management and appraise its significance within the context of operational risk.

Introduction

In this chapter, we turn our attention to operational risk, which you will find is a catch all term for a number of risk areas. The first section examines the notion of business risk – this is the risk that a firm is not able to deliver a satisfactory return for its owners, in other words, the business is no longer viable. There can be a number of contributory factors to this risk and these are outlined. The next risk area to be explained is financial risk, being the risks arising from borrowing.

A major theme of the chapter is introduced next – Operational Risk – this is any risk that is neither credit risk nor market risk. Operational Risk is defined by the Basel Committee as the risk of loss resulting from inadequate or failed internal processes, people or systems or from external events. Remaining with the Basel Committee, the chapter then explains the Basel general categories of loss events, which are – internal and external fraud, employee practices and workplace safety, client products and business practices, damage to physical assets, business disruption and system failure, and execution, delivery and process management. The business lines defined by the committee are outlined next, with their significance lying in the fact that firms use these categories to calculate their capital charge under Basel II. Whilst it can appear quite straightforward to categorise risk into neat headings, the reality is that the boundaries between these areas are not as clear and straightforward as we would like and the text will move on to discuss this. The section concludes with an explanation of regulatory and reputational risk

Operational risk policy is the next topic to consider, where the principles and policies that underpin the policy are explained. The operational risk framework is described next – you will be familiar with much of this through your knowledge of the risk management lifecycle. The stages of this are: operational risk policy, identification of risk, measurement and assessment of risk, mitigation, monitoring and finally the reporting of risk. As with any policy, there can be barriers on the ground to the implementation of it and this is the next topic up for discussion.

We then move on to consider the benefits of operational risk management, and these can be both direct and indirect benefits, before concluding this section with an examination of the key industry developments in this field.

The next broad theme of the chapter is responsibility for operational risk. Once risks have been identified and assessed, then appropriate controls must be put in place to manage the risks. The occurrence of fraud within financial services and the steps taken to manage this is discussed next. Risk can present itself during periods of change and a checklist for implementing an effective control framework is explained. The implementation of operational risk management is discussed next, with a particular focus on how the culture of the organisation affects the management of risk. This section then moves on to consider the responsibilities of particular groups within the firm – the individual, the business, the risk function, senior management, internal and external audit. This section on operational risk responsibilities concludes by explaining the three lines of defence model.

The final major discourse of the chapter is business continuity management – The steps that need to be followed to develop a business continuity plan are discussed, before discussing the topic of crisis management with particular reference to the events of 9/11. The section concludes with an explanation of the regulatory issues surrounding business continuity management.

1 Business risk

QUICK QUESTION

Business risk is a new concept for this course. What do you think we mean by it?

Write your answer here before reading on.

In essence, **business risk** is the risk that a firm may be unable to trade (carry out its business) in a manner which delivers a profitable return to the business owners (i.e. the shareholders) – that is to say it is a non-viable business. This manifests itself in a variety of ways and the component parts of this business risk can derive from disparate sources. It may be regarded as the probability of loss inherent in a firm's operations and the environment in which it operates (such as competition and adverse economic conditions) that may impair its ability to provide returns on investment. It is also associated with political changes or changes in the competitive environment perhaps with the emergence of a strong competitor in an erstwhile benign market.

As you can imagine, business risk can come from a diverse range of sources, which includes:

Economic – consider the state of the airlines in 2008 when the price of oil products soared and this had the effect immediately of forcing many airlines to become potentially unviable and many did indeed become bankrupt. We saw the same trend continuing into 2009 whereby the costs of aviation fuel (which contributes one of the key underlying costs of the airline industry) was volatile and rising which had a marked effect on airlines around the world.

Political – it may be that a company is operating in another country and a political event such as an election, the removal of a government by a revolutionary coup or a change in government policy will have a transforming effect upon the ability of that business to produce or continue to produce viable results.

Competitive environment – a company that has enjoyed a relaxed marketplace with few competitors which is suddenly faced by a new keen and well-capitalised competitor with good products and services would immediately find its potential market being removed by the enthusiastic competitor.

Social and market forces – any kind of change in the public mood with regard to the acceptance of new practices or ways of behaving including grounds for something remaining socially acceptable may have a profound effect on a company's ability to remain competitive. The non-use of green practices with regard to energy or to the use of child labour in component or raw material manufacture for example may mean that customers boycott the finished product and turn to other sources. Organisations should ask themselves (and find answers to) questions addressing the nature of their business partners (who are they doing business with), the nature of their dependencies upon suppliers (who they are buying from), the products/services they are buying and selling (from an environmental and intellectual property point of view) together with the internal processes and people involved.

Technological – looking back, a good example of technological pressures was indeed the case of the video recording industry which had announced two standards. These were known as VHS and Betamax. Sheer market forces dictated that VHS was the favoured one and therefore suppliers of Betamax were forced into a weak position and became unviable. Similarly in the European marketplace post-MiFID some of the stock exchanges are being faced with having to improve their business models because of the potential of competing equity trading platforms using electronic trading technology. A good example from the derivatives industry was the requirement back in 1998-2000 for the Liffe market to reinvent its trading process in order to compete with the electronically traded German exchange Eurex.

More recently, the Kodak and Nokia companies have been forced to re-engineer their businesses as technology has overtaken them.

Shocks and natural events – any natural event linked to climate, weather or severe acts of God would of course have a profound effect on any business thus affected.

External stakeholders – a shareholder ultimately will be able to control businesses because they own them and therefore they can wield strategic power over the direction that businesses take; similarly institutional stakeholders and even regulatory agencies and environmental bodies including political cliques can exert power such that businesses can be affected demonstrating similar business risk sources.

Third parties – dependence upon third party suppliers will also occasionally provide sources of business risk. For example, if a supplier goes bust and is unable to provide its services to say a manufacturer who had been depending upon component parts from the supplier then the business of the manufacturer is itself put at jeopardy in turn. It may be that no alternative source exists or could be quickly brought to bear.

QUESTION TIME 1

The following table lists the sources of business risk. Complete the table with topical examples of where this risk could manifest itself.

Risk Area	Example
Economic	
Political	
Competitive environment	
Social and market forces	
Technological	
Shocks and natural events	
External stakeholders	
Third parties	

Write your answer in here then check with the answer at the back of the book.

Firms also face **financial risks** such as those arising from debt (borrowed capital and/or trade credit). Thus a firm will face these two sets of risks, the business risk as indicated above plus any financial risk arising from use of debt (borrowed capital and/or trade credit). Together these equate to the total corporate risk facing an enterprise.

Today, the financial risks are well exemplified and hopefully well understood in the light of immediate past experience across the banking and investment industries for example. As discussed earlier under the heading of liquidity risk, a company cannot run out of money or it will become insolvent and fail. Liquid cash and the availability of that cash are of paramount importance. The risk that a company will not have adequate cash flow to meet its operating expenses forms a fundamental element of liquidity risk.

A company's risks include financial risk, which is linked to debt, and business risk, which is often linked to the economic climate. If a company is entirely financed by shares, it would pose almost no financial risk, but it would be susceptible to business risk or changes in the overall economic climate.

In parallel with defining its business risks a firm will also need to design control measures to mitigate those risks. The more severe the risk the greater degree of difficulty, and almost certainly cost, there will be in controlling them.

Firms thus face many business and financial risks and the aggregate effect of these is the essence of enterprise risk management.

2 Key elements of operational risk

When you begin to consider the events that have actually been fatal for financial institutions, it is clear that they do not always come from either credit risk or market risk. It is to be hoped that institutions do not allow themselves to be so exposed to a type of credit risk that the entire institution is endangered. Likewise where a large market exposure is entered into the institution typically passes part of the risk across to other parties. Sometimes failures are the result of operational risk, not market or credit risk.

QUICK QUESTION

Why do you think that operational risk is responsible for a number of failures as opposed to market or credit risk?

Write your answer here before reading on.

Operational risk is inherent in all the activities of a financial firm not only due to the nature of the financial transactions themselves but also because financial firms are indeed businesses which employ staff, own property, hold assets, including data and other information, which belong to the institution and its clients. The approach to the management of operational risk for financial firms would not be designed to eliminate risk per se but to contain it within acceptable levels as determined by the senior management of the firms concerned. This ties in with the view expressed earlier in the course that we cannot exist profitably in a risk free environment. Each business will be different; banks are banks but each of them will have a different set of businesses, clients and activities. In this way the business of any financial institution will present its own different mix of business and risks.

Every function within a firm, be it front end or administrative or control, must manage the operational risks that arise from its own activities. Operational risk is all pervasive, with a failure in one area potentially impacting many others.

In risk management we often talk about credit risk and market risk and operational risk as being the three key types of risk. Of these, operational risk really sweeps up everything that doesn't fit into the first two categories and therefore many other types of risks for example reputational risk, strategic risk fall under the heading of operational risk. With this in mind therefore, it is possibly the most wide ranging and varied type of risk that managers need to address. The management of operational risk concerns managing the exposure to the frequency and severity of expected losses as well as unexpected losses. The resulting added-value to any company varies according to the level of ambition from management and also the rigour and expertise within the risk management process overall. Firms that invest in a firm-wide approach to the operational risk management practice will succeed in optimising their investment.

For some years now it has been observed how financial institutions have demonstrated particularly acute exposure to operational risk owing to the breakdowns of their controls and decision-making processes as well as the impacts received from events over which they have no control. Breakdowns in internal controls and corporate governance can lead to massive losses. Consider the cases of Barings Bank in 1995 and other institutions such as Northern Rock, HBOS, Lehman Brothers, Société Générale, UBS and MF Global in recent years. Therefore the successful application within a financial institution of a methodology to address and conquer operational risk management is of critical importance and therefore should prove of poignant interest to management, the Board, the shareholders, the stakeholders and employees of that organisation.

2.1 The Basel definition of operational risk

The Basel Committee on Banking Supervision formally defines operational risk as:

> *The risk of loss resulting from inadequate or failed internal processes, people and systems or from external events.*

It is a succinct, no-nonsense statement which encapsulates in a straightforward manner the key issues regarding operational risk. You may well have come across this definition within your own organisation.

In practical terms, operational risk addresses the risk of things going wrong with the day-to-day operating activities of the firm, which then results in financial loss.

It is important to learn and be comfortable with this definition. It addresses the origins of operational risk.

2.1.1 The Basel Committee definition

Remember that the Basel Committee definition does not include strategic risk, legal risk and reputational risk, although these types of risks may certainly be linked to (or result from) operational risk.

2.2 The Basel operational risk event types

Basel defines seven general categories of loss events. They are:

- Internal fraud
- External fraud
- Employee practices and workplace safety
- Clients, products and business practice
- Damage to physical assets
- Business disruption and system failures
- Execution, delivery and process management.

We will go on to look at each of these in turn.

Internal fraud: Losses due to acts of a type intended to defraud, misappropriate property or circumvent regulations, the law or company policy, excluding diversity/ discrimination events, which involve at least one internal party. These may take the form of any unauthorised activity and of course internal theft or fraud. Examples would include transactions intentionally not being reported, a type of transaction being unauthorised (with a monetary loss) and the intentional mismarking of a position(s).

External fraud: Losses due to acts of a type intended to defraud, misappropriate property or circumvent the law, by a third party. Here the events might relate to theft, fraud and systems security with examples being things like theft or robbery, forgery, cross firing of cheques, hacking damage and the theft of information involving monetary loss.

Employment practices and workplace safety: Losses arising from acts inconsistent with employment, health or safety laws or agreements, from payment of personal injury claims, or from diversity/discrimination events. Events here would relate to employee relations, perhaps losses resulting from compensation payments, benefits, termination issues or any kind of loss resulting from organised labour activity (perhaps with trade unions). It would also involve any environmental losses; these might be payments under general liability (accidents such slips, trips and falls) and any matter involving employee health & safety rule benefit events. Any compensation to members of the workforce would be included under this heading. The final example would be to cater for any kind of discriminatory events for which a loss was incurred.

Clients, products and business practice: Losses arising from an unintentional or negligent failure to meet a professional obligation to specific clients (including fiduciary and suitability requirements), or from the nature or design of a product. In this category there is greater scope than with many others for losses incurred with customers. They might be relating to suitability, disclosure and fiduciary matters which resulted in losses due to fiduciary breaches, guideline violations, suitability or disclosure issues (relating to Know Your Customer (KYC) shortcomings), retail customer disclosure violations, breaches of privacy, aggressive sales practices, account churning and switching, any misuse of confidential information or lender liability.

This will extend further into losses arising from improper business or market practices which give rise to antitrust, improper trade or market practices, market manipulation, insider trading (on firm's account), unlicensed activities and money laundering. Further categories or subsets of the client area would be product flaws and defects including model errors (e.g. calculations, price quotes, valuations) together with any kind of failure to investigate clients in line with established guidelines or exceeding client exposure limits. Finally, where any kind of advice or advisory service is provided, then losses resulting from disputes concerning performance would also appear in this category.

Damage to physical assets: Losses arising from loss or damage to physical assets from natural disaster or other events. We refer here to disasters and other major impact events. They may be truly losses resulting from natural disasters but also losses from external human causes, perhaps from terrorism, and vandalism.

Business disruption and systems failures: Losses arising from disruption of business or system failures. We all know that systems and technology can cause losses and Basel is no exception in including this as its sixth category. It refers to losses from systems in general and hardware, software, telecommunications, utility outages and systems disruptions in general.

Execution, delivery and process management: This is another large area of potential troublesome loss events. It will include all losses from failed transaction processing or process management, from relations with trade counterparties and vendors. The first area concerns transaction capture, execution and maintenance whereby a wide range of events would be caught including miscommunication, data entry, maintenance or loading error; missed deadline or responsibility, model or system malfunction; accounting error or entity attribution error; any other task not being performed correctly, delivery failure, collateral management failure or reference data maintenance error. It would extend further into monitoring and reporting activities where any failed mandatory reporting obligation or inaccurate external reporting event took place and where an incurred loss resulted.

Negligence when taking on new customers, any client permissions or disclaimers missing and legal documents which go missing or are incomplete constitute another of the types of examples under this category. With established clients, any error resulting in losses owing to unapproved access given to accounts, incorrect client records where a loss has been incurred or any type of negligent loss or damage of client assets will qualify for inclusion here. Similarly relationships with non-client trading counterparties which result in mis-performance or disputes will be booked here too. The final group for inclusion will be general trade vendors, perhaps disputes with technology or systems or outsourcing vendors.

2.3 The business lines defined in Basel

The operational risk event types that we have just looked at are those which the Basel Committee in co-operation with the industry identified as having the potential to result in substantial losses, although one may argue that the list is not exclusive. This is then used within Basel as the basis for the operational loss database, which follows the business lines and analyses losses accordingly. It is in these areas where substantial losses are anticipated.

QUICK QUESTION

The Committee defined eight business lines, what do you think they are?

Write your answer here before reading on.

The eight business lines defined by the Basel Committee which they deem to be applicable to banks are:

- Corporate finance
- Trading and sales
- Retail banking
- Commercial banking
- Payment and settlement
- Agency services
- Asset management
- Retail brokerage.

In Pillar One of the Operational Risk Standardised Approach under Basel II, the capital charge is calculated as a simple summation of capital charges across the eight business lines as follows:

Business lines	% of gross income
Corporate finance	18
Trading & sales	18
Retail Banking	12
Commercial Banking	15
Payment & Settlement	18
Agency Services	15
Asset Management	12
Retail Brokerage	12

Mapping risk events against these business lines is reasonably straightforward and to a large extent self-explanatory but managers must be careful to make the correct allocation. In many ways the potential for losses is similar across the seven listed categories.

From time to time the Basel Committee carries out reviews of operational risk loss data collection across a large number of banks. These studies deliver results which are interesting to observers in as much as they show the frequency by risk type and also across different business lines. Some risk types affect more than one business type being cross-dimensional. Perhaps the highest numbers of risk events have been proved to occur amongst external fraud and the execution and delivery and process management groups. In the business lines possibly retail banking exceeds others by a long margin.

2.4 Boundary issues with other types of risk

Credit risk would normally be taken to include settlement risk, but is a failure to complete collateral documentation credit risk or operational risk? Market risk could be taken to cover correlation risk, equity risk, interest rate risk, currency risk, commodity risk and credit spread risk – that is all of the risks which are dependent upon market movements rather than a failure of a particular counterparty.

Portfolio concentration risk is more likely to be an operational risk – but what is liquidity risk? This should appear under trading book issues within this definition. Transactional risk – execution error, broking error, settlement error and similar types of problem are operational risk. Operational control risk is another part of operational risk and typically includes rogue trading, money laundering, fraud, people risk, processing risk and security risk. Another part of operational risk is systems risk, together with contingency planning and telecommunication failure.

But there are a set of other risks – strategic risk is rather separate and clearly the planning and management of this are undertaken separately. But there are also the external events which clearly have a significant impact. What is a general shift in credit? This is still credit risk. Regulatory risk falls within operational risk, with disaster risk, legal risk, financial risk and taxation risk. What is clear even from this first analysis is that it is important to have a clear definition of risk types otherwise different people within the organisation will be using the same term but meaning different things - a recipe for disaster.

Systemic risk lies at the industry level, the risk of the entire industry being compromised by the collapse of a single firm leading to a domino collapse of many others (consider the events of 2008 with the actual or near failure of major British, Icelandic and other nation's banks or perhaps by the failure of a systemically important utility organisation such as an exchange, central securities depository or central clearing counterparty).

What about country risk, economic risk, political risk and taxation risk? All of these can be described as discrete risks and need to be managed by any institution.

2.4.1 Regulatory risk

If a firm experiences any form of operational risk then it is likely that this will not satisfy the regulators so therefore any sub-standard operational risk management approach may well lead to what we could call **regulatory risk**. In some ways a regulatory intervention or enforcement will show that a firm is not conducting its risk management correctly and that its operation is sub-optimal. In the UK the FSA (and its successors, the PRA and FCA) as the regulator has imposed major fines on many firms in recent years as a penalty for poor controls, inconsistent marketing messages to clients and the absence of adequate money laundering checks to name just a few examples.

2.4.2 Reputational risk

A consequence of regulatory risk in most cases will be a loss of reputation, hence **reputational risk**. Reputational risk can also be caused without the regulators getting involved as a result of customers receiving sub-standard service and deciding to join another supplier and for many other reasons. It is important to remember that operational risk potentially leads to regulatory risk and on, in turn, to a damaged reputation.

When a major operational risk occurs, there is an unexpected loss in the institution. The market takes a view on the event to see what it tells them about the institution –and the impact on the market value of the bank can be many times the actual loss suffered. It is about looking like you are not in control, that you are accident prone.

When an institution begins to lose its reputation in this way, there is generally no way back.

3 Operational risk policy

Good risk management and control lie at the heart of any successful business, particularly a financial services firm. They are an integral part of providing consistent returns to shareholders and clients. More serious however is the resultant damage to a firm's reputation should they fail to manage and control risks adequately. This may have an ongoing impact upon their share price and impair their ability to maintain their client base and indeed to retain talented employees. Regulatory risk exists over the horizon in as much as financial regulators are able to impose constraints upon the firms they supervise should they not manage risk matters satisfactorily.

Facing risks is an integral part of being in business as we discussed when looking in particular at strategic risk. Taking risk is central to any financial business and therefore operational risks are an inevitable consequence of being in business. The aim will be to achieve an appropriate balance between risk and reward based upon the firm's assessment of potential risk developments in both normal and stress conditions.

Banks and financial firms base their approach to risk management and control addressing five principles:

- **Business management is accountable** for all the risks they assume and are therefore responsible for the continuous and active management of risk exposures to ensure that risks and return are balanced. Therefore it is not acceptable to delegate the management of risk to an Operational Risk Department.
- An **independent control process** should be in place with respect to short-term profit incentives and longer-term interests. This has been on the public agenda when discussing the incentive schemes operated before the banking crisis and how much this focus on short-term rewards contributed to the crisis.
- **Risk disclosure** – a procedure whereby comprehensive, transparent and objective statements are made with respect to senior management, the firm's board, its shareholders, regulators and any other stakeholders.
- **Protection of earnings** by controlling risk at the level of exposures wherever and of whatever size taken.
- **Protection of the firm's reputation** by managing and controlling risks incurred in the course of business.

The risk management policies should include and define the following:

- Level of reporting of risk events
- To whom should risk events be reported
- What should be reported
- Investigation procedures
- Treatment of unexpected profits and near misses
- Risk appetite definition
- New business risk
- Risk limits
- KRI policy.

As you know from earlier studies, the policy and approach must start from the top of the organisation and be agreed and sponsored at Board level via a process of embedding into the firm's culture. As it is firm-wide and often requires significant cultural change, it must have the full and continued support of senior management to succeed. Different directors will each have their own risk appetites dependent on the nature of the role they undertake and their own backgrounds. This will colour the way that they will look at any particular issue and in particular risk discussions. For the senior management team to work effectively this will need to be addressed.

It is important for firms to identify and empower those individuals who are given the key responsibilities of managing the operational risk function. Key risk officers are the people in the organisation that manage operational risk. Line managers within the independent operational risk management function will be key officers, responsible for monitoring and reporting to the Board, senior business managers, the group risk management function (responsible for the firm's overall financial risk) and, via senior management, to regulators.

There are a number of objectives within the Basel framework. One that clearly emerges from the Sound Practices Paper is that responsibility sits with the Board, although there may be a series of delegations of authority. What is important to recognise is that delegations must be clearly understood and responsibility taken for actions. PRA rules state that, a firm should ensure that all employees are aware of their responsibility and role in operational risk management and are suitable and capable of performing these responsibilities. Failure to do this will result in the risk residing with the Board or an approved person.

This is not just to set the Board's minds at rest, rather it is to ensure that there is someone who is responsible and therefore has primary responsibility for the key risk indicators that the firm develops. Remuneration policies and job profiles will need to ensure that this ownership of risk is properly structured within the business. The firm will now have developed a framework of risks with each significant risk assigned a risk owner and a deputy.

Key risk officers may also be designated from within the business itself. If ownership of operational risk issues is assigned to the department or business process where they originate, then the relevant line manager will often be made responsible for risk management. For this reason, managers may have direct reporting lines through their own business lines and dotted lines into the risk management function.

The policy should provide clear responsibility and accountability for risk management at all levels. Staff throughout the organisation need to know precisely what is expected of them and why. If they are accountable for managing risk then they also require the necessary control and authority to be able to take action and implement risk reduction plans. The risk policy should include clear lines of authority, identify key risk officers to carry out prescribed actions, and define specific roles and responsibilities. The risk policy should also make clear the consequences of non-compliance for staff not observing the policy.

The approach should promote collaboration between functions, departments and across divisions as it is becoming increasingly recognised that many of the key operational risks occur at the interface between these boundaries. The cultural tendency to develop departmental silos should be addressed and cross-functional teamwork encouraged through incentives, education and a supportive organisational structure.

Collaboration with other risk management disciplines is becoming ever more important as understanding of the inter-relationship of financial risk increases.

A coherent, consistent and comprehensive approach should be defined that will provide a 'roadmap' to move the organisation from what might be a fragmented, non-strategic attitude to operational risk management to a more comprehensive, global and firm-wide methodology, and a common risk language throughout the firm. The approach lays out the framework or rules of engagement under which the firm will operate. This must be in unison with and support the overall business strategy.

Therefore the firm should aim to:

- employ a methodology that identifies and categorises all the operational risks that exist in the organisation
- employ a methodology for measuring and assessing the significance of all the identified risks
- work with line managers to agree the mitigating action required to reduce the risk exposure to acceptable levels
- monitor the effects of the mitigating action to ensure its success
- report and escalate risk issues to all levels of the organisation. This ensures that there is transparency and aids the decision-making process.

In practice, the framework described is rarely fixed and standardised immediately. It is more evolutionary to begin with, and its maturity will reflect the maturity of the organisation with respect to operational risk management. The process is iterative and will gain strength and expertise over time.

The process of developing the approach- rather like the risk management lifecycle - is cyclical and continuous and can result in refinements to the risk policy.

The strategy should be consistent throughout the firm. A common operational policy and terminology, which exists globally and across all functions, allows:

- A meaningful overall capital adequacy assessment to be performed across the organisation
- Objectivity when risk prioritisation needs to be performed
- A sense of fairness when rewarding or penalising risk performance.

Again, because the risk policy takes a firm-wide approach and cuts across departmental boundaries, there should be a central, independent risk management role responsible for the co-ordination and implementation of risk policies and procedures. Depending upon the size and type of organisation, this role may be set up as an independent department. Most large organisations have now developed an independent operational risk management function that reports into an overall group risk officer.

In order to control and manage procedures effectively, the firm will need to ensure explicit segregation of duties between the trading and support functions, such as front office, operations, accounting and risk monitoring.

3.1 The operational risk management framework

Following the agreement of the high-level risk policy, a risk management process must be implemented to enable the risk management function to achieve its aims. The diagram below describes a typical process, which includes the following stages:

- Operational risk policy
- Identification of risks
- Measurement and assessment of risks
- Mitigation (the reduction of potential risk impact and likelihood)
- Monitoring of risks
- Reporting of risks.

You will be familiar with this process through the risk management lifecycle that was described in Chapter 1 – with the main addition now being the link to the operational risk policy. In some firms the last two stages of this process may be handled by the internal audit function. The delineation is not a major issue; the salient point is that the six stages must all be carried out. A commitment to deliver successful results under such an approach will be rewarded over time as experience and greater quality come to the fore.

The Risk Management Process

3.2 Practical constraints of implementing an operational risk management framework

Risk management starts at the Board level and is then passed down through the organisation. Whilst committees can assign risk to departments and/or individuals, management by committee of a specific risk is rarely successful. That is not to say that committees do not have a role in terms of ratifying the requirements and setting the general standards, but a committee cannot manage a risk on a day-to-day basis. Quite simply a committee does not meet on a day-to-day basis.

QUICK QUESTION

Understanding the constituents of a risk management framework is one thing – implementing it successfully within an organisation is quite another. What do you think these difficulties are?

Write your answer here before reading on.

Some of the practical constraints of implementation are:

- **Data collection and management constraints:** in practice, it is very difficult to build a truly comprehensive data set – apart from the general lack of data, system constraints and a lack of standardisation mean that the required data feeds from disparate sources cannot be easily developed. This is particularly so in a large organisation. There is also relatively little availability of industry-wide data, as this depends on firms self-reporting and, by definition, it is not straightforward to gain an understanding of high impact, low-frequency events. Firms may also not be allowed to report for legal disclosure reasons.
- **Cultural constraints:** operational risk managers used to find that building momentum and demand for operational risk practices across the business was a constant struggle, but this is no longer the case as firms are capturing data more frequently. Business heads need to be convinced of the value that operational risk management will bring. If not implemented in a well-structured manner it is often seen as a cost to the business, and even a nuisance, rather than a real asset. Consequently, many firms have rolled out risk management frameworks piece by piece, attempting to gain the confidence and support of one area before moving on to another, as it may be that incremental change is easier to embed than structural change.
- **Resource and cost constraints:** firms continually underestimate the amount of time and resources required to implement identification and measurement systems. In an era of tight cost controls, resource constraints put a limit on how quickly or comprehensively implementation is carried out.
- **Indicator constraints:** it can be difficult to design risk indicators that monitor the full range of risks. There is a natural tendency to use indicators that are already available (such as existing management information) but these are often designed to monitor performance rather than risk. The extra cost and time required to design and maintain a truly comprehensive set of risk indicators is often prohibitive.

4 The benefits of operational risk management

'The essence of risk management lies in maximising the areas where we have some control over the outcome, while minimising the areas where we have absolutely no control over the outcome and the linkage between cause and effect is hidden from us.'

Peter Bernstein (Against the Gods)

4.1 Direct benefits

QUICK QUESTION

Having spent some time now studying operational risk, what do you think are its benefits?

Write your answer here before reading on.

The benefits of sound operational risk management within banks can be summarised as follows:

(1) A reduction of operating losses
(2) Lower compliance/auditing costs
(3) The early detection of unlawful activities
(4) Reduced exposure to future risks
(5) A lower capital charge under the regulatory environment in line with Basel recommendations
(6) Better decision making
(7) Improved rating, share price and reputation.

These benefits lead to greater resilience in the business and a better chance of the business growing and attracting further customers in line with its strategic objectives.

There are various benefits that spin off from the actual activity of operational risk. These are:

- Improved decision making and operational risk governance
- Improvements to risk and control assessment
- Better data capture, record keeping and analysis
- Improvements in stress and scenario testing leading to better modelling
- Better reporting and priority setting
- Greater clarity over risk appetite and tolerance
- Ability to use risk indicators more effectively.

A firm that utilises sound operational risk management will benefit in further ways beyond merely the risk management framework. It will also be able to attract and retain better quality staff to improve its resilience and business continuity.

5 Key industry developments

There have been two major sources of industry development. The first have been the series of corporate debacles, collapses and failures which collectively have led to the second source which is that provided by regulatory impetus. This is logical inasmuch as failures of firms, particularly financial institutions, will obviously result in governments and regulators talking action to correct the problem.

Another driver has been the pressure for improved corporate governance which, lies at the heart of sound risk management risk practices.

We will now look at both of these sources in turn.

5.1 Corporate failures

In the world of financial institutions there are so many examples to choose from and we will restrict ourselves here to a few of the higher profile ones. You may well have read of these cases but some additional detail is given. Collectively these plus other examples form the significant series of developments in the shape of operational risk failures which has led to the drivers for change.

- Barings – February 1995, a single derivatives operation in Singapore led to the collapse of a 230 year-old British bank with a loss of US$1.2billion.
- NatWest Markets – 1997, a single trader acting in a weak control environment lost £90 million due to mis-pricing options and concealing losses.
- Allied Irish Bank – 2002, the actions of John Rusnak a trader at AllFirst in Baltimore, a subsidiary of Allied Irish Bank, led to a loss of US$691 million through derivatives trading activity. Again an environment existed of poor controls, deferential management and lack of internal audit resources and understanding.
- National Australia Bank – 2004, a team of currency option traders recorded a loss of AUS$360 million which exposed poor levels of integrity, risk and control weaknesses, corporate governance and culture failures.
- Enron – 2002, the collapse of the whole company at the time recognised as the seventh largest corporate organisation in the United States. Although it was not a regulated business (such as a

financial firm) failures of corporate governance leading to massive fraud and complex corporate structures including concealed use of derivatives led to this huge failure. As a consequence of the collapse of Enron, Arthur Andersen the renowned external audit company itself folded mainly as a result of reputational damage and the United States government under George Bush enacted the Sarbanes-Oxley Act in 2002. The act was aimed at eradicating the underpinning reasons for poor quality financial reporting of some of the largest corporate organisations in the United States and imposed new public disciplines for controlling the appointment of external auditors.

- Société Générale – 2008, a loss of 4.9 billion Euros, ostensibly a fraud by a single trader in the Paris dealing room operating with massive positions in derivative markets. Systems and controls within the bank failed to challenge, mitigate or control the size of positions that were being managed in excess of the bank's net worth.
- Madoff Ponzi scheme – 2009, a loss of US$50 billion, amazingly this activity of Bernie Madoff was supposed to have gone on for 20 years and he was single-handedly was guilty of this malpractice. However the controls within his company and indeed the controls from the regulator the SEC in the United States fell woefully short of the necessary standard.
- MF Global – 2011, the company, a long-established clearing firm, collapsed from a huge loss incurred in the European debt market. This case highlighted deficiencies of vigilance from its clearing house, the Chicago Mercantile Exchange, and also demonstrated severe shortcomings in client asset protection practices in both London and the United States.
- JP Morgan Chase – 2012, a loss of $2 billion in a credit derivatives hedging programme. The bank's CEO famously described the bank as having been sloppy and stupid.

5.2 Regulatory initiatives

These are led by the activities of the Basel Committee which announced Basel II as its new Accord in 1999 but which took until 2007 to achieve wide international (but not complete) implementation. Amongst a great deal of substantial detail about operational risk management it also highlighted good corporate governance as a key process.

The European Commission has passed many directives and regulatory initiatives across the member states of the European Union including the Risk-Based Capital Directive, which was replaced by the Capital Requirements Directive (CRD), which is currently in operation in its fourth phase. Prior to these initiatives the Capital Adequacy Directive (CAD 3) contained explicit rulings about operational risk addressing such things as employees, processes, outsourcing and business continuity management.

Prior to being replaced in 2013 by the PRA and FCA in 2013, the FSA (the principal UK regulator for the past 10 years) implemented its Consultation paper CP142 in 2004. This addressed directly operational risk management within firms and was drawn up in line with CAD 3.

More recently the FSA introduced the Internal Capital Adequacy Assessment Process (ICAAP) which requires firms to think through not only the material risks that affect their business, including of course operational risk, but also the levels of capital that they need in order to provide prudential risk mitigation in support of their overall business.

In general the FSA initiatives were focussing on operational risk and encouraging firms to think for themselves. It was not a prescriptive set of measures but really was asking firms to be able to apply, justify and convince the regulator about their own approach to operational risk management. This is borne out in such initiatives as the ICAAP. Generally speaking the FSA's initiatives mirror the international supervisory approach for banks laid down by the Basel Committee.

5.3 The benefits of a good framework

A bank should seek to operate a total risk programme whereby they capture risks precisely and do this only once. They should also strive to align the management of those risks to the manner in which the organisation actually operates and against the objectives it wishes to achieve. This will include categorisation of risks and clarity on precisely where different types of risk are reported and reviewed.

It will be important to distinguish between:

- The activities of analysis, reporting and oversight where the concentration should be on doing the right things.
- The action or management activities effectively getting on with the job and doing it.
- The activities of assurance and compliance is addressed possibly by way of internal audit addressing whether the firm actually did carry out what they said they would.

Risk management can be summarised as being a set of **actions** used to **contribute** towards the **likelihood** of **achieving** and **surpassing planned objectives** of the organisation over a defined **timescale**.

QUESTION TIME 2

Consider the items from the definition above and expand upon what is meant by each word/phrase.

Write your answer here then check with the answer at the back of the book.

Culture cannot be over-emphasised. It lies as a fundamental element of the ability to establish a meaningful risk management framework. Accordingly therefore a bank should be able to answer positively that the senior management of the organisation cares passionately about the quality of its business. Similarly senior management must take operational risk management seriously. This will mean playing their part appropriately and using operational risk management as a key tool for effective business management.

Should a problem of culture exist within the firm, the organisation should ask itself whether the fundamental problem is the commitment or the competence of senior management. Or instead, does the problem lie with the operational risk concept itself? This is very much the standpoint where a regulator might be coming from when they investigate and interview banks about their risk management frameworks.

Furthermore, members of a bank's organisation should be clear as to what operational risk management actually means to them and what it should be achieving. All in all there is an absolutely basic need for a clear concept for risk management to be customised for any particular organisation. Remember that every business is different, banks are banks but each bank is dissimilar and therefore the assessment of risks, the risk management framework and the very culture of the way the bank is managed will vary from organisation to organisation.

QUESTION TIME 3

Your bank has decided to launch a new packaged account (current account plus benefits) product. You are required to produce a risk assessment identifying the key risks associated with this product and you are to propose appropriate mitigating controls. You should categorise the risks under the following headings:

- People risks
- Process risks
- Systems risks
- External risks

Write your answer here then check with the answer at the back of the book.

6 Business continuity management

6.1 Business continuity or contingency planning

In the same way that financial provisioning provides financial continuity, the ability to anticipate and plan for potential operational crises reduces the harm of unexpected losses. Firms should address and decide how best to keep their businesses operating and available (particularly for customers) in case of adverse events. Continuity or contingency planning may take the form of disaster recovery, succession planning or the production of other fall-back procedures to deal with potential crises or threats to the continuity operation of the business.

Both business continuity and business availability are important for management to address. This includes emergency response, crisis management and business resumption planning, covering a whole range of scenarios as identified by the business. Businesses have to understand the underlying risks and the potential impact of each type of disaster. A contingency plan needs to be drawn up, maintained, tested and checked regularly. It is also important to consider the magnitude of the risks which could result from these impacts. This will help determine which scenarios are most likely to occur, to make an assessment of their frequency and to which ones resources should be directed at the planning stage. Analysis of any potential disruption is required, ranging from minor mishaps to major catastrophes.

QUICK QUESTION

What events do you think would lend themselves to continuity planning?

Write your answer here before reading on.

Potential events that typically lend themselves to continuity planning are:

- Fire
- System failure
- Power failure
- Natural disasters (floods, earthquakes, tsunamis, hurricanes ....)
- Explosions
- Civil unrest, terrorist actions, police intervention
- Strikes
- Adverse weather (snow, storms, ice, flooding, stifling temperatures ....).

6.2 Guidance from the regulatory requirements

Principle Seven from Basel's Sound Practices Paper states that banks should have in place contingency and business continuity plans to ensure their ability to operate on an on-going basis and limit losses in the event of severe business disruption. Basel goes on to state that, this potential requires that banks establish disaster recovery and business continuity plans that take into account different types of plausible scenarios to which the bank may be vulnerable, commensurate with the size and complexity of the bank's operations.

Their statement begins with:

'For reasons that may be beyond a bank's control, a severe event may result in the inability of the bank to fulfil some or all of its business obligations, particularly where the bank's physical, telecommunication, or information technology infrastructures have been damaged or made inaccessible. This can, in turn, result in significant financial losses to the bank, as well as broader disruptions to the financial system through channels such as the payments system'.

The key here therefore is that there are a number of different scenarios that need to be considered.

Basel is explicit in that it states, 'Banks should identify critical business processes, including those where there is dependence on external vendors or third parties, for which rapid resumption of service would be essential. For these processes, banks should identify alternative mechanisms for resuming service in the event of an outage'. So this is asking the bank to look through each of its processes and identify which are critical and also those that rely on third party vendors or third parties. What this means is that for every third party used there should, if possible, be an alternative supplier.

Particular attention should be paid to the ability to restore electronic or physical records that are necessary for business resumption. Basel also states, 'Where such records are backed-up at an off-site facility, or where a bank's operations must be relocated to a new site, care should be taken that these sites are at an adequate distance from the impacted operations to minimise the risk that both primary and back-up records and facilities will be unavailable simultaneously'.

Basel continues, 'Banks should periodically review their disaster recovery and business continuity plans so they are consistent with the bank's current operations and business strategies. Moreover, these plans should be tested periodically to ensure that the bank would be able to execute the plans in the unlikely event of a severe business disruption.'

How severe can the disruption be? You will not be able to test unlikely events that easily. A viable test that could be performed might include a complete loss of systems for a day – perhaps – but for durations of say a week we would then be in the area of scenario analysis. At this stage, we start to look at the unexpected end of disaster recovery.

7 Business continuity policy

7.1 Business continuity plans (BCP) and disaster recovery (DR)

QUICK QUESTION

What do you think is the difference between business continuity plans and disaster recovery?

Write your answer here before reading on.

Business continuity plans (BCP) are concerned with ensuring that the firm is able to recover from an emergency such as utility disruptions, software failures and hardware failures – some of the key Operational Risk events as defined in Basel II.

Disaster recovery is the process of regaining access to the systems, data, hardware and software necessary to resume critical business operations after a natural or human-induced disaster. A disaster recovery plan (DRP) should also include plans for coping with the unexpected or sudden loss of key personnel. DRP is part of the larger process of business continuity planning.

With respect to technology and systems, a disaster could be any one or more of the following kinds of events, ranked by increasing severity:

(1) One or more of the applications that the firm uses to process its business is lost, either as a result of a software or hardware failure. The failure is in one of the firm's own systems, and it is the only firm affected.

(2) An external application, upon which the firm is dependent (such as one provided by an exchange or clearing house system or an information provider's system), is lost, either as a result of a software or hardware failure. Other user firms with which the firm trades are also dependent on this application.

(3) The firm is the victim of an event such as fire, flood, criminal or terrorist related activity, and has lost access to one of its key buildings. Other neighbouring businesses may also be affected.

Since 9/11 much attention has been paid to the most severe event. However a firm must also pay attention to less dramatic events under its BCP approach.

7.2 What is in the plan?

A disaster recovery plan is a comprehensive statement of consistent actions to be taken before, during and after a disaster. The plan should be documented and tested to ensure the continuity of operations and the availability of critical resources in the event of a disaster.

The primary objective of disaster recovery planning is to protect the organisation in the event that all (or part) of its operations and/or computer services are rendered unusable. Being prepared is the key. The planning process should minimise the disruption of operations and ensure some level of organisational stability and an orderly recovery after a disaster.

Other objectives of disaster recovery planning include:

- providing a sense of security
- minimising the risk of delays
- guaranteeing the reliability of standby systems
- providing a standard for testing the plan
- minimising decision-making during a disaster.

7.3 Obtain senior management commitment

Management must support and be involved in the development of the disaster recovery planning process. They should be responsible for co-ordinating the disaster recovery plan and ensuring its effectiveness within the organisation.

Adequate time and resources must be committed to the development of an effective plan. Resources could include both financial considerations and the effort of all personnel involved.

7.4 Establish a planning committee

A planning committee should be appointed to oversee the development and implementation of the plan. The planning committee should include representatives from all functional areas of the organisation. Key committee stakeholder members should include the operations manager and the data processing manager. The committee also should define the scope of the plan.

7.5 Perform a risk assessment

The planning committee should prepare a risk analysis and business impact analysis that includes a range of possible disasters, including natural, technical and human threats.

Each functional area of the organisation should be analysed to determine the potential consequence and impact associated with several disaster scenarios. The risk assessment process should also evaluate the safety of critical documents and vital records.

Traditionally, fire has posed the greatest threat to an organisation. Intentional human destruction, however, should also be considered. The plan should provide for the worst-case situation: destruction of the main building. It is important to assess the impact and consequences resulting from loss of information and services. The planning committee should also analyse the costs related to minimising the potential exposures.

In December 2006 the FSA published its Business Continuity Management Practice Guide (BCMP Guide) which is available from its website (www.fsa.gov.uk). Among its recommendations for leading practice in this area were the following.

(1) Planning considers wide area destruction involving significant loss of staff.
(2) Local authority and emergency services plans are taken into account by the firm.
(3) Procedures that are agreed with the firm's insurers are included in the plans.

7.6 Establish priorities for processing and operations

The critical needs of each department within the organisation should be carefully evaluated in such areas as:

- Functional operations
- Key personnel
- Information
- Processing systems
- Service
- Documentation
- Vital records
- Policies and procedures.

Processing and operations should be analysed to determine the maximum amount of time that the department and organisation can operate without each critical system.

Critical needs are defined as the necessary procedures and equipment required to continue operations should a department, computer centre, main facility or a combination of these be destroyed or become inaccessible.

A method of determining the critical needs of a department is to document all the functions performed by each department. Once the primary functions have been identified, the operations and processes should be ranked in order of priority: essential, important and non-essential.

7.7 Interdependencies

It is important to review the various dependencies and interdependencies. This diagram addressing 9/11 illustrates the point:

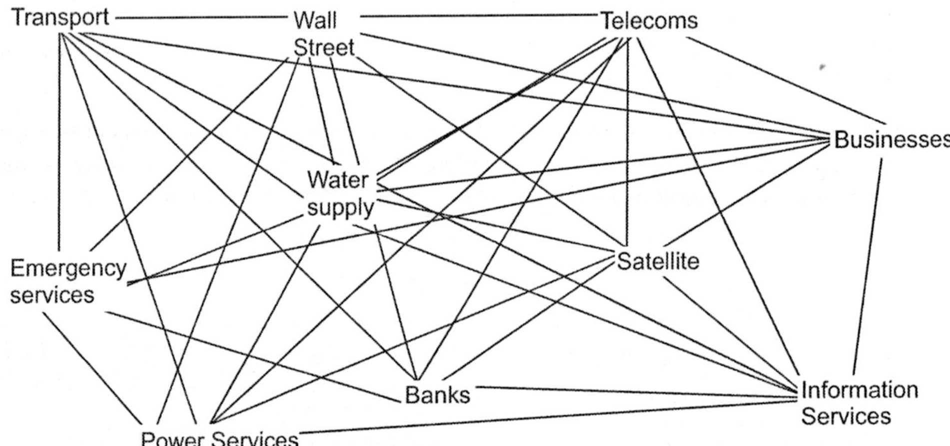

7.8 Organise and document a written plan

An outline of the plan's contents should be prepared to guide the development of the detailed procedures. Senior management should review and approve the proposed plan. The outline can ultimately be used for the table of contents after final revision. Other benefits of this approach are that it:

- helps to organise the detailed procedures
- identifies all major steps before the writing begins
- identifies redundant procedures that only need to be written once
- provides a 'road map' for developing the procedures.

A standard format should be developed to facilitate the writing of detailed procedures and the documentation of other information to be included in the plan. This will help ensure that the disaster plan follows a consistent format and allows for ongoing maintenance of the plan. Standardisation is especially important if more than one person is involved in writing the procedures.

The plan should be thoroughly developed, including all detailed procedures to be used before, during and after a disaster. It may not be practical to develop detailed procedures until back-up alternatives have been defined.

The procedures should include methods for maintaining and updating the plan to reflect any significant internal, external or systems changes. The procedures should allow for a regular review of the plan by key personnel within the organisation.

The disaster recovery plan should be structured using a team approach. Specific responsibilities should be assigned to the appropriate team for each functional area of the company. There should be teams responsible for administrative functions, facilities, logistics, user support, computer back-up, restoration and other important areas in the organisation. The structure of the contingency organisation may not be the same as the existing organisation chart.

The contingency organisation is usually structured, with teams responsible for major functional areas such as:

- Administrative functions
- Facilities
- Logistics
- User support
- Computer back-up
- Restoration
- Other important areas.

The management team is especially important because it co-ordinates the recovery process. The team should assess the disaster, activate the recovery plan, and contact team managers. The management team also oversees documents and monitors the recovery process. Management team members should be the final decision-makers in setting priorities, policies and procedures.

Each team has specific responsibilities that must be completed to ensure successful execution of the plan. The teams should have an assigned manager and an alternate in case the team manager is not available. Other team members should also have specific assignments where possible.

7.9 Develop testing criteria and procedures

It is essential that the plan be thoroughly tested and evaluated on a regular basis (at least annually). Procedures to test the plan should be documented. The tests will provide the organisation with the assurance that all necessary steps are included in the plan.

Other reasons for testing include:

- determining the feasibility and compatibility of back-up facilities and procedures
- identifying areas in the plan that need modification
- providing training to the team managers and team members
- demonstrating the ability of the organisation to recover
- providing motivation for maintaining and updating the disaster recovery plan.

7.10 Test the plan

After testing procedures have been completed, an initial test of the plan should be performed by conducting a structured walk-through test. The test will provide additional information regarding any further steps that may need to be included, changes in procedures that are not effective, and other appropriate adjustments. The plan should be updated to correct any problems identified during the test. Initially, testing of the plan should be done in sections and after normal business hours to minimise disruption to the overall operations of the organisation.

Types of tests include:

- Checklist tests
- Simulation tests
- Parallel tests
- Full interruption tests
- Cross industry tests involving suppliers and customers.

Key recommendations about testing in the FSA's BCMP Guide include:

- Critical suppliers are involved in tests at least annually.
- The firm should be prepared to supply evidence of its testing to its own customers, suppliers and regulators.
- To facilitate these recommendations, most exchanges and clearing houses offer their customers facilities to test whether their back-up facilities are able to communicate successfully with the providers' own systems.

7.11 Approve and update the plan

Once the disaster recovery plan has been written and tested, the plan should be approved by senior management. It is their ultimate responsibility that the organisation has a documented and tested plan.

Management is responsible for:

- establishing policies, procedures and responsibilities for comprehensive contingency planning
- reviewing and approving the contingency plan annually, documenting such reviews in writing.

If the organisation receives information processing from a service bureau, management must also:

- evaluate the adequacy of contingency plans for its service bureau
- ensure that its contingency plan is compatible with its service bureau's plan.

Whenever new applications are deployed, old applications are retired, new business units are opened or existing units closed, the plan will require updating. Depending on the nature of the change, it may be necessary to repeat some of all of the steps described above.

7.12 Conclusion

The key factor in business continuity planning is objectives. Just as we require objectives for our operational risk framework project, so we also need them for our business continuity plan.

Often plans try to ensure that you recover as quickly as possible. This would be equivalent to putting controls in place to prevent all errors from occurring. This is neither valuable nor possible.

QUICK QUESTION

A business continuity plan needs to reflect business realities, therefore what should the objective of the plan be?

Write your answer here before reading on.

There will be an element of loss so the objective is to manage that loss. Manage the event rather than letting the event manage the firm. The next point is to ensure that the firm will recover at least as quickly as its stakeholders expect and ideally quicker than the competition.

Disaster recovery planning involves more than off-site storage or back-up processing. Organisations should also develop written, comprehensive disaster recovery plans that address all the critical operations and functions of the business. The plan should include documented and tested procedures which, if followed, will ensure the ongoing availability of critical resources and the continuity of operations.

The probability of a disaster occurring in an organisation is highly uncertain. A disaster plan, however, is similar to liability insurance: in that it provides a certain level of comfort in knowing that if a major catastrophe occurs, it will not result in financial disaster. Insurance alone is not adequate because it may not compensate for the incalculable loss of business during the interruption or the business that never returns.

8 Crisis management

8.1 The event in Manhattan – 9 September 2011 (9/11)

CASE STUDY

9/11

One of the key elements arising from the analysis of the 9/11 event in Manhattan was that people were much harder to replace that systems and processes, consequently the initial emphasis should aimed towards the people issues that can be handled so poorly by Business Continuity Plans. Why were they so poor? Often they are capable of dealing with the "fire in reception" event, but not dealing with an earthquake. Some events appear so terrible that they are difficult to plan for. The staff that want to plan for such events are considered as morbid. However it is important to plan for such remote events, because there will not be sufficient time to plan after the event has occurred. That is why it is important to look at the low frequency high impact events that are so difficult to imagine.

Looking back at September 2001, the following observations are valid:

- Firms generally had designed business continuity plans, although there was still evidence of a lack of belief in their importance at senior level.
- Testing of plans was rarely completely integrated.
- The business analysis was often inadequate.
- Many plans did not take into account a major disaster.
- They were not fully effective.
- Some could not be found.
- Staff did not know what to do.
- Some firms took longer to recover than was really necessary.

The firms in the Twin Towers mostly had business contingency plans which they tried to put into effect, but there was evidence in some companies that the importance of contingency planning had not really been taken seriously. Stories are heard of senior executives who paid lip service to the principle since they doubted that the plan would actually work.

The business analysis that underpins the business continuity plan should have led directly from the detailed risk analysis and identification undertaken by the institutions – yet it was often seen as a separate document that did not fit into the structure at all. A business continuity plan is part of the risk control and mitigation structure – perhaps individually the most important of all.

There was also evidence of firms just going through the motions in respect of testing their plans. Single departments or offices would be evacuated for a short period and then the staff allowed to return. What the 9/11 event highlighted was that the use of the contingency site under stress conditions was actually central to the investigation of the adequacy of a business continuity plan.

Business continuity plans had another problem - there was only one plan. This would generally mean that it was only capable of dealing with comparatively minor events, for example a loss of utilities. It set out what were the key bits of equipment that would be required in the short-term prior to reusing the main properties. What they did not consider was the type of composite event experienced with 9/11, where there was likely to be relocation of significant levels of operation for a significant period without key staff being available.

Indeed the contingency sites for some of the companies in the twin towers were themselves in the twin towers, which is clearly inappropriate. In other cases the contingency plans were kept in the offices they related to – so if you lost use of the office you lost use of the contingency plan. Some of the lessons appear obvious – have the contingency plan at the contingency site, for example.

If there is a major event, there is the expectation that there will be significant loss. The market and customers are able to understand this and should be tolerant – as will the regulators. Where there is a problem is if the firm fails to recover as quickly as the market, regulators or customers expect.

8.2 Not all events will be equivalent to 9/11

This is the point where business continuity planning fits into the main Risk Identification exercise. It is the risk identified as part of that process which should be incorporated into this part of the planning. Again just as for the operational risk framework, it is necessary to set objectives for the operational risk plan, with different sets of objectives potentially in place for different types of event.

Is there just one BCP plan which tries to cover everything, or are there a series of plans that cover a series of different types of event – increasing in severity? If you only have one plan, then it tries to deal with both a fire in reception and an earthquake with the same set of solutions. The consequence of this can be that you over react to certain types of event, yet under react to others.

Clearly 9/11 was an extreme event, but most plans did not take into account what an extreme event really was and how that could impact the business.

The solution is to set up plans for extreme, serious, moderate and minor events, defining these in terms of the seriousness of their impact on the business. Ideally these should be in some form of database or data register so that changes to the structure or control environment can also immediately be considered in a Business Continuity Planning framework.

When business continuity planning is considered, or key person insurance taken out, firms go through an exercise to identify who are key to the business. One of the lessons from the 9/11 event was that these analyses were often flawed. In this case there were no new transactions to enter into in the short term, so all of the trading staff that would normally have been key were not actually required for the first week.

In looking at who is key to the business, this will vary depending on the nature of the event. In a case where there is to be no new activity, the key staff are attached to the control environment and processing areas, the legal and insurance teams, the communications people – but not the front office staff. If the event were a collapse of a major financial counterparty causing market turbulence then it is the front office staff that are key. So one plan for all events is clearly again not the answer – those that are key would need to know that the plan identifying them as key was being invoked.

What you would not want is a whole lot of staff that consider themselves to be important, but are actually not required, to be hanging around in times of crisis. So the exercise required is to scenario test the extreme events and then identify those staff that would become key in those circumstances – and then identify the actions to be taken if they are unavailable.

8.3 Planning and organising resources

There are a lot of things to do, which will add value to the crisis contingency plan. The objective should also be to build this into the main operational risk framework. Cutting corners in testing will invalidate the usefulness of the tests. If the test is too complex to undertake, try to simulate it using modelling techniques.

- Try to think the unthinkable
- Try to obtain someone independent to review your plan
- Ensure that managers and critical employees have at least two different methods of communication
- Test your plan fully on a regular basis – cutting corners will invalidate the test.

The work conducted in identifying which staff are available will need to take account of the specific circumstance of the employees. Each is likely to deal with an extreme event such as 9/11 differently. Some will not have been directly affected and may only have seen the events unfold on television – yet they could still be in shock or have post traumatic stress disorder. The effect is the same; they will be unable to work.

Some staff may have lost their friends, family and homes. They may not have a roof or food. Under these circumstances, whilst they are accounted for, they have needs that must be addressed prior to their returning as an asset to the company. To meet this demand it is likely that counsellors and staff specifically required to solve staff problems will be required. The way that your firm deals with hardship in this way will be part of the way that you will subsequently be judged.

Here are some additional things to think about:

- Media contacts
- In-flight transactions
- Defining critical assets and asset dependencies
- Mapping asset vulnerabilities
- The people chain
- The communications strategy.

8.4 The nature of crisis management

In a crisis it is self evident that various risks will exacerbate, so that when one type of risk worsens others will do so as well. This is particularly true with operational risk. Therefore being able to adapt and develop good organisational skills within a firm is of even greater importance in times of crisis. One of the key elements will be managing people as a resource addressing in particular the manner in which they communicate with and between each other.

Crises exacerbate composite threats so that in an extreme event, such as 9/11 in Manhattan, loss of staff, premises and communications all presented immediate attention together with the inability to travel, the loss of infrastructure plus the loss of basic utilities such as power and water. The mitigation of individual threats is somewhat more straightforward than mitigating waves of composite threats. If there is more than one threat, which would easily be expected in a crisis, then more resource and better organisational planning will be required and so on. If a firm takes the view that it is difficult to undertake this kind of analysis, it will not make the set of risks disappear, so the more that can be done by the firm the better. If a company's Board decided that they would only plan on the basis of a single threat, then that it is a risk-based choice that they will make hopefully consistent with their acquisition of insurance and their maintenance of a good control environment.

The important thing is to find a structured way to undertake fresh thinking about business continuity. It will be hard to carry out full tests but simulations should be performed. By doing so you will have a better understanding of the risks your firm is running and the likely impact of such an event upon your operations. It is also possible to acquire software database tools that will assist in implementing the contingency plan that is suitable for the event(s) that the firm actually confronts.

The organisation will need to have in place a graduated response ranging from minor events through to significant events onto major events and ultimately disasters. It will be important to make sure that the terms used are well-understood by all employees so that they will know roughly what to do in each case.

8.5 The control and command centre

The heart of the crisis in a disaster scenario will be the control centre or disaster room. This control centre and the staff within it will need to be able to make decisions - significant decisions - without obtaining what historically would have required approvals. As a result therefore there will be mistakes made and this consequence needs to be accepted by the company's management.

It is the ability to make a decision and proceed with that decision that is most crucial. Indeed, when training the team that will be situated in the control centre, putting them through some of the scenarios and seeing how they react will also be useful to the organisation. General guidelines can be provided against which the managers are able to judge the actions to take but these must become first nature under the stressed environment of a serious event. Not everything can be planned for and some of the expected solutions may fail but a good control and command centre that is able to take control and deal with issues is crucial for the successful recovery of the company. The key staff must remain calm and totally focussed on the job in hand.

8.6 Location of the control centre

Undertaking detailed thought about where you wish to site your control centre is vital. Ideally it should have a few similar services as your principal site or sites. The communication issues should be carefully evaluated. In terms of access consideration must be given to road, air and other forms of transport. Will staff be able to drive there? Will the airports be working? Will access over roads or bridges be required? Additionally, what telephone facilities will be available? Will there be more than one medium available or more than one provider of services?

Sometimes organisations may well use a control centre in a remote location. Consider for example London being the control site for a disaster taking place in India. There will still be a series of communication steps that will need to be taken locally. What is the likelihood that long range communications are still working when local communications have failed? The control centre site location therefore is a key decision. If it is to be a single site then it must be dependent upon as few of the main site's services as possible. If staff need to arrive there then it must be accessible. It may well be necessary to have more than one site available.

The plan of action for the control centre needs to be meticulously planned. There must be a suitable structure so that if an event occurs the staff will know immediately what to do and where to go. Every identified person who may have specific roles and responsibilities must have at least one, ideally more, deputies who can cover for their absence.

The control centre is the central decision-making unit with the authority to make decisions. Its team therefore has to be fully trained with adequate cover. Members of the team must know what to do and where to go and above all they must be able to communicate.

Some members of the team will possibly be impacted by the event. Others will simply be unable to arrive at the location. It is therefore important that a team of sufficient capability and strength of numbers can be created quickly in order to lead the firm towards recovery. This will mean they have the contact information for each member of the team and all their seniors and deputies who they would expect to be present. It may well be desirable for all staff to have portable communications equipment with them at all times which contains all up to date communications information.

In looking at the options under a crisis scenario the key test is to be able to satisfy yourselves that the plan will work.

As indicated earlier, efficiency of communications will be a key to success. The elements in the plan regarding communications should set out who is to be contacted, how often, when and by whom. It will also set out what is to be communicated because there generally there is no time to be wasted. Those to be contacted will include staff and customers, the market and the regulators. Each will have different needs and require to be contacted at different frequencies. Providing clear information to staff therefore is crucial. It may be that telephone lines are cut and that radio may be possible as a back-up medium in order to reassure the market and customers. It may be that the internet is still available when your own internal systems fail. It is necessary to consider the totality of scenarios and design a strategy to deal with issues on a progressive basis.

9 Information security

QUICK QUESTION

Think about what personal information your bank holds about you.

Write your answer here before reading on.

9.1 Information security principles

Information security broadly covers the practise of protecting information from unauthorised access, use, disclosure, destruction, manipulation and modification. Information security relates to information held in any form, be it physical or electronic, written or verbal. Information is a valuable commodity in any business, including banking – imagine if an investment bank developed an algorithm that enabled them to successful speculate on financial markets while minimising risks. Similarly, the client list of a stock broker's highest value clients is a source of competitive advantage. Losing this information would be a disaster. Therefore having robust information security measures in place is essential and is based around three basic principles:

- Confidentiality – information should only be accessible by those who have been granted access to it.
- Integrity – information should remain stored as it was intended to be and should remain intact and unaltered
- Available – information is only an asset to a business if it is available when it is required. Anyone who has legitimate access to information should be able to access it as and when they need it.

9.2 ISO2700

The International Standards Institute have issued a series of standards relating to information security:

- ISO 27001 – a specification for an information security management system.
- ISO 27002 – a code of practise for information security that establishes guidelines and principles for information security management.

- ISO 27003 – offers guidelines for implementing a information security management system.
- ISO 27004 – information security measurements, metrics and controls.
- ISO 27005 – prime standards relating to information security risk management.
- ISO 27006 – guidelines for receiving information security accreditation.

(Source: *ISO website*)

9.3 Information security policy

Every bank should have a clear information security policy that is communicated and understood across the organisation. A typical policy document would cover the following:

- Purpose – the rationale and overall objectives of the policy, stressing the importance of information security and the roles and responsibilities of staff.
- Aims and commitments – banks are likely to be bound by legislation relating to information security. In the UK, this will include the Data Protection Act. Failure to comply with this act can result in large fines. This section of the policy will make reference to such legislation and organisational specific aims and commitments.
- Protection of confidential information – this section goes into specific measures that must be taken in order to protect confidential information and will be broken down into sub-sections:
  - Storage – Areas where information should be stored (secured cabinets, authorised network drives etc.).
  - Access – Details of necessary security measures required (such as encryption) to ensure that only authorised persons can access confidential information.
  - Security – Guidelines on password protection and access rights.
  - Copying – Requirements for making back-up copies of data (physical and electronic).
  - Disposal – Guidelines of the permissions needed to dispose of information and details of the permitted data disposal methods (shredding, archiving etc.)
  - Exchange of information – Permissions that allow the exchange of information and approved methods. For example, some banks do not permit confidential information to be sent to personal devices such as Blackberry's.
  - Enforcement – A summary of the negative consequences arising from not adhering to the information security policy.
  - Use of information security technology – Guidelines on the controls in place around technology used to protect information, such as PCI DSS (Payment Card Industry Data Security Standard). PCI DSS users must adhere to 12 areas of compliance if they wish to use the technology.
  - Sharing information with third parties – banks are likely to share information with clients, vendors and outsourced operations. Clear guidance must be provided on the authorisation requirements needed to share information with these parties and the procedures for storing any information received.
  - Disaster recovery – the plans and escalation procedures in place should confidential information be compromised.

10 Business continuity management regulatory issues

10.1 The PRA and FCA's approach

Under the British PRA and FCA's Senior Management Arrangements, Systems and Controls requirements (known as SYSC), a firm must have robust governance arrangements. These include a clear organisational structure with well defined, transparent and consistent lines of responsibility, effective processes to identify, manage, monitor and report the risks it is or might be exposed to, and internal control mechanisms, including sound administrative and accounting procedures and effective control and safeguard arrangements for information processing systems.

In addition to these general requirements, a common platform firm (**meaning most regulated firms**) must take reasonable steps to ensure continuity and regularity in the performance of its regulated activities. To this end the common platform firm must employ appropriate and proportionate systems, resources and procedures.

It is easy to see that the general requirements of the British regulator in line with the EU standards under MiFID (The Markets in Financial Investment Directive) sets down clear standards for business continuity discipline to which firms should adhere.

The PRA states, for example, that the matters dealt with in a business continuity policy should include:

- Resource requirements such as people, systems and other assets, and arrangements for obtaining these resources
- The recovery priorities for the firm's operations
- Communication arrangements for internal and external concerned parties (including the PRA, FCA, clients and the press)
- Escalation and invocation plans that outline the processes for implementing the business continuity plans, together with relevant contact information
- Processes to validate the integrity of information affected by the disruption
- Regular testing of the business continuity policy in an appropriate and proportionate manner.

Business continuity has been a goal of chief technology officers and heads of risk for decades, but gradually the regulators of the financial services sector have also begun to pay more attention to the concept of interruption-free operations.

10.2 The Basel Committee

The Basel Committee similarly has focused on business continuity and has determined that high-level principles on business continuity would contribute beneficially to the resilience of the global financial system. A working group of the Joint Forum was established in early 2005 to develop the principles, which were published in a consultative paper in December 2005.

It drew attention to the fact that recent acts of terrorism, outbreaks of Severe Acute Respiratory Syndrome (SARS) and various widespread natural disasters had underlined the substantial risk of major operational disruptions to the financial system. It argued that financial authorities and financial industry participants have a shared interest in promoting the resilience of the financial system to such disruptions.

Financial authorities have been working closely with industry participants to establish a consensus as to what constitutes acceptable standards for business continuity. Much of this work to date has been focused at the national level. At the international level, while there have been several regulatory and private sector initiatives on the business continuity front, there has not been a concerted effort to draw together the lessons learned from major events and translate them into a set of business continuity principles that is relevant across national boundaries and financial sectors (i.e. banking, securities, and insurance). Furthermore, consistent with their focus on preserving the functionality of the financial system as a whole, financial authorities undertaking these initiatives have tended to give priority to critical market participants. The lessons learned from past experience, however, are applicable to a broader audience.

Basel's recommendations represent an effort to address these gaps. They are intended to support international standard setting organisations and national financial authorities by providing a broad framework within which more detailed business continuity arrangements might be developed that are more closely tailored to unique sectorial and local circumstances. The Basel principles also provide a consistent context for those arrangements and thereby promote a common base level of resilience across national boundaries.

The high-level Basel principles have been developed for two distinct but related audiences - financial industry participants and financial authorities. While these groups have different perspectives, roles and responsibilities in the event of a major operational disruption, both are integral in any meaningful effort to improve the financial system's resilience to such disruptions. The principles are not intended to be prescriptive, nor does their broad applicability mean a one-size-fits-all approach to business continuity. An organisation's business continuity management should be proportionate to its business risk (arising from both internal and external sources) and tailored to the scale and scope of its operations.

Basel outlines seven high-level principles that build upon traditional concepts of effective business continuity management in the following ways:

- **Principle 1** emphasises that the requirement for sound business continuity management applies to all financial authorities and financial industry participants and that the ultimate responsibility for business continuity management – not unlike the management of other risks – rests with an organisation's board of directors and senior management.
- **Principle 2** advises organisations that they should explicitly consider and plan for major operational disruptions. While this concept may be new for many organisations, it is considered important in light of the increasing frequency of such events.
- **Principle 3** states that financial industry participants should develop recovery objectives that reflect the risk they represent to the operation of the financial system. Financial industry participants that provide critical services to, or otherwise present significant risk to the operation of, the financial system should target higher standards in their business continuity management than other participants. This concept may be new for some financial industry participants. Because the steps necessary to improve the resilience of the financial system may be more costly than the steps such participants would choose to undertake on their own, financial authorities are encouraged to participate, as appropriate, in identifying recovery objectives that are proportionate to the risk posed by a given participant in order to achieve a reasonably consistent level of resilience.
- **Principle 4** stresses the critical importance of business continuity plans addressing the full range of internal and external communication issues an organisation may encounter in the event of a major operational disruption. The principle specifically recognises that clear, regular communication during a major operational disruption is necessary to manage a crisis and maintain public confidence.
- Principle 5 highlights the special case of cross-border communications during a major operational disruption. Given the deepening interdependencies of financial systems across national boundaries, this principle advises financial industry participants and financial authorities to adopt communication protocols that address situations where cross border communication may be necessary.
- **Principle 6** emphasises the need to ensure that business continuity plans are effective and to identify necessary modifications through periodic testing.
- Finally, to ensure that financial industry participants are in fact implementing appropriate approaches to business continuity management that reflect the recovery objectives adopted in accordance with Principles 1 and 3, **Principle 7** calls upon financial authorities to incorporate business continuity management reviews into their frameworks for assessing financial industry participants.

QUESTION TIME 4

Explain why business continuity management has gained increasing prominence over recent years.

Write your answer here then check with the answer at the back of the book.

11 Responsibility for the management of operational risk

11.1 Procedures and rules-based controls

CASE STUDY

BP

When Tony Hayward became CEO of BP, in 2007, he vowed to make safety his top priority. Among the new rules he instituted were the requirements that all employees use lids on coffee cups while walking and refrain from texting while driving. Three years later, on Hayward's watch, the Deepwater Horizon oil rig exploded in the Gulf of Mexico, causing one of the worst man-made disasters in history. A U.S. investigation commission attributed the disaster to management failures that crippled the ability of individuals involved to identify the risks they faced and to properly evaluate, communicate, and address them. Hayward's story reflects a common problem. Despite all the rhetoric and money invested in it, risk management is too often treated as a compliance issue that can be solved by drawing up lots of rules and making sure that all employees follow them. Many such rules, of course, are sensible and do reduce some risks that could severely damage a company. But rules-based risk management will not diminish either the likelihood or the impact of a disaster such as Deepwater Horizon, just as it did not prevent the failure of many financial institutions during the 2007 banking crisis.

11.2 Establishing controls

The establishment of controls follows the process of identification and assessment of risks in the operational risk management cycle. It is important that controls are set at a suitable level in order to address appropriately the risks that they have been set up to mitigate. In the same way that risks and performance can be measured by indicators so can controls utilising the concept of key control indicators

(KCIs). A KCI will be something which sets in place a scoring mechanism to measure the effectiveness of the control.

When identifying controls it is important to identify the independent controls which mitigate a risk. Where controls operate in sequence, if the first control should fail then subsequent controls would be unlikely to provide any additional benefit in mitigating relevant risks. It is important therefore that all controls are checked to ensure that they are all independent of each other otherwise they may imply a false sense of well-being and security.

Sometimes controls can be put in place to mitigate more than one risk. In practice however it is unlikely that the application of the control is exactly the same every time. Often the control can be the same but applied differently in different parts of the business. It is most important to be able to define not just what the control is but the purpose of the control and therefore to be able to assess its viability and usefulness. Internal audit groups will also, as part of their general work and review, check that controls are meaningful.

Controls are the most common method of mitigating risks. They are very much part of management's influence and it is important to make sure that the controls are reviewed on a meaningful and regular basis.

However it is worth pointing out that there are other controls to mitigate risk such as avoidance of risk altogether by ceasing business in the particular product or business activity to which the risk is attached. Similarly transferring the risk to another party entirely for example through insurance or maybe through some sort of modification to the business model, whilst it may not eradicate the risk completely, will change the risk such that the nature of the risk is altered. It is important to remember however that with insurance the potential pay-out from the insurance will not be immediate nor will it be absolute and is therefore not a complete answer to the question.

11.3 Types of controls

There is more than one type of control. The most common ones are referred to as **preventative** and **detective**. However **directive** and **corrective** controls also exist. We summarise these as follows:

Directive controls – These provide a degree of direction for the firm and typically take the form of policies, procedures, processes or manuals.

Preventative controls – The essence of these controls is to prevent the risk or event from happening in the first place. They are often automated such as computer validation techniques on input data or system checks to prevent limits being breached. There might be access codes to prevent personnel from entering certain parts of the building or from visitors being able to gain entry to an office area. In many ways such controls are regarded as the most useful because they stop something happening in advance of the event.

Detective controls – These take place after the event has occurred and the principal purpose is to identify immediately that the risk event has occurred and to mitigate it. Typical detective controls in the operation of banks would be any kind of reconciliation or checking to detect or crystallise an error which can then be acted upon and corrected.

Corrective controls – These act again after the event has happened and mitigate the effects of the event through corrective action. Typical such controls are following up on outstanding reconciliation items or elements contained in risk reports or taking action following risk monitoring and escalation.

QUESTION TIME 5

Under which of these headings would the following controls fall?

- A ban on all employees taking calls when driving
- An insistence that employees use handrails when climbing or descending stairs
- Searching for a cash difference
- Balancing a cash till
- A flow chart detailing how to open a money transmission account

Write your answer here then check with the answer at the back of the book.

11.4 Fraud as the enemy

No financial institution can countenance fraud. Two of the seven Basel operational risk event categories address fraud – external and internal.

Internal controls are simply policies and procedures that are implemented to deter or prevent business related internal theft by employees. They form part of the environment and ethics within which work is carried out. Most of these controls involve accounting systems and the related records of the business. When effective internal controls are in place, employees will usually have to collude to facilitate a theft. Collusion occurs where two or more employees work as accomplices or co-conspirators to steal money or property from the business, thereby defeating a control procedure. Family members may well be tempted to collaborate together in this manner and many firms have in place specific employment rules and conditions to prevent that.

Today, more than ever, employee theft has become a major problem for small businesses. Business owners, faced with long workdays do not have the time to watch over these employees to make sure that there is no pilfering going on. Simple internal control procedures can stop employees from stealing money and property from the business. Internal controls are simple policies that segregate duties and implement safeguards that make it harder for employees to steal. Often, when strict internal controls are implemented and working properly, it takes collusion between two or more employees to facilitate a theft scheme. The dual control procedures that you will be aware of from your own office are an example of this.

There are many types of frauds, but the most common is asset misappropriation. This type of fraud can be facilitated by skimming, cash theft, payroll theft, cash sales theft, billing schemes, accounts receivable schemes, impersonal account fraud and just about every system that deals with cash is vulnerable to thefts. Understanding how fraudsters can manipulate systems will help you understand how to stop them with internal controls.

11.5 Segregation of duties

Simple rules concerning segregation of duties will help prevent theft and other risk events.

Duties reflect the recording, authorisation, reconciliation, and custody of assets and processes.

QUICK QUESTION

Image that you are running your own small business. What controls could you put in place to minimise the possibility of employee fraud?

Write your answer here before reading on.

Here are some examples of the procedures you could put in place:

(1) Never let the same person handle cash coming into the business (custody) and record the receipt of that cash in the accounting records.

(2) Never let the same person that signs the cheques and authorises payments record the transactions into the accounting records.

(3) Never let the same person reconcile the bank statements and the cash accounts and write or sign payment orders or make money transfers.

(4) Never let the person that has the authority to make payments, do so alone. Always have two signatories on each payment.

(5) Never let the bookkeeper that enters transactions on a daily basis in the accounting system make general book keeping entries that override the system.

(6) Never let the person that records the transactions into the accounting system deposit money or cheques at the bank.

(7) Never let the same person record payroll and sign off the payroll amounts.

There are many others, but this is the general idea. If you look at all of these rules, you will notice that each one separates accounts receivable and sales.

These ideas, in a modified form, can be applied in the real cases such as Nick Leeson to whom reference was made elsewhere in this course.

11.5.1 Accounts receivable

Control is possible by segregating duties and not allowing the same person to handle cheques or automated payments and make accounting entries.

Some simple business examples might behave like this – a payment comes in from a customer on their account and it never arrives at your bank. The bookkeeper takes the cheque and makes a deposit in a similarly named bank account that the employee has set up with another bank. Do banks check the names on cheques? Not necessarily, and you can sign a cheque Mickey Mouse and the bank will process it. The advent of automated pay in terminals in bank branches has made it more likely that this type of fraud can occur. Now, in this fraud, the accounts receivable has to be removed or the customer will complain when they receive their next month's bill. The accounts receivable is written off to an expense account. This type of fraud cannot be performed with an accounting system that has built in controls over the entries that are allowed. Account receivables should never be able to be written off to any other account besides cash. Some standard software allows this type of fraud to be committed due to the lack of controls present within the system.

Fraud also occurs when a cheque is stolen and then the next cheque that comes in is applied to the stolen account and so on. The bookkeeper cannot take a holiday or this type of fraud will be discovered. A common check for this type of fraud is to guard against employees who do not use their holiday entitlement.

Sales are either stolen off the books or on the books. If sales are stolen off the books, the employee does not have to worry about making an entry into the accounting system to cover the theft. Sales are skimmed and never make it to the register. The inventory in this type of theft will reflect a sale, because, in the case of a restaurant for example, the beer is consumed or the meal is still eaten. Comparing weekly purchases to weekly sales for each category of food and alcohol will show distinct patterns. These sales patterns will be surprisingly accurate with little deviations between one week and the next. Inventory being stolen out the back door will also cause this relationship to be skewed. Accordingly, if the sales percentages are showing a strong variance, then employees are stealing either sales or food.

On the books sales are a little harder and will usually involve the making of general journal entries to write off sales or inventory so the cash accounts will not be off. Remember that a booked sale raises the cash account and that cash account on paper must reconcile with the bank records each month. It is surprising how many businesses do not properly reconcile their bank accounts.

11.6 Change management

Change management is an activity which will face every firm. No business can afford to resist change or else it will become obsolete. Change in environment, technology will face every organisation on a regular basis. However, generally speaking, rules based change management practices always fail. You cannot assess risk by rules alone! Over time rules based practices will increase your workload (actually that usually happens on day one), slow down the rate of change, frustrate staff, and ultimately increase the change risk as well-intentioned workers find ways to get their job done despite the rules!

To understand why rules based approaches fail you have to go back to the key principles of change management, which are:

- Changes should be planned and deployed in a controlled way to avoid service disruptions.
- The level of planning and control used should be determined by an objective risk assessment (this is key – rules often conflict with this principle).
- The level of risk should be mitigated by the appropriate level of planning and testing (balanced approach – hard to get right with rules).
- Clear judgment is required when business drivers or technical constraints significantly influence the risk vs. mitigation balance in one direction or the other.

11.7 A checklist for implementing control systems

These eight ideas are a guide for establishing an effective controls framework.

(1) **Create a positive work environment**

A positive work environment encourages employees to follow established policies and procedures and act in the best interests of the organisation. Fair employment practices, written job descriptions, clear organisational structure, comprehensive policies and procedures, open lines of communication between management and employees, and positive employee recognition will all help reduce the likelihood of internal fraud and theft.

(2) **Implement internal controls**

Internal controls are measures that ensure the effectiveness and efficiencies of operations, compliance with laws and regulations, safeguarding of assets, and accurate financial reporting. These policies and procedures should address the following points:

- **Segregation and separation of duties**: As discussed above, no employee should be responsible for both recording and processing a transaction.
- **Access controls**: Access to physical and financial assets and information, as well as accounting systems, should be restricted to authorised employees.
- **Authorisation controls**: Develop and implement policies to determine how financial transactions are initiated, authorised, recorded, and reviewed.

(3) **Employ honest people**

Of course, this is the goal of every company, but it is easier said than done. Dishonest employees will ignore a firm's attempts to provide a positive work environment, and will search for ways to defeat even the most comprehensive internal controls.

Pre-employment background checks are an excellent way to cut down on employing dishonest employees.

QUICK QUESTION

What factors should comprise a suitable background check?

Write your answer here before reading on.

A thorough pre-employment background check should include:

- Criminal history for crimes involving violence, theft, and fraud
- Civil history for lawsuits involving collections, restraining orders, and fraud
- Driving licence check for numerous or serious violations
- Education verification for degrees from accredited institutions
- Employment verification of positions, length of employment, and reasons for leaving.

(4) **Educate employees**

Firms should inform employees about their policies and procedures related to fraud, the internal controls in place to prevent fraud, the organisation's code of conduct and ethics policies, and how violations of these policies will be disciplined. Every employee should sign a form to verify receipt of this material. Ideally this should be covered during induction training.

Employees should receive further annual training on these topics and on the definition of what is considered fraudulent behaviour, and sign an acknowledgement each time.

(5) **Create an anonymous reporting system**

Every organisation should provide a reporting system for employees, vendors, and customers to report anonymously any violations of policies and procedures – whistleblowing.

The firm should promote and encourage the use of the reporting system whenever possible, and take the reports seriously. The fact that they are anonymous does not mean they are any more or less credible; they should be investigated just as thoroughly as any reported misconduct.

(6) **Perform regular (and irregular) audits**

Every company should have regular assessments; but random, unannounced financial audits and fraud assessments can help identify new vulnerabilities, and measure the effectiveness of existing controls. Audits also let employees know that fraud prevention is a high priority for the organisation, imposes an impediment to temptation and keeps any potential wrongdoers uncomfortable enough that they may cease their fraudulent activities or leave the company.

(7) **Investigate every incident**

There is no point in implementing a procedure if it is not going to be acted upon. The organisation should investigate every incident and report, no matter how large or small. A thorough and prompt investigation of policy and procedure violations, allegations of fraud, or warning signs of fraud will present the facts needed to make informed decisions and reduce losses.

(8) **Lead by example**

Senior management and business owners must set an example for employees. A cavalier attitude toward rules and regulations by management will soon be reflected in the attitude of employees. All employees – regardless of position – should be held accountable for their actions.

Implementing these recommendations can dramatically reduce the opportunity for employee theft and protect the assets of the business. If a firm suspects fraudulent activity by an employee, it should seek professional assistance to conduct the investigation. Management must determine what is necessary to protect the business and prevent a recurrence.

11.8 The appropriateness of rules-based methods

As you now know, risk management is too often treated as a compliance issue that can be solved by drawing up lots of rules and making sure that all employees follow them. However rules-based risk management misses many kinds of risks that organisations face. A better approach will be a framework that allows executives to tell which risks can be managed through a rules-based model and which require alternative approaches.

Three categories of risk are normally observed:

Preventable risks – These are internal risks, arising from within the organisation, that are controllable and out to be eliminated or avoided. These include illegal, unethical, or inappropriate actions, as well as breakdowns in operational processes. These are typically covered by internal control schemes. These kinds of risks are best controlled through active prevention: monitoring operational processes and guiding people's behaviours and decisions toward desired norms. This can be done via rules-based compliance approaches.

Strategic risks – These are different from preventable risks because they are not necessarily undesirable. For example, developing a new technology platform may be seen as taking a strategic risk over the proven, existing set of legacy systems that support a bank's operations. Strategic risks cannot be managed through a rules-based control model. Instead, a firm needs a risk-management system designed to reduce the probability that the assumed risks actually materialise and to improve the company's ability to manage or contain the risk events should they occur.

External risks – Organisations cannot prevent external risks from happening. So managers need to forecast what these risks might be and develop ways to lessen their impact. They cannot be avoided, only managed. The model for addressing external risks is the use of open and explicit risk discussions. The format might be brainstorming (for near-term issues) or scenario analyses (for longer-term issues).

Each approach requires quite different structures and roles for a risk-management function. Many organisations tend to label and compartmentalise their risk management functions along business lines (credit risk, operational risk, financial risk) and this may inhibit discussion of how different risks interact. They say that one way to provide this integrative approach is to anchor their discussions in their existing strategic planning functions, in part because that function already serves as an integrated function in most large organisations. Most organisations discount the role of risk management because it is not intuitive and runs counter to many individual and organisational biases. Risk management focuses on the negative. It runs exactly counter to the can do culture most leadership teams try to foster when implementing strategy. Many tend to emphasise risk avoidance and the rules-based compliance approach. However, the concept of broader risk management is beginning to take root.

12 A risk-based management approach to controls

12.1 Identifying and categorising risks

When identifying risks, a firm needs to consider not only its own processes and systems, but also its relationships with its clients, the nature of its products and the wider business environment.

As you know, risk identification is the first step in understanding how operational risk affects the firm, raising awareness of risk issues and assessing the culture of the organisation. It can be a difficult exercise due to the diverse nature of risk causes and the difficulty in distinguishing cause from effect. Risk identification lies at the heart of the operational risk management culture of an organisation. If managers fail to identify a risk, they will fail to measure it, mitigate it and consider it and so on.

It is important to remember that risk identification will not be just a single exercise that can be completed and then forgotten about; it is clear that operational risks do change over time both in their likelihood and in their type. The risk identification will therefore need to be a live process that is regularly revisited to ensure that it remains current and applicable to the nature of the business being conducted.

The purpose of identifying operational risks is to understand, record and categorise a firm's operational risks. By doing this the firm can create a basis for establishing its risk profile and risk appetite, an understanding of the types of risk it faces and its level of exposure. There is a need to do this in order to:

- provide information to management on which to make decisions and take action to ensure a controlled environment
- establish the chain of events relationship of operational risk and understand where they occur throughout the firm
- provide a basis for risk measurement and assessment which may, for example, be used for capital allocation purposes
- set boundaries to differentiate between operational risk and other risk types (such as market and credit) and assign ownership for their mitigation
- develop a common language for discussing, assessing and managing risk that allows clear and transparent communication and decision-making.

Referring back to your study of Risk Identification, self-assessment and risk categorisation would be useful techniques to employ at this stage. You may wish to refresh your knowledge of these topics at this point.

13 Implementing operational risk management

As we discussed at the start of this course, risk management starts at the board level and is then passed down through the organisation. Whilst committees can assign risk to departments and/or individuals, management by committee of a specific risk is rarely successful. That is not to say that committees do not have a role in terms of ratifying the requirements and setting the general standards, but a committee cannot manage a risk on a day-to-day basis.

To understand how to manage risk and to implement systems that really work it might be a good idea to look at how people manage risks in extreme environments. Managing risk in war is a powerful example. Strategy, planning, training, rehearsal and operational excellence are all vitally important but without character, sense of purpose, a just cause, judgement, courage and love for country and comrade they will be defeated and they may lose their lives.

In business, unless the Board displays the same understanding of how to lead, effectively bringing the employees with them, then no matter how diligent its governance structure, processes and systems, its plan will not survive contact with the reality of human character, judgement and behaviour.

Throughout history evidence shows us that human communities only function and sustain themselves when their people:

- have a clear moral purpose
- truly care for each other
- co-operate and make good decisions about how to obtain the scarce resources they need in a hostile environment
- do all these things in a way that sustains their environment for future generations.

13.1 Importance of culture

Unless the culture is right it has to be changed is a well established maxim. Another salient quote is, culture eats strategy for breakfast. This is a quotation from a very senior executive responsible for safety at one of the major oil and gas companies. The point he was making is that managing risk in high risk endeavours such as his ultimately boils down to the character, judgement and behaviour not just of individuals but of social groups in the workplace. This is what can be referred to as culture. Every workplace has its own culture.

QUICK QUESTION

Write down a sentence that describes your understanding of culture.

Write your answer here before reading on.

Put simply, culture is the way we do things around here. It is the way that the firm acts and thinks collectively and is evident in the layout of premises, the way that people communicate, dress and work. It is important that boards and senior executive groups fully understand the culture of their business, influence it and set a good example by way of leadership and therefore stimulate the culture in a way that not only mitigates risks but also enhances the value of the business they are leading.

13.2 Better decision making

It is clearly desirable to make sensible decisions when running businesses including banks. As part of this managers should understand the context within which decisions are taken regarding operational risk. Good operational risk governance across a business will provide the Board with increased confidence that material risks which impact on the business objectives of the firm are being managed effectively. Corporate governance sits at the top of everything and provides greater assurance to the Board and to shareholders on the effectiveness of internal controls operating and utilised within the bank.

Explicit operational risk management together with good governance provides the basis for developing a consistent and effective framework for the firm. It is establishing this sound framework that is the most essential part of implementing the firm's approach.

Operational risks are inevitable. There will be many small events over which the firm must maintain control. Operational risks are therefore inherent in a bank's business activities as will be typical of any large business enterprise. It is not cost effective to attempt to eliminate all operational risks and in any event it would not be possible to do so. Losses from operational risk of small significance are expected to occur and will be accepted as part of the normal course of business. However those of material significance will occur rarely and a bank will need to reduce the likelihood of these and their impact in accordance with its risk appetite.

Effective risk management must underpin all the commercial decisions that a bank takes. The larger the bank the greater the business spread and therefore risk. Those who manage banks of any size must understand the risks that both the banks and the bank's clients take owing to the nature of both the spread and depth of the relationships that they have between them.

13.3 The operational risk cycle

The cycle of activity in managing operational risk has controls as an important step in the overall loop. Once risks are identified and measured the next job is to control them. This control covers any measure whether organisational, or by using technology. Controls are there to be defined and implemented. Beyond that the task is for the controls to be checked and reviewed periodically to see if they are operating effectively and smoothly. This latter task falls to internal audit groups within firms.

When setting up an operational risk programme it is important to recognise that operational risk management exists throughout an organisation, from the Board to the newest recruit. As such it is not sufficient just to identify the owners of the risk and the owners of the controls, but rather there is the need to ensure that risk and risk ownership are monitored as they percolate throughout the business. Each and every member of the staff, including agents and contractors, must be part of this process.

Line managers will own risks and some will own the controls which are in place to mitigate those risks. Clearly a signpost that does not tell you where you are or where to go is of no value. Likewise operating a control environment where the controls either are ineffective, cost more than the expected loss or duplicate existing controls is clearly wasteful. One of the problems here can be that vigilant internal auditors have recommended the implementation of additional controls as a result of the identification of a specific event or failure. Such an additional control may itself duplicate a control that should have identified the error, but failed to do so. Rather than implementing an additional control, the effectiveness of the original control should be improved.

If the controls are not achieving any real degree of mitigation, then they are probably of doubtful value. Another result of this part of the work can be that duplicate controls are identified; that is controls which would only identify the same control failures that another control is already identifying. Risk managers are also likely to identify controls which are either inefficient or ineffective.

To do this, measures will be required covering the throughput of the control. Information is also required on errors corrected and errors that still occur. As a consequence of this analysis, a view can be taken on the effectiveness of the controls and whether they need to be enhanced. Part of this enhancement could be training or reporting, rather than a change to the actual control.

14 The individual

14.1 The nature of organisation's and those who work within them

Everyone has experience of other people's behaviours and attitudes to working with others in an organised manner for an employer.

This diagram below demonstrates some basic axioms.

People/Organisations	
WILL	WON'T
Do what is important to them	Take seriously regulatory initiatives that they can't believe in
Do things which demonstrably and measurably add value	Keep doing things unless the value arising is evident

A firm can only achieve a risk management culture when there is **alignment** between the goals of risk management and the goals of the organisation. Hence, an organisation will have to set this in place as a specific goal.

It is at the individual level where this can be made to work.

14.2 Individuals' contribution

Individual members of staff should be made to feel part of the full risk management framework and to be made aware through their company's efforts of the importance of the individual contributions they make to the overall control system. At a personal level it is necessary to retain the ability to question and think about what one is doing. Members of staff should be encouraged to check and review and be able to work things out from first principles.

Similar to senior members of staff at board level staff should be prepared to challenge on matters and issues or events where they don't feel comfortable and be able to report their feelings either anonymously via a formal whistleblowing policy or directly to their line manager. Individuals who are performing their jobs well should be able to analyse elements of their job and the job processes upon which they are engaged in order to address risk issues as they occur.

Above all, members of staff should be willing to share information and be encouraged to communicate efficiently and effectively with one another. They should remember that they are working for organisations and that therefore controls are important and effectively a way of life within an organisational structure.

Any information that is not explicit can lead to error and misunderstanding which lead directly to operational risk events. The ability to work sensibly and to apply sound thinking and common sense is of basic importance.

15 The business

Operational risk management is, quite simply, good management and close to quality management. As management in financial services and banking is effectively dealing with people – in a continuous process and ever changing environment – there cannot be an easy answer or a simple model.

Mistakes and failures, manifested by operational risk losses, happen daily in every financial services organisation. Some are negligible, some more serious - very rarely they can be very critical. The general environment for financial services continues to change dramatically. It will call for significant and continuous adjustment in the way firms do business and adapt their operations.

As a result, Operational Risk will primarily be driven by:

New products	Product sophistication
New distribution channels	New markets
New technology	Complexity (IT-interdependencies, data structures)
E-Commerce	Processing speed
Business volumes	New legislation
Role of non-government organisations	Globalisation
Shareholder and other stakeholder pressure	Regulatory pressure
Mergers and acquisitions	Reorganisations
Staff turnover	Cultural diversity of staff and clients
Faster ageing of know-how	Rating agencies
Insurance companies	Capital markets

The diagram below illustrates that banking as a business can expect to experience losses.

Some of these will be expected in the course of normal business. For example credit card losses, defaulting mortgage payments, small cases of fraud and the like and these will be factored into the normal costs of doing business and will sit in the diagram to the left of the mean loss line under the heading expected losses. This is typical of any business where certain losses can be expected to occur and are factored into the cost of doing business. Such losses are manageable, they can be mitigated and the cost of control and loss can be passed on in the price of doing business to customers.

To the right of the vertical mean loss line as the curve shows there could be extremely serious losses in conditions of great market or economic stress whereby a loss could be critical to the survival of the enterprise. Before that case is reached there will also be more moderate stresses climbing to levels of more severe stress. All of these potential outcomes and losses can be covered by economic capital together with disaster recovery planning, continuity plans and standby facilities including insurance, capital and other buffers. It is the unexpected losses which lie to the right of the mean loss line in the diagram which are effectively addressed by Basel III and its recommendations with respect to prudential risk management.

Risk Appetite concepts (diagram not to scale)

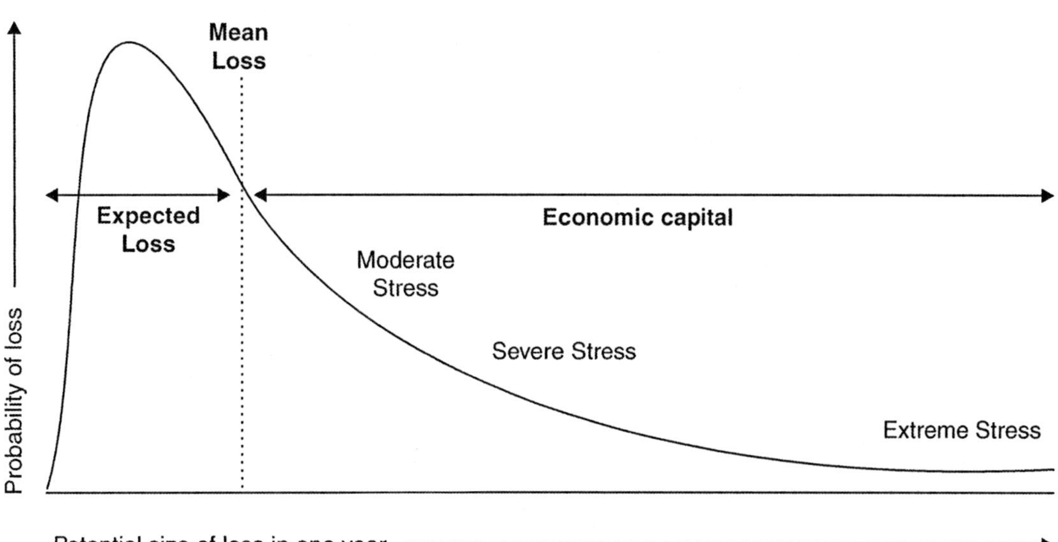

Source – Barclays PLC

Potentially larger but increasingly less likely levels of loss are illustrated in the chart above. Since the level of loss at any given probability is dependent on the portfolio of exposures in each business, the statistical measurement for each key risk category gives the bank clearer sight and better control of risk-taking throughout the organisation. Specifically, this framework enables the bank to:

- Improve management confidence and debate regarding the bank's risk profile
- Re-balance the risk profile of the medium-term plan where breaches are indicated, thereby achieving a superior risk-return profile
- Identify unused risk capacity and thus highlight the need to identify further profitable opportunities
- Improve executive management control and co-ordination of risk-taking across businesses.

16 The risk function

16.1 Risk management function

To ensure the integrity of risk management decisions every business group should have access to an operational risk control unit, the head of which would report functionally to the group head of operational risk and on to the risk committee of the firm. The primary role of the control unit will be to confirm the effective implementation of the appropriate risk framework in the business group and to ensure transparent assessment and reporting of operational risks through to senior management.

The foundation of the operational risk framework is the definition by all functions of their roles and responsibilities so that, collectively, they can ensure that there is adequate segregation of duties, complete coverage of risks and clear accountability. By organising and analysing in this way firms develop control objectives and standards to protect assets and interests based upon the types of operational risk events that may possibly arise. These will range from everyday reconciliation activities and the problems resulting through to potentially serious and severe events such as fraud. It is important to recognise within the firm that errors and accidents will always happen and that even where it is possible it is not always cost-effective to do so.

The principle aim of the operational risk management function is to take overall responsibility for the development and implementation of operational risk control principles, frameworks and processes across the firm. There will be interfaces from the risk management function across to colleagues in financial groups, compliance and the legal department. The critical elements in the risk control process should be to support the business lines of the firm by undertaking the following measures.

- First, to **identify risks** through the continuous monitoring of activities. This will include portfolios, new business and any complex or unusual transactions.
- **Measuring quantifiable risks** by using methodologies and models which have been independently validated and approved.
- To **establish risk policies** to reflect the firm's risk principles and risk appetite which are consistent with the changing business requirements of the firm and developing international best practice.
- **Comprehensive risk reporting** to stakeholders and to management at all levels.
- To **control risk** by monitoring and enforcing compliance with the risk principles including the policies, limits and regulatory requirements under which the firm operates.
- **All these processes must be coordinated** involving all relevant control and logistics functions. This will ensure that the overall approach is conducted in a comprehensive and holistic way including the assurance that transactions can be booked in a manner that will permit appropriate ongoing risk monitoring, reporting and control.

17 Senior management

17.1 Overall responsibility

In managing operational risk the establishment of the risk control framework and the corporate governance measures under which it operates lies full square with the Board.

The firm will require a proper well-functioning Board which is committed to the right culture of leadership to embed the culture of risk appetite and control within the firm. It is they who must provide the effective leadership and conduct for the firm to follow. The Board itself will need to comply with good corporate governance standards as laid down by such definitions as the Financial Reporting Council's Combined Code and operate sub-committees of the Board with respect to various matters including – one of the most important – that of the Risk Committee. The risk committee should be under the chairmanship of a member of the Board and have as a member of its group the Chief Risk Officer (CRO) acting for the bank.

17.2 Senior management's role

The general role of senior management will be to make themselves aware of the major operational risks facing their firm. They should therefore have a full understanding of the business. In many large banks they will operate in a silo environment where individual business units will each contribute their own thinking and operational risk management approaches which will then be aggregated at group level.

Senior management must approve and review the operational risk framework and ensure that that framework is audited by independent, trained and competent staff. The Board must ensure that there is a segregation of duties between internal audit and operational risk management. Both of these disciplines are necessary to support the business. Both will have unfettered access to the Board itself and operate independently. The role of the operational risk management group is to provide the centre of excellence and expertise that supports the business lines in establishing the risk and control assessment framework under which they will operate. The internal audit group can be regarded more as a checking mechanism to review the processes that are being followed, to ensure that these processes are being followed, to spot and report upon gaps that are being found in the procedure, to evaluate that the firm is actually practicing what it preaches in terms of following its own procedures and finally to suggest gaps and in the control environment which are not operating smoothly. Internal audit can often suggest new risks that are not currently being addressed in a changing business environment.

17.3 Development of the framework

A challenge to the Board will be the very development of risk frameworks, providing the necessary budget and resources together with trained and competent expertise to fulfil the necessary functions. They will be responsible for the development of policies and procedures and to ensure that these are consistently implemented throughout the organisation. This will be a major challenge, particularly in very large institutions. Another very important element will be that of communication whereby it is essential that the Board ensures that staff working in the firm understand their responsibilities. The importance of communication cannot be underestimated in that it must work effectively downwards, upwards and also across the organisation. The bank should be looking for a standard, holistic way of working which is improved over time and is thoroughly understood by all who take part in it. Operational risk remains an issue of importance to everyone working for the firm.

17.4 Establishing the right culture

Businesses must make sure that the right culture is in place and this is established by the Board. The following could be suggested as demonstrating the right sort of culture:

- A motivated workforce
- Excellent morale
- Staff of high integrity
- Ability to understand and take personal responsibility
- A broad commitment to improve
- The appropriate environment in which to manage risks and to challenge
- High levels of personal expertise
- A collective awareness of risk
- The ability to manage change.

As discussed earlier, the culture of the firm fundamentally demonstrates its own personality or the way we do things around here. It will reflect the core beliefs and attitudes of the workforce. The culture will be slow to develop and will be strongly influenced by the leadership of those who run the firm at board level. Within the overall culture of the company there will be a risk culture which is effectively mirroring the organisational awareness of risk and its management within the firm. There should be an understanding of the firm's risk appetite and the ability of individual members of staff to understand their personal role, to understand the manner in which the job they do affects others within the firm and helps to deliver a stronger end product.

The cultural element is a major factor in providing the right sort of control environment under which people operate within the firm. It is therefore a major defence mechanism in order to prevent there being an opportunity for fraud. Fraud cannot be tolerated within a bank or any financial institutions for that matter and should be anathema to all concerned. However, things being as they are with human organisations, a lax environment may well lead to events of fraud – both internal and external.

Although the cultural elements are fairly intangible, if managed well the effects can be very substantial for the benefit of the firm. Some key issues linking to this will be the manner of the leadership presented, the quality and integrity of staff, the extent of change to which the organisation is being impacted, the effectiveness of the control environment and the reward practices in terms of recognising the efforts of those concerned.

17.5 Challenge and escalation

One of the key watchwords is that of challenge. This applies equally in the boardroom where it is precisely the role of non-executive directors to challenge arguments and to contribute to debate and thus arrive at more sensible strategic decisions for the benefit of the firm. It also resides within the staff cohort as a whole such that there should be the ability to challenge things which seem to be wrong. This will lead to the ability to escalate issues to the supervisors or managers above and also to report early on any matter that may lead to an operating loss, loss of customers or loss of reputation. So therefore an escalation policy which would involve a whistleblowing and escalation policy understood by all staff will play its part together with a no blame culture where it will not be deemed incorrect for a member of staff to report or escalate an issue upwards. Instead it should be encouraged that people remain vigilant and contribute to an active risk awareness and mitigation in the manner in which they undertake their own jobs.

The benefits of an ongoing commitment to improvement in knowledge and expertise will benefit the firm by being better able to recruit and retain good quality staff.

17.6 Regulatory requirements

Regulators expect firms to manage their risks and this is fundamentally a senior management responsibility which can be achieved only by having the right governance structure in place plus well-performing systems and controls. It is therefore necessary for boards to review their business, to identify and manage risks that are identified and to ensure that information about risk is being openly communicated throughout the firm. This can only be done with sufficient motivation and participation.

The phrase, no risk plan means no risk management! is worth contemplating.

The Board is responsible for setting appropriate policies and to procure the necessary resources including the appointment of supervisors. Individual senior managers must take appropriate steps to ensure that the business they are running is properly organised and capable of being controlled. This is an explicit requirement of the UK regulators – the PRA and FCA – under its controlled functions approach.

Responsibility should be explicit and set out clearly for individual managers, supervisors and members of staff to follow. There should be a clear division of responsibilities across the team and overall a clear overall framework within which to operate.

18 Internal and external audit

The purpose of audit is to provide an independent review. Audit comes in two forms, internal audit and external audit.

The essence of audit is to ensure that all functions, procedures and controls within a banking organisation are checked to be adequately controlled, up to date and operate in accordance with the operating manuals and existing documentation.

Naturally a lot of audit activity is to do with the books and records of the company but another very important area covered by audit, both internal and external, is that of risk control and assessment of the risk management system. Essentially internal audit is addressing these matters for the purposes of the senior management of the company. On the other hand external audit is primarily there to report to the members of the company, being the shareholders, in line with the governance requirements of the UK Companies Act 2006. Such external auditors have to operate within auditing standards as laid down by the Auditing Practices Board and must check and comment on financial reporting statements in accordance with statements of standard accounting practice as laid down by the Auditing Practices Board.

18.1 The purpose of internal audit

Essentially, internal audit acts as a dry run or test platform for an external audit. The teams involved provide input to the operational risk management information available to the firm and operate to check and comment upon the risk indicators and controls as utilised by the firm.

Internal audit always acts independently of senior management yet its scope and the objectives of its tasks are decided and mandated by the senior management. Internal audit should have an unrestricted mandate to access records and to operate across the firm by checking, challenging and reviewing practices. The internal audit activity reports directly to the board. Its purpose is to report and provide a follow up providing an action plan upon which management can move forward.

18.2 The role of external audit

QUICK QUESTION

How would you describe the role of external audit?

Write your answer here before reading on.

As indicated, external audit operates for the purpose of reporting to the members and shareholders of a company. Essentially it has to provide an opinion as to whether the financial statements give a true and fair view of the reports of the company. They have to decide and declare whether the records are materially correct (i.e. true) and are not misleading (i.e. they are fair). Normally a clean audit opinion is delivered but sometimes a qualified opinion is given by the external auditors.

External audit projects can be carried out on a risk basis and/or on a controls basis.

18.3 Stages of an external audit

A normal audit programme would be entered into via a letter of engagement. This would be followed by a team identifying the systems and controls within the firm and investigating the accounting system and document flow with all relevant departments within the firm.

The auditors would check to see whether the controls were in place and to test those controls to see whether the results of the control framework were either effective or ineffective in practice. Very often substantive testing is undertaken to check large numbers of transactions as backing information. The auditors would be engaged in reviewing the financial statements.

Much of the external work revolves around regulatory mandates whereby such things as client money and safe custody practices, regulatory prudential returns and record keeping in general are adequate against regulatory requirements.

Internal and external audit share a common goal providing assurance to the Board that risk control processes and practices are appropriate to the business and are indeed effective. Both functions operate independently of management and report directly to the board.

Internal audit operates as part of the organisation and from within. They therefore have certain advantages in being able to sense changes of style in the control culture. In some ways they operate as an organisation's internal checkers being on the spot they are able to spot breaches of standards, process and controls.

Internal audit is an ongoing activity which permits a company to have risk assessment done on a continuous basis. External auditors, on the other hand, carry out their assessment with reference to a set point in time - for example, at the end of the financial year. A key facet of internal audit will be one of challenge and asking line managers those difficult questions. In any business environment where there is a lack of challenge perhaps because of the inability or the incompetence of internal auditors to ask the right questions or to understand the products and issues they are checking can only lead to operational risk problems. A good example of this was the case of National Australia Bank in 2006 where auditors were kept at arm's length and probably did not have sufficient ability to audit the dealings of the rogue traders involved in that case sufficiently well either.

Working in parallel with the internal and external auditors is the Audit Committee of the Board, which comprises independent non-executive directors drawn from the Board. This committee provides a key role for the Board overall in terms of oversight and provides a critical link between the Board and the professional auditors. In almost all banks there will be a separate Risk Committee as well as the Audit Committee.

19 Three lines of defence model

The three lines of defence model is one approach to safeguarding the internal control framework. It is the Prudential Regulatory Authority's (PRA) preferred (but not prescribed) approach.

19.1 The framework in practice

19.1.1 1st line of defence

This describes the **controls** an organisation has in place to deal with its day-to-day business. Controls are designed into systems and processes and assuming that the design is sufficient to appropriately mitigate risk, compliance with process should ensure an adequate control environment. There should be adequate managerial and supervisory controls in place to ensure compliance and to highlight control breakdown, inadequacy of process and unexpected events.

19.1.2 2nd line of defence

This describes the **committees and functions** that are in place to provide an oversight of the effective operation of the internal control framework. These committees review the management of risk in relation to the particular risk appetite of the business, as determined by the board. The effectiveness of the second line is determined by the oversight committee structure, their terms of reference, the competence of the members and the quality of the management information and reports that are considered by these oversight committees.

The second line is re-enforced by the advisory and monitoring functions of risk management and compliance. Risk management defines and prescribes the financial and operational risk assessment processes for the business; maintains the risk registers and undertakes regular reviews of these risks in conjunction with line management. Compliance advises on all areas of regulatory principles, rules and guidance, including leading on any changes, and undertakes monitoring activity on key areas of regulatory risk.

One would expect these functions to report upon their work undertaken and significant findings to the appropriate executive risk oversight committees in the second line. These functions may also report to the board's audit committee or a board risk committee in the third line (depending upon the committee structures of the organisation).

19.1.3 3rd line of defence

This describes the **independent assurance** provided by the **board audit committee**, a committee of non-executive directors chaired by the senior independent director, and the **internal audit function** that reports to that committee.

Internal audit undertakes a programme of risk-based audits covering all aspects of both the first and second lines of defence. Internal audit may well take some assurance from the work of the second line functions and reduce or tailor its checking of the first line.

Clearly the level of assurance taken will depend on the effectiveness of the second line, including the oversight committees, and internal audit will need to coordinate its work with compliance and risk management as well as assessing the work of these functions. The findings from these audits are reported to all three lines, i.e. accountable line management, the executive and oversight committees and the board audit committee.

This third line role likens internal audit to that of a goalkeeper in a football match. When the ball is lost in midfield (the first line) and the defence (the second line) fails to pick up the opposition's attack, it is left to the goalkeeper (as the third line) to save the day. There is a reasonable expectation that internal audit will identify the weaknesses in both the first and the second lines and failure to do so may lead to significant loss to the organisation.

QUESTION TIME 6

Referring to the three lines of defence model, how does this manifest itself in your firm?

Write your answer here then check with the answer at the back of the book.

19.2 The PRA, FCA and internal audit

The PRA and FCA, as regulators to the financial services industry, have statutory objectives. For the PRA these are:

- to promote the safety and soundness of banks, building societies, credit unions, insurers and investment firms
- to secure protection for policy holders.

The statutory objectives of the FCA are:

- to secure an appropriate degree of protection for consumers
- to protect and enhance the integrity of the UK financial system
- to promote effective competition in the interests of consumers.

The PRA and FCA place significant reliance on the work of internal audit when assessing the risk that individual organisations present to achieving the above objectives. The PRA and FCA place internal audit under regular close scrutiny as part of its risk assessment visits. They are particularly concerned with internal audit's independence, its standing with the board and senior executive management and the influence it exercises across the organisation.

19.3 Use in other sectors

Although the above model has been described above as typically applied in a financial services organisation, it is equally relevant to other sectors and industries. The model of management control in the first line, oversight challenge in the second and independent assurance in the third line is universal in application.

KEY WORDS

Key words in this chapter are given below. There is space to write your own revision notes and add any other key words or phrases you want to remember.

- Business risk
- Financial risk
- Operational risk
- Regulatory risk
- Reputational risk
- Directive controls
- Preventative controls
- Detective controls
- Corrective controls
- Preventable risks
- External risk
- Three lines of defence model
- Business continuity plan
- Disaster recovery

REVIEW

Now consider the main points that were introduced in this chapter. These are listed below. Tick each one as you go through them.

- Business risk is the risk that a business is no longer viable. This can come about as a result of a number of factors, including economic, political, the competitive environment, social and market forces, technology, shock and natural events, external stakeholders, or third parties.
- Financial risk is those risks that arise as a result of borrowing.
- Operational risk is the risk of loss resulting from inadequate or failed internal processes, people or systems or from external events.
- The Basel Committee has defined seven categories under which loss events can occur.
- The Committee has further defined business lines that are used by firms to calculate their capital charge.
- The principles and policies that drive the management of operational risk must come from the top of the organisation.
- The operational risk framework is similar to the risk management lifecycle with the addition of the operational risk policy.
- The implementation of an operational risk policy can be constrained by difficulties collecting and managing data, cultural issues, resource and cost constraints along with indicator constraints.
- The benefits of operational risk management are both direct and indirect.
- Operational risk has come into the public domain through a number of corporate failures, and regulatory initiatives have been developed in the operational risk field.
- Control measures can be preventative, detective, directive or corrective.
- One of the ways in which a bank will minimise the occurrence of internal fraud is through the introduction of dual control procedures.
- Periods of change present risks to firms but these can be minimised through the adoption of guidelines to establish appropriate controls.
- Business continuity planning allows organisations to recover and maintain operations after a major disruption.
- The steps required to develop a business continuity plan are: obtain senior management buy-in; establish a planning committee; conduct a risk assessment; establish priorities for processing and operations; determine interdependencies; write up the plan; develop testing criteria and procedures; test the plan; and finally approve and update the plan.
- Culture is another way of describing how an organisation acts and this can have a profound effect on the management of risk.
- Individual members of staff must feel part of the firm's risk management process.
- Businesses will experience both expected and unexpected losses.
- The risk management function must be able to confirm the effective implementation of the risk framework.
- Senior management must approve and review the operational risk framework and make sure that it is independently audited.

- Both internal and external audit are concerned with assessing the risk management framework of the company.
- With the Three Lines of Defence Model, the first line is internal controls, the second line is the committees and functions of the organisation in the management of risk and the third line is independent assurance.
- The objectives of a Business Continuity Plan are to manage the loss arising from the event and restore operations as quickly as possible.
- Firms must have a number of Business Continuity Plans to cover a number of possible events.
- Both the PRA, FCA and the Basel Committee require banks to have Business Continuity Plans in place.

chapter 10

REGULATORY RISK

Contents

Learning objectives

On completion of this chapter, you should be able to:

- critically review the International and UK regulatory risk environment.

Introduction

The chapter opens with a discussion around the topic of self-regulation and its relevance to the banking industry, with particular reference to events of the recent banking crisis.

We then move on to the large topic of corporate governance – this is the set of relationships between directors and stakeholders, through which objectives are set and monitored. The chapter describes the Combined Code, before moving on to consider the Walker Report of 2009 which sought to examine corporate governance in the UK financial sector and make recommendations. The development of corporate governance in the UK is described next, before a discussion ensues regarding the leadership role of the board of directors in a firm. The role of audit and the Audit Committee is described next, before we turn our attention to the Risk Committee and the Remuneration Committee. After this, we re-visit the topic of due diligence, this time with particular focus on corporate governance. The requirement for risk management to be embedded in the culture of the firm is emphasised again at this juncture, before considering a description of the benefits of risk management to the business. The section on corporate governance concludes with an explanation of moral hazard.

Our attention then turns to the work of the Prudential Regulatory Authority (PRA and the Financial Conduct Authority (FCA), the UK regulatory bodies that succeeded the Financial Services Authority (FSA) in 2013.

Having considered regulation in the UK, we widen the geographical view by summarising the work of the European Banking Authority. At this point in our analysis, we are ready to turn our attention to Basel. We start this analysis by considering what is meant by risk based capital and the development of the first Basel Accord. Basel II is then discussed – this Accord set out the three Pillars which you may have heard of. The requirements of these pillars are explained – Pillar 1 set out the amount of capital that banks had to maintain to cover credit, market and operational risks. Pillar 2 allowed regulators to determine if additional capital was required to cover any risks that were not included in Pillar 1, and Pillar 3 required banks to publish certain information (on risk, capital and risk management) in an attempt to improve market discipline. Basel III has been developed in response to the banking crisis and the implications of this are discussed in the next section. As you will learn, the upshot of Basel III is that banks have to hold greater amounts of capital to absorb potential losses and the management of liquidity risk has been tightened. The ways in which a bank will quantify operational risk is explained next, before the chapter ends with a discussion on the regulators view on stress testing.

1 Self-regulation and statutory regulation

It is possible to argue that the financial community, including the banking industry, should be able to regulate itself. Every scandal or crisis and economic emergency seems to result in a public response for yet more bureaucratic regulation from government and more boxes to tick. The consequences of that can be increased costs, poorer regulation and reduced competition. The cost of the regulation has to be passed on by banks and financial companies to their clients thus affecting the wider community as a whole.

There has been a lot of focus in recent years on further regulation of the banking system. This has been fostered by reports written by committees and their chairmen and has led to the clamour for better regulation and better corporate governance applied to and conducted within the banking industry.

An alternative approach other than binding up banks with red tape might well be to force or encourage them to regulate their own behaviour. Thus far, self-regulation has not worked because of the way the state underwrites risk in the banking system. Consider the fact that the government, the Bank of England and the FSA all felt that the major British banks that were rescued by taxpayers in 2008-2009 were too big to fail. This situation lead to severe degrees of moral hazard being taken by those who were instrumental in running and operating banks, a problem which even today has not yet been solved. When banks take risks, they gain from the upside but the taxpayer is often left with the costs of bailouts when things go wrong. An alternative focus therefore might be to make sure that banks bear the costs of the risk they underwrite. A possible step could be a risk-based deposit insurance system where banks pay premiums based on the risks they take. There could much better mechanisms for an orderly winding-up of failed banks and sophisticated financial institutions which run into trouble. In the capitalist model there are those that argue that banks should be able and indeed allowed to fail just like any other form of business. Banks for some reason are different because the wider economic community and everyone in the economy depends upon them for oiling the wheels of the economy and providing the wherewithal for people to conduct their normal lives. This then is the conundrum for self-regulation.

Banks could issue debt capital which automatically could become equity capital if the institution became insolvent. If such steps were taken there could be a major improvement in market discipline without the need for complex regulation.

There is some evidence from history to offer optimism that deregulation could work. In the days before the government regulated the banking system and underwrote deposits, banks held much more capital. They also had special mechanisms such as double liability for shareholders to signal to their customers that they had to operate conservatively. It is incentives that matter not the rules.

The global might of modern banking and financial regulation has increased enormously in recent years and indeed compliance and regulation has now become an industry in itself with the associated costs that have passed on

The message is consistent: There is no point trying to avoid scandals and crises by having bureaucrats writing more and more rules. There will always be a need for new rules as those who have to operate within the rules think of even smarter ways of bending them or navigating their way around them. The key surely must be a financial system where prudent behaviour runs in the very being of the industry as part of the way business is done as a result of self-interest.

Many observers take the view that self-regulation just isn't the same thing as external regulation. The meaning behind this is that in the Credit Crunch period those that ran certain banks were too busy frantically taking risks and stoking up the securitisation money-making machine to take any notice of some of the principles that had been laid down by the regulators. One can argue therefore that banks will never regulate themselves other than purely cosmetically. Even if each bank were to agree that it would make collective sense for each and every bank to observe certain practices and to desist from others, the temptation to defect from this agreement would prove irresistible as soon as the next financial boom started to ratchet up and the next sure thing money-making wheeze was touted by a new breed of financial engineers.

So in balance therefore, it may be that there just has to be regulation from outside. The UK, after all, experienced the first run on a bank for over 100 years in September 2007 with the Northern Rock episode and such an incident in the wholesale market could be just as possible bringing a highly leveraged institution down as would a sudden withdrawal of deposits from the likes of a Northern Rock.

Highly leveraged institutions are inherently vulnerable to the temporary disappearance of either their funding liquidity or the liquidity available in the market. As long as their assets have long maturities and are rather illiquid and their liabilities have short maturities this vulnerability to a liquidity crunch will always be present regardless of the details of their funding practices. There is no such thing as a safe highly leveraged institution, regardless of the soundness of its assets if held to maturity.

Another fundamental factor is that regulators and central banks have decided that non-deposit taking financial institutions can be too big and too systemically important to fail, thus putting investment banks and potentially also hedge funds above a certain size in the same situation that the deposit banks have been in for a long time. We have witnessed the rescue of Bear Stearns in 2008 and 10 years before that the 1998 rescue of Long-Term Capital Management by the Wall Street community. Indeed it is also possible to describe Northern Rock as a non-deposit taking institution because the majority of its funding came from the wholesale money markets rather than retail depositors.

If an institution is inherently vulnerable and too big to fail, it must be regulated from the outside. Self-regulation in the financial sector has been weak.

2 Corporate governance

2.1 What is corporate governance?

QUICK QUESTION

What is your understanding of corporate governance?

Write your answer here before reading on.

Corporate governance is a set of relationships between a company's directors, its shareholders and other stakeholders. It also provides the structure through which the objectives of the company are set, and the means of achieving those objectives and monitoring performance, are determined.

Although mostly discussed in relation to large quoted companies, governance is an issue for all corporate bodies, commercial and not for profit, including public sector and non-governmental organisations.

There are a number of elements in corporate governance:

(a) The management, awareness, evaluation and mitigation of risk are fundamental in all definitions of good governance. This includes the operation of an adequate and appropriate system of control.

(b) The notion that overall performance is enhanced by good supervision and management within set best practice guidelines underpins most definitions.

(c) Good governance provides a framework for an organisation to pursue its strategy in an ethical and effective way and offers safeguards against misuse of resources, human, financial, physical or intellectual.

(d) Good governance is not just about externally established codes; it also requires a willingness to apply the spirit as well as the letter of the law.

(e) Good corporate governance can attract new investment into companies, particularly in developing nations.

(f) Accountability is generally a major theme in all governance frameworks, including accountability not just to shareholders but also other stakeholders.

(g) Corporate governance underpins capital market confidence in companies and in the government/regulators/tax authorities that administer them.

Do not assume that recognised codes of practice such as the Combined Code which follows immediately below and experience of the past mean that there is nothing new for boards to do or that some companies could not make more effective use of the established guidance. Establishing an effective system of internal control is not a one-off exercise. No such system remains effective unless it develops to take account of new and emerging risks, control failures, market expectations or changes in the company's circumstances or business objectives. Every business must undertake systematic reviews of its strategy with respect to where it stands in the marketplace and the business cycle and in respect of the regulatory environment and competitive situations. This will affect its approach to both business and risk management.

2.2 The Combined Code

The Financial Reporting Council (FRC) is the UK's independent regulator responsible for promoting confidence in corporate governance and reporting. It promotes high standards of corporate governance through the Combined Code (see below), but does not monitor or enforce its implementation by individual boards. It sets standards for corporate reporting and actuarial practice and monitors and enforces accounting and auditing standards. Also it oversees the regulatory activities of the professional accountancy bodies and operates independent disciplinary arrangements for public interest cases involving accountants and actuaries.

Good corporate governance should contribute to better company performance by helping a board discharge its duties in the best interests of shareholders. If it is ignored, the consequence may well be vulnerability or poor performance. Good governance should facilitate efficient, effective and entrepreneurial management that can deliver shareholder value over the longer term. The Combined Code on Corporate Governance is published by the FRC to support these outcomes and promote confidence in corporate reporting and governance.

The Combined Code, originally published in 1998, was updated most recently in 2008. There are at the time of writing two versions in operation; those of 2006 and 2008. The latter being created in order to reflect changes resulting from a review conducted in 2007. The Code sets out standards of good practice in relation to issues such as board composition and development, remuneration, accountability and audit and relations with shareholders. All companies incorporated in the UK and listed on the Main Market of the London Stock Exchange are required under the Listing Rules to report on how they have applied the Combined Code in their annual report and accounts. Overseas companies listed on the Main Market are required to disclose the significant ways in which their corporate governance practices differ from those set out in the Code.

The Combined Code contains broad principles and more specific provisions. Note that although it strictly applies only to listed companies, firms of any size may (and do) use it as a set of standards upon which to base their approach to good corporate governance.

The Code is not a rigid set of rules. Rather, it is a guide to the components of good board practice distilled from consultation and widespread experience over many years.

There are two broad sections of the Combined Code which address companies and institutional shareholders respectively. The companies section addresses four areas: directors, remuneration, accountability and audit and finally relations with shareholders.

Taking these in turn the salient points are as follows. The first and second groups refer to directors and their remuneration. The principles are:

The Board – every company should be headed by an effective board, which is collectively responsible for the success of the company.

Chairman and Chief Executive – there should be a clear division of responsibilities at the head of the company between the running of the board and the executive responsibility for the running of the company's business. No one individual should have unfettered powers of decision.

Board balance and independence – the board should include a balance of executive and non-executive directors (and in particular independent non-executive directors) such that no individual or small group of individuals can dominate the board's decision taking. [The new shorthand for non-executive directors is NEDs].

Appointments to the board – there should be a formal, rigorous and transparent procedure for the appointment of new directors to the board.

Information and professional development – the board should be supplied in a timely manner with information in a form and of a quality appropriate to enable it to discharge its duties. All directors should receive induction on joining the board and should regularly update and refresh their skills and knowledge.

Performance evaluation – the board should undertake a formal and rigorous annual evaluation of its own performance and that of its committees and individual directors.

Re-election – all directors should be submitted for re-election at regular intervals, subject to continued satisfactory performance. The board should ensure planned and progressive refreshing of the board.

Remuneration – levels of remuneration should be sufficient to attract, retain and motivate directors of the quality required to run the company successfully, but a company should avoid paying more than is necessary for this purpose. A significant proportion of executive directors' remuneration should be structured so as to link rewards to corporate and individual performance.

Remuneration procedure – there should be a formal and transparent procedure for developing policy on executive remuneration and for fixing the remuneration packages of individual directors. No director should be involved in deciding his or her own remuneration.

The principles listed under the third grouping of accountability and audit provisions are:

Financial reporting (part of accountability and audit) – the board should present a balanced and understandable assessment of the company's position and prospects.

Internal control – the board should maintain a sound system of internal control to safeguard shareholders' investment and the company's assets.

Audit committee and auditors – the board should establish formal and transparent arrangements for considering how they should apply the financial reporting and internal control principles and for maintaining an appropriate relationship with the company's auditors.

The principles involved in the fourth segment (with respect to shareholders) are as follows:

Relations with shareholders – there should be a dialogue with shareholders based on the mutual understanding of objectives. The board as a whole has responsibility for ensuring that a satisfactory dialogue with shareholders takes place.

Constructive use of the AGM – the board should use the AGM to communicate with investors and to encourage their participation.

Institutional shareholders – institutional shareholders should enter into a dialogue with companies based on the mutual understanding of objectives.

Shareholder voting – institutional shareholders have a responsibility to make considered use of their votes.

QUESTION TIME 1

Obtain a copy of the Annual Report for your firm and identify how they are meeting the demands of the Code.

Write your answer here then check with the answer at the back of the book.

2.3 Further UK initiatives

Since the publication of the Combined Code a number of reports in the UK have been published about specific aspects of corporate governance.

- The Turnbull report (1999, revised 2005) focused on risk management and internal control.
- The Smith report (2003) discussed the role of audit committees.
- The Higgs report (2003) focused on the role of the non-executive director.
- HM Treasury's white paper on reforming financial markets, 2009.
- The Turner report (March 2009) focused on post Credit Crunch regulation.
- The Walker report (July 2009) focused on bank governance (to be finalised in October 2009).

2.4 The Walker Report of 2009

The original Terms of Reference for the Walker Review was to examine corporate governance in the UK banking industry and make recommendations, including in the following areas:

- The effectiveness of risk management at board level, including the incentives in remuneration policy to manage risk effectively.
- The balance of skills, experience and independence required on the boards of UK banking institutions.
- The effectiveness of board practices and the performance of audit, risk, remuneration and nomination committees.
- The role of institutional shareholders in engaging effectively with companies and monitoring of boards.
- Whether the UK approach is consistent with international practice and how national and international best practice can be promulgated.

On 21 April 2009, the Terms of Reference were extended so that the review would also identify where its recommendations were applicable to other financial institutions.

The review made these five specific recommendations concerning risk governance within banks (from a total of 39 recommendations the review made overall).

Recommendation 23

The board of a BOFI (Banks and other Financial Institutions) should establish a board risk committee separately from the audit committee with responsibility for oversight and advice to the board on the current risk exposures of the entity and future risk strategy. In preparing advice to the board on its overall risk appetite and tolerance, the board risk committee should take account of the current and prospective macro-economic and financial environment drawing on financial stability assessments such as those published by the Bank of England and other authoritative sources that may be relevant for the risk policies of the firm.

Recommendation 24

In support of board-level risk governance, a BOFI board should be served by a CRO (Chief Risk Officer) who should participate in the risk management and oversight process at the highest level on an enterprise-wide basis and have a status of total independence from individual business units. Alongside an internal reporting line to the CEO or FD, the CRO should report to the Board Risk Committee, with direct access to the chairman of the committee in the event of need. The tenure and independence of the CRO should be underpinned by a provision that removal from office would require the prior agreement of the board. The remuneration of the CRO should be subject to approval by the chairman or chairman of the board remuneration committee.

Recommendation 25

The board risk committee should have access to and, in the normal course, expect to draw on external input to its work as a means of taking full account of relevant experience elsewhere and in challenging its analysis and assessment.

Recommendation 26

In respect of a proposed strategic transaction involving acquisition or disposal, it should as a matter of good practice be for the board risk committee to oversee a due diligence appraisal of the proposition, drawing on external advice where appropriate and available, before the board takes a decision whether to proceed.

Recommendation 27

The board risk committee (or board) risk report should be included as a separate report within the annual report and accounts. The report should describe the strategy of the entity in a risk management context, including information on the key exposures inherent in the strategy and the associated risk tolerance of the entity and should provide at least high-level information on the scope and outcome of the stress-testing programme. An indication should be given of the membership of the committee, of the frequency of its meetings, whether external advice was taken and, if so, its source.

2.5 Corporate governance history in the UK

Within the UK, corporate governance has been enshrined in the psyche of business for decades. In common with other countries changes to codes have generally been as a result of well publicised cases where the government of the time has felt compelled to act.

Previous reports on governance

Cadbury, Hampel, Turnbull and Higgs all produced reports and the Combined Code then tried to implement these standards consistently throughout the listed sector. The political imperative is quite clear. Governments of all persuasions have seen corporate governance as being a political imperative since there is no advantage to the ruling party in being seen as being soft on corporate activity.

At the heart of the issue is what corporate governance in a UK context really is. The board of a company have responsibility for the stewardship of that company and to balance the various conflicting demands of the various stakeholders.

QUICK QUESTION

List the stakeholders in your organisation.

These stakeholders should include:

- Shareholders
- Staff
- Customers
- Suppliers
- Tax authorities
- The wider public interest
- Regulatory bodies.

Write your answer here before reading on.

Each of these is looking for something different from the board. Corporate governance is about taking these conflicting requirements fully into account when designing a control and procedural structure which is suitable for the business. As such UK corporate governance codes have tended to be relatively benign documents which provide a set of guidance without formally requiring very much.

These codes are generally designed to focus on the narrowness of procedure rather than true governance. Nothing in a corporate governance code actually requires a business to make the right analysis of its trading position; rather they tend to focus on the level of oversight that is considered as being required by so-called independent individuals.

Accounting standards

With the advent of International Accounting Standards companies on a global basis should all be producing consistent accounts to enable global comparison. The UK accounting and finance industry embraces new standards with vigour and tries to make them work. The problem is whether they actually improve the ability of senior management to meet their corporate governance obligations.

With the increasing use of capital accounting through reserves and increasingly arcane accounting and measurement techniques, there must be significant doubt that most directors are capable of interpreting their own accounts yet alone those of their competitors. As accounts increase in length and complexity the challenge is maintain transparency and understanding. The current International Accounting Standards have become complex and in some cases at best unhelpful.

That being said, the UK finance profession fully understands the stewardship role and fiduciary responsibilities that exist. With a largely qualified profession of high quality specialists the presence of the relevant institutes adds additional credence to the role of finance in governance. Furthermore most firms have also implemented whistle blowing charters, although there is still the concern that nobody will hire a whistleblower.

When corporate governance goes wrong it is often the finance function that is in the best position to identify that there is wrongdoing. They are in a much better position than either internal or external audit who can only view issues periodically. With their engrained ethical standards UK chartered accountants in industry effectively act as the watchdogs of the corporate governance code.

2.6 The role of the board and its members

Boards that meet irregularly or fail to consider systematically the organisation's activities and risks are clearly not fulfilling their responsibilities. Sometimes the failure to carry out proper oversight is due to a lack of information being provided, which in turn may be due to inadequate systems being in place for the measurement and reporting of risk.

QUICK QUESTION

Describe your understanding of the role of the board in your organisation.

Write your answer here before reading on.

The board's role is to provide entrepreneurial leadership of the company within a framework of prudent and effective controls which enables risk to be assessed and managed. The board should set the company's strategic aims, ensure that the necessary financial and human resources are in place for the company to meet its objectives and review management performance. The board should set the company's values and standards and ensure that its obligations to its shareholders and others are understood and met.

The board should meet sufficiently regularly to discharge its duties effectively. There should be a formal schedule of matters specifically reserved for its decision. The annual report should include a statement of how the board operates, including a high level statement of which types of decisions are to be taken by the board and which are to be delegated to management.

All directors, both executive and non-executive, as members of the board, must take decisions objectively in the interests of the company.

QUICK QUESTION

What do you understand of the role of the chair of the board of directors?

Write your answer here before reading on.

The chair of the board is responsible for leadership of the board, ensuring its effectiveness on all aspects of its role and setting its agenda. The chair is also responsible for ensuring that the directors receive accurate, timely and clear information. The chair should ensure effective communication with shareholders. The chair should also facilitate the effective contribution of non-executive directors in particular and ensure constructive relations between executive and non-executive directors. It is recommended that the chair should meet separately with non-executive directors without the executive directors being present to discuss matters of policy and control independently and also for the non-executive directors to meet alone in order to review the performance of the chair under the leadership of the senior non-executive director.

The chair is also responsible for ensuring that the directors receive accurate, timely and clear information. Management has an obligation to provide such information but directors should seek clarification or amplification where necessary.

Boards and their chairs are supported by the company secretary. Under the direction of the chair, the company secretary's responsibilities include ensuring good information flows within the board and its committees and between senior management and nonexecutive directors, as well as facilitating induction and assisting with professional development as required. Every public company must have a company secretary, who is one of the officers of a company and may be a director. Private companies are not required to have a secretary; in this case the role is normally performed by the company secretary and may be done by one of the directors, or an approved person. The Secretary of State may require a public company to appoint a secretary where it has failed to do so.

Whatever the duties of the secretary, their ultimate loyalty must be to the company. This may mean the secretary coming into conflict with for example a director or even the chief executive. If, for example, one of the directors has a clear conflict of interest between their duties to the company and their personal interests, the company secretary should ensure that the board minutes reflect the conflict. If the conflict prevents a director from voting and being counted in the quorum at the board meeting, the proper procedure should be followed. Throughout corporate governance matters the issues of conflicts of interest are key in that they must be recognised and managed in an appropriate manner.

As part of their role as members of a unitary board, non-executive directors should constructively challenge and help develop proposals on strategy. Non-executive directors should scrutinise the performance of management in meeting agreed goals and objectives and monitor the reporting of performance. They should satisfy themselves on the integrity of financial information and that financial controls and systems of risk management are robust and defensible. They are responsible for determining appropriate levels of remuneration of executive directors and have a prime role in appointing, and where necessary removing, executive directors, and in succession planning.

The Combined Code asserts that, except for smaller companies, at least half the board, excluding the chair, should comprise non-executive directors determined by the board to be independent. A smaller company should have at least two independent non-executive directors.

The board's responsibility to present a balanced and understandable assessment extends to interim and other price-sensitive public reports and reports to regulators as well as to information required to be presented by statutory requirements. The directors should explain in the annual report their responsibility for preparing the accounts and there should be a statement by the auditors about their reporting responsibilities. The directors should report that the business is a going concern, with supporting assumptions or qualifications as necessary.

The board should, at least annually, conduct a review of the effectiveness of the group's system of internal controls and should report to shareholders that they have done so. The review should cover all material controls, including financial, operational and compliance controls and risk management systems.

The Walker report made many references to NEDs and stressed the importance for firms to ensure that the NEDs are independent, fully trained, competent and are well supported by the firm. NEDs and executives should not operate as opposing camps within a firm. The accent should be on effective co-operation under strong leadership. Basically the tone of some of the most recent reports issued in 2009 is that NEDs should raise their game and undertake more of a full-time role.

Employees of course play a vital role in an organisation in the implementation of strategy; they need to comply with the corporate governance systems in place and adopt appropriate culture. Their commitment to the job may be considerable involving changes when taking the job (moving house), dependency if in the job for a long time (not just financial but in utilising skills that may not be portable elsewhere) and fulfilment as a human being (developing a career, entering relationships).

Employees will focus on how the company is performing, and how the company's performance will impact on their pay and working conditions. UK company law has required the directors to have regard to the interests of the company's employees in general as well as the interests of its members. Other European jurisdictions have gone further in terms of employee participation.

Employees also have information requirements. Surveys suggest that the most interesting information for employees is information concerned with the immediate work environment and which is future-orientated. There are a number of ways on which this information can be provided:

- An organisation-wide employee report
- Organisation-wide information on financial results, but breaking down information on personnel or sales to a unit level
- Including statements by managers on their individual activities
- Producing separate inserts about each division.

2.7 Audit committees and auditors

The board should establish an audit committee of at least three, or in the case of smaller companies, two independent non-executive directors. In smaller companies the company chairman may be a member of, but not chair, the committee in addition to the independent non-executive directors, provided he or she was considered independent on appointment as chairman. The board should satisfy itself that at least one member of the audit committee has recent and relevant financial experience.

QUESTION TIME 2

You will now be familiar with the role of the audit committee. Describe what its roles and responsibilities are.

Write your answer here then check with the answer at the back of the book.

Audit committee

One of the key elements of corporate governance in an organisation is the establishment of the necessary Board committees to fulfil an effective corporate governance framework. One of these, the Audit Committee, has clear responsible for oversight and reporting to the Board on the financial accounts and adoption of appropriate accounting policies, internal control, compliance and other related matters. In essence this vital responsibility is essentially backward-looking relating to the effective implementation by the firm's executive of policies decided by the Board as part of the strategy of the organisations.

The Audit Committees of all banks have responsibility to bear a heavy load in the demanding part of their role with respect to financial reporting and internal control. This burden has been increasing greatly in recent times owing to the increased amount of regulatory oversight applied to banks. The Audit Committee should focus on the correctness of financial statements as well as the need to review and report on the effectiveness on the bank's internal controls. Risk governance on the other hand is largely handed over now to Risk Committees of the Board. Indeed this was a recommendation of the 2009 Walker Report which addressed the issues of corporate governance in banks and financial institutions. However it is customary now in all banks to have a Risk Committee in addition to an Audit Committee which takes on the principal burden of being responsible for the management of risk reporting directly to the Board.

Internal audit

The increasing prominence of the internal audit functions in major companies is to be welcomed. They have a clear role in corporate governance and reporting lines to both the Chair and the Audit Committee, where such a committee exists. This enables them to look at the key values of the company and the primary responsibilities of the board and to ensure that these are met.

Of course the role of the internal audit function should go much further than that. They are no longer a tick box function seeking to hammer failures that are in effect inconsequential and result in expensive controls being implemented that themselves detract value. Rather they are akin to an internal consultancy function seeking to improve the business of their company.

Maintaining an adequately trained and independent internal audit function is crucial to the ongoing corporate governance of a firm. Without such a function there is nobody checking that actions are actually delivered.

2.8 The risk committee

The board of directors has risk management responsibilities that are defined not only by best practices and guidelines, but also by laws and regulation. The risk committee must assist the board in assessing the different types of risk to which the organisation is exposed.

Management is responsible for executing the organisation's risk management policy. The risk committee must exercise oversight, and must provide evidence about it. The members of the committee must have direct access to, and receive regular reports from management.

The risk committee must be composed of at least three members and must have a majority of non-executive directors, at least one of whom shall also typically be a member of the Audit Committee. At least one person must be a risk expert. The Chairman of the Committee must be a non-executive Director.

The duties of the risk committee are to:

(1) Learn about the actual risks and the control deficiencies in the organisation.

(2) Help the board define the risk appetite of the organisation.

(3) Exercise oversight of management's responsibilities, and review the risk profile of the firm to ensure that risk is not higher than the risk appetite determined by the board.

(4) Monitor the effectiveness of risk management functions throughout the company. Ensure that infrastructure, resources and systems are in place for risk management and are adequate to maintain a satisfactory level of risk management discipline.

(5) Monitor the independence of risk management functions throughout the organisation.

(6) Review the strategies, policies, frameworks, models and procedures that lead to the identification, measurement, reporting and mitigation of material risks.

(7) Review issues raised by internal audit that impact the risk management framework.

(8) Ensure that the risk awareness culture is pervasive throughout the enterprise.

(9) Fulfil its statutory, fiduciary and regulatory responsibilities. This is commonly the most difficult task.

2.9 The remuneration committee

The remuneration committee's (sometimes referred to as REMCO) overall responsibility is to develop a remuneration policy to attract, retain and motivate those people of the highest calibre who have the skills needed to achieve the company's objectives year on year and which balances the interests of the shareholders, the company and its employees. It will be so structured as to perform effectively the task of creating the policy for the remuneration of the executive directors, the executive committee, the chairman and the company secretary and review the ongoing appropriateness and relevance of such remuneration policy. The remuneration of the non-executive directors will usually be a matter for the chairman and the executive directors but this may be a matter for the whole board or indeed the shareholders to address. At all times, no persons shall be involved in any decisions as to their own remuneration.

The remuneration committee should consult the chairman and/or chief executive about their proposals relating to the remuneration of other executive directors. The remuneration committee should also be responsible for appointing any consultants in respect of executive director remuneration. Where executive directors or senior management are involved in advising or supporting the remuneration committee, care should be taken to recognise and avoid conflicts of interest.

The chair of the board should ensure that the company maintains contact as required with its principal shareholders about remuneration in the same way as for other matters.

The REMCO should address all executives whose remuneration exceeds that of the median of the executive board members. In many financial institutions, of course, there may well be several highly paid managers and traders / dealers who will meet this criterion. The identities of high-end earners should be disclosed. Note how the bonus culture point, so strongly raised by observers towards banks in in the wake of the Credit Crunch links in to remuneration transparency in corporate governance. A good example is Fred Goodwin's pension and bonus provisions at the time of his exit from the RBS Group.

2.10 Due diligence

Due diligence is part of corporate governance – you will be familiar with this term from your earlier studies.

QUICK QUESTION

Define due diligence.

Write your answer here before reading on.

Due diligence is a term used for a number of concepts involving either the performance of an investigation of a business or person, or the performance of an act with a certain standard of care. It can be a legal obligation, but the term will more commonly apply to voluntary investigations. A common example of due diligence in various industries is the process through which prior to a takeover a potential acquirer evaluates a target company or its assets for acquisition. The same holds true for a legal agreement or an assessment of a potential supplier's services whereby a process of due diligence checking would be undertaken to ensure that everything was correct and that there were no unforeseen surprises lurking in the future, which might present a loss or risk impact outcome.

Thus in business transactions, the due diligence process varies for different types of companies. The relevant areas of concern may include the financial, legal, labour, tax, IT, environment and market/commercial situation of the company. Other areas include intellectual property, real and personal property, insurance and liability coverage, debt instrument review, employee benefits and labour matters, immigration, and international transactions.

QUESTION TIME 3

When else might due diligence be carried out?

Write your answer here then check with the answer at the back of the book.

2.11 Due diligence in risk oversight

When addressing risk scenarios, firms will carry out a due diligence study with respect to the risk assessment process and set in place a management approach to deal with the perceived risks. The purpose of the exercise is to carry out a rigorous examination of the sources and implications of risk. These will include risk identification, an impact and severity assessment and the establishment of a plan as to how to put in place an effective mitigation approach.

Consider risk assessment with respect to money laundering. The tax revenue authority (HMRC) in the UK presents guidance on how to perform due diligence checks with respect to its money laundering requirements. Businesses must identify and assess the risks of their being used for a money laundering or terrorist financing activity, mitigate these as far as possible by putting appropriate procedures and controls in place and monitor regularly, adjusting as necessary to keep them relevant and up to date.

Firms are advised that risk assessments will probably fall within the following areas:

- Customers – type and behaviour
- Products and services
- Delivery channels, e.g. cash over the counter, electronic, wire transfer, cheque
- Geographical areas of operation or destination of funds or goods.

Firms should identify the money laundering and terrorist financing risks that are relevant to the business, and:

- assess the risks presented by the particular client, product, delivery channel mechanism and geographic area of operation
- design and implement controls to manage and mitigate these assessed risks
- monitor and improve the effective operation of these controls, and
- record appropriately what has been done, and why.

A risk-based approach should balance the costs to the business and its customers with a realistic assessment of the risk of the business being used for money laundering or terrorist financing. It focuses effort where it is needed and will have most impact. Businesses can decide for themselves how to carry out their risk-assessment, which may be simple or sophisticated in accordance with the business they operate.

The business should be asking:

- What risk is posed by the customers?
- Is the risk posed by the customer's behaviour?
- How does the manner in which the customer interfaces with the business affect the risk?
- What risk is posed by the product mix that the customer is using?

Risk assessment must also include the review and monitoring of the money laundering and terrorist financing risks to the business. The risk-based approach of the business will be informed by the monitoring of patterns of business, for example:

- A sudden increase in business from an existing customer
- Uncharacteristic transactions which are not in keeping with the customer's known activities
- Peaks of activity at particular locations or at particular times
- Unfamiliar or untypical types of customer or transaction.

Once the business has identified and assessed the risks it faces of being used for money laundering or terrorist financing, it must ensure that appropriate controls are put in place to lessen these risks and prevent the business from being used for money laundering or terrorist financing.

Managing and mitigating the risks will involve:

- applying customer due diligence measures to verify the identity of customers and any beneficial owners
- obtaining additional information on higher-risk customers
- conducting ongoing monitoring of the transactions and activity of customers with whom there is a business relationship; and
- having systems to identify and scrutinise unusual transactions and activity to determine whether there are reasonable grounds for knowing or suspecting that money laundering or terrorist financing may be taking place.

2.12 Culture and leadership

A firm's risk culture encompasses the general awareness, attitude and behaviour of its employees to risk and the management of risk within the organisation. The internal operational risk culture is taken to mean the combined set of individual and corporate values, attitudes, competencies and behaviour that determine a firm's commitment to and style of operational risk management. The internal control culture includes, amongst other things, clear lines of responsibility and segregation of duties.

As you know, risk management should become part of an organisation's culture. It should be embedded into the organisation's philosophy, practices and business processes rather than be viewed or practiced as a separate activity. When this is achieved, everyone in the organisation becomes involved in the management of risk.

The chief factors therefore which have a bearing on the mechanics of this process of building the right culture include the quality of the corporate governance within the firm, as set and embedded downwards from the executives and leaders at the top of the organisation.

The UK regulators, the PRA and FCA, sets great store by leadership in its outlook regarding good corporate governance. A similar point was made strongly in the Walker report, which regarded leadership as the most important attribute in managing companies effectively.

This points up the key role of the chairman and CEO of any firm who, in the main, provide corporate leadership.

2.13 How risk management adds value

QUICK QUESTION

What are the benefits that accrue from effective risk management?

Write your answer here before reading on.

By addressing the main factors which contribute to the company's risk and control culture a firm will be able to deliver better results. This will manifest itself in any of the following direct benefits:

- Greater certainty over risk management decisions
- Increased awareness and buy-in (embedding within the firm) of the importance of effective risk management
- Better informed decision making
- Stronger client relationships and greater customer loyalty
- Reduced capital charges from regulators and central banks
- Improved stock market perception and stronger share prices
- An enhanced corporate reputation in the marketplace
- Fewer shocks and unwelcome surprises
- Reassurance for staff, stakeholders and governing bodies
- Enables quick assessment and grasp of new opportunities
- Supports strategic and business planning
- Enhances communication within and between firms
- Supports the effective use of resources
- Promotes continuous improvement
- Helps to focus the internal audit programme
- Ensures robust contingency planning
- Improves the ability to meet objectives and achieve opportunities.

The main aim is to ensure that the firm understands risk and regards risk managers as senior internal appointments, providing the holders of these roles with the necessary support and resources to fulfil them. The benefits of risk management vary depending on how it is planned and how widely it is embraced throughout the firm. Minimalist approaches are likely to deliver limited benefits and could just turn into a bureaucratic tick box exercise. The real benefits are obtained by linking risk management into the existing management and planning processes, and realising that it is a two way process, both of feeding information up through the institution to help strategic planning, but also providing support, resources and direction downwards to help manage the risk effectively.

2.14 Moral hazard

The phrase moral hazard refers to the risk that the presence of a contract will effect on the behaviour of one or more parties. The classic example is often deemed to originate from the insurance industry, where coverage against a loss might increase the risk-taking behaviour of the insured. The fact that the loss is protected in some tangible way means that the risk appetite of the insured is skewed. When applied to the behaviour of managers and executives in a financial trading firm, one can infer how the issue of moral hazard may increase the likelihood of irrational behaviour towards risk taking.

As indicated, moral hazard is the prospect that a party insulated from risk may behave differently from the way it would behave if it were fully exposed to the risk.

Moral hazard is related to information asymmetry, a situation in which one party in a transaction has more information than another. The party that is insulated from risk generally has more information about its actions and intentions than the party paying for the negative consequences of the risk. More broadly, moral hazard occurs when the party with more information about its actions or intentions has a tendency or incentive to behave inappropriately from the perspective of the party with less information.

Such situations arise because an individual or institution does not take the full consequences and responsibilities of its actions, and therefore has a tendency to act less carefully than it otherwise would, leaving another party to hold some responsibility for the consequences of those actions. For example, a person with insurance against car theft may be less cautious about locking his or her vehicle, because the negative consequences of losing it are (partially) the responsibility of the insurance company.

Moral hazard also arises in a principal-agent problem, where one party, called an agent, acts on behalf of another party, called the principal. The agent usually has more information about his or her actions or intentions than the principal does, because the principal usually cannot completely monitor the agent. The agent may have an incentive to act inappropriately (from the viewpoint of the principal) if the interests of the agent and the principal are not aligned.

In 2008, during the bailout of AIG, Fannie Mae and Freddie Mac in the United States, the phrase moral hazard became popular, typically in conjunction with the phrase privatising profits and socialising losses. The problem according to many observers was that the rescue of the banks (including those in the UK which were saved by the British government) echoed the case of Long Term Capital Management (LTCM), the collapsed US hedge fund in 1998 as these rescues increased moral hazard, or the risk that investors would enter into contracts in bad faith. Knowing that the government was there to help them, banks and other investors were free to make irresponsible commitments.

Financial bail-outs of lending institutions by governments, central banks or other institutions can encourage risky lending in the future, if those that take the risks come to believe that they will not have to carry the full burden of losses. Lending institutions need to take risks by making loans, and usually the most risky loans have the potential for making the highest return. So called too big to fail lending institutions can make risky loans that will pay handsomely if the investment turns out well but will be bailed out by the taxpayer if the investment turns out badly. Profit is privatized while risk is socialized.

However, now that the magnitude of the government rescues of banking institutions in various countries has now been made so abundantly clear, it may be that nobody will again assume that the government will bail them out if they lend foolishly.

3 The FSA's objectives

Under the previous British regulatory model, which was phased out in 2013, the FSA along with the Treasury and the Bank of England forms the triumvirate of the approach to financial market regulation in the UK. This has been the model for the last decade. Each of the three has its own role and the FSA effectively operates as an outsourced service set up by HM Treasury in order to fulfil its tasks. The enabling legislation which set up the FSA was known as the Financial Service and Markets Act 2000 (often abbreviated to FSMA 2000).

3.1 The role of the FSA

FSMA 2000 required that the FSA exercised its powers and carried out its duties in such a way as to meet its four statutory objectives. These basic responsibilities drove its approach to the manner in which it set about all its tasks. They were as follows.

(1) **Market confidence** – to maintain confidence in the financial system. This means the financial system operating in and from the UK, including all of the firms involved in regulated financial services, as well as the related financial markets and exchanges.

(2) **Financial stability** – contributing to the protection and enhancement of the UK financial system.

(3) **The protection of consumers** – to secure the appropriate degree of protection for consumers (note, this does not necessarily mean preventing **all** risk of loss to consumers). In considering what is the appropriate degree of protection, the FSA should have regard to the different degrees of risk involved in different kinds of investment, the differing levels of experience and expertise of consumers, the needs of the consumers for advice and accurate information and the general principle that consumers should take responsibility for their decisions.

(4) **The reduction of financial crime** – to reduce the extent to which it is possible for firms within the financial system to be used for purposes connected with financial crime.

3.2 The FSA rulebooks

In order to meet its statutory objectives, the FSA had prepared a regulatory text (generally referred to as the FSA handbook, or just the handbook). FSMA 2000 gives the FSA the power to write rules into its handbook. Firms working within the regulated financial services industry were restricted to those which the FSA authorises and to those exempt from the need for authorisation because they are classified as designated professional bodies (DPBs) – the latter being subject to their own rules, which may differ from those of the FSA.

4 UK regulatory reform

At the Queen's speech on 25 May 2010, the Coalition Government announced that it would introduce a Financial Services Regulation Bill. At the time little detail on the bill was published apart from the reiteration of two comments that the Conservatives made in opposition. First, that the FSA would be abolished and secondly that the Bank of England would be placed at the heart of the UK's financial system with both control of macro-prudential policy and oversight of micro-prudential regulation.

In June 2010 the Chancellor of the Exchequer announced the creation of an Independent Commission on Banking (ICB), chaired by Sir John Vickers. The purpose of the ICB is to formulate policy recommendations covering structural measures that are designed to reform the UK banking system and promote stability and competition, including the complex issue of separating retail and investment banking functions.

On 26 July 2010, the Treasury published the Coalition Government's first consultation document on the proposed reforms. The consultation document was called, a new approach to financial regulation: judgement, focus and stability. The Treasury published a second consultation document in February 2011 which was called, 'A new approach to financial regulation: building a stronger system'. Both consultation documents confirmed the essential elements of the reforms in that the FSA will be abolished and in its place will be established:

- A new macro-prudential regulator, the Financial Policy Committee (FPC), established within the Bank of England.
- A new prudential regulator, the Prudential Regulation Authority (PRA), established as a subsidiary of the Bank of England.

- A new conduct of business regulator, originally entitled the Consumer Protection and Markets Authority, but subsequently changed to the Financial Conduct Authority (FCA).

In March 2011 the FSA published its paper setting out initial thoughts concerning the regulatory approach of the FCA. This was followed in May 2011 with the FSA and the Bank of England publishing a paper on the PRA's regulatory approach for banks and larger investment firms. A paper on the PRA's approach to insurers was also published on 20 June 2011.

On 16 June 2011, the Treasury published a consultation document and white paper entitled, 'A new approach to financial regulation: the blueprint for reform' (the White Paper). The White Paper is a significant milestone because it provides further detail on the Government's regulatory reform proposals and sets out for the first time a draft of the Financial Services Bill (which was originally called the Financial Services Regulation Bill) which will make the necessary changes to existing legislation.

The ICB published its Final Report on 12 September 2011. The introduction of the Vickers measures are on a separate track from the other elements of the bill before parliament. It is likely that any resulting Vickers reforms will be implemented by 2015 with some elements not until 2019.

All of these changes are designed to lead to the stage whereby the existing FSA can hand over its responsibilities to the members comprising the new regulatory structure.

4.1 The move to a new structure for regulation

Under the Government's reforms, the UK moved to a new twin peaks style of regulation. The Financial Policy Committee (FPC), within the Bank of England, is responsible for protecting the stability of the financial system as a whole and macro-prudential regulation. The Prudential Regulation Authority (PRA) is a subsidiary of the Bank of England, supervising deposit takers, insurers and a small number of significant investment firms. The FCA is responsible for regulating conduct in retail and wholesale markets (including both exchange-operated markets and over-the-counter (OTC) dealing); supervising the trading infrastructure that supports those markets; and for the prudential regulation of firms not prudentially regulated by the PRA.

Under the move to the new PRA and FCA structure, many firms, including banks, ware responsible therefore for reporting to both regulators and the boundary issues addressing the powers of both regulators will need to be carefully constructed.

The FCA has taken charge of the product regulation and financial promotion powers including regulation of consumer activity within the UK marketplace. It is a very substantial regulatory body and will employ most of the resources of the current FSA.

On the other hand the PRA is the body that is charged with a statutory duty to supervise participants in the marketplace. There is a commitment to take a judgement led approach to supervising firms.

Under the new world of the FCA and PRA regulation, banks can expect a more judgment-based supervisory approach. In reality under the new FCA world the regulator will expect to identify their target audiences and design products which meet that group's need. They will want to exercise their authority in order to test products that they can deliver fair outcomes to the consumer and in conjunction with this to make sure that robust approval processes are in place to ensure that the product ends up in the right hands. The FCA has the power to intervene in respect of products where they feel particularly that there is an inherent flaw in the design of a product or where there has been widespread promotion or selling to customer groups for whom the product is likely to be unsuitable. There will certainly be a strong incentive to forestall mis-selling such as with Payment Protection Insurance against which banks have had to make so much provision for customer repayment in their current activities.

In 2012 the FSA was in a transitory role and planned the transfer of its powers across to the new framework but at that time supervision across the banking and other financial sectors was overseen by the Financial Services Authority.

Banks could look forward to the fact that the activities of accepting deposits and effecting or carrying out contracts of insurance were going to be specified PRA-regulated activities. The activity of dealing in investments as principal is also a PRA-regulated activity to be designated only by the PRA.

New systems and processes would need to be developed by retail banks in order to demonstrate that the FCA's objectives are at the forefront of their product design and development. The FCA has adopted a preventative approach in its intervention activities and will have a lower risk appetite for issues affecting a whole sector or type of product. They will intervene earlier in a product's lifecycle by supervising the stages of product design and governance as well as point of sale processes, marketing and complaints.

Banks will be required to think through their products to a greater degree and consider any market level issues that their products could create.

4.2 The Prudential Regulatory Authority (PRA)

The PRA was the authority responsible for the prudential supervision of deposit takers, certain investment firms and insurance companies.

The PRA will adopt a more judgement based approach to supervision. The UK Treasury has presented for discussion key elements in the PRA's judgement based approach to supervision and these elements include:

- The nature and intensity of the PRA's supervisory approach will be commensurate with the level of risk a firm poses to the stability of the system. This appears to be identical to the FSA's risk based approach to supervision.
- Supervisors will focus on the big picture and on understanding where the main risks to the stability of the financial system lie.
- The PRA will be forward looking, seeking to assess whether, on the balance of risks, there are vulnerabilities in firms' business models, capital and liquidity positions, governance, risk management and controls that cast into doubt their future financial soundness. The focus of supervision will go well beyond assessing compliance with rules.
- Where potential threats to the safety and soundness of an institution are identified, the PRA will take supervisory action at an early stage to reduce the probability of disorderly failure.
- Firms will be expected to consider the underlying purpose of PRA rules when managing their businesses.
- The PRA will expect the firms it regulates not to engage in creative compliance with its rules and policies and not to engage in regulatory arbitrage designed to mask the riskiness of their activities or financial exposures.
- For those firms posing greater risk to the stability of the UK financial system, the PRA's approach will be more intensive.
- The PRA will ensure that major judgements involve its most senior and experienced individuals, using a process which is both rigorous and well documented.

The Treasury clearly envisages the PRA following a style of supervision that is more judgement based than that adopted by the FSA following the financial crisis. In addition this style of supervision will be more intensive for those firms that have been deemed to pose a greater risk to the UK financial system.

4.3 PRA supervisory assessment

The PRA's supervisory assessment covers all relevant entities within a consolidated group. The assessment will include the following:

Business risk

PRA supervisors will assess business risk at the level of the sector or of the firm as appropriate. For firms that pose the greatest risk to the stability of the financial system, the analysis will include a review of the drivers of profitability, firms' risk appetite and performance targets, and the assumptions under which these targets have been set. Peer analysis will form an important part of the assessment.

Financial strength

The PRA will regularly assess the key elements which determine a firm's financial strength in relation to the size and type of business it carries out. For example, the PRA will examine the quantity and quality of capital that a firm needs to support its activities on a forward looking basis. The PRA will also examine the adequacy of a firm's liquidity in quantitative and qualitative terms, in order to assess its ability to meet its liabilities (actual and contingent) on an ongoing basis. The PRA will also assess the robustness of a firm's internal systems and controls and senior management oversight in relation to capital and liquidity management. The PRA will conduct two types of stress testing: bottom up idiosyncratic stress tests of individual banks and sector wide stress tests undertaken to support other authorities such as the European Banking Authority. Firms will also be expected to implement reverse stress testing to identify the scenarios most likely to cause financial distress. In addition, firms will be expected to develop recovery plans with the PRA forming a judgment on each plan's credibility.

Risk management and governance

The PRA will assess the quality of a firm's risk management functions, including via spot checks designed to assess a firm's ability to respond to unforeseen events. Related to this, the PRA will also take into account a firm's culture, as this factor is considered to have a significant influence on business strategy.

Resolvability

The development of credible and effective resolution plans form a key part of the PRA's assessment process. In assessing resolvability the PRA will consider whether the domestic and, if relevant, overseas authorities have in place a resolution plan for a firm. Also, as a minimum, all firms will be expected to be able to demonstrate that they can produce a single, consistent view of depositors' funds to enable the Financial Services Compensation Scheme to implement rapid payout, and to protect connectivity to payment systems.

4.4 Why this radical change?

QUICK QUESTION

Why do you think that this change was necessary?

Write your answer here before reading on.

Hector Sants, the FSA's CEO, has said that there was little or no evidence that the financial services industry had significantly changed its attitude towards consumers. Whilst the FSA's Treating Customers Fairly (TCF) initiative may have created further awareness of the issue, complaints against financial services firms had significantly increased from 2.7 million in 2006 to 3.5 million in 2010.

In addition, there have also been a number of mis-selling scandals, including the long running payment protection insurance (PPI) saga in which the British Bankers Association lost its legal challenge to new regulatory provisions and guidance concerning the handling of complaints related to PPI. It was estimated by the FSA that the costs relating to compensation for PPI complaints handling could be between £0.8 billion and £1.3 billion over five years, with wider costs of the package ranging between £1.1 billion and £3.2 billion.

4.5 The role of the FCA

The FCA has a single strategic objective of protecting and enhancing confidence in the UK financial system. It also has three operational objectives:

- Securing an appropriate degree of protection for consumers
- Promoting efficiency and choice in the market for financial services
- Protecting and enhancing the integrity of the UK financial system.

The Government also proposes that the FCA must, so far as is compatible with its objectives, discharge its general functions in a way that promotes competition. Following on from the objectives the FCA must have regard to six high-level regulatory principles including one relating to proportionality whereby restrictions imposed should be proportionate to the expected benefits.

The FCA's strategic objective in summary states that:

'The FCA will develop a model of regulation that recognises the variety of ways in which different types of firm, product or activity, affect its ability to deliver its objectives, both in individual markets and in the financial services sector as a whole. This approach will recognise that there are important differences between wholesale and retail markets – but also important links that could pose risks to confidence in the UK financial system'.

For the purposes of the FCA's operational objective to secure an appropriate degree of protection for consumers, the term 'consumer' is a very broad one covering at one end, infrequent purchasers of financial products to, at the other end, investment banks engaging in sophisticated transactions. The FCA will recognise the differences across this spectrum.

Many questions arise when considering the differentiated approach and the approach towards different types of consumers. A key one is whether the FCA will have the quality and quantity of staff to be able to deliver this type of regulation. Another important question is that you can differentiate only so far before you make regulation completely unworkable for the industry.

4.6 The supervisory approach of the FCA

The key points regarding the FCA's supervisory approach include:

- The FCA will place particular focus on firms' culture as a potential root cause of poor outcomes for retail or wholesale consumers, recognising its determining role in a firm's regulatory behaviour. The FCA will look to firms' senior management to set, embed and maintain a firm-wide culture that supports choice and an appropriate degree of protection for consumers.

- The FCA's core markets regulatory activities will continue to be centred on: supervising the infrastructures which support trading of financial instruments; supervising the markets for the issuing of securities, including acting as the UK competent authority for listing; and maintaining a broad oversight of both on-exchange and OTC markets and detailed monitoring to prevent market abuse.

- The FCA will focus its direct supervision of trading infrastructures on a relatively small number of entities which provide key services to the markets – particularly recognised investment exchanges and multilateral trading facilities.

- The FCA's approach to the regulation of markets for capital fund raising will generally follow the FSA's approach and will mainly be concerned with ensuring the integrity and efficiency of markets, ensuring adequate disclosure of information and providing a level playing field for market participants.

- In the primary markets, the FCA will perform the functions that the FSA currently performs as the UK Listing Authority. The FCA will continue to be responsible for reviewing and approving prospectuses and circulars, determining eligibility for listing and maintaining the Official List.
- The FCA will also police the ongoing compliance of issuers and major shareholders with the ad hoc and periodic disclosures required under the Disclosure and Transparency and Listing Rules. The FCA will authorise and monitor the performance of sponsors and, if proposed reforms are enacted, primary information providers. The major regulatory tool in this area will remain ensuring that disclosures made by issuers, both in key documents such as prospectuses, and on a continuing basis, provide the information required to protect investors.

It is not clear how the change in culture will be effected. The FSA's treating customers fairly (TCF) initiative and the emphasis on firm culture and senior management responsibility has been ongoing for some years now but consumer complaints have risen significantly. In relation to capital raising activity and primary market regulation it appears that it will be pretty much business as usual when the FCA takes over. In relation to direct supervision of trading infrastructures there it is not clear as to how the new regime will differ.

5 European Banking Authority (EBA)

5.1 The new ESAs

The European Banking Authority was established by the European Parliament and the European Council on 24 November 2010. It is one of three European Supervisory Authorities (ESAs).

It officially came into being on 1 January 2011 and took over all existing and ongoing tasks and responsibilities from the previous body, the Committee of European Banking Supervisors (CEBS). It is based in the City of London.

There are three new EU Supervisory Authorities (ESAs). The EBA is one of these together with the European Securities Markets Authority (ESMA) in Paris and the European Insurance & Occupational Pensions Authority (EIOPA) in Frankfurt. These are parts of a new EU regulatory oversight system called the European System of Financial Supervisors (ESFS) and the key players are the European Supervisory Authorities – ESAs – introduced in January 2011.

These three ESAs now have considerable powers over domestic regulators such as the FSA. Each ESA has a full time chairman and a full time CEO. A Board of Supervisors is drawn from the 27 national authorities plus European Economic Area (EEA) countries (Norway, Iceland and Liechtenstein). A management board is selected from the Board of Supervisors, and there is a permanent staff of around 70.

The role of these ESAs is:

- the development of a single European rulebook
- to prepare draft laws for EU Parliament
- to draft binding technical standards that are legally binding in EU Member States
- to be able to override national regulation
- to have additional responsibility for consumer protection.

5.2 The EBA's role

The EBA acts as a hub and spoke network of EU and national bodies safeguarding public values such as the stability of the financial system, the transparency of markets and financial products and the protection of depositors and investors.

The EBA has broad responsibilities, including preventing regulatory arbitrage, guaranteeing a level playing field, strengthening international supervisory coordination, promoting supervisory convergence and providing advice to the EU institutions in the areas of banking, payments and e-money regulation as well as on issues related to corporate governance, auditing and financial reporting.

Its 2012 work programme identifies four areas of EBA's activities and aims to define the main objectives and corresponding priorities for its activities. The first three areas, Regulation, Oversight, and Consumer Protection are representing the core functions of the EBA that are laid down by the EBA regulation. The support functions summarised as 'operations' play a critical role in ensuring that the EBA can perform its core functions.

The main objective of the EBA in the regulatory policy area is to play a leading role in the creation of the single rulebook for the EU banking system. Based upon the current CRD IV/CRR proposals, to be adopted in the course of 2012, about 200 deliverables will be expected from the EBA. Most products are expected to be finalised by 2013-2014.

Based upon the capacity available at both the EBA and at the national authorities, the following policy areas have been identified as having priority:

- Capital and capital buffers
- Liquidity
- Remuneration
- Leverage ratio.

In the context of crisis prevention and crisis resolution, the EBA is expected to set further technical standards but also to coordinate and, where applicable, to participate actively in the management of cross border crisis events.

5.3 Financial Groups Directive (FGD)

This is a financial regime applying to EU-based companies whose activities span both the banking and investment sectors and the insurance sector. It lays down requirements for the company's capital positions and is intended to improve the stability of the financial system, thereby protecting customers.

6 Risk-based capital

The holding of sufficient levels of capital is one of the central techniques used by regulators to enforce resilience in banks and other financial institutions. Risk-based capital as a concept is the blending of the assessment of the amount of risk faced by an organisation against the level of capital to be held to provide resistance to that risk.

6.1 Adoption by leading regulators

In 1988, the Basel Committee on Banking Supervision (BCBS), with the endorsement of the G-10 Governors, published the first international capital framework for banks, entitled International Convergence of Capital Measurement and Capital Standards (Basel I Accord). In 1989, the Office of the Comptroller of the Currency (OCC), Board of Governors of the Federal Reserve System, Federal Deposit Insurance Corporation (FDIC), and Office of Thrift Supervision (OTS) in the United States finalised the general risk-based capital rules to implement Basel I for U.S. banks. Risk-based capital is also a method developed by the National Association of Insurance Commissioners (NAIC) in the United States to measure the minimum amount of capital that an insurance company needs to support its overall business operations.

Risk-based capital is used to set capital requirements considering the size and degree of risk taken by the organisation, be it a bank or an insurer. For banks, the measures involve credit and market risk in the main with operational risk also taken into account resulting from Basel II thinking.

6.2 Benefits afforded by risk-based capital approaches

Economic capital and other advanced risk-based capital methodologies enable financial institutions to quantify the risks they face, the capital needed to cover them and the real risk-adjusted returns that are being made.

While interest in such frameworks is increasing in the wake of the move to risk-based prudential regulation including Basel II, the overriding benefits are the ability to enhance strategic and tactical decision-making and optimise shareholder wealth.

Risk-based capital management can help organisations to spot threats and weaknesses, to identify opportunities that may be missed by competitors and target investment where it can earn its best return.

It can also help to align risk appetite with capital allocation and communicate the tangible strengths and potential of the business to analysts, investors and rating agencies.

However, risk-based capital management is only as good as the reliability of the data, validity of the assumptions and quality of application that underpin it. Data may be incomplete or inconsistent. Even if the desired data is available, it could be dangerous to give too much credence to model outputs without the sense check of experience and intuition. Risk-based capital management cannot exist in a vacuum; it requires expert implementation, development and a period of bedding-in to be credible and relevant to the business.

6.3 The PRA's view

In accordance with the second principle, the PRA adopts a risk-based approach to supervision. This means that it focuses its resources on mitigating those risks which pose a threat to the achievement of its statutory objectives (with most resource being expended on the greatest risks) and that it has regard to the efficient and economic use of its resources. One of the key directions of this is to focus on the capital strength of the firms it supervises.

Since 1991, capital requirements at UK banks have, in large part, been dictated by the 1988 Basel Accord (i.e., Basel I), as agreed by the Basel Committee on Banking Supervision. The purpose of that regime was to make capital requirements more risk sensitive and commensurate with the degree of risk inherent in banks' balance sheets. This regime required banks to hold minimum levels of capital equal to 8% of risk-weighted balance sheets assets. The risk weights assigned to various asset classes were designed to reflect the degree of uncertainty surrounding the payoff of broad asset classes and, in that sense, reflected their intrinsic credit risk.

While Basel I was generally perceived as a step forward in making capital requirements more risk sensitive, the FSA (and the Bank of England as the predecessor supervisor) required additional capital charges to compensate for several recognised shortfalls. The Basel I regime, in particular, did not consider a number of other key risks, including interest rate, legal, reputational and operational risks, that had the potential to produce losses and lead to bank failure. For that reason, UK supervisors set individual capital guidance, also known as trigger ratios, based on firm-specific reviews and judgments about, among other things, evolving market conditions as well as the quality of risk management and banks' systems and controls. These triggers are reviewed every 18-36 months, which gives rise to considerable variety in capital adequacy ratios across firms and over time.

6.4 FSA findings on bank practice

Prior to being replaced, the FSA has produced some reports on its analysis on the risk-based capital ratios and individual capital requirements set by the regulator with respect to British banks. Their analysis reported on a significant positive association between the risk-based capital ratios and capital requirements suggesting that British banks increase and decrease ratios in response to higher or lower capital requirements. This association appeared to be more pronounced at larger banks, banks with lower capital cushions and banks that are less exposed to market discipline. Additionally, this relationship was stronger during more favourable economic conditions and indicated that, on average, banks raise capital ratios more in response to higher capital requirements in such a climate. This result is not surprising given that it may be easier (i.e. less costly) to raise capital and adjust balance sheet make-up during such conditions.

The FSA also found with respect to economic conditions a negative association between capital ratios and the rate of GDP growth for all banks in the UK. This negative relationship afforded further credence to policy makers' concerns about pro-cyclicality and some evidence supporting the need for regulatory intervention.

With respect to pro-cyclical bank practices however it was far from clear for a number of reasons. First, when looking only at large banks, the FSA found no statistical association between risk-based capital ratios and economic conditions. This finding was not consistent with the idea that these banks are short-sighted in their capital management practices or that large bank capital management practices may accentuate economic cycles. Also the analysis done by the FSA was conducted during a period of significant economic downturn in the United Kingdom.

On the issue of capital quality, the FSA found a significant positive association between total risk-based capital ratios and a proportion of Tier 1 regulatory capital. This finding suggested that banks that rely to a greater extent on higher quality Tier 1 capital tended to maintain higher total risk-based capital ratios on average. Since this type of capital is generally more costly, this finding is not necessarily surprising as optimising banks, in their capital management practices, consider the relatively higher adjustment costs associated with this type of capital. The implication therefore is that by requiring banks to maintain a higher proportion of better quality Tier 1 capital the mandate may also raise the profile of capital adjustment costs in banks' capital management practices and therefore call into question the motivation for cost minimising banks to maintain higher risk-based capital ratios overall.

Banks tend to mitigate expected market reactions with respect to their funding costs or access to certain capital market activities in line with their business activity by holding higher capital ratios. Market forces play important roles in UK banks' capital management practices and this supports ongoing efforts by regulators to improve and harness market discipline, which is done in the Pillar 3 process under the Basel practice.

7 Basel II

The original Basel Accord that we have just looked at was agreed in 1988 by the Basel Committee on Banking Supervision. The 1988 Accord, now referred to as Basel I, helped to strengthen the soundness and stability of the international banking system as a result of the higher capital ratios that it required.

Basel II was the second of the Basel Accords, (now extended and effectively superseded by Basel III), which are recommendations on banking laws and regulations issued by the Basel Committee on Banking Supervision.

Basel II, initially published in June 2004, was intended to create an international standard for banking regulators to control how much capital banks need to put aside to guard against the types of financial and operational risks banks (and the whole economy) face. One focus was to maintain sufficient consistency of regulations so that this does not become a source of competitive inequality amongst internationally active banks. Advocates of Basel II believed that such an international standard could help protect the international financial system from the types of problems that might arise should a major bank or a series of banks collapse. In theory, Basel II attempted to accomplish this by setting up risk and capital management requirements designed to ensure that a bank had adequate capital for the risk it exposed itself to through its lending and investment practices. Generally speaking, these rules mean that the greater risk to which the bank is exposed, the greater the amount of capital the bank needs to hold to safeguard its solvency and overall economic stability.

Basel II (or Basel 2) was a revision of the previously existing framework, which aimed to make the framework more risk sensitive and representative of modern banks' risk management practices.

There are four main components to the framework:

- It is more sensitive to the risks that firms face: the framework includes an explicit measure for operational risk and includes more risk-sensitive risk weightings against credit risk.
- It reflects improvements in firms' risk-management practices, for example the internal ratings-based approach (IRB) allows firms to rely to a certain extent on their own estimates of credit risk.
- It provides incentives for firms to improve their risk-management practices, with more risk-sensitive risk weightings as firms adopt more sophisticated approaches to risk management.
- The new framework aimed to leave the overall level of capital held by banks collectively broadly unchanged.

7.1 The Capital Requirements Directive

The Basel Accord was implemented in the European Union via the Capital Requirements Directive (CRD), which was designed to ensure the financial soundness of credit institutions (banks and building societies) and certain investment firms. The CRD came into force on 1 January 2007, with firms applying the advanced approaches from 1 January 2008.

The CRD framework was revised by the introduction of Basel II, initially published in June 2004. The Basel II framework introduced the concept of three pillars.

As indicated, the Basel II Accord has been implemented in the European Union via the Capital Requirements Directive (CRD). This includes the UK. It affects banks and building societies and certain types of investment firms. The new framework consists of three pillars.

Pillar 1 of the new standards sets out the minimum capital requirements firms will be required to meet for credit, market and operational risk.

Pillar 2 refers to the supervisory review process. Under Pillar 2, firms and supervisors have to take a view on whether a firm should hold additional capital against risks not covered in Pillar 1 and must take action accordingly.

The aim of Pillar 3 is to improve market discipline by requiring firms to publish certain details of their risks, capital and risk management.

The Basel II framework describes a more comprehensive measure and minimum standard for capital adequacy that national supervisory authorities were working to implement through domestic rule-making and adoption procedures. It sought to improve on the existing rules by aligning regulatory capital requirements more closely to the underlying risks that banks face. In addition, the Basel II framework intended to promote a more forward-looking approach to capital supervision, one that encourages banks to identify the risks they may face, at the present moment and in the future, and to develop or improve their ability to manage those risks. As a result, it is intended to be more flexible and better able to evolve with advances in markets and risk management practices. The efforts of the Basel Committee on Banking Supervision to revise the standards governing the capital adequacy of internationally active banks achieved a critical milestone in the publication of an agreed text in June 2004, which has since been enhanced.

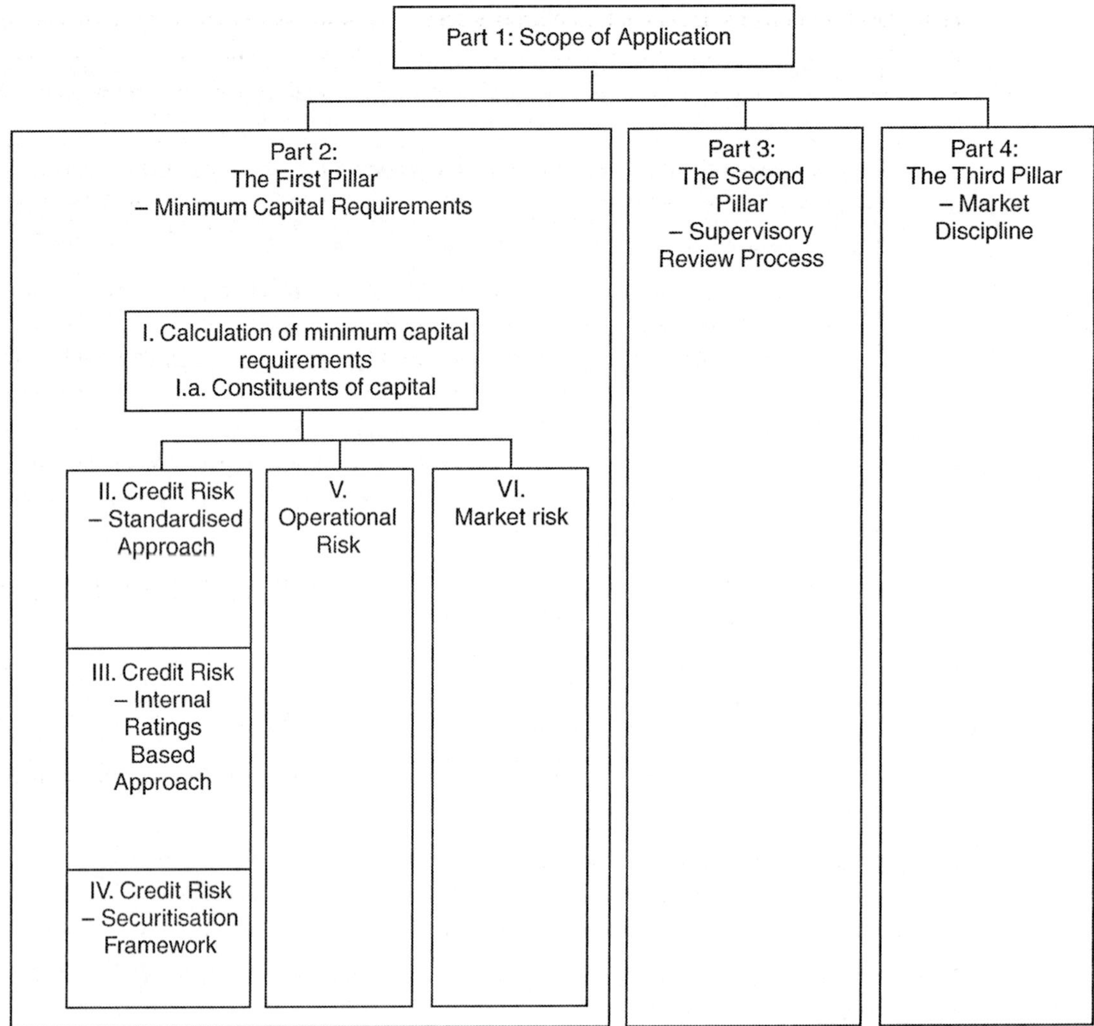

Basel II came into force on 1 January 2008. At that time, the CRD amended two of the most significant existing directives (the Banking Consolidation and Capital Adequacy Directives) for the prudential regulation of credit institutions and investment firms across the EU. Closely related to the revised Basel Framework, it introduced a modern, risk-sensitive prudential framework based on the three Pillars, which to reiterate were:

- Pillar 1: minimum capital requirements – a quantification of the risks arising from firms' credit, trading and other businesses.
- Pillar 2: supervisory review – the establishment of a strong constructive dialogue between a firm and the regulator on the risks, the risk management and capital requirements of the firm.
- Pillar 3: market discipline – robust requirements on public disclosure intended to give the market a stronger role in ensuring that firms hold an appropriate level of capital.

The CRD was therefore a major piece of legislation, and was designed to have a major impact on the prudential regulation of firms across the EU, particularly in terms of relating capital levels much more closely to risks. It was also billed as a single market measure, intended to harmonise standards to a degree and to make it easier for firms to do business and to compete across the EU Member States.

We will now look in more detail at the requirements under each of these pillars.

7.2 Pillar 1 of Basel II

Pillar 1 of the Basel II capital framework revised the 1988 Accord's guidelines by aligning the minimum capital requirements more closely to each bank's actual risk of economic loss.

First, Basel II improves the capital framework's sensitivity to the risk of credit losses generally by requiring higher levels of capital for those borrowers thought to present higher levels of credit risk, and vice versa. Three options are available to allow banks and supervisors to choose an approach that seems most appropriate for the sophistication of a bank's activities and internal controls. These are:

- Under the standardised approach to credit risk, banks that engage in less complex forms of lending and credit underwriting and that have simpler control structures may use external measures of credit risk to assess the credit quality of their borrowers for regulatory capital purposes.
- Banks that engage in more sophisticated risk-taking and that have developed advanced risk measurement systems may, with the approval of their supervisors, select from one of two internal ratings-based (IRB) approaches to credit risk. Under an IRB approach, banks rely partly on their own measures of a borrowers' credit risk to determine their capital requirements, subject to strict data, validation, and operational requirements.

Second, the Basel II framework established an explicit capital charge for a bank's exposures to the risk of operational risk losses caused by failures in systems, processes, or staff or those that are caused by external events, such as natural disasters. Similar to the range of options provided for assessing exposures to credit risk, banks will choose one of three approaches for measuring their exposures to operational risk that they and their supervisors agree reflects the quality and sophistication of their internal controls over this particular risk area.

By aligning capital charges more closely to a bank's own measures of its exposures to credit and operational risk, the Basel II framework encouraged banks to refine those measures. It also provided explicit incentives in the form of lower capital requirements for banks to adopt more comprehensive and accurate measures of risk as well as more effective processes for controlling their exposures to risk.

7.3 Pillar 2 of Basel II

Pillar 2 of the Basel II capital framework recognises the necessity of exercising effective supervisory review of banks' internal assessments of their overall risks to ensure that bank management is exercising sound judgement and has set aside adequate capital for these risks.

Supervisors (meaning regulators) will evaluate the activities and risk profiles of individual banks to determine whether those organisations should hold higher levels of capital than the minimum requirements in Pillar 1 would specify and to see whether there is any need for remedial actions.

The Basel Committee expected that, when supervisors engage banks in a dialogue about their internal processes for measuring and managing their risks, they will help to create implicit incentives for organisations to develop sound control structures and to improve those processes.

Under Basel II, the Supervisory Review Process of Pillar 2 has two key elements:

- Firms should have a process for ensuring that they hold capital consistent with their risk profile and strategy – the name for this is the Internal Capital Adequacy Assessment Process, or in short form, ICAAP.
- Supervisors should review that process and strategies and if they identify weaknesses or deficiencies should take appropriate prudential measures, including the setting of a higher capital requirement – this was called the Supervisory Review and Evaluation Process or the SREP.

Responsibility lies with the firms

A central assumption in the new rules was that the formulation of the internal capital adequacy assessment process would be the duty and responsibility of the institution itself. The supervisory authorities' role is to set forth a number of basic principles and requirements for the work and subsequently to assess whether the outcome meets the basic goals. The institutions themselves (banks and others) must solve the approach to the achievement of this based on the requirements imposed by the authorities and on the specific operations conducted by the individual institution. More specifically, the institution must ensure that a functioning interface is in place between the definitions, concepts and benchmarks that the institution and the respective supervisory authority use in order for assessment and follow-up to be possible. An important and obvious example is the manner in which capital is defined in line with the EU Directives and this will be relevant when determining legally binding capital adequacy.

Responsibility for the internal capital adequacy assessment process lies with the institution's own board of directors and senior management, while the supervisory authority's fundamental task is to assess whether the board and senior management of the institution have complied with their responsibility in an adequate manner. If not, the institution must take appropriate action.

Pillar 2 is one of the most important features in Basel II. Within its scope, institutions and supervisory authorities must work both together and independently in order to achieve a comprehensive and flexible assessment of risks, risk management, and capital requirements. The basic idea is that institutions within the framework of Pillar 2 identify all of the risks to which they are exposed. This involves a wider spectrum of risks than those that form the basis for the capital adequacy calculation within Pillar 1, i.e. credit risks, market risks and operational risks.

QUICK QUESTION

Based on your knowledge of different types of risk, what other risks do you think would be included here?

Write your answer here before reading on.

It involves, amongst other things, the following additional risk assessments.

- **Strategic risk** – institutional changes and changes in fundamental market conditions which may occur.
- **Earnings risk** – current income may develop less favourably than expected.
- **Reputational risk** – the risk of adverse perception of image of the institution in the market, in the media or with clients for example.
- **Liquidity risk** – the risks of difficulties in raising capital in certain situations.
- **Concentration risk** – exposures concentrated on a limited number of customers, a certain sector or geographic area and so leading to vulnerability.
- **Business cycle risk** – through lending or otherwise firms may be vulnerable to business cycle risks.

The ICAAP

The Internal Capital Adequacy Assessment Process (ICAAP) is a requirement where the financial institution needs to assess:

(1) The adequacy of Pillar 1 minimum capital requirements.

(2) How much total shareholders' funds are required in order to meet the firm's strategy and ensure that the minimum capital requirements are not breached.

(3) Ensure that all the material risks of the group are understood by the Board and there is appropriate and proportional risk management action being taken.

Pillar 2 requires risk to be presented and debated in an intuitive manner to the Board both in order to prove the use test and to ensure buy in and understanding by the Board.

7.4 Pillar 3 of Basel II

Pillar 3 leveraged the ability of market discipline to motivate prudent management by enhancing the degree of transparency in banks' public reporting. It set out the public disclosures that banks must make that lend greater insight into the adequacy of their capitalisation.

The Basel Committee believed that, when marketplace participants have a sufficient understanding of a bank's activities and the controls it has in place to manage its exposures, they are better able to distinguish between banking organisations so that they can reward those that manage their risks prudently and penalise those that do not.

8 Basel III

Basel III is the third iteration of the stages of development of banking standards and sound practices. Implementation of the Basel III requirements – an international regulatory framework – will start from 2015 in an effort to improve regulation, supervision and risk management, in the banking sector.

New banking regulations, effective from 2015, have been the centre of much debate for some time, as banks struggle to meet the requirements proposed by the Basel Committee on Banking Supervision (BCBS).

8.1 The need to move to Basel III

QUICK QUESTION

Which events prompted the need for Basel III?

Write your answer here before reading on.

The crisis in financial markets over 2008 and 2009 prompted a strengthening of the Basel rules to address the deficiencies exposed in the previous set of rules.

The Basel III proposals sought to strengthen the regulatory regime applying to credit institutions in the following areas:

- enhancing the quality and quantity of capital
- strengthening capital requirements for counterparty credit risk (and in CRD III for market risk) resulting in higher Pillar I requirements for both
- introducing a leverage ratio as a backstop to risk-based capital
- introducing two new capital buffers: one on capital conservation and one as a countercyclical capital buffer
- implementing an enhanced liquidity regime through the Net Stable Funding Ratio and Liquidity Coverage Ratio.

The Basel III proposals are a long-term package of changes commencing 1st January 2013 and, based on the Commission's timetable, the transition period is expected to run until 2021.

The Basel III proposals will be implemented into EU law through changes to the existing CRD – referred to as CRD IV. CRD IV, which will include an EU Regulation and an EU Directive (implemented through national law). This will be a key instrument through which the European Commission intends to introduce substantive parts of the new European supervisory architecture, including the development of the Single Rule Book for financial services.

The single rule book which the UK signed up to at the June 2009 European Council is intended to replace separately implemented rules within Member States. The principle of maximum harmonisation will be applied to the adoption of CRD IV. This principle requires that national legislative implementation should not exceed the terms of the original EU legislative proposal, and therefore prohibits the gold-plating of EU legislation when it is transposed into national law.

8.2 The start of Basel III

In December 2009, the BCBS set out its concrete proposals, named Basel III, in response to the financial crisis of the preceding few years.

It stated, the objective of the Basel Committee's reform package is to improve the banking sector's ability to absorb shocks arising from financial and economic stress, whatever the source, thus reducing the risk of spillover from the financial sector to the real economy.

As part of the Basel III rules, the minimum requirement for banks' tier-one capital ratio (ratio of equity capital to risk-weighted assets [RWA]) has been raised from 2% to 4.5%.

Effective as of 2019, lenders will also need to add a conservation buffer of 2.5%, meaning banks must hold a total core capital equal to 7% of their RWA.

BCBS has highlighted that in the most recent phase of the crisis there has been a significant spill-over of risk between the banking sector and sovereigns, as governments increased their debt in an effort to stabilise their banking systems and economies. As a result, debt-to-gross domestic product (GDP) ratios in a number of economies increased by as much as 10-25 percentage points. It was therefore clear to many observers that the economic benefits of raising the resilience of the banking sector to shocks are immense.

While some believe that these new rules will be too harsh, others – such as Lord Turner, the chairman of the UK's Financial Services Authority – have said that they do not go far enough to protect the system. Turner has stated that raising tier-one capital ratios to between 15% and 20% would be more appropriate. He questioned whether the proposals are the best and indeed are radical enough.

Basel III is in simple terms the answer to what was missed and caused massive problems in the economic crisis.

8.3 Elements of Basel III

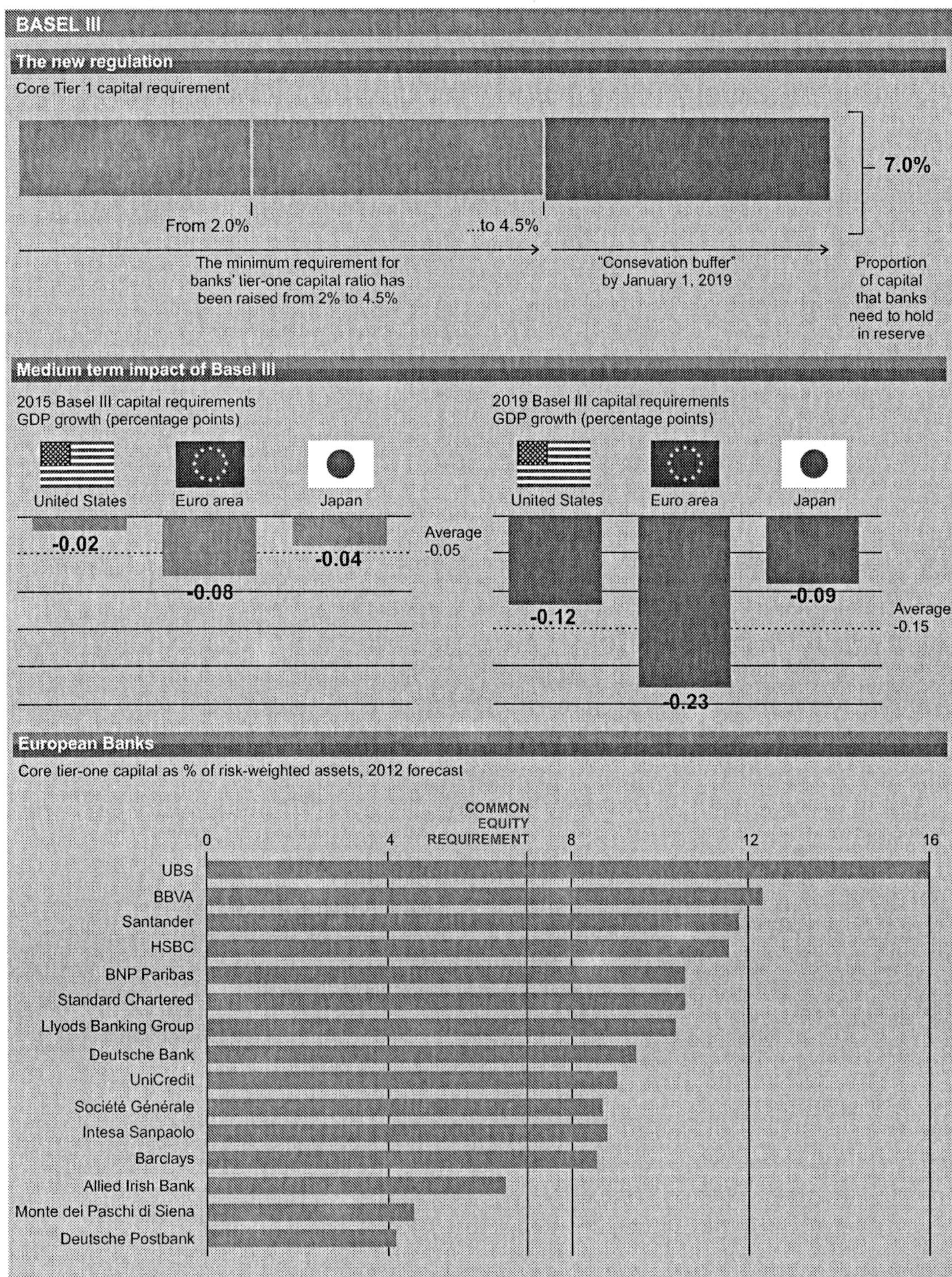

BASEL III
The new regulation
Core Tier 1 capital requirement
7.0%
From 2.0%
...to 4.5%
The minimum requirement for banks' tier-one capital ratio has been raised from 2% to 4.5%
"Consevation buffer" by January 1, 2019
Proportion of capital that banks need to hold in reserve
Medium term impact of Basel III
2015 Basel III capital requirements GDP growth (percentage points)
United States
Euro area
Japan
-0.02
-0.08
-0.04
Average -0.05
2019 Basel III capital requirements GDP growth (percentage points)
United States
Euro area
Japan
-0.12
-0.23
-0.09
Average -0.15
European Banks
Core tier-one capital as % of risk-weighted assets, 2012 forecast
COMMON EQUITY REQUIREMENT
0
4
8
12
16
UBS
BBVA
Santander
HSBC
BNP Paribas
Standard Chartered
Llyods Banking Group
Deutsche Bank
UniCredit
Société Générale
Intesa Sanpaolo
Barclays
Allied Irish Bank
Monte dei Paschi di Siena
Deutsche Postbank

8.4 Basel III – Calibration of the capital framework

Calibration of the Capital Framework

Capital requirements and buffers (all numbers in percent)

	Common Equity (after deductions)	**Tier 1 Capital**	**Total Capital**
Minimum	4.5	6.0	8.0
Conservation buffer	2.5		
Minimum plus conservation buffer	7.0	8.5	10.5
Countercyclical buffer range*	0 – 2.5		

* Common equity or other fully loss absorbing capital

Phasing in Basel III

Annex 2: Phase-in arrangements (shading indicates transition periods)
(all dates are as of 1 January)

	2011	**2012**	**2013**	**2014**	**2015**	**2016**	**2017**	**2018**	**As of 1 January 2019**
Leverage Ratio	Supervisory monitoring		Parallel run 1 Jan 2013 – 1 Jan 2017 Disclosure starts 1 Jan 2015					Migration to Pillar 1	
Minimum Common Equity Capital Ratio			3.5%	4.0%	4.5%	4.5%	4.5%	4.5%	4.5%
Capital Conservation Buffer						0.625%	1.25%	1.875%	2.50%
Minimum common equity plus capital conservation buffer			3.5%	4.0%	4.5%	5.125%	5.75%	6.375%	7.0%
Phase-in of deductions from CET1 (including amounts exceeding the limit for DTAs, MSRs and financials)				20%	40%	60%	80%	100%	100%
Minimum Tier 1 Capital			4.5%	5.5%	6.0%	6.0%	6.0%	6.0%	6.0%
Minimum Total Capital			8.0%	8.0%	8.0%	8.0%	8.0%	8.0%	8.0%
Minimum Total Capital plus conservation buffer			8.0%	8.0%	8.0%	8.625%	9.125%	9.875%	10.5%
Capital instruments that no longer qualify as non-core Tier 1 capital or Tier 2 capital			Phased out over 10 year horizon beginning 2013						
Liquidity coverage ratio	Observation period begins				Introduce minimum standard				
Net stable funding ratio		Observation period begins						Introduce minimum standard	

8.5 The current status with Basel III

In Spring 2012 banks were earning returns that were unattractive to private investors. This had the effect of preventing credit from being granted to companies and households which has the ongoing impact of damaging the broader economy and diminishing growth within economies.

One of the prime reasons for this was the effect of regulation. There were so many new rules to deal with. The Dodd-Frank Act in the United States is a powerful example together with Basel III.

The new Basel III capital standards require banks the whole world over to have larger buffers of capital through which to absorb losses. Under this new regime banks will hold about three times as much equity as they used to under the old one. In some places the cushion could be even greater. At the time of writing Europe is split over how strictly the Basel III rules should be enforced and countries such as Britain and Sweden are pushing for a stricter regime than the rest of the European countries. But higher levels of capital mean lower returns on equity.

This is leaving the regulators with a difficult conundrum to balance. For example, many of Europe's banks need to bolster their capital buffers but few will be able to entice investors since they promise such low returns. Banks will struggle to generate the capital they need from profits. Many banks therefore might seek therefore simply to reduce the size of their loan books instead.

In the future profits are bound to be smaller. The banking system has operated on too little capital before. The cost of bank borrowing is going up as new rules regarding bank debt are introduced. The new rules make it less likely that governments will have to step in to save banks (as happened in many places in 2008-2009) and their creditors.

It is also difficult to separate the effect of regulation from the state of the broader economy. In Europe and America so many companies are attempting to rebuild their balance sheets but unemployment and property failures are reaping a toll of bad debts. Over time things will improve in the economy which will enable provisions to be reduced; demand will increase and with it commercial profit.

8.6 Accent on strengthening liquidity risk management

Under Basel III the three pillars of the standard Basel approach with which everyone is now fully familiar will continue as mutually reinforcing pillars of the structures.

Much of its new requirements address the management of liquidity risk trying to ensure the banks are better at managing liquidity risk in the future, a skill that was sorely lacking in many banks during the credit crunch of 2007-2009. This is to be achieved by the introduction of a leverage ratio together with short and medium-term quantitative liquidity ratios. Another measure that Basel III introduces in order to set aside reserves for future downturns is what they call a counter-cyclical capital buffer. These are all new under Basel which, together with the tighter definitions and boosting of Tier 1 capital (equity), sit at the heart of the Basel III proposal.

The two measures addressing liquidity management are known as the liquidity coverage ratio (LCR) and the net stable funding ratio (NSFR).

Furthermore Basel III is addressing derivatives and securities and increasing the capital charges for all organisations involved in those marketplaces.

Oddly enough the area of operational risk is possibly the least affected area of Basel III which remains very much unchanged from the Basel II requirements.

Other banks, and buy side institutions including asset managers will be affected by Basel III. There is an effort to reduce exposure to higher risk-weighted assets and to limit the issuing of credit in difficult markets and building buffers during good times. One measure that Basel III introduces is a limit on dividend payouts and staff compensation for banks that are experiencing difficulties. It is a basic requirement under Basel III that the regulators are seeking to increase the loss absorbability of capital.

So the following ratios will be introduced.

- **Leverage ratio** – to counter the build-up of an excessive on- and off-sheet leverage. The ratio is intended to constrain leverage in the banking sector and introduce a financial safeguard against model risk and measurement error.
- The **Capital Conservation Buffer** – here the idea is that restrictions will be imposed when capital levels fall within the conservation range and therefore distribution of capital via dividends, share buy-backs and discretionary bonus payments will be restricted once the trigger level is reached. The minimum capital conservation ratios will be applied expressed as a percentage of earnings.
- The **Counter-cyclical Buffer** – here the proposal is for a counter-cyclical buffer to act in addition to the capital conservation buffer with an aim of providing a defence against the build-up of system-wide risks associated with excess aggregate credit growth. This measure will be deployed by national regulators and such deployment is expected to be infrequent. Internationally active banks are likely to be subject to a small buffer on a more frequent basis since credit cycles are not always correlated across national jurisdictions. The buffer can vary between zero and 2.5% of risk-weighted assets as decided by the local supervisory body.
- **Net Stable Funding Ratio (NDFR)** – the purpose of this measure is to ensure stable funding on an ongoing, viable entity basis over one year in an extended firm-specific stress scenario where a bank encounters and customers become aware of decline in profitability, downgrade events or any material event that calls into question the reputation or credit quality of the institution.
- The **Required Stable Funding** – a set of supervisory assumptions relative to the liquidity risk profile of a bank's asset and off balance sheet exposures. It represents what supervisors believe should be supported with stable funding (i.e. assets that are more liquid and more readily available to act as a source of liquidity in stressed market conditions).
- **Incremental Risk Capital Charge**, which is calculated based on a risk measure that includes default risk as well as migration risk for unsecuritised credit products held in the trading book at a 99.9% confidence level under a one-year capital horizon and a minimum liquidity horizon of three months.
- **Comprehensive Risk Capital Charge**, which is calculated based on a risk measure that can be applied to banks' so-called correlation trading portfolios and captures not only incremental default and migration risks, but all price risks at a 99.9% confidence level and a one-year capital horizon.

8.7 Stress testing again

Not surprisingly, stress testing rules also apply. Under Basel III banks must have a comprehensive stress testing programme for counterparty risk which enables:

- Trade capture and exposure aggregation by counterparty
- Regular stress testing of market risk factors
- Stress testing to be performed at least monthly
- It to address all counterparties
- A reduction of exposure to concentrations of directional sensitivities.

8.8 Wrong way risk

Wrong way risk occurs when exposure to a counterparty is adversely correlated with the credit quality of that counterparty. Wrong way risk, as an additional source of risk, is rightly of concern to banks and regulators.

In short it arises when default risk and credit exposure increase together. The terms wrong-way risk and wrong-way exposure are often used interchangeably. Ordinarily in trading book credit risk measurement, the creditworthiness of the counterparty and the exposure of a transaction are measured and modelled independently. In a transaction where wrong-way risk may occur however this approach is simply not sufficient and ignores a significant source of potential loss.

Basel II highlighted the issue of wrong-way risk as an area which should be specifically addressed by banks in their risk management practice as far back as 2001. In recent months however wrong-way risk has come more sharply into focus as an area of concern for risk managers and one that may have been neglected by many.

There are a number of reasons for this. In part it is due to the advancements in credit derivative trading that bring creditworthiness into the trading book as a market factor. It also is due to the sub-prime crisis in 2007, the subsequent market volatility and the increasing attention being paid to credit risk.

Basel III addresses this phenomenon and requires that banks should identify exposures which generate wrong way risk. This can be done by stress testing and scenarios in order to identify any possibility of severe shocks. Should risk factor relationships change banks may well be affected. Hence Basel III states that banks should monitor by product, industry, and region as relevant to their business.

Regular reporting to board and risk committees about incidences and mitigation steps must be performed.

9 Quantifying operational risk

Since the Basel Accord was first designed banks' activities have become more complex and diverse. This has been due to a number of factors but principally is has been globalisation, changes to the regulatory approach and improved technology which itself has led to the development of e-commerce. To this one can add large volume transactions and the development of outsourcing models. However perhaps the most important thing has been the growing number of operational loss events ranging right from Barings Bank in 1995 through to Enron in 2001 and others highly publicised ones since. This has led to the development of the view that operational risk management is to be regarded as a comprehensive and inclusive discipline which is comparable in banks to credit and market risk management within the overall gamut of risk management.

Taking the fundamental operational risk management process of identification, followed by assessment, then monitoring, and by control and mitigation, this led to the Basel II approach whereby there must be a capital charge included to cover operational risk.

Under the Basel rules, this may be provided by three distinct approaches for determining the exact amount of capital – the basic indicator approach, the standardised approach and the advanced measurement approach. The intention behind Basel is that all banks hold sufficient capital to mitigate the risks they are taking in their business. You will recall that these were discussed earlier in this chapter when we looked at Basel II.

KEY WORDS

Key words in this chapter are given below. There is space to write your own revision notes and add any other key words or phrases you want to remember.

- Corporate governance
- Financial Reporting Council
- Risk committee
- Remuneration committee
- REMCO
- Due diligence
- Moral hazard
- Financial Policy Committee
- Financial Conduct Authority
- Prudential Regulation Authority
- European Banking Authority
- Risk based capital
- Pillar 1
- Pillar 2
- Pillar 3
- Wrong way risk

REVIEW

Now consider the main points introduced in this chapter. These are listed below. Tick each one as you go through them.

- The recent financial crisis has increased the demand within society for more regulation in financial services.
- Corporate governance is the set of relationships between directors and stakeholders, through which objectives are set and monitored.
- The Combined Code was established by the Financial Reporting Council to set out standards relating to board composition, remuneration, accountability, audit and relations with shareholders.
- The Walker Report made five risk governance recommendations.
- Stakeholders in organisations have differing interests in the Board. Corporate governance seeks to take these into account when developing controls and procedures.
- The Board of Directors is led by the Chair and their role is to provide entrepreneurial leadership to the organisation.
- The Audit Committee is appointed by the Board and its role is to monitor and review the effectiveness of the audit activities within the organisation – this extends to both internal and external audit.
- The Risk Committee must assess the different types of risks faced by the firm.
- The Remuneration Committee establishes the remuneration policy for the organisation.
- An example of due diligence with regard to corporate governance is the money laundering checks carried out by a bank.
- To be effective, risk management must be embedded in the culture of the organisation, and this must be led from the top of the firm.
- Moral hazard occurs when a person's behaviour is affected by their protection from risk.
- The FSA's statutory objectives are market confidence, financial stability, the protection of consumers and the reduction of financial crime.
- In response to the banking crisis, the regulatory landscape of the UK financial services industry has been altered.
- The Financial Policy Committee of the Bank of England is responsible for the stability of the UK financial system.
- The Prudential Regulation Authority supervises deposit takers, insurers and a small number of significant investment firms.
- The Financial Conduct Authority regulates retail and wholesale markets.
- The European Banking Authority is a network that seeks to maintain European financial stability and protect depositors and investors.
- Basel I used a risk based capital approach, and the FSA adopted a risk-based approach to supervision.
- Basel II introduced three Pillars that were used by firms and regulators.
- Pillar 1 sets out minimum capital requirements – this is done with the standardised and internal ratings-based approaches.
- Pillar 2 is concentrates on supervisory review. The regulator will review the activities of a firm to determine if more capital needs to be held.

- Pillar 3 is concerned with market discipline and transparency – firms are required to publish information which will inform on their capital adequacy.
- The Basel III Accord is being phased in as a result of the banking crisis and the perceived flaws in the existing arrangements.
- Basel III requires that banks hold larger amounts of capital reserves to absorb potential losses.
- Steps have also been taken under Basel III to improve the management of liquidity risk.
- Wrong way risk arises when default risk and credit exposure increase at the same time and Basel III requires that banks identify this through stress testing and scenarios.
- A bank will quantify the capital charge for operational risk using the provisions of Basel II.

chapter 11

THE IMPACT OF THE GLOBAL BANKING CRISIS 2007/8

Contents

Learning objectives

On completion of this chapter, you should be able to:

- examine the impact of the global banking crisis of 2007/2008.

Introduction

The banking crisis that started in 2007 has had global ramifications. This final chapter seeks to delve into the origins of the crisis, before discussing the potential solutions that have been put in place to avoid a repetition of the situation. However, you need to be aware that the effects of the crisis are still being felt and whilst the content of this chapter was current at the time of writing, by the time you study this chapter, the situation will have moved on.

The chapter opens with a re-examination of systemic risk, before moving on to outline the factors that contributed to the banking crisis. One response to the crisis was the establishment of the European Systemic Risk Board and the work of this body is explained next. The impact of the crisis is explained covering areas of weakness within firms and the lessons that have been learned. This section moves on to reflect upon the global impacts of the crisis and the response of regulators to it. The chapter concludes with a ranging discussion on the future of European Monetary Union.

1 Systemic risk

QUICK QUESTION

Systemic risk was introduced earlier in this study text.

What is it?

Write your answer here before reading on.

In financial markets, **systemic risk** is the risk of collapse of an entire financial system or entire market, as opposed to the risk associated with any one individual entity, group or component of a system. It can be defined as financial system instability, potentially catastrophic, caused or exacerbated by idiosyncratic events or conditions in financial intermediaries. It refers to the risks imposed by inter-linkages and interdependencies in a system or market, where the failure of a single entity or cluster of entities can cause a cascading failure, which could potentially bankrupt or bring down the entire system or market. Hence, major institutions or elements of market infrastructure present systemically important issues to the rest of the well being of the marketplace. From this it can be seen that a serious disruption at one particular firm, be it a trading entity such as RBS, or a key trading, clearing or settlement utility (that is a firm upon which the whole market depends) could potentially cause a domino effect throughout the financial markets toppling one institution after another. Such an event would lead to a crisis of confidence and, as was seen in 2008, led to a situation of being too big to fail; witness the case with those British banks which the Government supported by bringing them into public ownership.

The problems with RBS in October 2008 caused unprecedented damage to confidence in the financial system, as markets realised that some institutions that had previously been judged too big to fail turned out not to be. The effects of the banking crisis on market confidence was dramatic and rapid. Systemic risk is essentially results from the contagion of disruption spreading from firm to firm. It can also result from the failure of systems which many, if not all firms depend upon for their daily operations. This might be the electronic trading platform of an exchange, an international bank payments system or a central counterparty or settlement provider such as a central securities depository (CSD).

1.1 The credit crunch

QUICK QUESTION

There has been much public debate as to the cause of the banking crisis and credit crunch – however, it is agreed that there were a number of contributory factors.

List what you think these factors were.

Write your answer here before reading on.

With so much attention paid to systemic risk following the Credit Crunch events of 2007 through to 2009, it is evident to see why the issue of effective management of this type of risk had proved so difficult before. There are just so many moving parts to it. It is not simply a question of regulation alone, the subject involves, inter alia:

- Risk granting mechanisms within lending institutions
- The reliability of the services of credit ratings agencies
- The effectiveness of systems used by firms for credit risk assessment
- Complexity of financial products
- Understanding of complex products by those who market them
- Risk-taking by trading institutions
- Efficient corporate governance within firms
- Senior management understanding of risk
- The recognition by firms of the role and contribution of risk officers
- Implementation by firms of efficient risk management practices
- Systems for imposing bank liquidity ratios and capital charges
- Regulatory structures and resources
- Regulatory audit quality
- The quality of the regulatory risk assessment of firms overseen
- Reward and bonus cultures within financial institutions.

1.2 The European Systemic Risk Board

In response to the global financial crisis, the European Commission tasked a High Level Group, chaired by Jacques de Larosière, a distinguished French Central Banker who had served as the Managing Director of the International Monetary Fund (IMF) and was then appointed as the Governor of the Bank of France, to consider how the European supervisory arrangements could be strengthened both to protect its citizens better and to rebuild trust in the financial system. Among its many conclusions, the Group highlighted that supervisory arrangements should not only concentrate on the supervision of individual firms but also place emphasis on the stability of the financial system as whole.

In 2009, the de Larosière report recommended, among other things, that an EU level body be established with a mandate to oversee risk in the financial system as a whole. This was to become the European Systemic Risk Board (ESRB). On 16 December 2010 the legislation establishing the ESRB came into force.

1.2.1 Its mission, objectives and tasks

According to the ESRB Regulation:

The ESRB shall be responsible for the macro-prudential oversight of the financial system within the Union in order to contribute to the prevention or mitigation of systemic risks to financial stability in the Union that arise from developments within the financial system and taking into account macro-economic developments, so as to avoid periods of widespread financial distress. It shall contribute to the smooth functioning of the internal market and thereby ensure a sustainable contribution of the financial sector to economic growth.

For this purpose, the ESRB shall carry out the following tasks:

- determining and/or collecting and analysing all the relevant and necessary information
- identifying and prioritising systemic risks
- issuing warnings where such systemic risks are deemed to be significant and, where appropriate, make those warnings public
- issuing recommendations for remedial action in response to the risks identified and, where appropriate, making those recommendations public
- when the ESRB determines that an emergency situation may arise, issuing a confidential warning addressed to the Council and providing the Council with an assessment of the situation, in order to enable the Council to adopt a decision addressed to the European Supervisory Authorities (ESAs) determining the existence of an emergency situation
- monitoring the follow-up to warnings and recommendations
- cooperating closely with all the other parties to the European System of Financial Supervision (ESFS); where appropriate, providing the ESAs with the information on systemic risks required for the performance of their tasks; and, in particular, in collaboration with the ESAs, developing a common set of quantitative and qualitative indicators (risk dashboard) to identify and measure systemic risk
- participating, where appropriate, in the Joint Committee of the ESAs
- coordinating its actions with those of international financial organisations, particularly the International Monetary Fund (IMF) and the Financial Stability Board (FSB) as well as the relevant bodies in third countries on matters related to macro-prudential oversight
- carrying out other related tasks as specified in Union legislation.

2 The impact of the global banking crisis

The credit crunch, as the economic crisis was originally dubbed, has undermined faith in the banking and investment system and thrown up huge questions for savers, governments and the financial industry. It has destroyed institutional and private investor wealth on a huge scale, undermined many of the investment theories and reputations of the past generation, unveiled large-scale criminal activity and created immense private investor cynicism towards the banking industry – which is being forced into a radical reappraisal of its structure.

The events that started in 2007 clearly exposed the vulnerabilities of financial firms whose business models depended too heavily on uninterrupted access to secured financing markets, often at excessively high leverage levels. This dependence reflected an unrealistic assessment of liquidity risks of concentrated positions and an inability to anticipate a dramatic reduction in the availability of secured funding to support these assets under stressed conditions.

A major failure that contributed to the development of these business models was weakness in funds transfer pricing practices for assets that were illiquid or significantly concentrated when the firm took on the exposure. Some improvements have been made, but instituting further necessary improvements in liquidity risk management must remain a key priority for financial services firms. This has become one of the prime focuses of the Basel Committee and is factored into Basel III rules very strongly.

2.1 Areas of weakness within financial firms

A number of areas of weakness were identified that required further work by firms to address, including the following (in addition to liquidity risk management issues):

- Failure of some boards of directors and senior managers to establish, measure, and adhere to a level of risk acceptable to their firms
- Pay and reward schemes that conflicted with the control objectives of the firm
- Inadequate and often fragmented technological infrastructures that hindered effective risk identification and measurement
- Institutional arrangements that conferred status and influence on risk takers at the expense of independent risk managers and control personnel.

2.2 The principal learning points from the crisis

The events of 2007-2009 demonstrated on a very large scale the vulnerabilities of firms whose business models depended heavily on uninterrupted access to secured financing. Many firms relied on excessive short-term financing of long-term, illiquid assets. This included banks in the UK such as HBOS. Firms that were least affected by this had the ability to resist short-term funding because they had access to other sources of funding such as deposits and other liquidity pools including central bank lending facilities.

Some firms' business models also relied on excessive leverage which, combined with doubts about the realisable value of the firm's assets, heightened solvency and business model concerns among the firm's creditors and counterparties.

The American tri-party market for re-purchase agreements (repos) also was severely disrupted. Securities dealers had come to rely on the repo market for funding themselves against securities. Increasingly however, as time passed, illiquid and hard to price securities were consequently vulnerable to disruption in that market. With a heightened concern of credit risk, borrowers failed to anticipate the amounts of collateral that their clearing banks would require when providing intra-day funding for a weak borrower with a deteriorating collateral pool.

The bankruptcy of Lehman Brothers and in particular Lehman Brothers International (Europe) (LBIE) highlighted the risk of relying on the re-hypothecation of client securities as a source of funding. Many counterparties of LBIE elected to hold accounts that allowed Lehman to re-hypothecate securities positions to obtain funding. After LBIE declared bankruptcy, prime brokerage customers sought to withdraw from these arrangements. However these clients were deemed as unsecured creditors of the LBIE estate and found themselves without access to their positions. The failure of Lehman Brothers generated concern amongst hedge fund customers relating to the fact that, in certain instances, their prime brokerage free credit balances and other assets in the UK were not subject to segregation. In many cases customers decided to withdraw from these arrangements. In more recent times a similar story has occurred with the collapse of MF Global in October 2011.

Firms also failed to realise that two important sources of funding, securities lending and money market funds, could impose further demands on liquidity during periods of stress. At the time of the Credit Crunch many firms acknowledged that, if robust funds transfer pricing practices had been in place earlier, they would have not have carried on their trading books the significant levels of illiquid assets that ultimately led to such large losses and would not have built up significant contingency liquidity risks associated with off-balance sheet exposures.

A key lesson of the crisis, drawn by both firms and regulators, was that complex corporate structures hindered effective contingency funding. Firms found that complex corporate structures, often created to arbitrage tax and regulatory capital frameworks, also imposed significant constraints on the flow of funds across the firm between legal entities. As a result, firms now acknowledge the importance of the bottom-up approach to contingency planning which includes the preparation of contingency funding arrangements at the individual legal entity level.

Some interesting observations post-credit crunch that were revealed showed that one overarching observation was that weaknesses in governance, incentives and infrastructure undermined the effectiveness of risk controls and contributed the systemic vulnerability of banking. These failures reflected four challenges in governance:

- The unwillingness or inability of boards of directors and senior managers to articulate, measure and adhere to a level of risk acceptable to the firm.
- Arrangements that favoured risk takers at the expense of independent risk managers and control personnel.
- Compensation plans that conflicted with the control objectives of the firm.
- An inadequate and often fragmented infrastructure that hindered effective risk identification and measurement.

A key weakness in corporate governance is what stemmed from what several firms admitted was a disparity between the risks that their firms took and those that their boards of directors perceived that their firms were actually taking.

Within firms the stature and influence of revenue producers clearly exceeded those of risk managers and control functions. Since those times, virtually all firms have strengthened their authority of their risk management functions and increased the resources devoted to them. Nevertheless, firms still face considerable challenges to developing the necessary infrastructure and management information systems.

There was an imbalance between risk and rewards in the approaches to remuneration. There is broad recognition that industry compensation practices were driven by the need to attract and retain talent and were often not integrated with the firms' control environments. Among the critical weaknesses that the firms cited are the following:

- Historical compensation arrangements evidenced both insensitivity to risk and skewed incentives to maximise revenues.
- The accrual of compensation pools historically did not reflect all appropriate costs.
- Schemes for measuring individual performance often failed to take into account true economic profits, adjusted for all costs and uncertainty.

Firms have more recently been considering changes to their compensation regimes, including modifications to the accrual of bonus pools, the allocation of pools to business units and individuals, and the form of compensation paid out, with the goal of aligning practices with the control objectives of the firm better. Among the changes that have been, or are being, put in place or considered are:

- tying bonus accrual and performance measurement more directly to economic profit by incorporating the costs of risk, liquidity, and capital
- integrating the input of control functions with performance evaluations
- reviewing deferred compensation plans with an eye toward longer vesting and distribution periods.

Overall the credit crisis highlighted the inadequacy of many firms' IT infrastructures in supporting the broad management of financial risk undertaken by the firm. This was in some cases a result of poor integration of data that had resulted from firms' multiple mergers and acquisitions. Building more robust infrastructure systems required a significant commitment of financial and human resources on the part of firms but today are viewed as being critical to the long-term sustainability of improvements in risk management.

Firms were criticised post-credit crunch for their inability to conduct firm-wide stress testing. No doubt banks have sought since that time to improve their ability in this field but it is still likely that many firms do not have the ability to perform regular and robust firm-wide stress tests easily.

Although OTC derivatives were highlighted as being a contributor to the Credit Crunch in fact the industry had taken great efforts to reduce backlogs of unconfirmed over-the-counter derivatives positions. As a result they appear to have significantly mitigated a substantial systemic risk from levels that could have occurred. Many firms had been streamlining business processes to achieve same-day matching in adopting and implementing standard technology platforms and improving collateral management practices and reducing notional amounts of CDS outstanding through portfolio compression ("tearing up" of outstanding netting contracts). The Dodd-Frank initiative in the United States and European Market Infrastructure Regulation (EMIR) in Europe since then have both acted to improve the manner in which OTC derivatives will be traded and administered post-trade from 2013.

2.3 Improvements to be made in risk management

There are some areas of continuing weakness, which the regulatory agencies have focused upon in order to enhance the resilience of financial institutions and to promote global financial stability.

The four most important firm-wide risk management practices which differentiate better performance from worse during the crisis were:

- Effective firm-wide risk identification and analysis
- Consistent application of independent and rigorous valuation practices across the firm
- Effective management of funding liquidity, capital and the balance sheet
- Informative and responsive risk measurement and management reporting.

Implementing these practices comprehensively across large, complex organisations requires considerable resources and expertise. It was evident that many firms still fell short in these areas during the crisis.

2.4 Events and developments

There are so many facets to the global banking crisis that the intention in this section is to put forward some summarised points about some of the major matters that have been experienced over the last few years.

We will now look at a new world order affecting economies, regulation and marketplaces. Let us look at some of these in turn.

2.4.1 Western markets

During 2008 financial institutions were fighting for their very survival. Enormous banks such as Citibank, UBS and Merrill Lynch were forced to make billions of dollars worth of asset write-downs. This forced out some chief executives and these firms repeatedly returned to their shareholders and the market to raise new capital. Bear Stearns almost failed but was taken over by J.P. Morgan in March 2008 at the instigation of the American financial authorities and Lehman Brothers were the largest ever corporate default in September of the same year.

In 2008 some US$1,600 billion was cut from the global market capitalisation banks.

In the United Kingdom various banks' control was effectively taken over by the government using public finance including RBS and Lloyds Banking Group. The same story reached into Ireland, Belgium, Iceland and various other countries.

2.4.2 The United States

In the US the crisis has affected housing, unemployment, banks and banks' stock prices and in general the wealth of every American family. As a nation state it has the largest economy in the world but also the largest debt. In 2013 however although it is not business as usual the American economy is in reasonable shape and is recovering better than the troubled Eurozone and its impact across the entire European Union.

2.4.3 Lehman Brothers

Lehman Brothers was one of the biggest players on Wall Street and its collapse on 15th September 2008 had as significant an impact on the American economy as the terrorist attacks of 9/11 in 2001. It was the Lehman collapse that truly marked the high crisis point of that very troubled year of 2008. In the aftermath of that the Barack Obama administration enacted the Dodd-Frank Act in July 2010 which addresses all aspects of the crisis and it seeks to correct as many of the errors and gaps that were unveiled as possible. The business of Lehman Brothers itself was taken over by Barclays in the case of the American activities and Nomura elsewhere.

2.4.4 Central banks

Central banks in many Western economies have held their interest rates at record low levels and they have adopted also a programme of quantitative easing (to be discussed shortly) in addition as the only other possible levers they have at their disposal to breathe life into their economies. There is continuing concern over a contracting world economy. The Bank of England's governor, Mervyn King, has made public speeches in 2012 reemphasising his concern about the weakness of the UK position as it is so much exposed to the Eurozone crisis.

2.4.5 Financial job cuts

By about the end of 2008, since the start of the Credit Crunch in the latter part of 2007 it was reported that over 130,000 jobs had been lost by international banks. The largest of these were Lehman Brothers and Bear Stearns where companies which effectively came to an end but others including Citigroup, Bank of America, UBS and Commerzbank, to name some large institutions, also shed thousands of jobs. The banks that did not do so in the main were the Japanese banks. There were a few British and European banks that did not really fall victim to the credit crunch including banks such as Banco Santander and Standard Chartered Bank. All in all therefore there were mixed fortunes for banks in general and much depended upon the risk taking appetite of their boards and the degree in which they had become involved in securitisation and credit default obligation markets.

2.4.6 UK house prices

UK house prices narrowly increased in May 2012 leaving national house prices on average about 0.7% lower than their level one year previously. The economic downturn has also meant that there have been far fewer housing starts in the UK and there is a lack of supply such that there has been a shift in the market from purchasing houses to renting. Together with the inability to obtain a mortgage under much more strict lending conditions from British banks this has resulted in great difficulty for young people and young couples to be able to get a foot on the housing ladder. Housing prices are now deemed to be roughly five times average incomes. Mortgage rates of interest are still relatively low but up-front deposit requirements have increased markedly and only the finest credit quality borrowers are successfully securing mortgage loans. The higher cost of bank capital is also having its impact upon the UK housing market because banks have to charge higher mortgage rates. Overriding everything, there is also the continuing fear in the market about the stability of the Euro which is undermining general confidence.

2.4.7 Fortis Bank's rescue

Fortis Bank was rescued by the Dutch and Belgian authorities as they became a victim of the credit crunch in 2008. Since then BNP Paribas has taken control of the bank and as a result will become the largest deposit taking bank in continental Europe. The Belgian state still retains the single largest shareholding in BNP Paribas and BNP Paribas holds three quarters of the Fortis Bank's stock.

2.4.8 US monoline insurers

Monolines, companies like Ambac, FGIC and MBIA and others who insure bonds in the United States were rescued by the American government in the financial crash. Some of the issues were exacerbated by the involvement of monolines in the credit default swaps market because they purchased CDS as insurance on risky deals. These had to be negotiated with banks to provide an outlet for the monocline agencies.

2.4.9 Ratings agencies

Ratings agencies have been criticised for their role in the credit crisis. They were deemed too slow to react and errant in their analysis of securitised debt which they were asked to rate. This resulted in the US Department of Justice filing a civil lawsuit against Standard & Poor's in 2013, accusing them of defrauding federally insured financial institutions by issuing credit ratings that were overly optimistic and not objective.

There has recently been a clamour to downgrade, limit or regulate the ratings agencies. To limit data would almost inevitably lead to a more conservative stance by the agencies, and poorer-quality assessments, which would not help issuers. Many argue for more competition in the ratings business. There are about 80 agencies around the world and competition is generally a good thing. However, Standard & Poor's, Moody's and Fitch provide more than 95 per cent of credit ratings in western markets. The chief issue is to resolve the question of who pays – issuers or investors – and devising a business model that gives the rating body sufficient independence. Whether regulators can help much is debatable. Banks themselves have been critical of Brussels' idea of mandatory ratings rotation, which would risk pushing issuers even further towards the agencies. What is required is better regulation rather than greater regulation of ratings agencies.

2.4.10 Quantitative easing

As the world suffers its worst recession since the Second World War, policy makers are searching for the best tools to limit the downturn. Central banks have rapidly lowered interest rates in order to reduce the cost of borrowing. They have turned to quantitative easing as a further means to promote economic recovery. The hope is to stimulate spending in the economy now.

So far, it has been to no avail. Confidence disappeared from banks, companies and households in the autumn of 2008 and unemployment rose fast in 2009. Without an obvious source of fresh demand, central banks are moving to open the way to more unorthodox approaches to address the crisis. One of those is quantitative easing (QE).

QUICK QUESTION

What is your understanding of quantitative easing?

Write your answer here before reading on.

The idea behind QE is to increase demand in the economy by the central bank creating new money. The difficulty is to ensure the correct level of QE as if it were to be overplayed then it could lead to inflationary pressures and begin to destroy confidence in the economy in general. It must however be sufficiently aggressive to have its desired effect. A tricky balancing act! QE works by the Central Bank buying financial assets and so it injects funds into the economy.

QE has been utilised extensively in the United States and the UK since the economic crisis began.

2.4.11 UBS

The very fact that UBS even continues to exist as an integrated banking franchise, let alone plan for the future, has surprised many. Few other big casualties of the credit crunch were suspected of having such hidden problems; fewer still held the same systemic importance for their home countries as UBS did for Switzerland.

When the Lehman collapse was announced it seemed to many observers that the next mighty bank to collapse might well have been UBS. However this has not transpired.

Since the late part of 2008 UBS has weathered a number of storms which have impacted its business. Criticism abounds of its trying to run a universal bank with investment banking and private wealth banking side by side. Many have urged to break up the monolith. Rogue trader events in London, issues with the United States tax authorities and various other matters have also taken their toll.

The story of how the bank avoided collapse is as important for the wider industry as for Switzerland, offering crucial lessons. At a time when global regulators are rewriting the rule book, forcing institutions to hold more capital to guard against another financial crisis and imposing sweeping limits on riskier activities, UBS has at the same time faced the task of rebuilding its franchise brick by brick, business unit by unit.

2.4.12 Short-selling

You will remember that short selling is the practice of selling assets that have been borrowed from a third party with the intention of buying identical assets later on to return to the third party. At the time of the credit crunch and after that date short selling restrictions were brought in by various governments particularly in continental Europe, in the main addressing the shorting of financial equities. It was evident at one time that European regulators had an inadequate understanding of how shares were traded with the short selling bans that were introduced in Italy, France, Belgium and Spain.

According to research in the United States, Hong Kong and other places, the short selling bans across markets in 2008 did not prevent declines in the prices of financial stocks but presented a significant cost on capital market operations. The focus on short selling as introduced by regulators changed investors' perception of the practice and also had, as a result, a lasting impact on the securities lending industry.

Although the crisis originated in the US and Europe, and the focus of global attention has been on the policy response of those governments, all of the major players in the international system now need to move quickly to respond. This includes developing countries, who now contribute a large share of the global economy and trade flows, and the international financial institutions (IFIs), who help oil the workings of the international system and promote widely shared development.

2.4.13 Emerging markets

Investors used to regard government debt as risk-free. This is plainly no longer the case considering what has happened in Portugal, Ireland, Greece, Italy and Spain. The market today has started to price in a bigger probability of default amongst industrialised countries than among investment-grade companies. Confidence seems to be stronger with emerging markets but not that this is a totally constant position everywhere. The BRICs (Brazil, Russia, India and China) and the CIVETS (Colombia, Indonesia, Vietnam, Egypt, Turkey and South Africa) are now attracting far more investment and in general investors are taking more account of the potential for greater returns in emerging markets now that the returns on traditional Western markets are so poor. A particular attraction of the CIVETS is that they represent a diverse and dynamic set of economies with young, growing populations.

2.4.14 Global regulation

Driven by G20 on the wake of the economic crisis, financial reform is today high on the agenda both on a domestic and a global basis with initiatives such as Dodd-Frank, Basel III and the EU's initiatives via its new regulatory bodies – known as the European Supervisory Authorities, which were became operative form January 2011.

The Basel Committee on Banking Supervision, which sets international rules that national regulators then implement, decided in 2010 to require banks to hold more capital and tighten the definition of what counts as core tier 1 capital (essentially shareholder funds). The regulators have essentially tripled the required ratio of core tier 1 capital to risk-weighted assets and over the next few years will force banks to start subtracting a series of deductions so that core tier 1 capital mirrors more closely the basic definition of equity plus retained earnings.

A lot of attention has been focused on making banks safer. It has been suggested that some very large banks should be broken up. This includes banks such as RBS and UBS and others. The key emphasis lies between separating depositors and the normal run of the mill retail banking against investment banking activities including advisory, capital raising and proprietary trading. Against this backdrop banks that are deemed to be too big to fail by their own national governments are under particular scrutiny. The G20 leading nations have asked the Financial Stability Board to look at ways to address the systemic risk posed by global banks and markets.

2.4.15 Market manipulation

In 2008, the Wall Street Journal published an article suggesting that LIBOR rates (the amount at which banks will lend to one another) were being manipulated by some banks and brokers. At the time, LIBOR was calculated by the British Banker's Association, who published the rate based on lending rates submitted to them each day from large banks such as Barclays and RBS.

An investigation revealed that a number of banks and brokers had been colluding to manipulate the LIBOR rate in order to generate additional profits on their trading positions that were valued using LIBOR. This resulted in heavy fines for the likes of Barclays, UBS and ICAP.

The aftermath of the LIBOR scandal lead to additional investigations into market manipulation. In 2013, more than 30 FX traders from 11 financial institutions had been fired or suspended in relation to allegations of key FX benchmarks being manipulated. In May 2014, a gold derivatives trader at Barclays. received a fine and industry ban for manipulating gold prices in order to prevent paying out $3.9m on an option sold to a client.

All of these incidents undermine the integrity and reputation of the financial services industry and also highlight that scandals are still rocking the industry despite increased scrutiny and regulation.

2.5 The Basel Committee's response to the global banking crisis

In September 2009, the Group of Central Bank Governors and Heads of Supervision, the oversight body of the Basel Committee on Banking Supervision, met to review a comprehensive set of measures to strengthen the regulation, supervision and risk management of the banking sector. These measures will substantially reduce the probability and severity of economic and financial stress.

President Jean-Claude Trichet, who chairs the Group, noted that the agreements reached among 27 major countries of the world are essential as they set the new standards for banking regulation and supervision at the global level.

Central banks and supervisors responded to the crisis by strengthening microprudential regulation, in particular the Basel II framework. They were to work toward the introduction of a macroprudential overlay which includes a countercyclical capital buffer, as well as practical steps to address the risks arising from systemic, interconnected banks.

The authorities reached agreement on the following key measures to strengthen the regulation of the banking sector:

- Raise the quality, consistency and transparency of the Tier 1 capital base. The predominant form of Tier 1 capital must be common shares and retained earnings. Appropriate principles will be developed for non-joint stock companies to ensure they hold comparable levels of high quality Tier 1 capital. Moreover, deductions and prudential filters will be harmonised internationally and generally applied at the level of common equity or its equivalent in the case of non-joint stock companies. Finally, all components of the capital base will be fully disclosed.
- Introduce a leverage ratio as a supplementary measure to the Basel II risk-based framework with a view to migrating to a Pillar 1 treatment based on appropriate review and calibration. To ensure comparability, the details of the leverage ratio will be harmonised internationally, fully adjusting for differences in accounting.
- Introduce a minimum global standard for funding liquidity that includes a stressed liquidity coverage ratio requirement, underpinned by a longer-term structural liquidity ratio.
- Introduce a framework for countercyclical capital buffers above the minimum requirement. The framework would include capital conservation measures such as constraints on capital distributions. The Basel Committee were to review an appropriate set of indicators, such as earnings and credit-based variables, as a way to condition the build up and release of capital buffers. In addition, the Committee will promote more forward-looking provisions based on expected losses.
- Issue recommendations to reduce the systemic risk associated with the resolution of cross-border banks.

The Committee was also going to assess the need for a capital surcharge to mitigate the risk of systemic banks.

As you will know, the Basel Committee went on to issue concrete proposals on these measures, which became what we now refer to as Basel III. The plans was to ensure that these measures would result over time in higher capital and liquidity requirements and less leverage in the banking system, less pro-cyclicality, greater banking sector resilience to stress and strong incentives to ensure that compensation practices are properly aligned with long-term performance and prudent risk-taking.

The following principles were endorsed to guide supervisors in the transition to a higher level and quality of capital in the banking system.

- Building on the framework for countercyclical capital buffers, supervisors should require banks to strengthen their capital base through a combination of capital conservation measures, including actions to limit excessive dividend payments, share buybacks and compensation.
- Compensation should be aligned with prudent risk-taking and long-term, sustainable performance, building on the Financial Stability Board (FSB) sound compensation principles.
- Banks will be required to move expeditiously to raise the level and quality of capital to the new standards, but in a manner that promotes stability of national banking systems and the broader economy.

Supervisors were to ensure that the capital plans for the banks in their jurisdiction are consistent with these principles.

2.6 Basel III

The Basel III rules text was issued in November 2011 and sets out the Basel Committee's framework on the assessment methodology for global systemic importance, the magnitude of additional loss absorbency that global systemically important banks (G-SIBs) should have and the arrangements by which the requirement will be phased in. At the same time a cover note to the rules text set out the Committee's summary and evaluation of the public comments received on its July 2011 consultative document. The rules text was finalised following a careful review of the public comments received. The work of the Basel Committee formed part of a broader effort by the Financial Stability Board to reduce the moral hazard of global systemically important financial institutions (or GSIFIs).

3 The future of European Monetary Union

3.1 Introduction

For some years now, any suggestion that European Monetary Union was in trouble met with a hostile response, but since then the problem has become blatantly more obvious and much has been written on it in the press. The Greek Government issues and subsequent remedy and later the Spanish problem (with again its temporary fix) have highlighted that the issue will not lie down and be settled once and for all. Much work still needs to be done and it will not be easy. Austerity is an unwelcome bedfellow yet it seems as if no one can escape from its impact. The European crisis is having a crippling effect upon global business and impacts hugely, as government ministers have attested, to the economy of the UK. The 10th anniversary of the introduction of the currency has been achieved but where are we now, how did we get there and where do we go from here?

3.2 The pensions time-bomb

It has long been evident that there would be a large imbalance in the effect of the pensions commitments on different member states. This continues to be a key problem and will certainly have to be taken into account when the structure of the Eurozone is re-assessed. It was decided that the UK should certainly not join the euro, given that UK pension liabilities were largely backed by independent pension funds (some €1 trillion) while very similar expectations equivalent in France and elsewhere were an off balance sheet liability of the State. Very oddly, the Commission claimed that the UK pension funds needed topping up. But what about the others? The problem persists on unchanged policies. The French made a very modest change in increasing the retirement age from 60 to 62.

This problem has been recognised for a decade but it would have taken at least another before it was obvious in actual budgetary outflows. We knew that another shock might hit earlier – and one now has. There have been rifts in the Eurozone for some time, partly because of the convergence of interest rates to a level which was not right for everyone. The apparent benefit to the weaker countries proved to be a dangerous trap, leading to an over-borrowing (e.g. Greece), or an unsustainable asset price bubble in Ireland. The more general financial crisis did not cause, but simply precipitated, the crisis.

3.3 Political leadership

It has been evident for a long time that European politicians have been dragging their feet and David Cameron the UK Prime Minister (at the time of writing) has repeatedly declared publically that the European Union needs to take the necessary action to put its house in order and reminded his counterpart leaders that the rest of the world is being impacted by the failure to tackle the root cause within Europe. It is easy to see that the crisis in Europe has been addressed with certain numbers of initiatives which could be described as being, too little too late. Collectively, even in 2012, markets were still volatile and erratic without any clear view that the European question has been solved. The matter is all to do with confidence. Without confidence financial markets will not be able to reach equilibrium.

3.4 Attempts at a solution

Most of the solutions to the Eurozone crisis have involved throwing money at the problem sometimes indirectly by borrowing from third parties, but more usually by quantitative easing, but this will only buy time. The main concern has been with the banking system which was inadequately reformed after the 2008 crash and many banks continue to hold the debt of the less stable countries although the figures have now been reduced. In spite of Germany's objections to a fiscal union and a no bail out clause, the support fund now looks like needing at least €1 trillion. The European Financial Stability Fund was based on packaging high risk debt into tranches which they hoped would achieve AAA status. Financial markets have short memories.

Long-term refinancing operations (LTROs) have been around for years in the euro zone – but the European Central Bank launched them in a new form in early 2012 to tackle the debt crisis. Essentially, they involve the central bank lending money at a very low interest rate to euro zone banks, which has led to the term free money.

The injection of cheap money means that banks can use it to buy higher-yielding assets and make profits, or to lend more money to businesses and consumers – which could help the real economy return to growth as well as potentially yielding returns.

Banks can use assets such as sovereign bonds as collateral for the loans – although they can no longer use Greece's bonds as collateral after the country was downgraded to a default rating by Standard & Poor's, one of the chief ratings agencies. This initially helped to boost some of the more troubled sovereign bonds in peripheral countries such as Spain and Italy, as their yields fell because they were being used as collateral for the operations.

Eurobonds guaranteed collectively by the Eurozone member states would achieve little. If these are the pro rata liabilities of each State, they certainly would not have the AAA rating (which several of them have actually now lost) assumed. Bonds of even the Netherlands, Austria and Finland, surely core countries, have at times traded at around 100 basis points above Germany. If they are jointly and severally liable, this would in the last resort fall on the Germans, which they certainly won't accept and if they do, it would even threaten their own rating.

Current proposals would enforce fiscal discipline on German lines on weaker members. This will inevitably mean tax rises and expenditure cuts and a sharp contraction in the economies which will adversely affect everyone. Given that the exchange rates of these countries are uncompetitive, the only alternative to devaluation (the classic remedy) is deflation.

Internal devaluation by deflation is actually working quite well in Ireland where the problem was an unsustainable property bubble which could not be checked by interest rate policy. The country's finances were sound enough but they then made the mistake of guaranteeing the banks.

If quantitative easing effectively increases the money supply proportionately across the Eurozone, it could generate inflation in all relevant countries. If this caused prices in Germany to rise, which might seem unthinkable, and (possible but not inevitable) the weaker countries could take the opportunity to create an internal devaluation by holding down nominal prices, this would offer some of the benefits of devaluation and also reduce the real cost of Euro debt. To be effective without damage, it would have to be unanticipated inflation and the ECB would then need to convince markets that this had created a one-off adjustment rather than a continuing propensity to inflate.

3.5 A fiscal union?

It is in theory possible, but difficult, to create a monetary union without a fiscal union. The essential conditions are balanced budgets and great labour market flexibility, including wage flexibility. Even unions which had those, such as the Latin Monetary Union, could not survive with all the strains that hit them. In fact, all such unions (unless they preceded political union) eventually came to an end.

Recent proposals would involve a botched fiscal union. It is hard to know what this means. Politically, it would fall far short of a federal union (which would require a very different constitution) but economically may go even further as even these typically give more freedom, on tax and expenditure to members.

There seem to be two main issues, greater transfer of funds from the stronger to the weaker members – but will the Germans accept that? – and far more central control of broad economic policy in member states – but who would take the decisions?

It has been argued that one cannot have monetary union without something approaching a common tax system. This is the reverse of the truth: the only economic weapon left to member states for dealing with asymmetric shocks would then be on the 'expenditure' side. What is now being proposed is actually more central control of expenditure.

A full fiscal union would have to include only those who had signed up for it. Any country considering signing up for such a union would be well advised to compare their properly calculated balance sheet as a nation with those of the intended partners. This would obviously mean looking at the present level of formal debts, projected budgetary cash flows and other figures which are at least in theory readily available to the enquirer but they would need to look much deeper. There are several other ways in which the nation's solvency (and therefore whether it will contribute to, or make claims upon, the group as a whole) can be seriously affected.

Part of the deal will and indeed already does involve substantial fiscal transfers which probably fall outside the scope of the intended Eurozone rules. This will be viewed differently by different countries. Voters in the paying countries will not like this while the beneficiaries will take a different view. They may, but should not be, encouraged to delay taking internal remedial action. Help should be carefully designed to ease the transition rather than to postpone action.

In the United States, the individual states have their own credit ratings even though the country is far better placed to act as a union having a much higher degree of labour mobility then multilingual Europe. The Australians have complex arrangements for leaving their states with a degree of control over some taxes and expenditure, calculating the federal contribution on perceived standard needs rather than on actual expenditure.

3.6 A two-speed Europe?

Some members under the leadership of Germany could form a smaller Eurozone with transfer capabilities, proper central sanctions on government expenditure and a central bank capable of being a lender of last resort. Those staying outside would divide into three categories: the opt out countries, notably the UK, Denmark and Sweden, who would not join. Those like Greece and maybe others which would leave the Eurozone, devalue and default and an intermediate group who are committed to membership and will have to choose one side or the other.

A multi-speed Europe would raise several major problems, most obviously about which assets and liabilities could be converted into a new currency, the impact on the banking system and the inequitable way in which the inevitable loss of capital assets would be distributed partly to the benefit of the well advised who will have already moved their money.

This raises a very delicate diplomatic problem. The inner group would not want outsiders having an equal say in their relevant discussions and for them the unanimity rule on tax policy would not work. The non-members, including the UK, would need to negotiate considerably less interference, particularly in financial regulation and employment policy in case these could be abused by the fiscal union group to force us to share their uncompetitive practices. Economists need to ensure that those negotiating really understand what is at stake. It would be politically unwise to see this as an opportunity to bring back powers from Brussels but countries must take great care to ensure that their own markets are protected.

The weaker countries would have to be given the right to opt out of the Eurozone, raising very difficult questions which may, or may not, involve default. It must be made absolutely clear that their debts, both internal and external, were entirely their own responsibility - an aim intended, unsuccessfully, to be achieved by the Stability and Growth Pact.

3.7 Plans for the future

The essential step is to make it absolutely clear that each member state is responsible for its own debts. They could then make their own arrangements, on the classic gold standard procedures, for maintaining external balance: surely there should be a living will procedure as proposed for banks for dealing with the inevitable occasional default in a less damaging way. Convergence would cease to be an intelligent tactic for investors and interest rates on each country's debt would reflect investor perception of its government actions and give early warning of possible troubles to come. There would remain the problem of how to adjust interest rates to deal with internal problems when the international balance was perceived to be satisfactory.

One remedy could be achieved economically, but certainly not politically, by countries accepting Germany's Bundesbank as the monetary authority and voluntarily adopting their currency. This could well be the right answer for smaller EU members. Note issues and the monetary base would then be the responsibility of the central bank or currency board of the country concerned.

Countries which leave the Eurozone and others (even outside the EU) might well find that a new euro becomes widely used as a secondary currency. It may even become the currency of choice for internal contracts, a role which the US dollar once had. This might reach the stage when they would accept a process to euroise and partly or wholly abandon their own currencies. A currency board could be used which would have, these days, to involve any lender of last resort holding euros not only against banknotes but against the prudential reserves of banks.

QUESTION TIME 1

(a) How did the banking crisis affect your firm?

(b) Since the time this book was written what developments have there been in the banking crisis?

Write your answer here then check with the answer at the back of the book.

KEY WORDS

Key words in this chapter are given below. There is a space to write your own revision notes and add any other key words or phrases you want to remember.

- The European Systemic Risk Board
- Quantitative easing
- Short selling

REVIEW

Now consider the main points that were introduced in this chapter. These are listed below. Tick each one as you go through them.

- A large number of factors contributed to the 2007 banking crisis.
- One response to the crisis from the European Commission was the establishment of the European Systemic Risk Board.
- Firms were vulnerable to the financial crisis as their funding models were dependent on unlimited access to secured funding. The existence of complex funding structures compounded the problem.
- Leading into the crisis, many Boards were not aware of the level of risk being carried by their firms.
- The remuneration packages in firms did not align the rewards offered to some employees to risk.
- Regulators and central banks have responded to the crisis by strengthening microprudential regulation and the Basel II framework.
- At the time of writing, the Eurozone crisis is ongoing and there seems to be no single solution.

chapter 12

CYBER AND ELECTRONIC SECURITY RISKS

Contents

Learning objectives

On completion of this chapter, you should be able to:

- understand the background and context of cyber crime and the risks it poses to both banks and society
- examine a range of cyber threats and how they are used to facilitate criminal activity
- identify and explain the risks that cyber crime poses to governments, companies and individuals
- examine cyber crime prevention, policy planning and governance approaches
- explain the steps involved in cyber incident planning.

Introduction

This chapter covers one of the biggest risks to society in the 21st century: cyber crime. The widespread use of technology has become pivotal for individuals, companies and national governments and has provided a wealth of benefits, from being able to send emails from a smart phone through to being able to transfer money across the globe instantaneously. However, this chapter considers an increasing problem that plagues the use and application of technology called cyber crime. This chapter looks at the risks cyber crime poses and the prevention and planning measures that can be used to mitigate it.

1 Overview and background of cyber crime

The term cyber crime is used to cover a wide range of offences carried out with aid of technology. It is sometimes referred to as computer crime or electronic crime. Cyber crime is broadly defined as:

Any offence committed using a computer device, personal computers, computer networks, the Internet in general, telecommunications systems, message boards, internal communications systems such as intranets and mobile devices, including smartphones.

(Source: *Cyber Crime & Warfare. Peter Warren & Michael Streeter, 2013*)

The banking industry is a logical target for cyber crime. In the US alone it is estimated that $1.2 trillion dollars of electronic money transfers are made each day using the CHIPS system. (Source: *Federal Reserve website*). As the global economy gets bigger, the opportunities for cyber criminals to steal money from banks will increase. An added complexity of cyber crime for banks is the proximity of the attacks: A hacker could target multiple banks in various locations from a different continent.

QUESTION TIME 1

(a) Make a list of all of the electronic devices that you have used at work today.

(b) Write down all of the information security risks that you can think of for each electronic device that you have used.

Write your answer here then check with the answer at the back of the book.

1.1 Types of cyber crime

Many cyber crimes aim to achieve the same outcomes as non-cyber crimes. For example, a Denial-of-Service (DoS) attack could be achieved by using a computer virus to shut down a banks payments network. The non-cyber equivalent of this crime could be to physically attack bank branches and ATMs. Regardless of the method used, both aim to cause panic and disruption. In fact, some cyber crimes such as phishing combine people skills with computer skills.

The main reason for the increasing levels of cyber crime is the internet, which has connected computer networks and databases across the world. While the internet has revolutionised communications and commerce, it has also provided new opportunities for cyber criminals. Cyber crimes can be split into nine main categories, which will be discussed in detail later on in this chapter:

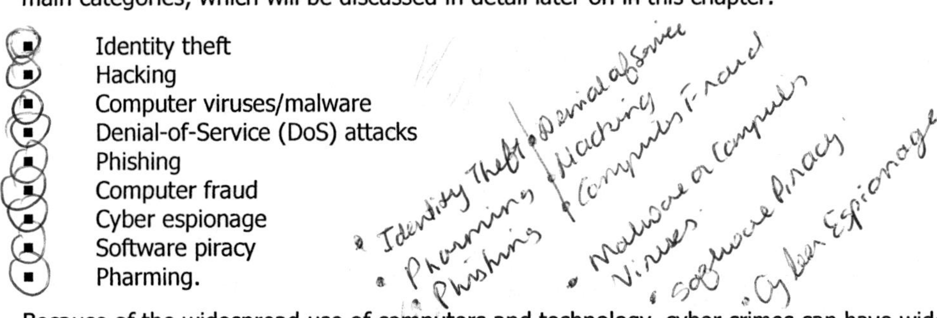

- Identity theft
- Hacking
- Computer viruses/malware
- Denial-of-Service (DoS) attacks
- Phishing
- Computer fraud
- Cyber espionage
- Software piracy
- Pharming.

Because of the widespread use of computers and technology, cyber crimes can have wide ranging adverse effects for different groups. Some examples are detailed below:

- Individual risk: individuals could be victims of identity theft.
- Company risk: Companies could be victims of DoS attacks and computer fraud.
- National risk: Governments and government agencies could be victims of cyber espionage.

These risks will be explored in more detail later on this chapter.

1.2 History of cyber crime

Cyber crime has existed since computers were created, but the potential scale and severity of cyber crime was not fully realised until the 1970s. Since then, there have been some notable incidents that have shaped the cyber crime landscape today:

- 1981 – Ian Murphy is tried as a felon for breaking into AT&T's computers.
- 1988 – Cyber criminals attempt to steal $70 million from First National Bank of Chicago.
- 1995 – First recorded incident of 'phishing'.
- 2003 – 'Titan Rain' launches co-ordinated attacks on American computers. This is an example of APT (Advanced Persistent Threats) – a coordinated and sustained cyber attack that targets specific networks.
- 2010 – Stuxnet computer worm is discovered that attacks Programmable Logistic Controllers.

1.3 The costs of cyber crime

Putting an exact figure on the global cost of cyber crime is difficult due its scale, but the World Bank estimates that it costs in the region of $400 billion per year. However, one of the main problems of trying to quantify the true cost of cyber crime is that companies who suffer from cyber crime are sometimes reluctant to disclose attacks. This is because of the reputational damage that cyber attacks can cause. Imagine a company that generates most of its revenue from selling to customers over the internet. Any cyber attack that compromised customer information (such as names, addresses, payment details) would damage customer confidence in using the internet in order to place sales orders.

CASE STUDY

Zeus

Zeus is a sophisticated piece of malware that has been used to target bank customers. It first appeared in 2007 and is designed to steal money from bank customers.

Zeus targets computers that use Microsoft Windows. It is termed a Trojan horse as it is very difficult to detect. Zeus then uses stealth techniques to steal personal information form computers, which is then used to fraudulently take money form bank accounts. Such is the scale and grandeur of Zeus that criminals have devised their own Zeus business model. Programmers will create their own version of Zeus, which they sell to others. Zeus will then unleashed on unknowing victims. The money is then stolen from bank accounts and laundered by a different set of people, called 'mules'. This makes tracking down the programmers who devise and modify Zeus very difficult to catch.

In January 2014 it was reported that 190 customers of an unnamed European bank lost between €1,700 and €40,000 each due to Zeus malware derivative called 'Luuuk'.

2 Threats – sources and types

Cyber crime threats come from a variety of sources and sometimes have a variety of different names (e.g. viruses and malware are often used interchangeably to describe the same type of threat). A key point to consider with regards to the list below is that cyber criminals often use a combination of threats to achieve their goals, such as using phishing and pharming in conjunction with one another in order to commit identity theft. This is what makes cyber crime so difficult to combat – the threats are constantly evolving and are often used in conjunction with one another.

2.1 Identity theft

Identity theft involves using someone else's identity in an attempt to derive benefits by using the stolen identity. One of the most common purposes of identity theft is to access the bank details of the victim. Identity theft pre-dates cyber crime, but the advent of technology has allowed identity theft methods to become more sophisticated:

- using hand-held card readers to skim information about credit cards, allowing cloned cards to be made
- using wireless networks to obtain information about contactless debit and credit cards
- using personal information from social networking sites
- using systematic attacks to find out passwords and security question answers
- breaching network security by using spyware
- using hacking and phishing techniques (covered below).

2.2 Hacking

Hacking is the activity of gaining unauthorised access to telecoms systems, networks and databases. However, not all hacking is a criminal offence. Companies often hire hackers (called 'white hat' hackers) to test the strength of their computer security. Hackers with criminal intentions are called 'black hat' hackers. While some illegal hackers use their skills for monetary gain (by stealing valuable information of committing fraud), some illegal hacking is based on ethical motives. For example, some hackers are interested in stealing information that will aid political or environmental causes.

2.3 Computer virus/malware

Computer viruses and malware are used to illegally gain access to computer systems in order to cause disruption or to gather information. Malware is a catchall term used to describe any intrusive software. Computer viruses are now very easy to spread due to the internet and the widespread use of email. For example, viruses are often spread by attaching the virus to a (seemingly) harmless link or attachment in an email. It is only when the link or attachment is opened that the virus infects the computer.

Another common form of malware is called a Trojan Horse. This is a piece of malicious software that runs on a computer without the computer user realising it is even there.

2.4 Denial-of-Service (DoS) attacks

DoS attacks aim to make a computer or network unavailable or unusable to end users. They are usually conducted by disrupting networks through disconnecting or slowing internet connections or by depleting network resources (such as memory or file space).

2.5 Phishing

Phishing is an attempt by criminals to persuade people to divulge personal data. Common phishing attacks involve a criminal organisation acting as a reputable company (such as a bank) and sending out emails asking for personal information. Sophisticated phishing emails will include logos of reputable companies and can often be hard to differentiate from genuine emails from reputable companies.

2.6 Computer fraud

Computer fraud involves using computers to commit fraudulent activity. In 2012, Jay Moore set up a fake shopping website called Freshshop. He used payment details from customers on this site to hack into payment systems and gain access to over 340,000 debit and credit cards. This information was sold to criminal gangs and resulted in fraudulent losses of £27 million. Using computers to commit and hide fraudulent activity in banking has already been covered in chapter 7, as highlighted by the crimes committed by Jerome Kerveil.

2.7 Cyber espionage

This is the practise of obtaining information without the permission of the owner of the information. Cyber espionage could be as simple as an employee walking past a colleague's computer that is unlocked and viewing confidential files. On a wider scale, cyber espionage could involve using a combination of hacking, malware and phishing to steal valuable company secrets.

2.8 Software piracy

This is the practise of illegally using, copying or distributing software without having the necessary permissions and licenses. Software piracy is essential theft, as it is using intellectual property without permission.

2.9 Pharming

Pharming involves redirecting website traffic to a bogus website. If an end-user is redirected to a bogus website, they may be asked for personal details such as credit card information, which is then used to commit identity theft.

3 Risks to individuals, companies and countries

When considering the risks of cyber crimes it is useful to use a top-down approach, from countries through to companies and then individuals. This is because threats to a country are likely to trickle down and also effect companies and individuals. Take for example a DoS attack on the UK electricity grid. If there was an extended power outage, the majority of companies would have to cease trading and most individuals would be unable to work. The effects would be far reaching.

3.1 Risks to countries

QUICK QUESTION

What are some of the key risks that governments must consider with regards to cyber attacks?

Write your answer here before reading on.

- **Disruption to utilities** – Water, power and heating are readily available and sometimes taken for granted in many countries. In 2013 alone, there were 256 cyber attacks on US energy utilities (Source: Reuters, 20 May 2014). If a cyber attack can disrupt or shut down a utility, it causes widespread panic and disruption – just imagine not being able to heat your home for two weeks during the winter. This makes utilities a prime target for criminals and terrorists.
- **Infiltration of the financial system** – In many ways an attack on a country's financial system is similar to an attack on a utility. The UK's money transmission and payment system is heavily reliant on computers – therefore any cyber-related disruption could bring everyone to a halt, with nobody being able to withdraw money, make payments or receive their wages. Worst still, a cyber attack on one country's financial system could cause a global meltdown: Suppose that hackers manage to fraudulently cause the price of US Government bonds to crash. This could result in a global sell off of securities around the world and a financial crash, all induced by cyber crime.
- **Theft of government secrets** – The amount of sensitive data that a government holds is incredible, ranging from social security and tax records through to national security information, such as the location of weapons and military personnel.
- **Cyber war** – As with many other areas of cyber crime, the techniques used are based on old methods. If two countries were at war, they would try and attack key areas of infrastructure, such as utilities, food supplies and industry to weaken their enemy. In bygone years, this would have been achieved through physical force. However, the same outcomes can now be achieved via computers.

3.2 Risks to companies

McAfee break the risks of cyber crime to companies into six distinct areas:

- **The loss of intellectual property and business confidential information** – Information is a valuable asset for a company. Consider the online retailer Amazon, who have invested heavily in proprietary algorithm to minimise the cost of inventory management. These algorithms would be of great value to competitors. Likewise banks have designed their own credit scoring models.Similarly, a company's strategy and business plans could be stolen by hackers and held to ransom to stop them being leaked.

- **Cyber crime related monetary losses** – The scope of corporate losses from cyber crime are broad. Imagine if a hacker managed to steal money from the bank accounts of 200 customers. The bank will lose money by having to reimburse the customers for the money that has been stolen. The bank will then have to pay to investigate how the hacker managed to breach their security measures. Worse still, the customers who were affected by the crime could sue the bank (a Yahoo email user sued a web portal company for negligence when his username and password were stolen by a hacker).
- **The loss of sensitive business information, including possible stock market manipulation** – A growing area in cyber crime relates to mergers and acquisitions: Hackers target banks, lawyers and accountants in order to steal information relating to potential merger and acquisition deals. The hackers can then use this information to make trades based on this restricted information.
- **Opportunity costs, including service and employment disruptions, and reduced trust for online activities** – All of the money spent by a company on mitigating cyber crime is money that could be invested elsewhere to increase profits – by developing new products or improving efficiency. Therefore the cost of cyber crime is high. By the same token, a cyber attack could leave a company unable to operate for a certain amount of time. This would again hit the bottom line and the company and cause reputational damage (as discussed below).
- **The additional cost of securing networks, insurance, and recovery from cyber attacks** – To mitigate the high risks relating to cyber crime, companies must incur significant costs. Section 4 of this chapter covers the mitigation methods available, which all add additional layers of cost to a company. As the level and sophistication of cyber crime increases, the costs will also increase as companies invest to stay one step ahead of the criminals.
- **Reputational damage** – Cyber crime can have a devastating effect on a company's reputation. In a survey conducted by IBM, 61% of the companies surveyed said that cybercrime was the greatest IT – related threat to their reputation (Source: *Reputational Risk and IT: IBM Global Technology Services Research Report 2012*). If a company's website or customer electronic interfaces (such as online payment systems) are compromised by cyber crime this can result in losing customers. This helps to explain why some corporate cyber crimes are not reported in the media – companies are very sensitive to the detrimental reputational effects of cyber crime that they are loathed to let the public know about them.

(Source: *MacAfee: The economic impact of cybercrime and cyber espionage, July 2013*)

3.3 Risks to individuals

- **Liability and compensation claims** – Electronic communication carries high risk. Incorrect, misleading or illegal statements can lead to an individual being sued for compensation and reputational damage. Therefore an individual could be sued for damages even though they were not responsible for the electronic compensation – the communication could have been posted on their website by a zombie computer or emailed from their email account by malware.

QUICK QUESTION

What are some of the adverse that an individual would suffer if someone was able to steal their identity?

Write your answer here before reading on.

- **Identity theft**

  The risks of identity theft are far reaching for an individual. If someone was able to gain access to an individual's name, address, national insurance and date of birth, they could potentially:

  - steal money from the bank accounts of the victim
  - open new lines of credit and spend money under the name of the victim
  - gain access to social security benefits, such as medical care and unemployment benefit
  - provide an alias if arrested by the authorities
  - gain employment and falsify tax returns using the identity of the victim.

  If the identity thief managed to achieve any of the above outcomes it would cause significant disruption and stress to the victim. It would be necessary for the victim to freeze all of their bank accounts while the authorities conducted their investigation. Likewise, if money were stolen from the victim it would take time for the bank to investigate the theft before the money could be reimbursed.

- **Physical loss of technology** – Increasing numbers of individuals are using technology as part of their working lives, such as using remote computer access to work from home. Entrepreneurs are likely to have key technology that they use to run their businesses, such as websites and customer databases. Therefore if technology is disrupted by cyber crime individuals will not be able to carry out their work and daily routines.

4 Guidance

The increasing threat of cyber crime has induced governments, companies and industry bodies to consider frameworks that will help to combat cyber crime. CPNI and GCHQ offer best practise guidance for companies in general, whereas CBEST is a banking specific framework.

4.1 CPNI guidance

The Centre for the Protection of National Infrastructure (CPNI) suggest a series of key controls that will enable an organisation to defend themselves against the latest and most common cyber attacks (Source: CPNI website):

- maintaining an inventory of authorised and unauthorised software and devices
- ensuring secure configurations for hardware and software on all networks and devices
- continuous vulnerability assessment and remediation
- malware and virus defences
- data recovery capability
- controlled use of administrative privileges
- maintaining, monitoring and analysis of audit logs
- incident response and management
- secure network engineering.

4.2 GCHQ guidance

GCHQ (Government Communication Headquarters) is a British organisation. They have published research that suggests that basic risk management can prevent up to 80% of cyber attacks. They suggest that companies need to consider ten steps in order to improve their cyber security: (Source: *10 Steps to Cyber Security, CESG 2012)*.

- **Home and mobile working policy** – develop a policy and train staff to adhere to it.
- **User education and awareness** – maintain user awareness of cyber risks and establish a staff training programme.
- **Incident management** – establish an incident response and disaster recovery capability.
- **Information risk management regime** – establish the company's risk appetite and engage the board over cyber risk in order to establish an effective governance procedure.

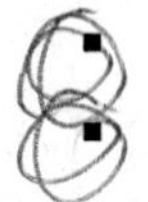

- **Manage user privileges** – limit user privileges and monitor user activity.

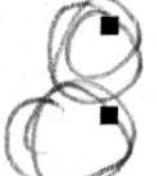

- **Removable media controls** – produce a policy to control all access to removable media.

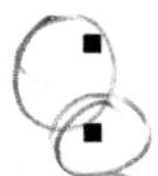

- **Monitoring** – establish a monitoring strategy and produce supporting policies.
- **Secure configuration** – ensure the secure configuration of all systems.
- **Malware protection** – establish anti-malware defences that are relevant to all business areas.
- **Network security** – monitor and test security controls.

4.3 CBEST

CBEST is a framework spearheaded by the Bank of England to protect the UK financial system form cyber attacks. The framework is designed to improve UK financial services firms' resilience to cyber attacks. CBEST will test cyber defences by using advanced cyber attacking techniques to see if they breach the target firms defences. The outcomes of these tests will identify any improvements that need to be made with regards to people, processes and technology. CBEST offers the following guidance to UK financial services firms:

- Firms should use the consistent cyber threat intelligence available to them.
- Firms should use CBEST intelligence to understand the latest cyber threats and to improve their responses to threats.
- Firms should undertake tests that mimic real cyber attacks.
- Firms should undergo a best practise cyber test audit.
- Firms should sign up to a code of conduct.

5 Methods of attack

The methods used by cyber criminals to achieve their objectives are dynamic and constantly evolving to overcome the latest computer security measures.

5.1 Social engineering

This method of attack involves using deception and subterfuge to gain information from people. This information is then used to work out passwords that can be used to gain access to computer systems. A typical social engineering example would be someone within an organisation receiving a phone call from someone who they believe works for a trusted source (such as a supplier, a client or a vendor). The bogus caller will entice the employee to give them information that will then be used to commit a computer security breach.

5.2 Botnets and zombie computers

Botnets pose one of the biggest systematic threats to electronic and information security. A botnet is an automated program that takes unauthorised control of a computer, and the computer becomes a 'zombie computer'. Botnets infect computers using a variety of methods, such as spam and malware. The end goal of the creators of botnets is to infect as many computers as possible, in order to create a network of botnets. The botnet network can then be mobilised to commit coordinated actions.

A common use of botnets is to commit DoS attacks. A large botnet network could simultaneously access a website, with the high volume of web traffic causing the site to become so slow that it is unusable, or causing the site to crash.

5.3 IP spoofing

IP spoofing is a technique used by hackers to gain unauthorized access to computers. The hacker will send messages to a computer that are interpreted as messages coming from a trusted host (such as a trusted web server). This allows the hacker to gain access to the computer. Once the hacker has gained access, they may commit further computer crimes, such as turning the computer into a zombie computer or unleashing spam.

5.4 Spam

Nearly everyone who has used email will have experienced spam. It is unsolicited email. Some spam is harmless and is just a (sometimes irritating) sales and marketing method. However, some spam is sent with an ulterior criminal motive:

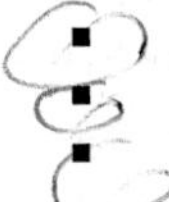

- The email infects the computer with some form of malware.
- The email redirects the computer to a website that will infect the computer with malware.
- The email redirects the computer to a website selling illegal goods or services.

5.5 Advanced persistent threats (APTs)

APTs are a sophisticated cyber espionage technique. The term gained credence due to attacks on government computer networks, such as the Stuxnet worm, which targeted the computer hardware of the Iranian government. They are dubbed advanced because they use the latest malware and hacking techniques to attack their targets. Because of their advanced nature, some APTs will go unnoticed by the target. They are also systematic and malignant in nature and attack over long periods of time, gradually working their way through the defences of their target.

6 Prevention, policy planning and governance

With so many evolving cyber threats to deal with, it is forgivable to think that trying to prevent cyber crime is ultimately futile. However, there are many prevention methods available, both from a people and a technology perspective.

6.1 Prevention

Education is a key weapon in cyber crime prevention. As the ICICI Bank case study shows, some people are not aware that they are at risk from cyber crime. Harmless information such as an update of seemingly trivial information on a social networking site could result in them being a victim of cyber crime. Therefore, increasing awareness of the following basic cyber crime prevention techniques is essential in reducing cyber crime:

- choose strong, secure passwords and do not share them
- be diligent with personal information – if in doubt, do not share it
- update computer security regularly
- think carefully before opening unknown emails and accessing unknown links
- secure all networks
- protect sensitive data using encryption
- use the latest firewall and anti-virus/malware software
- remember that cyber crime could happen to you – cyber criminals prey on carelessness. For example, some Apple Mac users think that they will never contract malware or viruses because the majority of malware is aimed at Microsoft Windows. This does not mean that Apple Macs are immune from cyber crime.

In order to increase awareness, education needs to start as soon as possible. Howard Schmidt, a former Cyber Security Co-ordinator for President Obama has said:

'Those people in business need to know about financial risk, about sales risks or the international disruption of rare earth materials, perhaps, but they all need to know about cyber risks.'

(Source: *Cyber Crime & Warfare. Peter Warren & Michael Streeter, 2013*)

CASE STUDY

ICICI Bank

In 2010 ICICI Bank in India was forced to pay compensation to a customer over a phishing incident. The customer received an email from ICICI Bank asking him to provide his online banking username and password, otherwise his account would be closed down. Without realising that the email was bogus, the customer replied with the requested details. The phishers then withdraw money from the customers account.

When the customer discovered that money had been stolen from his account, he complained to ICICI Bank. However, ICICI Bank refused to reimburse the customer, as they claimed that he had negligently disclosed confidential information. Therefore the customer took the case to court where a judge ruled that ICICI Bank must compensate the customer for the stolen funds plus loss of interest and expenses.

6.2 Policy planning

Due to the increasing threats of cyber crime, companies need to have an up to date cyber security plan in place.More and more guidance on cyber security policy planning is becoming available. For example, in February 2014 the US National Institute of Standards and Technology (NIST) introduced the NIST Cyber security framework. The purpose of the framework is to provide a set of standards and best practises that enable companies to manage their cyber security risks. The Cyber security framework acts as a baseline and some companies would be expected to go beyond the steps suggested in the framework to ensure that they have robust cyber security. The framework is designed in addition to existing risk management and cyber security plans.

The framework is based around five core functions:

- **Identify** – develop the organisational understanding to manage cyber security risk to systems, assets, data and capabilities
- **Protect** – develop and implement the appropriate safeguards to ensure delivery of critical infrastructure services
- **Detect** – develop and implement the appropriate activities to identify the occurrence of a cyber security event
- **Respond** – develop and implement the appropriate activities to take action regarding a detected cyber security event
- **Recover** – develop and implement the appropriate activities to maintain plans for resilience and to restore any capabilities or services that were impaired due to a cyber security event.

  (Source: *Framework for Improving Critical Infrastructure Cybersecurity, National Institute of Standards and Technology, February 2014*)

The five core functions are designed with a company's senior management in mind. They provide a concise summary of cyber security threats and an overview of how the company is geared to deal with these risks in line with existing cyber security guidelines and best practises.

6.3 Governance

Governance of cyber security can be a difficult area for some companies. The reason for this is that some companies do not have the necessary skills and experience to provide effective cyber security governance. Risk oversight in most large organisations is the responsibility of the board. However, if the board lacks cyber crime expertise, it may be necessary to create a separate enterprise risk committee on the board to provide specialist focus on cyber security. The enterprise risk committee can report to the board on cyber risks and the resources required to mitigate these risks. The NIST Cyber framework provides the following guidance on the governance of cyber risk:

- An organisation's assessment of cyber security risk and potential risk responses considers the privacy implications of its cyber security program.
- Individuals with cyber security-related privacy responsibilities report to appropriate management and are appropriately trained.
- Process is in place to support compliance of cyber security activities with applicable privacy laws, regulations, and Constitutional requirements.
- Process is in place to assess implementation of the foregoing organisational measures and controls.

  (Source: *Framework for Improving Critical Infrastructure Cybersecurity, National Institute of Standards and Technology, February 2014*)

7 Cyber incident planning

A logical response from companies to the threat of cyber crime is to focus on prevention: building robust firewalls, using the latest anti-virus software and running scans to detect malware. However, it is important to consider what action would be taken should a cyber incident take place – that is, what plans are in place should the cyber defences be breached and a cyber crime is committed? McKinsey suggest that a **cyber incident response plan** should contain six parts (Source: *McKinsey & Company: How good is your cyber incident response plan? December 2013, by Tucker Bailey, John Brandley and James Kaplan*).

- **Incident taxonomy** – terminology used in the plan should be standardised across the organisation in line with industry standards.
- **Data-classification frameworks**– incident response categories should be based on the various types of data held by the company. For example, the response taken to the loss of intellectual property would be different to the response taken for the loss of non-material historic financial data.
- **Performance objectives** – clear response objectives should be set for each incident type and each data type. For example, a performance objective the loss of confidential customer information could be finding out how many customers have been affected within four hours.
- **Definition of response-team operating models** – this part of the plan will specify the roles and responsibilities and escalation processes in the event of a cyber incident occurring. They will tie back to the data-classification framework.
- **Identification and remediation of failure modes** – the cyber incident recovery plan must be enhanced in response to newly identified failure modes.
- **Key tools for using during incident response** – the plan will include procedural guides and guidelines for documenting the response in governance, risk, and compliance applications. Checklists will provide step-by-step instructions to specific individuals.

QUESTION TIME 2

Think about some typical cyber incidents that the bank that you work for should consider as part of a cyber incident plan.

Write your answer here then check with the answer at the back of the book.

KEY WORDS

Key words in this chapter are given below. There is space to write your own revision notes and add any other key words or phrases you want to remember.

- Cyber crime
- Identity theft
- Hacking
- Computer viruses/malware
- Denial-of-Service (DoS) attacks
- Phishing
- Computer fraud
- Cyber espionage
- Software piracy
- Pharming
- Cyber crime prevention
- Cyber policy planning
- Cyber incident planning
- Cyber governance
- Social engineering
- Botnets
- Zombie computers
- IP spoofing
- Spam
- Advanced persistent threats (APTs)

REVIEW

Now consider the main points that were introduced in this section. These are listed below. Tick each one as you go through them.

- Cyber crime is a huge threat and the adverse effects have dire consequences.
- The threats of cyber crime are varied and evolving. Cyber criminals also use a combination of cyber crime techniques to achieve their outcomes.
- The risks to a government from cyber crime include disruption to utilities, infiltration of the financial system, theft of government secrets and cyber war.
- The risks to a company from cyber crime include loss of intellectual property business confidential information, money losses, opportunity costs, security costs and reputational damage.
- The risks to an individual from cyber crime include liability and compensation claims, identity theft and physical loss of technology.
- Methods of attack used by cyber criminals include social engineering, botnets and zombie computers, IP spoofing, spam and APTs.
- Prevention of cyber crime is focuses around educating people about the risks and prevention methods available. There are also a multitude of technical prevention methods available such as firewalls, ant-virus software and encryption devices.
- Cyber crime policy planning is critical for all companies that are subjected to cyber threats.
- Cyber governance can be difficult for some companies, as they do not have the necessary expertise available.
- If a company suffers from a cyber attack they should have a detailed cyber incident plan in place.

SOLUTIONS TO QUESTION TIMES

SOLUTION TO QUESTION TIME QUESTION IN CHAPTER 1

Question Time 1

There is no specified answer to this Question Time as your response will be driven by the organisation that you work for.

SOLUTION TO QUESTION TIME QUESTION IN CHAPTER 2

Question Time 1

The answer to this question will vary depending upon your personal circumstances. However here are some examples.

Risk	Reduction measures
Injury whilst in the gym	Carry out a warm up Receive advice from qualified staff in the gym
Wrist injury whilst typing an assignment on a laptop	Buy a separate keyboard with wrist support to attach to laptop when required
Impact injury when in a car crash	Selecting a new car with more emphasis on safety features such as number and type of airbags

SOLUTIONS TO QUESTION TIME QUESTIONS IN CHAPTER 3

Question Time 1

Whilst your answers will depend upon what you have been doing today, here are some examples.

Risk	▪ The house could catch fire ▪ I could break an ankle
Certainty	▪ The stock market will fluctuate ▪ Weather events will occur
Probability	▪ It is 85% probable that I will arrive home on time ▪ It is 98% probable that my pc will operate normally
Uncertainty	▪ The weather in 10 days time ▪ The value of the FTSE in 6 months

Question Time 2

Again, the exact response you have will be driven by your personal circumstances, but here is an example for your guidance:

What can go wrong?	How frequently does it happen?	What are the consequence?
My car does not start	Once every two years	Missed train leading to missed meeting and lost business for my bank
The train is delayed by more than 15 minutes	Once a week	Reprimand from manager re timekeeping Need to work part of my lunch break to make up time

Question Time 3

The advantages of ranking are:

- It provides a simple, powerful method for viewing the range of risks the business faces.
- It provides an evaluation of the effectiveness of the control environment.
- It focuses management's attention on the most important risks.
- It can be used with minimal hard data so if historical data is not available, useful subjective measurement can still be performed.
- It can capture a wide range of risk possibilities – from large, strategic risks to everyday, more detailed issues. For this reason it can be effective at all levels of an organisation.

- It can be used to anticipate loss by ranking the potential risks of new situations. This means it is forward looking as well as backward looking.
- It encourages a risk-aware culture and a more transparent risk environment.

The disadvantage of ranking is:

- It is subjective, and may present an over-simplified view. All subjective assessments should be validated by quantitative assessment also by using real loss data and also the input of an independent party, such as internal audit.

SOLUTION TO QUESTION TIME QUESTION IN CHAPTER 4

Question Time 1

A preventative control, as the name would imply, is a control which is designed to prevent the event from ever happening. An example would be the operation of dual control procedures when counting the contents of a night safe wallet in a bank branch. A detective control should find an error after the event – for example if you check your bank statement online and compare this to your own record of transactions passing through your personal account, then this is an example of a detective control. In this situation, should you have made a mistake in recording the transactions in your own records, then this will come to light during the reconciliation process. Detective controls are split into internal and external. An internal control aims to find the error before it comes to light in the outside world. An external control is one where we detect errors and losses once they have become known outside of the organisation.

SOLUTIONS TO QUESTION TIME QUESTIONS IN CHAPTER 5

Question Time 1

Effective risk reporting brings a number of benefits; the key ones can be summarised as:

- Raising awareness of risk issues across the organisation. This is achieved by ensuring that all relevant parties are provided with the reports and that the reports provide a comprehensive and consistent picture of the organisational risk profile using a common and acceptable risk language.
- Understanding the risk profile across the business. This suggests a consistent means of sizing or measuring risk.
- Ensuring that resources can be allocated to address areas where the risk profile is considered too high. In this context we mean that there is an understanding of risk tolerance or appetite that provides insight into where the operational risks under consideration are acceptable or not and that the reporting structure explicitly recognises this.
- Influencing product pricing by ensuring that it reflects both the reward profile and the risk profile. This suggests that risk assessment and mitigation should be fully considered for all products and reported as part of the product sign-off process.
- Meeting external expectations (shareholders, regulators, etc.) as to the quality of risk management and governance.

- Reporting that includes for example Key Risk Indicator data or consider impending changes (internal or external) will help ensure that management can take preventative measures where the data suggests a potential problem will arise if no action is taken.

Question Time 2

Identification

The first stage in the risk management lifecycle is Identification. It is the means by which an organisation identifies potential threats to the achievement of business objectives by considering what can happen, why it might happen and how it happens. It is fundamental to successful risk identification that the process is undertaken by reference to business objectives – this ensures that the exercise focuses on the key themes. Risk identification must be undertaken on a regular basis to ensure that the focus of risk management activity is targeted at those risks relevant to the organisation. As such, each subsequent stage in the Lifecycle is dependent on the accurate identification of risk.

Risk identification should provide a means of drawing out the broad impacts, both financial and non-financial of the risks identified. This will allow for the early prioritisation of activity.

There are a number of tools that may be employed, ranging from workshops involving those with detailed knowledge of the business and the threats arising to structured techniques including SWOT analysis.

The main benefits of risk identification are:

- It helps reduce surprises by drawing out possible risk exposures
- It can highlight risk concentrations and/ or dependencies
- It provides a basis for more informed decision making
- It tends to build business ownership through participation
- It helps target subsequent risk management activity.

Assessment

Assessment is the process by which previously identified risks are subjected to a structured means of considering their materiality and likelihood. The key elements in risk assessment are:

- The categorisation of risks identified
- Consideration of the causes that lie behind the risks
- Consideration of the nature of the event(s) that may arise should the risk occur
- Consideration of the controls currently in place
- An assessment as the both the probability of the risk occurring and the impact(s) should it do so.
- Logging the output in a risk register or database.

The categorisation process will establish a consistent basis for further analysis, including for the risk profile of activities that span multiple business lines. The assessment of probability and impact is fundamental to informing discussions on risk management priorities and mitigation strategies. This analysis will also help inform decisions on the cost/benefit profile of mitigation options.

The main benefits of risk assessment are:

- It develops a clear understanding of the cause, impact and event profile of risks identified
- It creates that basis for informed decisions as to appropriate risk mitigation approaches
- It creates the basis for setting risk appetite
- It creates a repeatable process so enabling changes in risk profile to be tracked over time
- It assists the in the identification of the most appropriate individual/ business to address issues highlighted.

Mitigation

Mitigation is the process by which the organisation puts in place measures to bring its risk down to an acceptable level. This level is generally referred to as risk tolerance or risk appetite.

There are basic methods of risk mitigation:

Risk avoidance: Avoiding the source of risk altogether for example by exiting the business that generates the risk.

Risk sharing: Reducing the risk by sharing it with a third party, for example through a joint venture.

Risk transfer: Transferring the risk to a third partying exchange for a fee, the most familiar example if which is insurance.

Risk acceptance: Recognising that due to the probability and/ or impact it is worth running the risk and not putting in place specific mitigation. This is likely to arise for very low probability risks where the cost of mitigation is not justified.

The implementation of controls is one of the most widespread risk mitigation techniques. Controls can be applied to:

(a) reduce the likelihood of the event occurring in the first place, such as access controls to prevent unauthorised entry to systems; or

(b) to reduce the severity of the event such as sprinkler systems to limit the spread of a fire once it starts.

The benefits of risk mitigation are:

- It reduces the overall level of risk run by the organisation
- The consideration of risk appetite drives a more objective debate as to which risks should be addressed and in which order
- It targets resources at risks by reference to their likelihood and severity, so ensuring best value.

Risk Monitoring

Risk monitoring refers to the process by which changes in the risk profile are tracked. Having tracked change sit is a natural step to report them to appropriate parties – for this reason monitoring and reporting tend to be seen as one overall stage in the risk lifecycle. The specifics of what is tracked will depend on the nature of the business profile but at the minimum are likely to include changes in the level of gross risk, changes in the level of residual risk, changes in the effectiveness of the control environment, losses over the period and a summary of emerging issues.

The main benefits of risk monitoring and reporting are:

- It raises the awareness of risk issues across the organisation
- It improves the understanding of the changing nature of business risk profiles
- It can help prevent losses through the early reporting of deteriorating positions
- It provides a means of engaging business executive attention.

SOLUTIONS TO QUESTION TIME QUESTIONS IN CHAPTER 6

Question Time 1

There are a number of reasons why a bank would want to issue a credit policy. These are:

- It gives a consistency of approach to credit throughout the organisation. As banks have grown over the years, it has become more important to have this consistency. Therefore the customer will not encounter a different approach from different parts of the organisation – this lack of uniformity would prove confusing for customers and would undermine their confidence in the organisation as a whole.
- It improves customer service. If the bank has a consistent approach to its credit, this means that customers will not receive mixed messages either from different parts of the bank, or from different individuals within the same organisation.
- Lending managers know clearly what the parameters of their lending authority are – this applies to both the amounts they are authorised to lend and also the conditions that attach to this lending – for example the amounts a credit manager may lend can be driven by the quality and quantity of security offered by the customer.
- The policy helps to position the governance of credit in the bank and will explain how the credit function of the bank will be structured. For example, what credit may be sanctioned by local management, what credit is sanctioned centrally and so on.
- It allows a Credit Risk Committee through the Credit Policy to determine and communicate the credit risk appetite of the organisation.
- A credit policy can determine what credit products will be offered by the bank, what is included in these products and what qualifying criteria customers must satisfy in order to access these products.
- Finally the credit policy will specify how the portfolios of credit managers within the organisation will be monitored.

Question Time 2

Prior to the introduction of automated credit scoring techniques, most bank branches has a lending manager employed on the premises – this person was called the Branch Manager and, in addition to their credit duties, they had overall responsibility for the branch. If a customer (business or personal) wished to apply for credit, then normally they would be interviewed by this Branch Manager. Depending upon the amount of credit requested, it may have been permissible for the manager to sanction the loan personally, or it may have had to be referred to either a regional or centralised credit department within the bank. Much of the administration of the branch would be overseen by an Office Manager and team of supervisors.

Once credit scoring was introduced, the need for these Branch Managers disappeared. Credit could be assessed by a more junior member of staff as they would input the customer's details into the system and receive a sanction/decline decision that could be communicated to the customer.

As a result, the Office Manager was now in a position to run the branch and the traditional Branch Managers would have exited the organisation.

The introduction of direct banking (Internet Banking and Contact Centres) further reduced the need for customers to deal with their local branch and further reduced the amount of staff employed in branches.

Question Time 3

No matter who the customer is, the checks should be similar, including:

- A careful review of the borrower's financial position - their cash flow commitments and past financial statements.
- A detailed consideration of the customer's earnings, profit margin, profit forecast and the schedule of outstanding debt.
- Analysis of industry standards including the economic circumstances, interest rates, competition, product cycles and general economic growth (or the reverse).
- Setting some controls and limits as to the terms or conditions of the loan. These will include limiting the amount of the loan, establishing by when the loan must be repaid and the frequency of repayments together with the interest rate at which it will be repaid. This might be straight or it might have some variety to it.
- Establishing a collateral requirement for the loan itself. Clearly this will be more likely to be required in the event of larger loans.

Question Time 4

Whilst we can't be too specific about these as they may vary from time to time, we can have a look at some commonly encountered items of security and their indicative discount rates:

Cash deposit

Normally, the bank would take 100% of the value of the cash deposit that has been pledged as security. This is because the value of this security will not decrease as the funds will be placed in a separate account. In addition, it is normal to expect the value to increase over time as interest is earned on the deposit and added to it.

Guarantee

This may be valued at 100% – but this will be determined by whether or not the guarantee is supported or unsupported. A supported guarantee is one where the guarantor provides additional security which is looked at only in the event that the guarantor is not able to fulfil their guarantee obligation if called upon. The extent to which this supporting security can be looked to is limited to the amount covered by the guarantee.

Residential property

Normally residential property is taken at around 80% of the market value. This will allow for a potential drop in the value of the housing market.

There will be additional items to think about if the bank only holds a second charge against a property. This is the situation where the customer has granted security over their property to their mortgage provider in the first instance and then grants your bank a subsequent security over their property in support of an advance. For example, the customer may have a residential property valued at £150,000, and have granted this property in security to the Midshires Building Society for their mortgage – let's say the outstanding mortgage is £50,000. We could calculate the value of the second security thus:

Value of property	£150,000
Less Discount – 80%	120,000
Outstanding Mortgage	50,000
Security Value	£70,000

Therefore, for security purposes, this property is valued by the second security holder at £70,000.

Irrevocable mandate

This is a security that we would normally encounter when dealing with bridging finance. Bridging finance can be either open ended or closed ended. This distinction will affect the security discount factor.

Normally for closed bridging, the full value of the security is taken, but for open bridging a reduced figure in the region of only 80% of the value of the security is usually taken. The reason for the difference is that open bridging is a riskier proposition as we do not have a firm settlement date for the sale of the customer's existing property – hence the more conservative view.

Life assurance policy

Around 75% of the value of the policy is taken for security purposes. This will cover any potential shortfall in the value of the policy.

Gilts

Gilts, or government securities, are a less risky form of investment than shares as they are issued by the government to support their medium to longer term borrowing requirements. They therefore carry little risk. Additionally, as the price of gilts tends to be much more stable than shares banks will place a less conservative discount value against them. Hence a discount factor of around 75% is normally applied here.

Shares

There are a number of different types of share that can be offered as security. These are split into:

- Alternative Investment Market (AIM) shares
- FTSE shares
- Unquoted shares.

These are given varying discount values primarily due to the marketability of the investment type and the volatility of the market in which the investments are ultimately traded. The figures we should be considering here are:

- AIM shares – generally we look to take around 25% of the value of these shares.
- FTSE shares – generally we look to around 50% of the value of these shares.
- Unquoted shares – generally no value is placed on these shares due to their very limited marketability.

SOLUTIONS TO QUESTION TIME QUESTIONS IN CHAPTER 7

Question Time 1

Liquid assets would include:

- Listed shares
- Government securities
- The second hand endowment market
- The second hand car market for relatively new cars in good condition.

Illiquid assets include:

- Property
- Specialised antiques and paintings.

Question Time 2

These scenarios might include such things as:

- What if our largest counterparty cannot pay or deliver?
- What if we lose funds from capital markets counterparties during flights to quality?
- What if the number of payments we are due to receive exceeds a normal day's typical level by a factor of 10?

- What happens if we experience reduced access to funds from all sources during credit crunches?
- What happens if our bank's systems fail to operate?
- What if our borrowing facility with our principal bank breaches its limit?
- What if our principal bank becomes bankrupt?
- What happens with respect to our collateral if the third-party custodian holding that collateral goes into liquidation?

In theory, of course, the list of possible scenarios is endless and it can readily be seen from the suggestions listed above how these overlap into other types of risk – credit, market and operational.

Question Time 3

The precise answer to this question will vary according to your circumstances and assets available. However, here is a possible order:

- How much cash do you have in savings accounts that you could use?
- Do you have any shares that you could sell?
- Could you approach a lender to borrow the money?
- Do you have any unencumbered assets you could sell quickly – such as your car?
- Do you have a life policy that you could surrender or sell?
- Whilst it is unlikely in this scenario, the final option would be to sell your house!

Question Time 4

Well known Black Swan events include:

- Hurricane Katrina
- The attack on the Twin Towers in 2001
- The BP Gulf oil spill
- The 2007 banking crisis.

Question Time 5

If the stock is priced at £115, then the return is:

10.5/115 x 100 = 9.13%

If the stock is priced at £103, then the return is:

10.5/103 x 100 = 10.19%

Question Time 6

The table below gives a broad indication of where various investments can be placed in a spectrum of overall investment risk.

NEGLIGIBLE RISK	NS&I deposit products Gilts (income) Gilts (redemption)
LOW RISK	Bank deposits Building society deposits Cash ISAs Annuities
LOW / MEDIUM RISK	Gilts (pre-redemtion capital) With-profits funds
MEDIUM RISK	Unit-linked managed funds Unit trusts and OEICs/ICVCs (UK funds) Investment trusts (UK) Residential and commercial property
MEDIUM / HIGH RISK	Unit-linked overseas funds Unit trusts and OEICs/ICVCs (overseas funds) UK single equities Commodities
HIGH RISK	Venture Capital Trusts Unlisted shares Warrants Futures and Options when used to speculate Enterprise Investment Scheme Enterprise Zone Property

Question Time 7

Again, the answer that you have here will be determined by the nature of the firm that you work for. It may be that you are employed in a small mutual organisation that perhaps have a senior manager who is responsible for internal audit, operational risk and all of the legal matters pertaining to the firm. If this is the case, then the firm will no doubt have a close working relationship with solicitors.

On the other hand, if you work for a large firm, the likelihood is that there will be an internal legal department in the organisation that manages all of the internal and external legal work of the firm. Probably the staff in this department are qualified solicitors as well as staff from within the organisation. However, it would also be expected that close links have been forged with external legal firms.

SOLUTIONS TO QUESTION TIME QUESTIONS IN CHAPTER 8

Question Time 1

Age 18 – 21: Low value

Age 50 – 60: High value

Living with parents: Low value

Living in rented property: Moderate value

Home owner: High value

Less than 2 years at this address: Low value

More than 10 years at this address: High Value

No credit searches in past 3 months: High value

4 credit searches in past 3 months: Low value

1 credit search in past 3 months: Moderate value

Has landline phone: High value

Less than 2 years in current employment: Low value

2 – 5 years in current employment: Moderate value

More than 5 years in current employment: High value

Question Time 2

There is a wealth of information that is available to you in this situation.

The accessibility of this information will vary from bank to bank depending on how their databases are organised. If for example, information is stored around the customer, then retrieving it will be straightforward – usually some form of customer identifier will need to be input to the system and all of the relevant information becomes available. On the other hand, if the information is organised around different products of the bank, then this task will take more time.

However, the following sources should be used:

- The customer's account – looking at the run of the account will yield valuable information regarding the types of transactions going through the account, the frequency and source of lodgements to the account, whether or not the account operates either in credit or within any agreed overdraft facility.
- Standing order and direct debit information – this will tell you about the customer's regular financial commitments, the amount of these commitments, who the beneficiaries are, when they are due to expire. Standing orders and direct debits can also let you know if the customer has any life assurance policies, who their mortgage is with, what other loans they have, etc.
- Evidence of regular savings.
- Use of other areas within the bank – does the customer use specialist departments (perhaps for investment purposes), or do they maintain accounts in other branches of the bank. In order to get a full picture of the customer's affairs, you would be looking to access this information.

- Safe custody records – if the customer has deposited items with you for safe keeping, then this will give you more background information about their assets.
- Lending files – if the customer has borrowed from you in the past, the details and documentation will be recorded in a lending file. Reading through this will give you valuable information about past dealings with the customer, and will also let you know if this customer has honoured previous agreements with your bank.
- Customer profiles – most banks will maintain some form of standard customer profile document. This will have personal information about the customer, what their financial goals are, what products they have been offered in the past, the products they have taken and those they have decided not to take.

Question Time 3

You should state that viability covers a number of factors. These include:

Amount	Is the customer asking for the right amount of funding? Not too much and not too little? Is there documentary evidence available to show that the customer is borrowing the correct amount?
Purpose	Is the customer borrowing for a purpose that the bank is happy to support? Does the purpose fit in with the bank's Credit Policy?
Term	Is the customer taking the borrowing over a term that that makes the borrowing affordable? If borrowing is to finance the purchase of an asset, will the facility be fully repaid during the useful life of the asset?
Customer's stake	Is the customer showing their commitment to the project by making a contribution from their own resources?
Repayment	Can the customer afford the required repayments? Do you have evidence to back this up – for example, income and expenditure statements, cash flow projections, salary slips, etc.?
Past record	If the customer has borrowed from us previously, what was their repayment record? Did the customer keep all of the conditions/obligations they made to us when the facility was agreed?

SOLUTIONS TO QUESTION TIME QUESTIONS IN CHAPTER 9

Question Time 1

Risk Area	Example
Economic	The banks' reduced appetite to lend to business as a result of the banking crisis.
Political	A UK company operating in Greece when the Eurozone crisis hit.
Competitive environment	The original High Street coffee shop in the UK was the Seattle Coffee Company, who faced huge amounts of competition when other chains moved into the market.
Social and market forces	The increased demands by consumers for cars with low emissions and economic fuel consumption.
Technological	The ability of bank customers to manage their accounts online and through the use of mobile technology.
Shocks and natural events	The effects on businesses of the earthquake of 2011 in Japan.
External stakeholders	The louder voice of shareholders regarding the level of bonuses paid to senior employees can change the culture of an organisation.
Third parties	The external provision of specialist services by third party providers (for example, payroll) can affect the level of service received by employees and this impacts on customer service.

Question Time 2

Actions – only events that actually happen make any difference.

Contribute – risk management is part of a business. The business lines and risk management expertise must operate in parallel and together.

Likelihood – if there is no uncertainty, risk management will have no meaning.

Achieving – the essence is to achieve stability.

Surpassing – this means outperformance and a commitment to continuing improvement.

Planned – plans are not always realistic but the scope of ambition drives the nature of the actions required.

Objectives – without clarity of objectives action is ultimately meaningless.

Timescale – because risk means uncertainty it is essential to operate within a defined timescale.

Question Time 3

New Product Risk Assessment – Packaged Account

Risk Category	Risk	Mitigating Control(s)
People	Inadequate staff allocated to supporting the product	Undertake resourcing assessment and recruit staff pre-launch. Ongoing assessment of volumes and resourcing requirements to be undertaken.
	Insufficient training for staff selling the product	Undertake pre-launch staff skills assessment and implement training programme pre-launch. Repeat training regularly once in place.
	Staff fraud	Employment screening checks undertaken. Segregation of duties enforced with rigorous checking of all payments. All transactions subject to audit trails. Regular process audits undertaken.
Process	Misdirected marketing effort targets customers who do not meet product profile	Engage Marketing function to identify target market segments(s). Review and check all marketing schedules and customer selection criteria prior to distribution.
	Procedural failures including co-ordination of service delivery by 3rd party suppliers	Business continuity plans developed and regularly tested. Seek verification of supplier BC arrangements.
	Predicted product sales targets not achieved	Undertake robust market analysis. Ensure product pricing strategy competitive. Design resourcing model so that staff brought on as volumes grow rather than heavily staff up in anticipation.
	Actual sales figures outstrip ability to support effective delivery	Undertake robust market analysis. Agree full resourcing budget requirements in advance and have fast track recruitment process in place including use of secondees for short term cover.
Systems	Systems failure	Disaster recovery plans implemented and regularly tested.
	Loss/ theft/ virus results in loss of customer data	Information security protocols implemented including password protection, system firewalls, data encryption.
	Systems designed to support new product does not deliver required functionality	IT function to be involved in design process. New system subject to rigorous pre-launch testing.

Risk Category	Risk	Mitigating Control(s)
External	Supplier failure	Apply business continuity plans including identification of alternative suppliers. Service Level Agreements introduced to monitor customer performance.
	Competitors launch equivalent product	Undertake ongoing market analysis and plan for product review and refinement over time.

Question Time 4

There are a number of possible reasons for this increased prominence, for example:

- Increased terrorist threats
- Regulatory requirements
- Reputational risk
- Financial loss if no plan in place
- Increasingly complex business arrangements.

Question Time 5

- A ban on all employees taking calls when driving – preventative
- An insistence that employees use handrails when climbing or descending stairs – preventative
- Searching for a cash difference – corrective
- Balancing a cash till – detective
- A flow chart detailing how to open a money transmission account – directive.

Question Time 6

Your answer will vary depending on where you work, but could include:

First line – cash handling procedures, branch door drills, fire alarm and evacuation testing.

Second line – the Operational Risk Department, the Compliance Function of the bank, the work of the Money Laundering Reporting Officer.

Third line – Audit Committee, the work of the internal audit department.

SOLUTIONS TO QUESTION TIME QUESTIONS IN CHAPTER 10

Question Time 1

There is no prescribed solution to this Question Time.

Question Time 2

The main role and responsibilities of the audit committee should be set out in written terms of reference and should include:

- To monitor the integrity of the financial statements of the company and any formal announcements relating to the company's financial performance, reviewing significant financial reporting judgements contained in them.

- To review the company's internal financial controls and, unless expressly addressed by a separate Board Risk Committee composed of independent directors, or by the board itself, to review the company's internal control and risk management systems.
- To monitor and review the effectiveness of the company's internal audit function.
- To make recommendations to the Board, for it to put to the shareholders for their approval in general meeting, in relation to the appointment, re-appointment and removal of the external auditor and to approve the remuneration and terms of engagement of the external auditor.
- To review and monitor the external auditor's independence and objectivity and the effectiveness of the audit process, taking into consideration relevant UK professional and regulatory requirements.
- To develop and implement policy on the engagement of the external auditor to supply non-audit services, taking into account relevant ethical guidance regarding the provision of non-audit services by the external audit firm; and to report to the board, identifying any matters in respect of which it considers that action or improvement is needed and making recommendations as to the steps to be taken.

Question Time 3

Due diligence exercises may be applied in so many scenarios; examples include:

- Corporate takeovers
- Appointment of strategic suppliers
- Hiring executives
- Regulatory reviews
- Undertaking business contracts
- Acquiring new technology
- Commencement of a joint venture with another firm
- Reviewing legal agreements
- Environmental assessments
- Information security
- Money laundering
- Intellectual property
- Financial stability of banks, new clients or counterparties
- Investment decisions.

SOLUTION TO QUESTION TIME QUESTION IN CHAPTER 11

Question Time 1

Due to the nature of this question, there is no prescribed solution. If you work in BRS or LBG, then you have been affected greatly both internally and externally by the crisis. On the other hand, you could be working for a firm which, whilst it was not greatly affected internally by the crisis – such as National Australia Group – the business will still have faced many challenges caused by the effect of the crisis on the financial sector and the domestic and global economy.

SOLUTION TO QUESTION TIME QUESTIONS IN CHAPTER 12

Question Time 1

There is no definitive answer to this question as it depends on the nature of your job, but some points to consider include:

(a) Electronic devices that you may have used include smart phones, telephones, tablets, laptops, and computers.

(b) Smart phones are reliant on mobile networks and wireless networks. These networks may not necessarily be secure and information from the smartphone could have been stolen.

An information security risk relating to telephones is that we do not know for sure who we are talking to. Criminals can pose as anyone on the phone and use this method to gain sensitive information from unknowing recipients.

Tablets, laptops and computers are carry similar information security risks. They are vulnerable to computer viruses, malware and various other risks that hackers use to steal information. Any information that these devices send or receive carries a risk as it could be bogus.

Question Time 2

Due to the nature of this question, there is no prescribed solution. Here are some cyber incidents that are relevant to banks:

Investment banks: Business sensitive information relating to a client has been stolen.

Retail banks: Money has been stolen from client accounts due to pharming.

All banks: The corporate website is unavailable due to a DoS attack.

All banks: Spam has caused the internal computer network to be infected with malware, making some computer applications unusable.

Clearing banks: Cyber espionage has allowed hackers to gain the bank account details and passwords of customers.

Credit unions: An APT has managed to disable the payment system of the bank, preventing customers from being able to send and receive money.

Retail banks: Malware has stolen the proprietary credit scoring model.

GLOSSARY

Glossary

Alternative investments	Non-standard investments such as antiques, paintings, vintage cars, etc.
APT	Advanced Persistent Threat. Persistent attacks on computers using the latest malware techniques.
Asset liability management	The procedure put in place by a bank to manage the risk of a mismatch between assets and liabilities due to either liquidity problems or changes in interest rates.
Asset liquidity risk	The risk that an asset cannot be sold due to a lack of liquidity in its market.
Audit Committee	The committee that reviews financial reporting as well as appointing and overviewing the work of the external auditors.
Basis risk	The risk of differences between the current price and the future or forward price.
Bond risk	The risk of the yield on a bond changing over its life. This can be brought about by economic prospects, government policy and interest rate movements.
Botnet	An automated program that takes unauthorised control of a computer, turning the computer into a zombie computer.
Bottom up analysis	An analysis of the risks that occur across the organisation to identify that risks faced by departments and the firm as a whole.
Boundary risk	Where different risk areas overlap.
Business continuity plan	The plans put in place to allow an organisation to recover after a major incident.
Business risk	The risk that a business is no longer able to provide a return for its owners.
Capital risk	The risk that a bank does not have enough capital resources to ensure that it can meet the minimum regulatory capital requirements set out by the bank's regulator(s). It can also refer to the risk of a capital loss on shares.
Cause	An activity or action that creates a risk event.
Central counterparty	An institution in one or more markets that sits between two trading parties and guarantees the performance of both, matching sellers to buyers and vice versa.
Change risk	The risk of losses or misfortunes arising as a result of change initiatives.
Collateral	Assets that are pledged as security for an advance.
Commodity risk	The risk of changes in supply/demand in the commodity markets which will alter force prices.
Computer fraud	Using computers to commit fraudulent activity
Computer virus/malware	Computer code used to gain illegal access to computer systems.

Concentration risk	The spread of a bank's lending over the number of borrowing customers.
Control risk	The threat that errors or irregularities in underlying transactions will not be prevented, detected and corrected by the internal control systems.
Corporate governance	The relationship between the Board and stakeholders, through which objectives are set and monitored.
Corrective controls	Controls that occur after an event has taken place and seek to mitigate the effect of an event through corrective action.
Counterparty risk	Another name for credit risk.
CPNI	The Centre for the Protection of National Infrastructure.
Credit event	A default event.
Credit exposure	Another name for credit risk.
Credit limit	The ceiling on the amount that a lender is willing to advance to an individual or organisation.
Credit policy	The document in a bank that will inform and standardise credit decisions throughout the business.
Credit ratings	An assessment of the creditworthiness of an individual, organisation or country.
Credit ratings agency	An organisation that assigns credit ratings borrowers and debt instruments.
Credit risk	The risk of a borrower not repaying all or part of a loan.
Credit risk committee	The committee that the credit risk officers in most banks will report to.
Credit risk premium	The premium paid on a riskier security to cover the position should a default occur.
Credit scoring	A procedure to assess credit applications. Factors from the application receive points and a threshold is set by the bank to determine whether or not the loan will be granted.
Currency risk	The risk presented when trading with foreign currencies that the exchange rate will move against you.
Cyber crime	Offences committed using computers, electronic devices and communication systems.
Cyber espionage	Obtaining information without the permission of the owner of the information.
Dashboard reporting	A form of high level report which presents a visual summary of key data.
Denial-of-Service (DoS) attacks	Computer attacks aimed at making computers and networks unavailable or unusable
Detective controls	Control measures that seek to find errors once they have occurred. They can be either internal (to find the errors whilst they are still within the organisation) or external (which detect errors once they have moved outside the organisation).
Directive controls	Control policies and procedures.

Disaster recovery — The process of reconnecting to systems, data, IT, etc. to allow operations to resume after a major interruption.

Distribution analysis — A statistic technique used to predict future events using historical data.

Diversification — The technique used in financial markets to spread activity and exposure in order to mitigate risk.

Due diligence — The checks made on a customer prior to granting them credit.

Earnings risk — The risk of loss arising from the interest rate gap between loans and deposits. It can also come from off-Balance Sheet exposures.

Economic capital — The amount of capital shareholders would choose to have in the absence of regulation.

Effect — The outcome of a risk event.

Equity risk — The risk of a fall in the value or return on shares.

European Banking Authority — A network of the EU and national bodies which seeks to safeguard the stability of the financial system, the transparency of markets and financial products and the protection of depositors and investors.

European Systemic Risk Board — An organisation set up by the European Commission to determine how banking supervisory arrangements could be strengthened in light of the banking crisis.

Expected loss — The loss that can be expected to arise from conducting an activity in the normal course of business.

Exposure at default — The amount of indebtedness at the time the credit goes into default.

External loss database — Information on losses experienced by other organisations.

External ratings — The use of specialised companies to assess the repayment ability of individuals and businesses.

External risk — A risk that comes from outside the organisation.

Financial Conduct Authority — The body responsible for the regulation of retail and wholesale markets in the UK.

Financial crime risk — The risk that a bank suffers losses as a result of internal and external fraud or intentional damage, as a result of financial crime.

Financial Policy Committee — The area of the Bank of England responsible for protecting the stability of the UK financial system.

Financial Reporting Council — The UK regulator responsible for promoting confidence in governance and reporting.

Financial reporting risk — The risk from a failure or inability to comply fully with the laws, regulations or Codes of Practice that govern a bank's operations.

Financial risk — The risks arising from borrowing.

Financial Services Authority — The current regulator of the UK financial services industry.

Funding liquidity risk	The risk that a bank cannot meet efficiently both expected and unexpected current and future cash flow and collateral needs without affecting either daily operations or its financial condition.
GCHQ	Government Communication Headquarters
Hacking	The activity of gaining unauthorised access to telecom systems, networks and databases.
Hedging	An activity intended to offset or mitigate the risk in a market.
Identity theft	Illegally using the identity of another person to derive benefits, such as opening new lines of credit.
Illiquid assets	Assets that are difficult to trade due to uncertainty as to their value or doubt as to the existence of a market.
Impairment	A deteriorating credit situation.
Inherent risk	The probability of loss or damage occurring as a result of the circumstances existing in an operating environment without any steps being taken to control or modify.
Insurable risk	A risk event that can be mitigating through the purchase of an insurance policy.
Insurance risk	The risk of financial loss through fluctuations in the timing, frequency and/or severity of insured events, relative to the expectations at the time of underwriting.
Interest rate risk	The risk that interest rates in the future will move against you.
Internal credit gradings	The amounts that individual sanctioning officers are permitted to lend.
Internal loss database	Information on losses suffered by your organisation.
Investment mandates	The rules under which a fund, portfolio or investment arrangement are to be conducted.
IP spoofing	A cyber crime technique used by hackers. The hacker will send a message to a computer that will be interpreted as coming from a trusted source. This allows the hacker to take control of the computer.
Judgemental scoring model	A method of credit scoring that uses the credit officer's past experience to assess the proposition, as well as the bank's own credit policies and decision tools.
Key risk indicators	A measure used to identify how risky an activity is. They indicate thresholds whose breach indicates the need for action by the firm.
Legal risk	The risk of losses or misfortune occurring as a result of failure to comply with the laws governing the bank's operations.
Liquidity risk	The risk that a bank is unable to meet its financial commitments as they fall due.
Loan to value	The amount of borrowing expressed as a percentage of the value of the asset being financed.
Loss given default	The likelihood of loss occurring on a particular exposure, expressed as a percentage of the exposure.

Manual underwriting — The assessment of a credit proposal by a credit officer as opposed to an automated credit scoring procedure.

Market liquidity risk — The risk that a bank cannot offset or eliminate a position at market price due to inadequate market depth or market disruption.

Market neutral arbitrage — A strategy to remove market risk by taking off-setting positions – often by taking different securities in the same company.

Market neutral securities hedging — A strategy of investing equally in long and short equity portfolios in the same sectors of the market.

Market risk — The risk of loss occurring as a result of movements in a market.

Market risk limits — Trading limits imposed upon dealing desks with the intention of managing the levels of risk taking.

Maturity — Either the life of a security or the final payment date of a loan or a financial instrument.

Maturity ladder — A tool used to measure future cash flows through a business arising from securities settlements.

Modelling — A system used by banks to assess credit risk. Credit scoring is an example of this.

Moral hazard — The possibility that a person's behaviour will be altered as they are protected from risk.

Netting — Setting off two or more cash flows, assets or liabilities against one another.

Normal distribution — A graph showing a range of observed outcomes in the shape of a bell curve.

Operational risk — The risk of loss resulting from inadequate or failed internal processes, people and systems or from external events.

Opportunity cost — The event that must be foregone when choosing an alternative course of action.

People risk — The risks arising from the poor management of staff.

Pharming — Redirecting website traffic to a bogus website.

Phishing — An attempt by criminals to persuade individuals to divulge personal data.

Pillar 1 — The minimum capital requirements set out under Basel II.

Pillar 2 — The supervisory review requirements set out under Basel II.

Pillar 3 — The market discipline requirements set out under Basel II.

Preventable risk — An internal risk that is avoidable.

Preventative control — A control measure that prevents the error from occurring in the first place – for example, a checking procedure.

Price level risk — The risk of prices in a market moving.

Pricing risk — The risk to the organisation of incorrect pricing either in the purchase or sale of its products and services.

Private equity	Shares in companies that are not traded on a stock exchange.
Probability of default	The likelihood that an asset (such as a loan) will go into default, expressed in percentage terms.
Property risk	The risk of adverse events in the property market.
Provisioning	Setting aside funds for future credit issues.
Prudential Regulation Authority	A subsidiary of the Bank of England that supervises deposit takers, insurers and some significant investment firms.
Quantitative easing	The central bank policy of injecting fresh funds into an economy through the purchase of securities on the market.
Ranking	The assessment of a firm's operations and activities against a menu of potential operational risk vulnerabilities.
Regulatory capital	The amount of capital a firm needs to hold as set out in the Basel Accord.
Regulatory risk	The risks associated with a banks non-compliance with the requirements of the relevant regulators.
Reputational risk	Risk arising from damage to the reputation of the organisation.
REMCO	The Remuneration Committee of a firm which develops the remuneration policy for the business.
Residual risk	The risk remaining after control measures have been taken.
Risk acceptance	Where risk has been identified and assessed. This covers the situation where the firm decides to accept the level of risk and not pass it on to another party.
Risk appetite	The level of risk that an organisation is willing to accept.
Risk avoidance	A risk mitigation strategy whereby the firm removes itself from the risk activity.
Risk based capital	The blending of the assessment of the amount of risk faced by an organisation against the level of capital to be held to provide resistance to that risk.
Risk Committee	A committee appointed by the Board to assess the different risks faced by the firm.
Risk identification	The on-going appraisal of a firm's internal and external environments to identify any risks that it may be facing.
Risk management lifecycle	The structured process for the management of risk, starting with risk identification and moving through assessment, mitigation and monitoring/reporting.
Risk map	A graph of information normally found on a risk register.
Risk Register	An internal document that lists risks identified by a business under risk categories.
Risk retention	An activity of risk mitigation whereby the organisation decides to accept the loss, or benefit of gain, from a risk when it occurs.

Risk sharing	A risk mitigation strategy where the potential for loss or gain from an activity is shared with a third party. For example, through a joint venture.
Risk transfer	A risk mitigation strategy that seeks to transfer the risk to another party – for example, through outsourcing or the purchase of an insurance policy.
Scenario analysis	An examination of key external losses and a consideration of whether they could occur within the firm.
Segmentation	The process of identifying sub-groups in a population with similar characteristics.
Sensitivity analysis	A technique whereby we consider the effect of the change of a variable in a complex model.
Short selling	The practice of selling assets that have been borrowed from a third party with the intention of buying identical assets later on to return to the third party.
Software piracy	Illegally using, copying or distributing software without having the necessary permissions and licenses.
Spam	Unsolicited email that can infect a computer with malware of redirect the computer to an illegal website.
Statement of means	Document produced as part of the credit risk assessment procedure to help identify the viability of the proposition.
Statistical loss	An estimate of how much actual losses can exceed expected losses over a given period of time.
Statistical scoring model	Credit scoring techniques that rely on statistical methods rather than a sanctioning officer's judgement.
Strategic risk	The risk of losses or misfortunes occurring as a result of strategic plans.
Stress loss	A loss that can occur as a result of an extreme event.
Stress testing	A form of testing that seeks to determine the stability of a system, process or entity. It works by testing the factors under review beyond their normal operating capacity.
Systematic risk	Another name for market risk, where the value of investments fall as a result of factors that affects all of the market – for example, investor confidence.
Technology risk	The risk of inadequate or malfunctioning technology resulting in loss or harm to the bank.
Three lines of defence model	A framework comprising controls, committees/functions and independent assurance. It is looked for by the FSA during ARROW visits.
Trading book	The range of financial instruments held by a firm.
Uninsurable risk	A risk event that an insurance company is not able to calculate the probability of it occurring.
Unsystematic risk	The risk that a share will fall in value, irrespective of the performance of the market as a whole.
Value ladder	Another name for a maturity ladder.

Venture capital	Private equity capital usually provided to early stage companies with a high potential for growth.
Volatility risk	The risk of sharp price movements within a market.
Wrong way risk	The risk that arises when default risk and credit exposure increase simultaneously.
Zombie computer	A computer that has been infected by a botnet that can be used to commit cyber crime.

INDEX

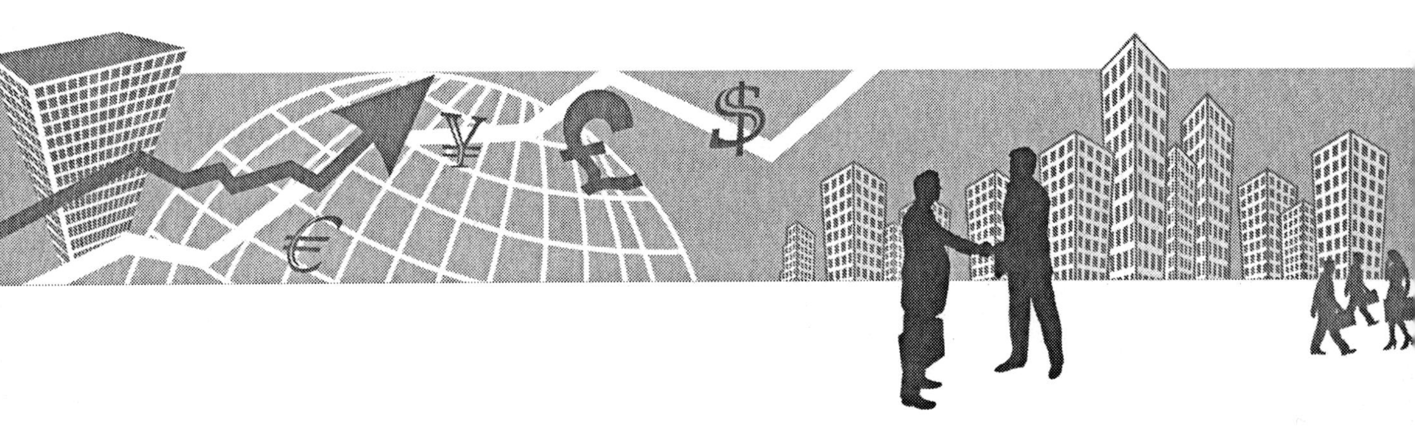